THE JEWS OF VIENNA AND THE
FIRST WORLD WAR

THE LITTMAN LIBRARY OF
JEWISH CIVILIZATION

Dedicated to the memory of
LOUIS THOMAS SIDNEY LITTMAN
who founded the Littman Library for the love of God
and as an act of charity in memory of his father
JOSEPH AARON LITTMAN
and to the memory of
ROBERT JOSEPH LITTMAN
who continued what his father Louis had begun
יהא זכרם ברוך

'*Get wisdom, get understanding:*
Forsake her not and she shall preserve thee'
PROV. 4: 5

The Littman Library of Jewish Civilization is a registered UK charity
Registered charity no. 1000784

THE
JEWS OF VIENNA
AND THE
FIRST WORLD WAR

◆

DAVID RECHTER

London
The Littman Library of Jewish Civilization
in association with Liverpool University Press

The Littman Library of Jewish Civilization
Registered office: 4th floor, 7–10 Chandos Street, London WIG 9DQ

in association with Liverpool University Press
4 Cambridge Street, Liverpool L69 7ZU, UK
www.liverpooluniversitypress.co.uk/littman

Managing Editor: Connie Webber

Distributed in North America by
Oxford University Press Inc., 198 Madison Avenue,
New York, NY 10016, USA

First published in hardback 2001
First published in paperback 2008

Catalogue records for this book are available from the
British Library and the Library of Congress

ISBN 978-1-904113-82-9

Publishing co-ordinator: Janet Moth
Designed by Pete Russell, Faringdon, Oxon.
Typeset by John Saunders, Production & Design, Eastbourne

Printed and bound in Great Britain by
CPI Group (UK) Ltd., Croydon, CR0 4YY

For my father,
who pointed me in the right direction

Acknowledgements

IT is a pleasure to thank the many people who have helped me during the research and writing of this book. At the Hebrew University in Jerusalem Ezra Mendelsohn gave his unstinting support, friendship, and intellectual guidance. I also owe a substantial intellectual debt to Robert Wistrich and Jonathan Frankel. I received an endless stream of good advice from Hannah Koevary and Laurie Fialkoff, with whom I worked at *Studies in Contemporary Jewry*. I am grateful to the staff at the libraries and archives I consulted in Jerusalem, Vienna, and New York. In Vienna and Stanford respectively Erwin Schmidl and Sonia Moss gave invaluable assistance in locating and providing sources. At the Stanford University Program in Jewish Studies Steve Zipperstein and Aron Rodrigue were welcoming above and beyond the call of duty and made my time there as a Visiting Scholar a pleasure. Then and later Mitch Hart provided much-needed humour and friendship. Vicki Caron read and made helpful comments on part of the work. In Oxford Peter Pulzer and Jonathan Webber have been consistently supportive. Laurien Berkeley did a thoroughly excellent editing job. Janet Moth gently guided the project to completion, immeasurably improving the end result. Naturally, many others have helped along the way, and I apologize to those I have neglected to mention.

I am grateful too for financial support from the following: the Lev Zion and Golda Meir funds of the Hebrew University in Jerusalem; the Memorial Foundation for Jewish Culture in New York; the Austrian Bundesministerium für Wissenschaft und Forschung; the Rosenfeld Project on Hungarian and Habsburg Jewry of the Dinur Center, Hebrew University; the Vereinigung für wissenschaftlichen Studienaustausch in Vienna; and the Conference on Jewish Social Studies, New York. Publication of the book was assisted by a generous grant from the Koret Foundation's Jewish Studies Publications Program.

I should also like to thank the following for permitting me to use material from previously published articles, in revised form, in Chapters 2, 3, and 4: the Center for Austrian Studies, University of Minnesota for 'Galicia in Vienna: Jewish Refugees in the First World War', *Austrian History Yearbook*, 28 (1997); Oxford University Press for '"Bubermania": The Jewish

Youth Movement in Vienna, 1917–1919', *Modern Judaism*, 16 (1996); and Oxford University Press, Inc. for 'Autonomy and its Discontents: The Austrian Jewish Congress Movement, 1917–1918', in Ezra Mendelsohn (ed.), *Studies in Contemporary Jewry*, xii: *Literary Strategies: Jewish Texts and Contexts* (© 1996 Oxford University Press, Inc.).

Finally, my greatest debt is to Lynne, Ella, and Noah, without whom none of it would have been either possible or worthwhile.

Contents

Note on Place-Names   xi

List of Abbreviations   xii

Introduction   1

1. The Political Culture of Viennese Jewry   16

2. The Refugees   67

3. Warring Youth   101

4. In Pursuit of Unity   129

5. A Jewish Revolution   161

Conclusion   187

Bibliography   191

Index   213

Note on Place-Names

Where places have commonly used English-language names, such as Vienna, Prague, or Bohemia, I have used these. Where no such obvious English version exists, I have used the German name of the time (e.g. Lemberg, Brünn), while indicating an alternative where it seems necessary or useful. In many cases those names are no longer in use, and their use was contested at the time. For the sake of convenience, when referring to the Austrian half of the Dual Monarchy I have generally used the shorthand 'empire', while 'monarchy' will be used to denote the combined Habsburg lands of Austria and Hungary.

Abbreviations

AOIB	Allgemeiner Österreichische-Israelitischer Bund
AR	Österreichisches Staatsarchiv, Archiv der Republik
ASW	*Amtsblatt der Stadt Wien*
AVA	Österreichisches Staatsarchiv, Allgemeines Verwaltungsarchiv
BIAW	*Bericht der Israelitischen Allianz zu Wien*
BJJ	*Blätter aus der jüdischen Jugendbewegung*
CAHJP, AW	Central Archives for the History of the Jewish People, Archiv Wien
CZA	Central Zionist Archives
EAC	Engeres Aktionskomitee
ECUAZ	Executive Committee of United Austrian Zionists
FT	*Freie Tribune*
IKG	Israelitische Kultusgemeinde
JDCA	Joint Distribution Committee Archives
JJ	*Jüdische Jugendblätter*
JK	*Jüdische Korrespondenz*
JNK	*Jüdischer Nationalkalender*
JZ	*Jüdische Zeitung*
LBIA, RW	Leo Baeck Institute Archives, Robert Weltsch Collection
LBIYB	*Leo Baeck Institute Year Book*
MI	Ministerium des Innern
MOIU	*Monatschrift der Österreichisch-Israelitischen Union*
NJM	*Neue Jüdische Monatshefte*
NNZ	*Neue National-Zeitung*
OW	*Dr. Bloch's Österreichische Wochenschrift*
PDW	Polizeidirektion Wien
SB	Stimmungsberichte
SBP	Siegfried Bernfeld Papers

SPOR	*Stenographische Protokolle über die Sitzungen des Hauses der Abgeordneten der österreichischen Reichsrates*
SW	*Selbstwehr*
WH	*Die Wahrheit*
WM	*Wiener Morgenzeitung*
YA	*Yidisher Arbeter*
YVA	Yad Vashem Archives
ZBB	*Zweimonats-Bericht für die Mitglieder der österreichisch-israelitischen Humanitätsvereine 'Bnai Brith'*
ZCO	Zionist Central Office, Berlin
ZCWA	Zionist Central Committee for Western Austria

INTRODUCTION

THE First World War was a disaster of unprecedented magnitude; it has been described as '*the* great seminal catastrophe' of the twentieth century, and as representing a 'profound caesura' in European history.[1] It is difficult to exaggerate the devastation wrought by the 'war to end all wars'. More violent and protracted than any previous conflict, this was 'total war', a cataclysm that killed and wounded tens of millions. Few areas were harder hit than eastern and central Europe, where the war's impact was incalculable, its consequences inescapable.[2] Here, the political and social landscape was radically transformed, as the war led to the collapse of the Russian, Habsburg, German, and Ottoman empires that had ruled the area for centuries. Peculiar to east central Europe was the extent and intensity of civilian suffering. The volatility of the eastern front, so different from the stagnant trench warfare of the western front, caused enormous hardship for the civilian population, precipitating a mass movement of refugees from eastern Europe.[3]

This eruption of chaos and violence directly affected the region's Jews. Many of the battles on the eastern front were fought in the most densely populated Jewish territory in Europe, devastating the infrastructures of Jewish life: expulsions, widespread anti-Jewish violence, and economic ruin were the result. Indeed, a common Jewish refrain was that while many

---

[1] The first description is from George F. Keenan's *The Decline of Bismarck's European Order*, quoted in Imanuel Geiss, 'World War I and East Central Europe: A Historical Assessment', in Béla K. Király and Nándor F. Dreisziger (eds.), *East Central European Society in World War I*, War and Society in East Central Europe, xix (New York, 1985), 27. The second comes from J. M. Winter, 'Catastrophe and Culture: Recent Trends in the Historiography of the First World War', *Journal of Modern History*, 64 (1992), 525.

[2] Nándor F. Dreisziger, 'The Dimensions of Total War in East Central Europe 1914–18', in Béla K. Király and Nándor F. Dreisziger (eds.), *East Central European Society in World War I*, War and Society in East Central Europe, xix (New York, 1985) 3–23.

[3] Michael R. Marrus, *The Unwanted: European Refugees in the Twentieth Century* (New York, 1985), 52–61. See also Imanuel Geiss, 'The Civilian Dimension of the War', in Hugh Cecil and Peter H. Liddle (eds.), *Facing Armageddon: The First World War Experience* (London, 1996), 17–20.

suffered gravely during the war, Jewish suffering was disproportionate and of greater severity.[4] Whatever the truth of such a claim, it certainly reflected a widespread Jewish perception of extreme vulnerability and powerlessness. During the war perhaps more than a million Jews were displaced from their homes in eastern Europe, whether as a result of flight from the invading Russian army, expulsion by the Russians when retreating, or deportation into the Russian interior. 'Death and destitution carved a wide swath through East European Jewry. . . . The First World War brought to an end a hundred-year period that, in retrospect, can be seen as something of a golden age in the history of the Jewish people.'[5] If the war was a 'caesura' generally, then clearly it was also such for the Jewish world.

But for the Jews the war was by no means over in November 1918. As Winston Churchill reportedly remarked to Lloyd George, 'the War of the Giants has ended; the quarrels of the pygmies have begun'.[6] Immediately following the armistice a wave of violent and bloody pogroms swept over large areas of Poland and Ukraine, and the western border areas of the Soviet Union. Much of the violence took place in regions where fighting still raged over disputed territories—between Poland and Ukraine, Poland and the Soviet Union, or between Ukrainians and the Red Army. In the midst of these wars all sides took the opportunity to prosecute an 'anti-Jewish war'.[7] Between November 1918 and the gradual calming of the situation in 1920–1, tens of thousands of Jews were killed, while hundreds of thousands were wounded and uprooted. It is barely an exaggeration to describe these events as the 'bloodiest disaster in modern Jewish history to that point'.[8]

Clearly the war and its aftermath was a period of prolonged and intense trauma for European Jewry as a whole, and for east European Jewry in particular. In Jewish memory, however, the Great War has been understandably overshadowed by the incomparably greater disaster of the Holocaust. Some have fashioned a link between the two. Omer Bartov, for example,

    [4] See e.g. *OW*, 8 Oct. 1914, pp. 683–4; 9 Mar. 1917, pp. 151–3; 28 Sept. 1917, pp. 617–19; *JK*, 23 Sept. 1915, pp. 1–2; 27 Jan. 1916, p. 1; 19 July 1917, p. 1.

    [5] Jonathan Frankel, 'The Paradoxical Politics of Marginality: Thoughts on the Jewish Situation during the Years 1914–21', in Frankel (ed.), *Studies in Contemporary Jewry*, iv: *The Jews and the European Crisis 1914–1921* (New York, 1988), 17.

    [6] Norman Davies, *White Eagle, Red Star: The Polish–Soviet War 1919–1920* (London, 1972), 21.

    [7] Ezra Mendelsohn, *Zionism in Poland: The Formative Years 1915–1926* (New Haven, 1981), 90.

    [8] Marrus, *The Unwanted*, 61. See also ibid. 63–4; Mendelsohn, *Zionism in Poland*, 88–91; Elias Heifetz, *The Slaughter of the Jews in the Ukraine in 1919* (New York, 1921).

calls the First World War 'the birthplace of industrial killing: Auschwitz could neither have been imagined, nor constructed and set to work, without the experience and memory of the Great War, where many of the architects and executioners of the "Final Solution" underwent their "baptism of fire"'.[9] Despite its self-evident importance, Jewish historiography on the First World War is notably undeveloped, in stark contrast to the overwhelming mass of work on the subject in general. Full-scale studies of European Jewry during the war are few and far between, and it is clear that the Holocaust has cast a giant shadow over the decades that preceded it.[10] By examining the wartime history of Viennese Jewry, one of Europe's largest urban Jewish communities, this book begins to correct this historiographical imbalance, hoping at the same time to 'rescue' the Great War as a historical experience for European Jews by cutting it adrift from the teleological moorings of the Holocaust.

To date, the great bulk of work on Viennese Jewry has focused on the period prior to the First World War. In particular, the role of Viennese Jews as creators and consumers of the much-celebrated phenomenon of *fin-de-siècle* Vienna, the 'experimental station for the end of the world', has received a great deal of attention.[11] There is, however, another, related, Jewish Vienna, that of Alfred Stern and Robert Stricker rather than Sigmund Freud and Arthur Schnitzler. In terms of their prominence and influence in Jewish circles, Stern and Stricker were the counterparts of Karl Lueger, the long-serving Christian Social mayor of Vienna. While the

[9] Omer Bartov, *Murder in our Midst: The Holocaust, Industrial Killing, and Representation* (New York, 1996), 23. On the relationship between the First World War and the Holocaust, see also ibid., ch. 2; George L. Mosse, *Toward the Final Solution: A History of European Racism* (New York, 1978), ch. 11.

[10] On European Jewry and the war, see Frankel (ed.), *Studies in Contemporary Jewry*, iv: *The Jews and the European Crisis*; Werner E. Mosse and Arnold Paucker (eds.), *Deutsches Judentum in Krieg und Revolution 1916–1923* (Tübingen, 1971); Mark Levene, *War, Jews and the New Europe: The Diplomacy of Lucien Wolf 1914–1919* (Oxford, 1992); David Joshua Engel, 'Organized Jewish Responses to German Antisemitism during the First World War', Ph.D. diss., University of California, Los Angeles, 1979.

[11] The phrase was coined by Karl Kraus in July 1914. See Edward Timms, *Karl Kraus, Apocalyptic Satirist: Culture and Catastrophe in Habsburg Vienna* (New Haven, 1986), 10. On this aspect of Vienna, see e.g. Carl Schorske, *Fin-de-siècle Vienna: Politics and Culture* (New York, 1981); Jürgen Nautz and Richard Vahrenkamp (eds.), *Die Wiener Jahrhundertwende. Einflüsse, Umwelt, Wirkungen* (Vienna, 1993). On the Jewish contribution, see Steven Beller, *Vienna and the Jews 1867–1938: A Cultural History* (Cambridge, 1989); Robert S. Wistrich, *The Jews of Vienna in the Age of Franz Joseph* (Oxford, 1989), chs. 15–18; Michael P. Steinberg, 'Jewish Identity and Intellectuality in *fin-de-siècle* Austria: Suggestions for a Historical Discourse', *New German Critique*, 43 (1988), 3–33.

internal political and social world of Viennese Jewry has received a share of its historiographical due, much work still remains to be done.[12] It is one of the aims of this book to consider the complex internal labyrinth of Viennese Jewish society on its own terms. A less glamorous world than that of Hermann Broch's 'gay apocalypse', certainly, but just as much a part of the Jewish story in modern Europe.

These were, of course, not mutually exclusive worlds, but the areas of overlap were limited. Theodor Herzl, for example, made it his life's mission to cross from one to the other; Sigmund Freud's involvement with the Jewish fraternal organization B'nai B'rith and his general concern with matters Jewish are well documented; Arthur Schnitzler wrote at length about Zionism and voted for the Jewish nationalists in the Viennese city council elections of May 1919; and Siegfried Bernfeld, leader of the wartime Jewish youth movement, was a disciple of Freud and later become a well-known psychoanalyst.[13] For all of these figures, it was antisemitism and the Jewish Question that repeatedly returned their focus to Jewish Vienna.[14]

The fact that Jews were disproportionately prominent in the Viennese press, in commerce and banking, in literary, theatrical, and musical life, and in the Social Democratic movement must play some role, if only tangential, in any consideration of Jewish Vienna. Most obviously, it was a significant factor in the persistence and virulence of Viennese antisemitism. Moreover, that so many of Vienna's publicly eminent Jews were entirely uninvolved in organized Jewish life (and yet brought so much opprobrium to Viennese Jews in general) was a constant irritant to Jewish activists. Here was an object lesson regarding the futility of any attempt to ignore the implications of being a Jew in Vienna. The Jewish press directed regular broadsides, for example, at Jews who occupied leading positions in the Viennese press or in

---

[12] On Viennese Jewry, see Wistrich, *The Jews of Vienna in the Age of Franz Joseph*; Marsha L. Rozenblit, *The Jews of Vienna 1867–1914: Assimilation and Identity* (Albany, NY, 1983); Harriet Pass Freidenreich, *Jewish Politics in Vienna 1918–1938* (Bloomington, Ind., 1991); Ivar Oxaal, Michael Pollak, and Gerhard Botz (eds.), *Jews, Antisemitism and Culture in Vienna* (London, 1987); Josef Fraenkel (ed.), *The Jews of Austria* (London, 1967); Avraham Palmon, 'The Jewish Community of Vienna between the Two World Wars, 1918–1938' (Heb.), Ph.D. diss., Hebrew University of Jerusalem, 1985.

[13] On Freud, see e.g. Yosef Hayim Yerushalmi, *Freud's Moses: Judaism Terminable and Interminable* (New Haven, 1991); Wistrich, *The Jews of Vienna in the Age of Franz Joseph*, ch. 16. On Schnitzler, see Arthur Schnitzler, *Tagebuch 1917–1919* (Vienna, 1985), 249.

[14] On Viennese and Austrian antisemitism, see Peter Pulzer, *The Rise of Political Anti-Semitism in Germany and Austria*, rev. edn. (London, 1988); Bruce F. Pauley, *From Prejudice to Persecution: A History of Austrian Anti-Semitism* (Chapel Hill, NC, 1992); Wistrich, *The Jews of Vienna in the Age of Franz Joseph*, ch. 7.

the Social Democratic movement but who refused to acknowledge Jewish interests. In a typical instance, the *Österreichische Wochenschrift* commented that the Social Democratic *Arbeiter Zeitung* was run by Jewish 'renegades', a fact which 'explained' the paper's unwillingness to protest against anti-semitism.[15]

For all the discussion about antisemitism and the role of Jews in Viennese culture, nowhere in the literature on Jewish Vienna is there anything substantial to be found about the war years. In most accounts it is a largely absent or unspoken presence—either the end-point of Habsburg Vienna or the beginning of the inter-war Austrian republic, rather than an object of attention in and of itself. But it is precisely the war's role as an end and a beginning, apart from its intrinsic significance, that makes it all the more important to investigate closely this crucial chapter in Viennese Jewish history, to explore how Viennese Jews made the transition from empire to republic.

By extension, the history of Viennese Jewry during the First World War is also, to a degree, the history of Austrian Jewry (Austria being defined here as the non-Hungarian parts of the Habsburg realm). In Jewish Austria, as in the empire in general, centre and periphery were in constant competition. During the war Vienna functioned as the 'capital' of Austrian Jewry to a greater extent than was normally the case. Regional political and administrative structures were weakened by the draft and by the chaos that reigned on the eastern front, while a good portion of the Jewish élite of Galicia and Bukovina fled westward. In this way, the general concentration of power and administration in the *Residenzstadt* found its echo in Jewish society. The major undertakings of Austrian Jewry in the war years—the welfare effort, and the Congress and youth movements—were largely Vienna-based, notwithstanding their pretensions and aspirations to an empire-wide embrace.

This is also a study of modern Jewish politics. Jewish political movements and ideologies emerged and developed in the latter half of the nineteenth century, in large part as a response to the inescapable Jewish Question.[16]

---

[15] See *OW*, 20 July 1917, p. 468. See also *JZ*, 25 Jan. 1918, p. 3; *YA*, 15 Nov. 1917, pp. 8–9.

[16] For definitions of modern Jewish politics, see Ezra Mendelsohn, *On Modern Jewish Politics* (New York, 1993), p. viii; Eli Lederhendler, *The Road to Modern Jewish Politics: Political Tradition and Political Reconstruction in the Jewish Community of Tsarist Russia* (New York, 1989), 3–10. For a different approach to the study of Jewish political culture, see Daniel J. Elazar and Stuart Cohen, *The Jewish Polity: Jewish Political Organisation from Biblical Times to the Present*

Jewish politics may be seen as part of the wider phenomenon of what has been called ethnopolitics—'the translation of ethnicity into political space'.[17] It should be noted, however, that this is a work of political history, not political science. It traces a dramatic episode in the volatile history of Jewish group identity—ethnic, national, and religious; as such, it is a case-study of ethnopolitics. The analysis here, as will become clear, is predicated on the assumption that in crucial respects Jewish politics mirrored the politics of other minorities.[18] This is not to imply that it was merely imitative; rather, it means that Jewish politics, as is true of Jewish history in general, cannot be isolated or extracted from its environment. Politics was central to Jewish society in pre-Holocaust eastern and central Europe, and Jewish politics was to a large degree about the public construction of Jewish identity. By examining the Jewish political sphere (the 'Jewish street', as it was commonly known), we can observe both the evolution of collective Jewish identities and Jewish attempts to deal with the Jewish Question. The political history of Jewish society, therefore, offers a valuable perspective on some of the most enduring questions of modern Jewish history in Europe—on emancipation and its discontents, on antisemitism, on the hardy perennial of Jewish identity.

Most of the existing literature on modern Jewish politics deals with the Jewish political heartlands of eastern Europe. Like so much in modern Jewish history, the Jewish political world can be conveniently divided along a loosely drawn east–west axis, with west European Jewry associated with a liberal, integrationist mode of politics and east European Jewry with an autonomous, 'auto-emancipationist' mode.[19] While this approach has much to recommend it, Viennese and Austrian Jewish politics do not fit entirely comfortably into either camp. It is, rather, an amalgam of east and

(Bloomington, Ind., 1985). On the shortcomings of this approach for the study of modern Jewish politics, see Lederhendler, *The Road to Modern Jewish Politics*, 8.

[17] Joseph Rothschild, *Ethnopolitics: A Conceptual Framework* (New York, 1981), 1. See also id., 'Recent Trends in the Literature on Ethnopolitics', in Ezra Mendelsohn (ed.), *Studies in Contemporary Jewry*, iii: *Jews and Other Ethnic Groups in a Multi-Ethnic World* (New York, 1987), 115–23; Walker Connor, *Ethnonationalism: The Quest for Understanding* (Princeton, 1994); Anthony D. Smith, *The Ethnic Revival* (Cambridge, 1981).

[18] For comparisons with the politics of other minorities, see Mendelsohn, *On Modern Jewish Politics*, ch. 6.

[19] See Jonathan Frankel, 'Modern Jewish Politics East and West (1840–1939): Utopia, Myth, Reality', in Zvi Gitelman (ed.), *The Quest for Utopia: Jewish Political Ideas and Institutions throughout the Ages* (Armonk, NY, 1992), 81–103; Mendelsohn, *On Modern Jewish Politics*, chs. 1–2.

west, their often uneasy coexistence reflecting many of the regional and cultural fault lines of Austrian society at large. In charting the development of Viennese and Austrian Jewish politics during the crisis of the war years, this work focuses westwards of most Jewish political studies, offering a 'central European' corrective to the east–west divide.[20]

Indeed, it is the hybrid nature of Viennese and Austrian Jewries that marks them out as different and unusual. As one contemporary observer wrote, Vienna was a 'central and focal point, where eastern essence and western culture flow into one another, where our forefathers' customs attempt to maintain themselves beside the demands of the new era, where assimilation, nationalism and Zionism collide with each other; in short, the scene of . . . an infinite range of Jewish-religious and Jewish-political aspirations'.[21] Of course, it was not unique in this; in fact, most Jewish polities encompassed a similar mixture, a result of the massive westward migration of eastern European Jews in the last decades of the nineteenth century. In Vienna, however, east and west were concentrated to a greater degree than in almost any other European city, and this compound nature was a defining characteristic of Viennese Jewry, a central and formative element in its collective life (as indeed was true of Habsburg Jewry as a whole). This was never more true than during the war, since, as just noted, Vienna was Austrian Jewry's 'capital' in this period, leading to an even greater degree of east–west mixing than in peacetime.

Typically for the politics of a minority, Jewish politics was firmly embedded in, and clearly reflected, the surrounding local and national political cultures. Almost the entire political spectrum of Austrian Jewry was notably loath to define a political identity against or outside the empire, remaining overwhelmingly *kaisertreu* until the very end of the war. Consequently, the agendas of Viennese and Austrian politics exerted a powerful influence on those of Jewish politics; so too, naturally, did more specifically Jewish concerns, whether local, empire-wide, or even international. While the emphasis here will be on the internal dynamics of Jewish society, the complex relationships between the minority group and the host society form an ever-present backdrop. The manifold intra-Jewish conflicts, for example, were often constrained by a pragmatic recognition of the predominance of

---

[20] On this, see Frankel, 'Modern Jewish Politics East and West', 86–8; Nethaniel Katzburg, 'Central European Jewry between East and West', in Yehuda Don and Victor Karady (eds.), *A Social and Economic History of Central European Jewry* (New Brunswick, NJ, 1990), 33–46.

[21] *WH*, 17 Dec. 1915, p. 6. For similar sentiments, see Samuel Krauss, *Die Krise der Wiener Judenschaft* (Vienna, 1919), 4–5.

Catholicism and its political expressions in Austria (most obviously the Christian Social Party) and the potential dangers to Jews inherent in that predominance. Similarly, the Austrian variant of radical pan-German nationalism represented a significant threat to the cultural and political pluralism that all Jewish parties deemed vitally necessary to the continued security of Jews in the empire. In the same vein, Viennese centralism, along with the related tensions between centre and regions that were endemic in the empire, were part and parcel also of Jewish politics and society. Finally, examining the politics of Viennese Jewry—along with Czechs, one of only two sizeable minorities in the city—offers a useful minority vantage-point on Viennese politics, in which the Jewish Question and antisemitism played such a prominent role.[22]

In eastern and central Europe Jewish politics was above all minority politics; this was, as already noted, its defining feature. In the latter half of the nineteenth century the demarcation lines between politicized ethnicity and full-blown nationality were often indistinct in this region, the development of various forms of Jewish nationalism being a case in point. Jewish nationalism, along with other forms of autonomous Jewish politics, reflected the growth of nationalist consciousness among the various minority peoples of the Habsburg and Russian empires.[23] In formulating their ideologies, Jewish nationalists of all stripes (whether Zionist, Diaspora nationalist, or socialist) looked to the models provided by other groups. As Rabbi Tsevi Hirsch Kalischer, one of the earliest exponents of a revived Jewish nationalism, wrote in 1862:

Why do the people of Italy and of other countries sacrifice their lives for the land of their fathers, while we, like men bereft of strength and courage, do nothing? . . . Let us take to heart the examples of the Italians, Poles and Hungarians, who laid down their lives and possessions in the struggle for national independence, while we, the children of Israel, who have the most glorious and holiest of lands as our inheritance, are spiritless and silent. We should be ashamed of ourselves.[24]

---

[22] John W. Boyer, *Political Radicalism in Late Imperial Vienna: Origins of the Christian Social Movement 1848–1897* (Chicago, 1981), 39, calls antisemitism one of 'the two principal modes of bourgeois politics in Vienna in the period 1848–1914'.

[23] For a discussion of the relationship between ethnicity and nationalism in the Jewish context, and the relationship between Jewish and other 'ethnonationalisms', see Gideon Shimoni, *The Zionist Ideology* (Hanover, NH, 1995), ch. 1.

[24] Quoted in Shlomo Avineri, *The Making of Modern Zionism: The Intellectual Origins of the Jewish State* (New York, 1981), 52. See also Mendelsohn, *On Modern Jewish Politics*, 103–13.

Kalischer, who was born in Sarajevo and lived for many years near Belgrade, could easily have expanded his list to include, for example, Serbs, Croats, Bulgarians, Greeks, Romanians, and Ukrainians. In a similar fashion, the-oreticians of Diaspora nationalism—such as the Russian Jewish historian Simon Dubnow and the lesser-known Austrians Siegmund Kaznelson and Max Rosenfeld—adapted the work of the Austrian Marxists Karl Renner and Otto Bauer, for whom the Jews failed to qualify as a nation. Jewish Dias-pora nationalists broadened the Austro-Marxist principle of personal, extra-territorial autonomy to include the Jews within its scope.[25]

An important consequence of the Jewish perception of catastrophe and vulnerability during the First World War was that many Jews paid renewed attention to their status as a non-territorial minority—i.e. a minority dis-persed throughout the region and without a substantial territorial 'base' in which it comprised a majority of the population. In this, as in so much else, Jewish politics took its cues from the surrounding societies. The war and immediate post-war years were the heyday of nationalism and ethnic self-determination, a time when every self-respecting national or ethnic group aspired to sovereignty or autonomy of one sort or another.[26] This was espe-cially true by the end of the war, with the collapse of the Habsburg and Russian empires. In these multinational areas more and more Jews were now prepared to define themselves in either ethnic or national terms.[27] But for Jews, perhaps more than for almost any other minority, the idea of political self-determination was particularly problematic, because there was no Jew-ish consensus as to what exactly Jews were—a nation, an ethnic group, a reli-gious community, or some combination of these. It is precisely these kinds of identity issues that bedevilled the Austrian Congress movement, an attempt to unite Austrian Jewry under one organizational umbrella.

The difficulties experienced in uniting the disparate elements of Austrian

[25] On Dubnow, see David H. Weinberg, *Between Tradition and Modernity: Haim Zhitlowski, Simon Dubnow, Ahad Ha-am, and the Shaping of Modern Jewish Identity* (New York, 1996), 194–204. On Austrian Marxism and the Jews, see Robert S. Wistrich, *Socialism and the Jews: The Dilemmas of Assimilation in Germany and Austria-Hungary* (London, 1982), 299–308; Jack Ja-cobs, *On Socialists and 'the Jewish Question' after Marx* (New York, 1992), ch. 4.

[26] See Geoff Eley, 'Remapping the Nation: War, Revolutionary Upheaval and State Forma-tion in Eastern Europe 1914–1923', in Peter J. Potichnyj and Howard Aster (eds.), *Ukrainian–Jewish Relations in Historical Perspective* (Edmonton, 1988), 205–46; Walker Connor, 'The Politics of Ethnonationalism', *Journal of International Affairs*, 27 (1973), 9–10.

[27] See Ezra Mendelsohn, 'Zionist Success and Zionist Failure: The Case of East Central Eur-ope between the Wars', in Ruth Kozodoy, David Sidorsky, and Kalman Sultanik (eds.), *Vision Confronts Reality: Historical Perspectives on the Contemporary Jewish Agenda* (London, 1989), 193–7; Frankel, 'The Paradoxical Politics of Marginality', 12–13.

Jewish society, even during the crisis situation brought about by the war, point up the rather problematic nature of any attempt to conceive of Austrian Jewry—divided as it was along socio-economic, religious, political, and cultural lines—as a single entity; 'Austrian Jewry', much discussed during the war, was something of a chimera. There was undeniably a strong Austrian patriotism among broad sectors of the empire's Jewish population, and the formulation of an explicitly 'Austrian Jewish' identity found some resonance, but all attempts to give concrete form to this amorphous sentiment of pan-Jewish solidarity ran aground. What indeed were the common interests of a poor Galician pedlar and a bourgeois merchant in Vienna or Trieste? Of a devoutly Orthodox Moravian Jew and a Zionist Prague student or a Jewish member of a liberal club in the Bohemian capital? Time and again it will be evident in this study that the centrifugal forces in Viennese and Austrian Jewry outweighed the centripetal.[28]

Notwithstanding the traumas of the war years and their aftermath, this was not merely a tale of unremitting Jewish woe.[29] For alongside the suffering and the travails, this period also saw the emergence of the Jews as autonomous agents of some significance in the international political arena. This startling development was facilitated by the apparent triumph of the principles of ethnic self-determination and nationalism. The British government's Balfour Declaration of November 1917, promising some sort of Jewish homeland in Palestine, was a major milestone. Almost equally remarkable was the presence of independent Jewish representation—the Committee of Jewish Delegations—at the Paris Peace Conference in 1919. This disputatious group consisted primarily of representatives of east European and American Jewries, and it played a decisive role in the formulation of the controversial Minorities Treaties adopted by the Peace Conference.[30] The immediate background to the achievements of the Committee of Jewish

[28] For an attempt to bridge these gaps by positing the existence of an overarching Austrian Jewish identity, see William O. McCagg, Jr., *A History of Habsburg Jews 1670–1918* (Bloomington, Ind., 1989).

[29] A somewhat similar point is made in relation to Jewish culture and politics in Aviel Roshwald, 'Jewish Cultural Identity in Eastern and Central Europe during the Great War', in Aviel Roshwald and Richard Stites (eds.), *European Culture in the Great War: The Arts, Entertainment, and Propaganda, 1914–1918* (Cambridge, 1999), 89–126. Roshwald writes on p. 124: 'The First World War was a double-edged sword that devastated traditional *shtetl* life and culture in Eastern Europe while simultaneously cutting away age-old obstacles that had hampered Jewish cultural and political self-expression.'

[30] On the Committee of Jewish Delegations and its role in Paris, see Oscar Janowsky, *The Jews and Minority Rights (1898–1919)* (New York, 1933), 309–83. See also Kurt Stillschweig, *Die Juden Osteuropas in den Minderheitenverträgen* (Berlin, 1936), 21–38.

Delegations, and to its ideological wranglings over issues of Jewish autonomy and minority rights, can be found in the Jewish experience in the war years; more concretely, in the Congress movements in the United States, Austria, and elsewhere, and in the Jewish National Councils of 1918–19. The Congress movements were attempts to forge representative Jewish organizations that could claim to speak for the Jews both in their own states and, collectively, in the international arena. (The Committee of Jewish Delegations, for example, claimed to represent nearly 12.5 million Jews.[31])

The Jewish National Councils of 1918–19 were an indirect outgrowth of the impulses and ideas underpinning the Congress movements. With the collapse of political structures at the end of the war, national groups across east central Europe established National Councils as a form of shadow government. These Councils played an important role in the transfer of power to the nationalities. Following suit, Jewish National Councils were established in many areas of the former Russian and Habsburg empires. Although a nationalist initiative, the Councils aspired to a pan-Jewish politics, hoping to become inclusive, all-party bodies that could reasonably claim to be Jewish 'governments' and exercise most of the functions of a government in internal Jewish affairs. No agreement could be reached, however, on precisely what constituted these internal Jewish affairs, because nobody could agree on what kind of group the Jews were. Despite these not inconsiderable obstacles, for a brief period the Councils became powerful institutions, assuming a leading role in the administration of the Jewish community, representing Jews to the external authorities, and organizing armed self-defence in the face of widespread anti-Jewish violence.[32] They were able to achieve all this because of the opportunities opened up by the political vacuum created at the war's end. Prior to the war Jewish communal administration in much of eastern and central Europe had been in the hands of either the liberal integrationists (often called assimilationists in eastern Europe), or the Orthodox, or a combination of the two. In the face of the fighting and chaos that enveloped many areas in the months following the war, the existing systems of Jewish governance and administration, like their counterparts in general society, were in disarray, opening a door through which the nationalists rushed.

[31] Janowsky, *The Jews and Minority Rights*, 310 n. 54. Stillschweig, *Die Juden Osteuropas in den Minderheitenverträgen*, 30, gives a figure of 9m.

[32] Mendelsohn, *Zionism in Poland*, 91–110; Shmuel Ettinger, 'Jews and Non-Jews in Eastern and Central Europe between the Wars: An Outline', in Bela Vago and George L. Mosse (eds.), *Jews and Non-Jews in Eastern Europe 1918–1945* (Jerusalem, 1974), 8–10.

Irrespective of their pan-Jewish agenda, the Councils were nationalist-dominated and consequently proved unable to draw the entire spectrum of Jewish society into their orbit. They were none the less remarkably successful, if only in the short term. In Vienna and Prague, to take just the most westerly cases, the Councils were virtually the only functioning Jewish organizations in the post-war months. In late October 1918 in Vienna the newly created Jewish National Council of German-Austria declared itself the 'sole legitimate representative body of the Jewish nation', whose task was nothing less than 'to guide the fate of the Jews'.[33] The same story was played out in much of Galicia, in many other parts of what was now Poland, and also in Ukraine, Lithuania, and elsewhere. Once the successor states to the Habsburg and Russian empires had consolidated themselves, this experiment in Jewish autonomy dissolved almost everywhere. As the only group in the area without any territorial base, and owing to terminal disagreements about the nature of Jewish identity and its political consequences, the viability of Jewish autonomy was in any case questionable. But, just as importantly, Jewish autonomy was predicated on the existence of a pluralist, multinational, and democratic state framework, while virtually all the successor states soon came to see themselves as nation-states, a development clearly inimical to the success of autonomous ethnopolitics, whether Jewish or otherwise. In this context, it is worth pointing out that Jewish Diaspora nationalism was at this stage a mostly liberal nationalist movement, and was therefore somewhat out of kilter with the prevalent exclusionary nationalist mood. Its socialist and extreme left-wing components were certainly influential, but it remained for the most part free of the kind of authoritarian, integral nationalist tendencies that played such a significant role in nationalist movements in central and eastern Europe generally.

While in one sense the events of this period may be interpreted as a Zionist success story, they should not consequently be viewed as part of the inevitable rise and rise of Jewish nationalism. Among Jews, as in society at large, nationalism emerged the victor; the Jewish experience in this regard resembles that of other minorities in eastern and central Europe. If nationalism was ascendant, it was by no means unchallenged. Left-wing radicalism, particularly following the Bolshevik Revolution, provided a serious ideological alternative. This was as true for Jews as for everyone else. In Vienna the Jewish nationalists reigned in fact for only a few months and did not regain power until 1932.

[33] *JZ*, 25 Oct. 1918, pp. 1–2.

Some contemporaries saw in these upheavals the final demise of 'Jewish liberalism', a long-delayed response to liberalism's diminished role in Austrian society.[34] Reports of its death, however, were premature (and in the Zionist case amounted to wishful thinking). A reflection of the much-discussed Jewish–liberal nexus in Austrian politics, Viennese Jewish liberalism emerged from the war bloodied but unbowed, and remained a force to be reckoned with, a viable political and cultural option for Jews throughout the 1920s and well into the 1930s.[35] Indeed, it will be argued here that Jewish liberalism in Vienna managed the passage from empire to republic more successfully than its non-sectarian counterpart in Austrian society. One of the principal conclusions of this book is that Jewish world-views survived the war remarkably intact, testimony perhaps to a continuing widespread Jewish faith in liberal ideas of progress.[36] If, as John Boyer has written, 'The war's profound social and psychological pressures revolutionized Viennese society', then in this respect the Viennese Jewish experience differed to some degree from that of the surrounding society.[37]

Despite these caveats, this period can none the less be regarded as revolutionary in the context of Jewish politics. Revolution is, of course, a relative notion; in Jewish politics it generally 'involved no bloodshed, no expropriation, not even in most cases any clear transfer of power, but rather the proliferation of rival power centers, movements, and ideologies'.[38] It is this type of 'revolution', a shift in political culture, that will be charted here. It was a

[34] See e.g. *WM*, 6 May 1919, p. 1; *JZ*, 2 May 1919, p. 1; 21 Nov. 1919, pp. 4–5; 28 Nov. 1919, p. 4; *OW*, 21 Feb. 1919, pp. 113–14; 13 June 1919, pp. 359–60. Freidenreich, *Jewish Politics in Vienna*, 38, appropriately calls it the end of the 'era of Liberal complacency'.

[35] On the Jewish–liberal connection, see Peter Pulzer, 'The Austrian Liberals and the Jewish Question 1867–1914', *Journal of Central European Affairs*, 23 (1963), 131–42; Wistrich, *The Jews of Vienna in the Age of Franz Joseph*, 141–63; Boyer, *Political Radicalism in Late Imperial Vienna*, 79–88; Freidenreich, *Jewish Politics in Vienna*, 29–36; Robert A. Kann, 'German-Speaking Jewry during Austria-Hungary's Constitutional Era (1867–1918)', *Jewish Social Studies*, 10 (1948), 241–2.

[36] For a similar kind of argument about the German Jewish *Bildungsbürgertum*, albeit from a different perspective, see George L. Mosse, *German Jews beyond Judaism* (Bloomington, Ind., 1985). In the same vein, David Vital has noted that after the war 'there was in Jewry no subsequent change of a *political* order, no great sweeping away of the old guard, no radical re-thinking of the basis of Jewish life. . . . it was *continuity* that marked the Jews once more in all their public and collective affairs'. See David Vital, 'Diplomacy in the Jewish Interest', in Ada Rapoport-Albert and Steven J. Zipperstein (eds.), *Jewish History: Essays in Honour of Chimen Abramsky* (London, 1988), 689.

[37] John W. Boyer, *Culture and Political Crisis in Vienna: Christian Socialism in Power 1897–1918* (Chicago, 1995), 380.

[38] Jonathan Frankel, 'Crisis as a Factor in Modern Jewish Politics 1840 and 1881–1882', in Jehuda Reinharz (ed.), *Living with Antisemitism* (Hanover, NH, 1987), 45.

shift brought about by the temporary ascendancy of a radical, nationalist, and mobilized mode of Jewish politics, more familiar in eastern Europe than in central or western Europe. An important part of this radical ascendancy was the successful adoption by Jewish activists of the type of 'mass' politics employed to such good effect by the Christian Social and Social Democratic movements in Vienna.[39] And while this Jewish 'politics in a new key'[40] was mild indeed by the extraordinarily violent standards of the era, for Viennese Jewry these were dramatic and unprecedented developments.

It has been suggested, referring to the string of Jewish successes on the international political and diplomatic stage during these years, that 'this series of genuine political achievements stretching from 1915 to 1920 is so out of the ordinary run of things that it almost defies explanation'.[41] These years of 'untold loss and of unprecedented political achievement'[42] remain a largely unexamined episode in the history of modern Jewish society and politics. For the Jews of Vienna and of the empire as a whole, both losses and achievements were immense. The Jews, István Deák has written, were 'the ultimate victims of the dissolution of the Habsburg Monarchy', a dissolution that came hard on the heels of a war which 'marked the apogee of Jewish participation in the life of Central Europeans'.[43] This book, then, offers a case-study of the Jewish experience on the home front in the crucible of war.

Following an introductory discussion of Viennese Jewry and its political culture, Chapter 1 surveys the contending forces within Viennese Jewish society—nationalist, liberal, and traditionalist Orthodoxy—both prior to and during the war. Chapter 2 examines the experience of Galicia in Vienna: the sudden arrival in the city of over 100,000 Galician (and Bukovinian) Jewish refugees, part of the mass flight from the eastern front. Although their num-

---

[39] On 'mass' parties in the Austrian context, see the remarks in Boyer, *Political Radicalism in Late Imperial Vienna*, 368–71.

[40] The phrase comes from Schorske, *Fin-de-siècle Vienna*, ch. 3.

[41] Frankel, 'The Paradoxical Politics of Marginality', 11. See also David Vital, *Zionism: The Crucial Phase* (Oxford, 1987), 89–92, 169–70, 190–1. To Simon Dubnow, for example, it appeared in May 1920 as though his 'ideal of autonomy for the twentieth century' was being realized. Quoted in Jonathan Frankel, 'S. M. Dubnov: Historian and Ideologist', in Sophie Dubnov-Ehrlich, *The Life and Work of S. M. Dubnov: Diaspora Nationalism and History*, ed. Jeffrey Shandler (Bloomington, Ind., 1991), 22.

[42] Frankel, 'The Paradoxical Politics of Marginality', 4.

[43] István Deák, 'The Habsburg Empire', in Karen Barkey and Mark von Hagen (eds.), *After Empire: Multiethnic Societies and Nation-Building. The Soviet Union and the Russian, Ottoman and Habsburg Empires* (Boulder, Colo., 1997), 137.

bers gradually fell to some 25,000–30,000 by the end of the war, the refugees' presence was felt in all areas of Viennese Jewish life. One striking consequence was that in the encounter between east and west, already a fixture of the Viennese Jewish scene, ambivalence increasingly yielded to abrasiveness. If this was true of the Jewish response, how much more so of the response of the Viennese population at large. The refugees became the catalyst for a sustained outburst of venomous antisemitism, initially aimed at the newcomers but soon trained on Viennese Jewry in general.

Chapters 3 and 4 discuss the most significant Jewish projects of the war years, the youth and Congress movements. These had much in common. Both were fuelled by the aspiration for Jewish unity in the empire, yet were riven and debilitated by internal strife; both were nationalist-initiated and nationalist-dominated; both were feasible and indeed conceivable only in the special circumstances of wartime Austria, and of Vienna in particular; both were Vienna-centred but empire-wide in their reach and ambition; and both fell far short of their goals. Together, they represent the final collective act of a self-consciously Habsburg Austrian Jewry attempting to assert itself as a coherent entity. Post-Habsburg Jewry is the subject of Chapter 5, which analyses Jewish responses to the end of the war and collapse of the monarchy, focusing on the fierce conflicts that raged within Viennese Jewry in the immediate post-war months. Many Jews feared, or hoped, that a revolution was taking place in the Jewish community, mirroring the historic upheavals taking place outside. As uncertainty reigned, the Jewish National Council stepped into the breach, supported by a Jewish militia, the first and only example of government-sanctioned armed self-defence in Austrian Jewish history. What began with a distinct bang, however, ended with something of a whimper, as the *status quo ante* was soon partially restored. None the less, the experience of the war years and the chaos of the war's end remained an open wound as the Jews of German-Austria slowly settled into their new society and began to rebuild their lives.

ONE

THE POLITICAL CULTURE OF VIENNESE JEWRY

F ROM just a few thousand in the Vormärz (pre-1848) era, Vienna's Jewish population increased rapidly after 1848, when restrictions on Jewish residence in the capital were relaxed.[1] In 1910 the Austrian census reported 175,318 Jews in Vienna, 8.6 per cent of the city's population.[2] According to estimates compiled by the Israelitische Kultusgemeinde (the Viennese Jewish community's official representative body) this increased to 186,848 by 1914, rising to 192,638 by 1918.[3] The first post-war Austrian census in 1923 gave a figure of 201,513 Jews in Vienna, 10.8 per cent of the total population.[4] Viennese Jewry on the eve of the First World War was a composite of three main waves of migration: from Bohemia and Moravia, the wealthiest group; from the western regions of Hungary, including a large Orthodox component and many middle-class immigrants with an affinity for German culture; and, from the 1890s until the outbreak of the war, from Galicia, the poorest, most Orthodox, and most socially cohesive group. A recent study offers a rough approximation of the regional derivation of Viennese Jews shortly before the First World War, estimating that about a quarter were Galician-born, a further quarter were probably of Hungarian origin, and half were either born locally or had arrived from Bohemia or Moravia.[5]

---

[1] On Viennese Jewry's exceptional growth rate, particularly after 1860, see Wistrich, *The Jews of Vienna in the Age of Franz Joseph*, 38–43; Rozenblit, *The Jews of Vienna*, 13–18.

[2] Wistrich, *The Jews of Vienna in the Age of Franz Joseph*, 42; Rozenblit, *The Jews of Vienna*, 17. At this time there were 1,313,000 Jews in cisleithanian Austria (i.e. excluding Hungary), 4.6% of the total population. See Wolfdieter Bihl, 'Die Juden', in Adam Wandruszka and Peter Urbanitsch (eds.), *Die Habsburgermonarchie 1848–1918*, iii: *Die Völker des Reiches*, pt. 2 (Vienna, 1980), 882–3.

[3] These statistics are from a draft report of Sept. 1919 on Kultusgemeinde activity from 1913 to 1918 (hereafter IKG Draft Report 1913–1918), CAHJP, AW, 102.

[4] Freidenreich, *Jewish Politics in Vienna*, 214.

[5] Ivar Oxaal and Walter R. Weitzmann, 'The Jews of Pre-1914 Vienna: An Exploration of Basic Sociological Dimensions', *LBIYB* 30 (1985), 400. For detailed analysis of the regional origins of Viennese Jewry, see ibid. 396–403; Rozenblit, *The Jews of Vienna*, 18–45; Wistrich, *The Jews of Vienna in the Age of Franz Joseph*, 43–54.

Implicit in this description is a link between socio-economic status and geographic origin, reflecting the major fault line within Viennese Jewry dividing 'west' from 'east' European Jews. Broadly speaking, local Jews and a preponderance of the immigrants from Hungary and the Czech lands were 'western', i.e. German-speaking, middle-class, and acculturated. Most of the Galicians, by contrast, were 'eastern', i.e. Yiddish-speaking, poorer, more Orthodox, and generally unacculturated.[6] Naturally, neither the cultural divide between east and west nor its economic concomitant was carved in stone. (The Hungarian Orthodox in Vienna, for example, combined resistance to religious reform with a degree of linguistic and social acculturation, speaking German and sporting modern dress.[7]) Yet even taking into account upward social mobility and acculturation, the east–west fissure remained a distinguishing feature of Viennese Jewish society and these categories can be useful as descriptive generalities that were current at the time.

The Jewish geography of Vienna bears this out. Jews lived in distinct residential enclaves that reflected both intra-ethnic and class preferences. Galicians, for example, were more likely than other Jews to live in close proximity to one another. Initially, Jews concentrated in three adjacent areas: the Inner City, primarily the site of government and commerce but also home to the aristocracy; Leopoldstadt, originally the Jewish ghetto of Vienna, with a mixed middle- and working-class population; and Alsergrund, a largely middle-class and professional district. By 1910 Jews were more dispersed, constituting more than 10 per cent of the population in six of Vienna's twenty *Bezirke* (districts). While Leopoldstadt remained home to nearly one-third of Viennese Jews, the majority lived in middle-class districts, with few in either the predominantly working-class areas or in the wealthiest districts (the working-class suburb of Brigittenau, part of Leopoldstadt until 1900, and the wealthy Inner City were the exceptions).[8] An interesting comparison to Jewish residential patterns and socio-economic profile (which incorporated extremes of wealth and poverty) can be found in the capital's only other numerically significant minority, the 100,000 Viennese Czechs. Points of contact between Bohemian and Mora-

[6] On Viennese Jewry's socio-economic profile, see Oxaal and Weitzmann, 'The Jews of Pre-1914 Vienna', 419–32; Rozenblit, *The Jews of Vienna*, ch. 3. On west and east European Jewries, see Ezra Mendelsohn, *The Jews of East Central Europe between the World Wars* (Bloomington, Ind., 1983), 6–7. [7] Freidenreich, *Jewish Politics in Vienna*, 116.

[8] See Rozenblit, *The Jews of Vienna*, ch. 4; Oxaal and Weitzmann, 'The Jews of Pre-1914 Vienna', 404–11; Wistrich, *The Jews of Vienna in the Age of Franz Joseph*, 57–8. On Galician residential preferences, see also Rozenblit, *The Jews of Vienna*, 96–7.

vian Jews and their non-Jewish Czech counterparts were minimal. The two groups lived in different areas, worked in different sectors of the economy—the Czechs were in the main lower-middle- or working-class—and spoke different languages (Czech and German). These differences serve to reinforce the point that Jews were a distinct and identifiable ethnic–religious presence in Vienna.[9]

What is of particular relevance here is how this presence manifested itself in the development of a Jewish political sphere. From the point of view of the Austrian authorities, Viennese Jewry constituted a legally sanctioned community to which all Jews resident in the city belonged, whether or not they paid communal taxes. 'Membership' in the Kultusgemeinde thus united, at least nominally, all Jews. Moreover, they certainly shared, to one degree or another, the *Schicksalsgemeinschaft* (community of fate) forced upon them by a perpetually self-rejuvenating Viennese antisemitism. Clearly, though, membership in the Jewish community—a *religious* community, as it was officially defined by the state—did not imply an interest in Jewish politics (many indeed denied that any such thing existed). While Jewish politicos regularly claimed to speak for all Jews, this was patently a rhetorical flourish rather than a seriously advanced claim. None the less, sufficient numbers were engaged on the Jewish street to achieve a critical mass of ethnopolitics, to create a self-sustaining and viable political life.

Bearing in mind the diversity of Viennese Jewry and its east–west divide, where does the Viennese Jewish polity fit in the context of Jewish political culture in central and eastern Europe, a culture best apprehended by an analysis that combines ideology and geography? In what Jonathan Frankel has called the 'western subsystem'[10] of Jewish politics, so called because it developed primarily in western Europe and the United States, Jews were regarded as solely a religious (rather than an ethnic or national) community and Jewish political goals were circumscribed accordingly. In this Jewish version of liberalism, politics was generally a part-time affair. Western Jewish organizations like the French Alliance Israélite Universelle, the German Centralverein der deutschen Staatsbürger jüdischen Glaubens (Central Association for German Citizens of the Jewish Faith), the American Jewish

---

[9] Michael John and Albert Lichtblau (eds.), *Schmelztiegel Wien—Einst und Jetzt. Zur Geschichte und Gegenwart von Zuwanderung und Minderheiten* (Vienna, 1990), 143–7; Wistrich, *The Jews of Vienna in the Age of Franz Joseph*, 46–7; Rozenblit, *The Jews of Vienna*, 95–6, 116–17; Monika Glettler, *Die Wiener Tschechen um 1900. Strukturanalyse einer nationalen Minderheit in der Großstadt* (Munich, 1972).

[10] Frankel, 'Modern Jewish Politics East and West', 83.

Committee, and the Anglo-Jewish Association saw themselves as advocates for their less fortunate 'co-religionists'—this in itself a telling term, implying that Jews were connected to one another by nothing more than religion. The leaders of these organizations assiduously championed the rights of Jews everywhere to equal rights and emancipation. As convinced liberals, they battled antisemitism by the eminently rational and optimistic means of persuasion and education; as liberals, too, they were suspicious of open and fully democratic politics, preferring what was called in Jewish political parlance *shtadlones*, i.e. intercession with the authorities. This was a philanthropic politics run by, but not necessarily for, an élite oligarchy of the great and the good. Their faith in the god of progress remained firm until well into the 1930s. Ezra Mendelsohn has aptly described this as an 'integrationist' form of politics, its adherents desiring 'to be recognized as being of their countries of residence, not merely in them, and at the same time [wishing] to retain a strong group identity and cohesiveness'.[11]

The nationalist or autonomist obverse of liberal integrationism was prevalent in eastern Europe, and influential also in the United States in the late nineteenth and early twentieth centuries. This was a post-liberal political culture in which Jews were defined as a nation rather than a religion, which was to be either relegated to a secondary role or dispensed with entirely. A revolutionary departure from both traditionalist and liberal Jewish self-perceptions, this nationalist self-definition implied a degree of political and cultural separatism. National self-determination, either in the form of autonomy in Europe or in an independent homeland in Palestine (or elsewhere), was central to the post-liberal world-view. Characteristically a full-time affair demanding from its followers an intense and all-embracing commitment, it diverged both in form and content from its western, integrationist counterpart: it was more radical and more democratic, striving for transformation rather than amelioration of the existing order; it was organized along explicitly political party and movement lines—Zionism and the Bund, for example—rather than along loose associational lines (religious, social, or welfare groups); and power and leadership positions were accessible not just to the wealthy but also to the professional and educated strata of Jewish society.[12]

Straddling both the east–west and the nationalist–integrationist divides

---

[11] Mendelsohn, *On Modern Jewish Politics*, 16. See also ibid. 6–17.
[12] See Frankel, 'Modern Jewish Politics East and West', 83–4; Mendelsohn, *On Modern Jewish Politics*, 17–23.

was traditional Orthodox Jewry, a particularly powerful, if somewhat besieged, force in east European Jewish society. For the Orthodox, the Jews were indeed a nation, or at least a unique and unified people, organically rooted in Torah and in Jewish tradition, i.e. a 'religious nation', not a nation in the secular, modern sense. The Orthodox vehemently rejected modern forms of both nationalism and integration. If thoroughgoing adoption of the mores of the surrounding non-Jewish society was anathema, a degree of linguistic and social acculturation was sometimes acceptable, as in the previously mentioned case of the Hungarian Orthodox in Vienna. In a sense, of course, the traditionalists were by definition anti-modern, concerned mainly with preserving and defending the social and religious *status quo*. But they were forced, by dint of the increasing strength of non- and anti-religious Jewish ideologies, to adopt modern political strategies in order to defend their interests. Their primary weapon in this mission was the Agudes Yisroel organization (League of Israel, also known as Agude). The Orthodox were akin to the Jewish liberals in that they preferred their politics to be part-time and kept within reasonable bounds; they were akin to the nationalists, and unlike the liberals, in that their Jewish identity was a full-time occupation.[13]

In terms of their relationship to the Jewish Question, the prime mover of Jewish politics, these three camps took divergent paths. The liberal integrationists felt that they could arrive at a *modus vivendi* with society at large and its demands upon Jews; the nationalists and autonomists assumed that nothing less than a complete transformation of the Jewish condition, and often of society as a whole, could solve the Jewish Question; while the Orthodox were content by and large to put their fate in God's hands, preferring tactical pragmatism to the elaboration of detailed political programmes. All three could be found in both east and west; nationalism and Orthodoxy, however, were strongest in eastern Europe and Russia, while integrationism held sway in western Europe and the United States. Finally, it is well to remember that these are descriptive models, 'ideal types' used not to impose rigid categories but rather to aid overall conceptualization of the Jewish political landscape.

Where, then, ought Vienna to be located in all this? Vienna was a hybrid

---

[13] On the Agude and what were sometimes called 'Jewish Jews', see Gershon C. Bacon, *The Politics of Tradition: Agudat Yisrael in Poland 1916–1939* (Jerusalem, 1996); Alan L. Mittleman, *The Politics of Torah: The Jewish Political Tradition and the Founding of Agudat Israel* (Albany, NY, 1996); Mendelsohn, *On Modern Jewish Politics*, 23–7.

Jewish polity, an admixture of east and west. Until the First World War a westernized liberal élite dominated Viennese Jewry, an élite conforming in some important respects to what David Sorkin has described as the 'sub-culture' of German Jewry. Some of the characteristics attributed to this sub-culture are applicable in part also to acculturated, German-speaking Viennese Jews—partial integration; an ideology of emancipation based on the idea of quid pro quo (rights for regeneration); the enthusiastic adoption of *Bildung*; the transference of allegiance from 'autonomous community to tutelary state'; embourgoisement; and the context of a semi-authoritarian (or partially enlightened) state.[14] Also evident was the influence of the Austrian strain of liberalism, 'permeated with the congenial but despotic rationalism, centralism, antifeudalism, opposition to church influence in government, and devotion to the use of the German language which were characteristic of Josefine absolutism'.[15] By far the wealthiest of those involved in Jewish affairs, this group constituted the power centre of Viennese Jewry, controlling the major communal institutions and enjoying good access to external sources of power and influence in Viennese and Austrian society.

Living cheek by jowl with this westernized élite were numerous Galician immigrants, all the more prominent and easily identifiable due to the fact that many retained traditional Jewish dress and spoke Yiddish. Given the fact that so many of the Jews in Vienna lived in reasonably close proximity, a degree of contact between the immigrants and the acculturated élite was inevitable. Mutual awareness, however, did not translate into mutual sympathy; antipathy, rather, was often the rule. Not surprisingly, both Jewish nationalism and Orthodoxy were strong among the Galicians. Although a long-time presence in Vienna—the World Zionist Organization established its first headquarters there—the nationalists were poorly represented in the city's formal Jewish power structures. Large potential reservoirs of their support, such as students and poor or working-class Jews (among whom Galicians were disproportionately represented), were disenfranchised by the liberal establishment's insistence that the right to vote in

[14] David Sorkin, *The Transformation of German Jewry 1780–1840* (New York, 1987), 5–8, 173–8. This parallel ought not to be pushed too far, as Sorkin's subculture was in place by 1840, at which time Viennese Jewry numbered only a few thousand.

[15] Andrew G. Whiteside, *The Socialism of Fools: Georg Ritter von Schönerer and Austrian Pan-Germanism* (Berkeley, 1975), 16. On Austrian liberalism, see also Pieter M. Judson, *Exclusive Revolutionaries: Liberal Politics, Social Experience, and National Identity in the Austrian Empire 1848–1914* (Ann Arbor, Mich., 1996).

communal elections be conditional on the payment of communal taxes. As regards Orthodoxy in Vienna, a mixture of east and west is once more evident, with Yiddish-speaking Galicians alongside more affluent, German-speaking, western Hungarians (primarily from western Slovakia and the Burgenland). The former were in general prepared to involve themselves in communal politics, while the latter were distinguished for many years by their separatist tendencies.[16] The war years saw a marked politicization and mobilization in Orthodox circles (true also of the liberals), leading to a greater readiness to engage, if somewhat ambivalently, in overt political action.

One notable political movement was absent from Vienna—the Jewish Left. Despite an economic profile that would seem to have provided at least some of the prerequisites for the growth of a left-wing Jewish subculture—found in the Russian Pale and eastern Europe, and throughout the world in cities where east European Jewish immigrants settled in force—such a movement did not take root in Vienna.[17] A sizeable sector of the Jewish economy in Vienna, for example, was characterized by small-scale artisanal manufacture, self-employment, and petty commerce, attributes it shared with both east European Jewry and the Viennese economy at large.[18] A number of factors, however, militated against the development in Vienna of a strong left-wing movement: the lack of a sweatshop proletariat; the absence of a thriving Yiddish culture; the relatively open nature of the host society, which despite ever-present antisemitism still offered Jewish newcomers the prospect of rapid upward social mobility; the fact that Galicians

[16] On the demographics of Jewish nationalism in Vienna, see Freidenreich, *Jewish Politics in Vienna*, 56–8. On Galicians in Vienna, see Klaus Hödl, *Als Bettler in die Leopoldstadt. Galizische Juden auf dem Weg nach Wien* (Vienna, 1994). On Orthodox demography, see Freidenreich, *Jewish Politics in Vienna*, 116–18.

[17] See Wistrich, *The Jews of Vienna in the Age of Franz Joseph*, 50; Hödl, *Als Bettler in die Leopoldstadt*, 172–7; Jack Jacobs, 'Written out of History: Bundists in Vienna and the Varieties of Jewish Experience in the Austrian First Republic', in Michael Brenner and Derek J. Penslar (eds.), *In Search of Jewish Community: Jewish Identities in Germany and Austria 1918–1933* (Bloomington, Ind., 1998), 115–33. For an overview of the Jewish Left, see Mendelsohn, *On Modern Jewish Politics*, 28–33.

[18] In 1910 approximately one-third of Jewish males fit into these rather elastic categories. See Wistrich, *The Jews of Vienna in the Age of Franz Joseph*, 66; Oxaal and Weitzmann, 'The Jews of Pre-1914 Vienna', 424–32. On the artisan class of east European Jewry, see Arthur Ruppin, *Soziologie der Juden*, i (Berlin, 1930), 431–52; Mendelsohn, *Zionism in Poland*, 7. The development of Viennese antisemitism owed much to this particular economic configuration. On the Viennese artisans and their antisemitism, see Boyer, *Political Radicalism in Late Imperial Vienna*, ch. 2; Wistrich, *The Jews of Vienna in the Age of Franz Joseph*, 227–9.

in Vienna were not fully fledged immigrants but rather internal migrants within their own state; and, finally, that in Galicia itself the Jewish Left was weaker than in many other parts of eastern Europe.[19]

The larger backdrop against which these forces were arrayed was the protracted crisis of the war and the eventual collapse of the monarchy. That they were living in the midst of crisis was a notion regularly articulated by many Jews; it is crucial in particular for an understanding of developments at the war's end. The war years effected a shift in the balance of forces within Viennese Jewish society. In the atmosphere of chaos and uncertainty that reigned at the war's end an almost revolutionary episode occurred in which the westernized norms of the liberal integrationist establishment were temporarily superseded by nationalist radicalism and activism more commonly associated with eastern Europe. What emerged clearly from these events was that east and west existed in an unstable equilibrium within Viennese, and indeed Austrian, Jewry. Both represent, in terms of the eastern and western models of Jewish politics and society, a middle way, central European polities incorporating both east and west yet neither wholly one nor the other. The entire panoply of Jewish politics existed here in constant and unresolved conflict. In turn, the larger context, the multinational Austrian empire, was similarly characterized by what eventually developed into a fatal tension between its constituent forces. Austria, however, was relatively tolerant and almost pluralistic in comparison with its neighbouring multinational empire, tsarist Russia. And it was this relative tolerance that allowed for the development of a unique Jewish political culture, unlike that of either its eastern or western neighbours.

THE POLITICS OF EMPIRE

For the Jews of the empire, the notion that they were part of 'Austrian Jewry', no matter how vaguely defined an entity that might be, was a significant element of their self-perception. An ardent dynastic patriotism played an important unifying role in Austrian Jewish society, with the conviction that the empire was 'good for the Jews' often the only common denominator to the most disparate and mutually hostile Jewish points of view. It was a

---

[19] On the Jewish Left in Galicia, see Shabtai Ungar, 'The Jewish Workers' Movement in Galicia on the Eve of World War One: The Failure to Unify' (Heb.), *Gal-ed*, 10 (1987), 121–46; Jonathan Frankel, *Prophecy and Politics: Socialism, Nationalism, and the Russian Jews, 1862–1917* (Cambridge, 1981), 169, 177–8.

belief forcefully expressed in Jewish responses to the outbreak of war. Echoing the general enthusiasm, the Austrian Zionists declared: 'we Jews lag behind none, but none, of the many nations united within the borders of the monarchy in our readiness to sacrifice for Kaiser and empire . . . [guided by] the categorical imperative of gratitude and love'. No nation, they stressed, 'suffers, sacrifices and fights more willingly . . . Jews are the most loyal among the loyal. . . . Like all Austrian Jews we are animated by fervent love for Kaiser and empire. . . . The intelligence and courage of Jewish officers and soldiers make them the élite of the army.'[20] The liberal *Österreichische Wochenschrift* was proud to announce the war's first Jewish casualty, furnishing proof that Jews were 'valiant comrades-in-arms'.[21] The Vienna Kultusgemeinde affirmed that Austrian Jews 'fight man for man, shoulder to shoulder with all loyal sons of the empire for the honour of the fatherland, they risk their lives for Kaiser and empire, they sacrifice life and property for the increase of the glory of our arms, for the prosperity of our beloved, wise, righteous Kaiser and his land'.[22]

There seems no reason to doubt the sincerity of these expressions of patriotism, although the note of special pleading, the desire to outdo all others in patriotic fervour, is unmistakable. For Jews in the Central Powers, there was an added dimension to their reaction to the outbreak of hostilities: the war was widely viewed as an opportunity to free Russian Jewry from tsarist oppression, thus neatly dovetailing general Austrian and particularist Jewish concerns.[23] The likelihood that Jews would be killing one

[20] *JZ*, 31 July 1914, p. 1; 18 Sept. 1914, pp. 1–2. The terms 'Jewish nationalist' and 'Zionist' will in general be used here interchangeably. When necessary, the difference between the former (emphasizing political and cultural work in the Diaspora) and the latter (stressing the centrality of Palestine) will be made clear.   [21] *OW*, 7 Aug. 1914, pp. 545–6.

[22] Protokolle der Plenar-Sitzungen, suppl., 18 Aug. 1914, CAHJP, AW, 71/15. See also *MOIU* 26 (July–Aug. 1914), 1–2. Jews on both sides of the war expressed such sentiments. On Germany, for example, see Jehuda Reinharz, *Fatherland or Promised Land* (Ann Arbor, Mich., 1975), 222–4. On Russia, see Salo W. Baron, *The Russian Jew under Tsars and Soviets*, 2nd edn. (New York, 1987), 156–7; M. Altshuler, 'Russia and her Jews: The Impact of the 1914 War', *Wiener Library Bulletin*, 27 (1973–4), 12–13.

[23] The Jewish press was tireless in its denunciations of Russian 'barbarism' towards Jews. See e.g. *WH*, 28 Aug. 1914, pp. 6–7; 29 Sept. 1914, p. 3; 13 Nov. 1914, p. 6; *OW*, 14 Aug. 1914, pp. 561–2; 21 Aug. 1914, pp. 579–80; 23 Oct. 1914, p. 722; *JZ*, 11 Dec. 1914, p. 2. See also Marsha L. Rozenblit, 'The Dilemma of Identity: The Impact of the First World War on Habsburg Jewry', in Ritchie Robertson and Edward Timms (eds.), *The Habsburg Legacy: National Identity in Historical Perspective*, Austrian Studies, v (Edinburgh, 1994), 146–7. More general condemnations of the 'war-mongers' of 'perfidious Albion' and 'superficial French civilization' were also common. See *WH*, 14 Aug. 1914, pp. 4–5; 6 Nov. 1914, pp. 3–4; 13 Nov. 1914, pp. 3–4; *OW*, 21 Aug. 1914, pp. 577–8. On the whole, the Zionist press was less preoccupied with these issues.

another in the name of a higher loyalty was glossed over and only very rarely mentioned in any public forum.[24] Apparently overriding this consideration (particularly in the earlier stages of the war) was the chance to prove themselves once and for all as equal and worthy citizens. Again and again, patriotism and heroism were emphasized in bathetic accounts of Jewish exploits at the front.[25] To the same end, the nationalists established a Jewish War Archive in Vienna to gather material to 'provide proof of the patriotism of Jews in Austria-Hungary and Germany during the war and thereby prepare them for future discussions concerning their status in these lands'.[26] Although a nationalist initiative, the War Archive received broad support.[27] Wall-to-wall Jewish patriotism was maintained until the very end, even when expressions of dissent were permitted and others were transferring allegiance from the empire to their own *Volk*.[28] From the Orthodox to the radical socialists of Po'alei Zion, Jews preferred a reformed Austria ruled by a strong and protective central power, combining guarantees of group autonomy for those who demanded it with constitutionally anchored equal rights for all citizens. Agreement of this sort, though, was at a premium. More common was a terminal fractiousness, a local version of the divisiveness and fragmentation that were characteristic of the Jewish public sphere

---

[24] See e.g. David G. Roskies, *Against the Apocalypse: Responses to Catastrophe in Modern Jewish Culture* (Cambridge, Mass., 1984), 135. While Russian Jews would do their patriotic duty, they would surely lack the zeal of German or Austrian Jews, commented a lead article in the *OW*, 14 Aug. 1914, pp. 561–3. It was 'tragic' that Jews should fight one another, lamented a Zionist commentator, but freedom would be the result of this 'battle against the Russians'. See *JZ*, 11 Dec. 1914, p. 1.

[25] For example: Jews 'deserve an honourable page in the annals of our monarchy. We have earned it with our blood' (*WH*, 16 Oct. 1914, p. 3). Or: the war 'has utterly eradicated' the idea that Jews are 'cowardly' or 'second-class citizens' (*WH*, 13 Nov. 1914, pp. 3–4). See also *WH*, 29 Jan. 1915, pp. 4–5; *OW*, 30 Oct. 1914, pp. 739–40; 11 Dec. 1914, pp. 855–8; *MOIU* 26 (Nov.–Dec. 1914), 1–2; Moritz Frühling (ed.), *Jüdisches Kriegsgedenkblatt*, nos. 1–6 (Vienna, 1914–18). On Jews in the Austrian army, see Erwin A. Schmidl, *Juden in der k. (u.) k. Armee 1788–1918* (Eisenstadt, 1989); István Deák, *Jewish Soldiers in Austro-Hungarian Society* (New York, 1990).

[26] Circular, n.d. (probably Jan. or Feb. 1915), CZA, Z3/154. See also the letters from late 1914 and early 1915 in CZA, L6/295; *JZ*, 1 Jan. 1915, p. 1; 29 Jan. 1915, p. 2; *Jüdisches Archiv. Mitteilungen des Komitees Jüdisches Kriegsarchiv* (Vienna, 1915–17).

[27] See e.g. the list of patrons in CAHJP, AW, 247/2. In Dec. 1917 J. S. Bloch suggested that the Kultusgemeinde create its own war archive. See Joseph Samuel Bloch, *Erinnerungen aus meinem Leben*, iii (Vienna, 1933), 237–41.

[28] Rozenblit, 'The Dilemma of Identity', 144–50. On the gradual dissolution of the bonds between the dynasty and its peoples, see Z. A. B. Zeman, *The Break-Up of the Habsburg Empire 1914–1918* (London, 1961); Robert A. Kann, *A History of the Habsburg Empire 1526–1918* (Berkeley, 1974), 497–520.

elsewhere in Europe.[29] Unity of purpose and action extended little beyond consensus about a common agenda—the need to deal with the pressing problems of refugee welfare and rising antisemitism. Practical co-operation proved elusive.

Jewish dynastic allegiance has often been remarked upon. Along with the court, army, bureaucracy, aristocracy, and the Church, an important role has been attributed to the Jews as an integrative force in the Habsburg lands.[30] Central to this argument is the perception that Jews constituted the backbone of a loyal, monarchy-wide, urban middle class. The idea of a Jewish bourgeoisie locked in a mutually beneficial embrace with a protective central authority has enjoyed wide currency. For Oscar Jászi, to give just one example, Jews were the constitutive element of capitalism, 'a very efficacious force in the unification and cohesion of the monarchy'.[31] Jewish publicists, too, saw fit to stress a particular Jewish affinity with the supranational Austrian idea, construing this affinity not just as a liberal or middle-class phenomenon but as one embracing the entire spectrum of Austrian Jewry. This was standard fare from the latter part of the nineteenth century. Adolf Jellinek, rabbi of the Leopoldstadt Temple from 1858 to 1865 and of the Kultusgemeinde's flagship synagogue, the Stadttempel (City Temple), until 1893, wrote in 1883 that Austrian Jews 'are Austrians first and last, they feel and think Austrian, they want a great, strong and mighty Austria. . . . Hence the Jews are thoroughly dynastical, loyalist, Austrian. . . . The Jews of Austria are therefore a very important constituent part of the multinational Empire. For they are the standardbearers of the Austrian idea of unity.'[32] To Joseph Samuel Bloch, Galician-born editor and publisher of the *Österreichische Wochenschrift*, and member of the Reichsrat (Austrian parliament) from 1883 to 1895, only the Jews were true Austrians: 'If one

---

[29] On this 'extreme divisiveness', see Ezra Mendelsohn, *Jewish Politics in East Central Europe between the World Wars* (Cambridge, Mass., 1984), 5–6.

[30] See e.g. Wistrich, *The Jews of Vienna in the Age of Franz Joseph*, 272–3, 665; Marsha L. Rozenblit, 'The Jews of the Dual Monarchy', *Austrian History Yearbook*, 23 (1992), 160–80. For a different perspective, see Steven Beller, 'Patriotism and the National Identity of Habsburg Jewry 1860–1914', *LBIYB* 41 (1996), 215–38.

[31] Oscar Jászi, *The Dissolution of the Habsburg Monarchy* (Chicago, 1966), 170. For other examples, see McCagg, *A History of Habsburg Jews*, 3–4; Ernst Bruckmüller, 'Die Rolle der Juden in der österreichischen Gesellschaft bis 1918', *Christliche Demokratie*, 7 (1987), 153–7; Nikolas Vielmetti, 'Liberalismus—Demokratie—jüdische Emanzipation in Österreich', *Christliche Demokratie*, 7 (1987), 166–70; László Peter and Robert B. Pynsent (eds.), *Intellectuals and the Future in the Habsburg Monarchy 1890–1914* (London, 1988), 1–7; Georg Franz, *Liberalismus. Die deutschliberale Bewegung in der habsburgischen Monarchie* (Munich, 1955), 189–98.

[32] Quoted in Wistrich, *The Jews of Vienna in the Age of Franz Joseph*, 164. See also ibid. 256.

could construct a specifically Austrian nationality, then the Jews would constitute its foundation.'[33]

Integral to this phenomenon was the widespread Jewish veneration of the emperor Franz Joseph.[34] Even under his successor, Karl I, however, there was no discernible breach in Jewish support for the dynasty, and Jewish leaders stressed their devotion right throughout the war. A lead article in Bloch's *Wochenschrift*, for example, reiterated that Jews were 'not only the most loyal supporters of the empire, but the only unconditional Austrians'.[35] Echoing this sentiment, Heinrich Schreiber, an influential figure in liberal circles, asserted that 'the oldest and most firmly established Austrians are actually the Jews. . . . There are no better and more authentic Austrians. . . . Only they acknowledge themselves without reservation to be Austrians.'[36] Robert Stricker, Vienna's leading Zionist personality, declared that 'there are no Austrian Jews who do not utterly affirm the existence of Austria and keenly wish for its free development in the interests of the Jewish *Volk*'.[37]

A corollary of this identification with the empire was the development of a Jewish version of the Austrian 'mission' or 'idea'. As a supranational entity Austria was deemed uniquely situated to be a force for reconciliation between nations and peoples, to mediate between eastern and western Europe. Within the confines of its own borders this was often expressed as a mission to bring enlightenment and western (which meant German-language) culture to the eastern reaches of the empire.[38] The Jews, supranational and possessing a special historical rapport with German culture, were particularly well suited to assist in these tasks, it was argued.[39] This coincidence of

[33] Joseph Samuel Bloch, *Der nationale Zwist und die Juden in Österreich* (Vienna, 1886), 41. Quoted in Wistrich, *The Jews of Vienna in the Age of Franz Joseph*, 270. See also Jacob Toury, 'Troubled Beginnings: The Emergence of the Österreichisch-Israelitische Union', *LBIYB* 30 (1985), 463.

[34] On Jewish devotion to Franz Joseph, see Wistrich, *The Jews of Vienna in the Age of Franz Joseph*, 175–81. A typically hagiographical tribute is Oskar Grün, *Franz Joseph der Erste in seinem Verhältnis zu den Juden* (Zurich, 1916).   [35] *OW*, 22 June 1917, p. 390.

[36] *OW*, 20 July 1917, pp. 454–5. See also *OW*, 19 July 1918, p. 442.

[37] *JZ*, 7 June 1918, p. 1. See also *JZ*, 9 Aug. 1918, p. 1. For similar sentiments from the Orthodox side, see *JK*, 28 Oct. 1915, p. 1; Jonas Kreppel, *Der Weltkrieg und die Judenfrage* (Vienna, 1915), 20–2.

[38] On the Austrian 'mission' and *Staatsgedanke*, see Fritz Fellner, 'Die Historiographie zur österreichisch-deutschen Problematik als Spiegel der nationalpolitischen Diskussion', in Heinrich Lutz and Helmut Rumpler (eds.), *Österreich und die deutsche Frage im 19. und 20. Jahrhundert* (Vienna, 1982), 33–59; Günther Ramhardter, *Geschichtswissenschaft und Patriotismus. Österreichische Historiker im Weltkrieg 1914–1918* (Munich, 1973), 57–62.

[39] See e.g. Bloch, *Der nationale Zwist und die Juden in Österreich*, 44–9; Isidor Singer, *Presse und Judenthum* (Vienna, 1882), 142–9; Stefan Zweig, *The World of Yesterday* (Lincoln, Nebr., 1964), 22–3. See also Toury, 'Troubled Beginnings', 463.

interests was emphasized during the war by Jewish nationalists in particular.[40] Nathan Birnbaum, a pre-Herzlian Zionist, later a Yiddishist, and
by the war years moving towards strict Orthodoxy, contended in December
1914 that it was Austria's 'unique historical task to solve the problem of the
national state, [as] only in such a [multinational] framework is the free development of the Jewish *Volk* possible'.[41] Approvingly citing the Czech
František Palacký's formulation of 1848—'If Austria had not existed, it
would have been necessary to invent it'—a lead article in the Zionist *Jüdische
Zeitung* remarked that the Jews 'have altruistically and loyally sustained the
Austrian state idea'. To grant Jews national status in an Austria reorganized
along national lines, argued the Zionists, would ensure the survival of
both.[42]

Such arguments were part of the broader wartime debate in Austria
about federally reorganizing the empire. Much of this debate focused on
the possibility of self-determination for the empire's national and ethnic
groups. Jewish contributions to this discussion illustrate at one and the
same time dynastic Jewish loyalism and the divergent styles of Jewish political praxis. The most explicit Jewish advocacy of structural reform of the
empire came from the nationalists. In 1906 the Austrian Zionist organization, responding to increasing pressure from proponents of *Gegenwartsar-
beit* or *Landespolitik* (political and cultural work in the Diaspora rather than
a solely political and Palestine-centred orientation), had called for the reorganization of the empire along national and democratic lines.[43] Influenced

[40] That Jews were uniquely well qualified to act as mediators between eastern and western
Europe, and were therefore a strategic asset to the Central Powers then occupying much of east-
ern Europe, figured prominently also in German Jewish apologetic literature of the war. See
Steven E. Aschheim, *Brothers and Strangers: The East European Jew in German and German Jew-
ish Consciousness 1800–1923* (Madison, Wis., 1982), 153–63. For examples of this genre, see
Wladimir W. Kaplun-Kogan, *Der Krieg. Eine Schicksalsstunde des jüdischen Volkes* (Bonn, 1915);
Felix Theilhaber, *Die Juden im Weltkriege* (Berlin, 1916).

[41] *JZ*, 25 Dec. 1914, p. 3. See also Nathan Birnbaum's remarks in *JZ*, 28 Oct. 1915, p. 1; Birnbaum, *Den Ostjuden ihr Recht* (Vienna, 1915); Hermann Kadisch, 'Die Idee des mitteleuropäischen Staatenbundes und das jüdische Volk', *JNK* 1 (1915–16), 96.

[42] *JZ*, 30 July 1915, p. 1. See also *JZ*, 2 Apr. 1915, p. 2; 28 May 1915, p. 1; 14 Apr. 1916, pp.
2–3; 30 June 1916, p. 1; 3 May 1918, p. 2; 14 June 1918, p. 1. On the wartime revival of the Austrian 'idea', see Stanley Suval, *The Anschluss Question in the Weimar Era* (Baltimore, 1974), ch. 12;
C. E. Williams, *The Broken Eagle: The Politics of Austrian Literature from Empire to Anschluss*
(London, 1974), 7, 17–18, 155.

[43] See Wistrich, *The Jews of Vienna in the Age of Franz Joseph*, 377–8; Rozenblit, *The Jews of
Vienna*, 170–6. The most important Austrian *Landespolitik* organizations were the Jüdische
Volkspartei (Jewish People's Party), formed in 1902, the Jüdische Nationalpartei (Jewish
National Party), established in 1906 in order to contest the 1907 Reichsrat elections (the first
with universal male suffrage), and the Jüdische Nationalverein (Jewish National Association), set

by both theories of Jewish autonomism elaborated by Simon Dubnow in Russia and the concept of non-territorial, personal-national sovereignty developed by Austrian Social Democrats Karl Renner and Otto Bauer (who denied that Jews constituted a nationality), the Zionists demanded that Jews too should enjoy national autonomy.[44] As long as far-reaching reform was little more than a vague prospect on the political horizon, they did not go beyond a framework of generalities calling for recognition of Jewish nationality and protection of Jewish national, cultural, and economic interests (however they might be defined).[45] During the war, however, when political reform and government recognition of Jewish nationality appeared imminent, sharp disagreements arose within nationalist ranks about what exactly was meant by the catch-all phrase 'national autonomy', and it became apparent that no consensus existed as to what the limits and contours of autonomy ought to be.

Jewish nationality was never officially recognized by the Austrian authorities. Formally defined as a religious minority, Jews were none the less on occasion categorized by Austrian officialdom as a *Volk*, and sometimes even as a nationality.[46] This ambiguity of status and the prospect of reform during the war aroused the hopes of Jewish nationalists for a *de jure* recognition of Jewish nationality.[47] Their ideas on reform were most consistently articu-

up in 1907 by the Zionist organization as its *Landespolitik* arm. See Adolf Gaisbauer, *Davidstern und Doppeladler* (Vienna, 1988), 458–74, 489.

[44] On Jewish autonomism, see Simon Dubnow, *Nationalism and History: Essays on Old and New Judaism*, ed. Koppel S. Pinson (Philadelphia, 1958), 131–42; Kurt Stillschweig, 'Nationalism and Autonomy among Eastern European Jewry: Origin and Historical Development up to 1939', *Historica Judaica*, 6 (1944), 27–68. For a more recent analysis, see also Matityahu Mintz, 'Jewish Nationalism in the Context of Multi-National States', in Jehuda Reinharz, Gideon Shimoni, and Yosef Salmon (eds.), *Jewish Nationalism and Politics: New Perspectives* (Heb.) (Jerusalem, 1996), 201–23.

[45] For the most comprehensive elaboration of a *Landespolitik* programme, see Hermann Kadisch, *Jung-Juden und Jung-Österreich* (Vienna, 1912).

[46] On the sometimes ambiguous status of the Jews in Austria, see Gerald Stourzh, 'Galten die Juden als Nationalität Altösterreichs?', *Studia Judaica Austriaca*, 10 (1984), 73–98; id., *Die Gleichberechtigung der Nationalitäten in der Verfassung und Verwaltung Österreichs 1848–1918* (Vienna, 1985), 233–40. Stourzh argues that the Jews enjoyed a *de facto* national status in certain areas of the empire. See also Kurt Stillschweig, 'Die nationalitätenrechtliche Stellung der Juden im alten Österreich', *Monatsschrift für Geschichte und Wissenschaft des Judentums*, 81 (1937), 321–40; id., 'Die nationalitätenrechtliche Stellung der Juden in den russischen und österreichischen Nachfolgestaaten während der Weltkriegsepoche', *Monatsschrift für Geschichte und Wissenschaft des Judentums*, 82 (1938), 217–48.

[47] For examples of their repeated calls for national and democratic reform of the empire during the war years, see the Nationalverein declaration in *JZ*, 21 Jan. 1916, p. 1; 'Denkschrift der national organisierten Judenschaft an die österr. Regierung', in *JZ*, 22 Mar. 1918, p. 1. See also

lated by Hermann Kadisch, an indefatigable ideologue of Jewish Diaspora nationalism. Kadisch took as his ideological inspiration the Jewish hero of the 1848 revolution in Vienna, Adolf Fischhof. Born and raised in Budapest, Fischhof studied medicine in Vienna and played a key role in the March uprising. He later became one of the first and most prominent advocates of a federalist and pluralist empire in which all nations would enjoy self-rule. In innumerable articles Kadisch similarly insisted that the continued existence of Austria, suitably democratized, federalized, and nationalized, was a 'historical necessity', and that Jews must be recognized as one of its constituent nationalities. Like his mentor he believed social and economic reform, democracy, and national reconciliation were indivisible and fundamental prerequisites for Austria's 'regeneration'.[48] It proved difficult for Kadisch and some of his like-minded colleagues to relinquish their devotion to an idealized version of Austria. In the early post-war period Kadisch and Robert Stricker (among others) somewhat wistfully advocated a monarchy-like federation of the successor states.[49]

Other Jewish calls for reform during the war were more muted and less radical, rarely propounding a distinct role for Jews in the new order. Instead, they promised that Jews would continue to be loyal and productive citizens, albeit in a hopefully more democratic and less internally riven Austria. Lead articles in the liberal *Wahrheit*, for example, repeatedly pointed out the benefits for all of greater democracy and increased co-operation among the peoples of the empire.[50] As the quasi-official Kultusgemeinde organ until shortly after the war, *Die Wahrheit* (published from 1885 to 1938) was sober and cautious, its concerns religious, social, and communal rather than political.[51] As constitutional reform became a topic of public discussion, however, the paper's leader writer grew bolder. By February 1918, for example, he could write: 'Austria-Hungary will sooner

---

JZ, 27 June 1917, pp. 1–2; 12 July 1918, p. 1. See also Boyer, *Culture and Political Crisis in Vienna*, 395–6, for Christian Social plans that recognized Jewish nationality in Galicia and Bukovina.

[48] On Fischhof, see Werner J. Cahnmann, 'Adolf Fischhof and his Jewish Followers', *LBIYB* 4 (1959), 111–39; Wistrich, *The Jews of Vienna in the Age of Franz Joseph*, 149–60. For Kadisch (1861–1934), see Hermann Kadisch, 'Die österreichische Nationalitätenfrage und die Juden', *NJM* 1 (1916–17), 300–6; id., *Die Juden und die österreichische Verfassungsrevision* (Vienna, 1918); Cahnmann, 'Adolf Fischhof and his Jewish Followers', 137–9; Gaisbauer, *Davidstern und Doppeladler*, 458–9 n. 45.

[49] For post-war federation proposals, see Ch. 5 n. 7.

[50] See e.g. *WH*, 4 Dec. 1914, pp. 3–4; 7 May 1915, pp. 3–4; 17 Sept. 1915, pp. 3–4; 14 Jan. 1916, pp. 3–4; 13 July 1917, pp. 3–4.

[51] Rozenblit, *The Jews of Vienna*, 183; Freidenreich, *Jewish Politics in Vienna*, 24–5; Jacob Toury, *Die jüdische Presse im österreichischen Kaiserreich 1802–1918* (Tübingen, 1983), 73.

or later be recast as a federation (*Staatenbund*) of all nations living within its borders.' In May 1918 he declared: 'A constitutional revision on the basis of nationality is unavoidable in Austria-Hungary.'[52] In contrast to Kadisch and other nationalists, however, liberals regarded the Jewish interest in democratic reform and 'national justice' from a primarily defensive perspective. Without reforms, *Die Wahrheit* feared, antisemitism would surely pose an ever greater threat as disgruntled nationalists vented their frustrations on the Jews.[53]

From the Orthodox side, the *Jüdische Korrespondenz*, Austrian Orthodoxy's leading organ, cautioned against precipitate Jewish action. Jews should remain alert but passive; engaging in premature politicking was mere demagogy.[54] Even as Jewish traditionalists began to organize in order to make their voices heard in the debate about constitutional reform and its implications for Jewish status, this was to remain the thrust of the paper's editorials and opinion pieces. There could be no independent Jewish role in Austrian politics and no explicitly Jewish opinion on constitutional issues beyond an emphasis on devotion to the Kaiser and loyalty to the empire. The only permissible collective demands were for equality before the law and the freedom to pursue Jewish religious and cultural affairs.[55]

The reluctance of liberals and the Orthodox to project an independent stance on the issue of reform is indicative of their generally reactive mode of politics. The activist bent of the nationalists, in this case their eagerness to project a vocal and unambiguously Jewish point of view in debates about constitutional reform, stood in sharp contrast to the liberal and Orthodox preference for restraint, caution, and strategic consultation with the authorities—in a word, *shtadlones*. Where the nationalists were political by intent and by definition, the liberals and Orthodox often portrayed themselves as political only by default, forced into open action against their will and better judgement. For most Austrian Jews, politics was in any case secondary for the first years of the war. Until late 1916 the demands of refugee welfare dominated organized Jewish life, subsuming (although not of course entirely extinguishing) other concerns. In addition to the refugee crisis that absorbed so much energy and attention, harsh restrictions on political activity had been imposed early in the war, severely curtailing the functioning of

[52] *WH*, 22 Feb. 1918, p. 4; 31 May 1918, p. 4.   [53] See e.g. *WH*, 22 Feb. 1918, pp. 3–4.
[54] *JK*, 19 Aug. 1915, p. 1; 28 Oct. 1915, p. 1.

[55] See e.g. *JK*, 4 Jan. 1917, p. 1; 11 Jan. 1917, p. 1; 22 Feb. 1917, p. 1; 25 May 1917, pp. 1–2; 12 July 1917, p. 1; 27 Sept. 1917, p. 1; 28 Feb. 1918, pp. 2–3; 7 Mar. 1918, pp. 2–3; 14 Mar. 1918, pp. 3–4.

the enormous network of *Vereine*, the social and political associations that were a central collective expression of ethnic society. Their ranks in any case depleted by the draft, Jewish associations, like their Czech counterparts, were largely dormant until the advent of the new regime of Karl I, following the death of Franz Joseph in November 1916.[56] The subsequent relaxation of political restraints, along with the new emperor's apparent commitment to structural reform of the empire, elicited a vigorous political response in Austrian society.[57] Jews were no exception to this, spurred also by their perception of an alarming increase in the volume and intensity of antisemitism. The result was a dramatic upswing in Jewish political life, among liberals, nationalists, and Orthodox alike.

JEWISH LIBERALISM

Prior to the Great War liberal integrationists controlled most of the formal and informal power structures of Viennese Jewish society, dominating the community's wealthiest institutions and political organizations. These 'Austrians of the Mosaic faith' were, in their own eyes at least, westernized and liberal in the mould of British, French, and American Jews.[58] Adhering predominantly to the non-Orthodox Viennese rite, a compromise between the demands of tradition and reform, they placed a high premium on decorum in religious ritual, striving in this way to convey a public image of propriety.[59] Their 'western' self-image, however, was more a matter of identification with German culture and political liberalism than geographic origin. Some of the liberal leaders were indeed Viennese-born, but a greater proportion had migrated to the capital from the Czech or Hungarian lands. (Few, though, were from Galicia.) This 'interlocking Jewish Liberal establishment' was made up mostly of middle- to upper-middle-class professionals and businessmen—women were excluded from leadership

[56] On ethnic *Vereine*, see Gary B. Cohen, 'Organisational Patterns of the Urban Ethnic Groups', in Max Engman (ed.), *Ethnic Identity in Urban Europe* (New York, 1992), 407–18; id., 'Liberal Associations and Central European Urban Society 1840–1890', *Maryland Historian*, 12 (1981), 1–11. On wartime Czech associations, see Karl M. Brousek, *Wien und seine Tschechen* (Munich, 1980), 26–7.

[57] On Austrian wartime administration, see Joseph Redlich, *Austrian War Government* (New Haven, 1929); Kann, *A History of the Habsburg Empire*, 487–97. On plans for reform, see Boyer, *Culture and Political Crisis in Vienna*, 382–419.

[58] For statements to this effect, see *OW*, 18 Oct. 1918, pp. 659–60; 25 Oct. 1918, pp. 673–5.

[59] On the Viennese rite, see Marsha L. Rozenblit, 'The Struggle over Religious Reform in Nineteenth-Century Vienna', *Association for Jewish Studies Review*, 14 (1989), 179–221.

positions—along with a small élite of parliamentarians, ennobled industrialists, and bankers.[60]

Of the impressive network of liberal organizations devoted to social, humanitarian, and educational concerns, the most important were the Israelitische Allianz zu Wien, B'nai B'rith, and the Österreichisch-Israelitische Union (Austrian–Israelite Union), all of which were based in Vienna but active throughout the empire. Only the Union conceived of politics as part of its work; the Allianz and B'nai B'rith, as local affiliates of international organizations, were avowedly non-political and went to great lengths to avoid any activity that could expose them to potentially damaging charges of foreign loyalties. They were, or so they liked to believe, above politics, preferring to focus on 'non-political' matters such as welfare, philanthropy, and education. During the war, though, with more than 100,000 Galician and Bukovinian refugees in Vienna, welfare took on a decidedly political hue and pitched the Allianz and B'nai B'rith willy-nilly into the political domain.

Modelled on the French Alliance Israélite Universelle, the Allianz in Vienna was formed in 1873. Its outlook was determinedly cosmopolitan. 'The protection of Jews, persecuted for their religious beliefs and denied their civic rights, was perceived . . . as an international humanitarian task that transcended national, separatist, and confessional boundaries.'[61] This agenda did not, however, preclude Austrian patriotism. The function of the Paris Alliance as purveyor of French *civilisation* in the Near East and North Africa was mirrored by the mission of the Viennese Allianz to spread German-language *Kultur* among the unenlightened Jewish masses of Galicia. Its supranational ideology made it in fact a model patriot organization, Germanophile in culture and liberal in political orientation. During the war the Allianz was fully occupied with the welfare effort, presiding over an enormous aid network for Jewish refugees in all the Austrian lands.

The Viennese branch of the fraternal philanthropic, charitable, and service organization B'nai B'rith was established in 1895. A self-styled 'ethical élite' of Viennese and Austrian Jewry, B'nai B'rith promoted a public image

[60] On the demographics of this group, see Freidenreich, *Jewish Politics in Vienna*, 23, 27–8, 38. The phrase 'interlocking Jewish Liberal establishment' appears ibid. 28. See also Rozenblit, *The Jews of Vienna*, 148–50. On the wealthy patrician élite of Viennese Jewry, see William O. McCagg, Jr., 'Jewish Wealth in Vienna 1670–1918', in Michael K. Silber (ed.), *Jews in the Hungarian Economy 1760–1945* (Jerusalem, 1992), 53–91.

[61] Wistrich, *The Jews of Vienna in the Age of Franz Joseph*, 72–3. On the Allianz, see ibid. 71–5; Nahum Michael Gelber, 'Die Wiener Israelitische Allianz', *Bulletin des Leo Baeck Instituts*, 3 (1960), 190–203.

of Jews as virtuous citizens. Nearly a quarter of local members were drafted at one time or another, and the organization's wartime activities were accordingly limited. Purely social gatherings were in any event abjured, as these were deemed inappropriately frivolous; nevertheless, a regular schedule of lectures and meetings was maintained. Here, too, welfare work dominated.[62] Both the Allianz and B'nai B'rith, despite being nominally non-political, were politically influential by virtue of their affluent memberships and the fact that their leaderships comprised a central part of the Jewish establishment. Besides their involvement in the politics of welfare, for example, both also became embroiled in the conflicts surrounding the Congress movement.

For the Union, politics was crucial. Established in 1886 by Jewish activists dissatisfied with the response of the Kultusgemeinde to the alarming increase in antisemitism during the previous decade, the primary goals of the Union were active defence against antisemitism and fostering of Jewish identity and pride. To the founders of the Union, the Jews were more than merely a religious community; they were a *Stamm* (tribe or ethnicity) with a distinct culture and heritage. This conviction gave rise to a greater willingness to be publicly assertive about Jewish rights and the promotion of Jewish education and culture. The political cast of the Union emerged most clearly in the 1890s, when it began to function as a pressure group, running and supporting candidates in local and national elections, and fighting a rearguard action against the declining fortunes of liberalism in the general political arena. In Jewish politics the Union quickly developed from an oppositional group into a leading force; it became, and remained, part of the establishment. Already by 1889, for example, it wielded considerable communal power and had secured a majority on the Kultusgemeinde's governing board.

The Union represented a marked shift within the liberal camp from an older generation's reluctance to engage in high-profile defence of Jewish rights to a more public affirmation of Jewish activism. That this was a shift

---

[62] B'nai B'rith ('Sons of the Covenant') was formed in the United States in 1843. A German branch was established in 1882. See Dennis B. Klein, *Jewish Origins of the Psychoanalytic Movement* (New York, 1981), 75. On B'nai B'rith in Vienna, see ibid. 75–84; Rozenblit, *The Jews of Vienna*, 149–50; Alexander Hecht, 'Die w. "Eintracht" als Erziehungsstätte', in *Festschrift anlässlich des fünfundzwanzigjährigen Bestandes des Israel. Humanitätsvereines 'Eintracht' (Bnai Brith) Wien 1903–1928* (Vienna, 1928), 70–1. On its wartime activity, see Arnold Ascher, '25 Jahre Eintracht', in *Festschrift anlässlich des fünfundzwanzigjährigen Bestandes des Israel. Humanitätsvereines 'Eintracht'*, 28–34; *ZBB* 19 (1916), 5, 24–7; 20 (1917), 77; 22 (1919), 202.

in degree rather than kind is pointed up by the gulf separating the Union from the nationalists, in terms of both style and content. At the root of the friction between the two groups was a fundamental disagreement over how to define the Jews—as *Stamm* or nation. By 1914 the Union claimed almost 8,000 members.[63] During the war the Union occupied itself with monitoring antisemitism and with making repeated, and largely futile, attempts to persuade the authorities to restrain anti-Jewish hostility. Although the Union was not involved in the welfare effort as an organization, its leaders and members were prominent in welfare work.[64]

The key figure in the creation of the Union and a good example of its brand of non-nationalist ethnic pride and assertiveness was Joseph Samuel Bloch. As a Reichsrat representative for an east Galician constituency, his outspoken defence of Jewish rights and indignant counter-attacks against antisemites paved the way for the Union's adoption of an unapologetically ethnic public profile. Bloch's insistence that Jewish political interests not only existed but ought to be vocally and defiantly pursued marked him as a radical in the context of Jewish liberalism. Over and above his importance as the public face of combative Judaism (in addition to his other accomplishments, he was an ordained Orthodox rabbi), Bloch introduced into the Jewish public sphere in Austria a new and more aggressive style of journalism. In 1884 he founded the *Österreichische Wochenschrift*, the paper's title alluding to Bloch's wish to provide a patriotic Austrian counterpart to the *Deutsche Wochenschrift*, edited by the Jewish German nationalist historian Heinrich Friedjung. Bloch's *Wochenschrift* became a forum for public debate on Jewish issues that far exceeded the scope of existing Jewish press organs, which tended to be less political in focus and less polemical in tone.[65]

[63] On the Union, see Wistrich, *The Jews of Vienna in the Age of Franz Joseph*, ch. 10; Freidenreich, *Jewish Politics in Vienna*, 23–36; Toury, 'Troubled Beginnings'; id., 'Years of Strife: The Contest of the Österreichisch-Israelitische Union for the Leadership of Austrian Jewry', *LBIYB* 33 (1988), 179–99. Membership figures are in Freidenreich, *Jewish Politics in Vienna*, 26–7.

[64] On the Union in wartime, see *OW*, 12 May 1916, pp. 314–19. Much of this report was excised by the censor, as was the whole of the Union's report of its previous year's activity. See *MOIU* 28 (Apr.–May 1916), 1–15; 30 (Jan.–Feb. 1918), 18. On the Union during the war, see also *Festschrift zu Feier des 50-jährigen Bestandes der Union Österreichischer Juden* (Vienna, 1937), ch. 1; *NNZ*, 25 Dec. 1914, p. 4.

[65] On the *Österreichische Wochenschrift* (which was published until 1920), see Toury, *Die jüdische Presse im österreichischen Kaiserreich*, 74–82; Bloch, *Erinnerungen aus meinem Leben*, iii. 265–9. On the importance of the press as an arena for Jewish politics, see Lederhendler, *The Road to Modern Jewish Politics*, 130–3; Yehuda Slutsky, *The Russian Jewish Press in the Nineteenth*

In formal terms, the premier Jewish political arena in Vienna was the liberal-dominated Kultusgemeinde. Why this was so, given that relatively few Viennese Jews paid communal taxes and even fewer participated in Gemeinde elections, requires some explanation. First established in 1852 (and given further legal definition in 1867, 1890, and 1896), the Kultusgemeinde functioned as a semi-autonomous administrative body, catering to the religious and welfare needs of Viennese Jewry. It was empowered by the state to charge fees for its services and to tax its constituents in order to raise the necessary revenue to carry out its manifold tasks—registering all Jewish births, deaths, conversions, and marriages in Vienna; building and maintaining synagogues, cemeteries, ritual baths, and a wide variety of philanthropic and welfare institutions for the elderly, the sick, and the indigent; supervision of religious education; and employment of communal rabbis. For the state, the Kultusgemeinde functioned as 'an agency of government', the state-sanctioned representative body on Jewish matters. In turn, the Gemeinde assumed for itself the role of Jewish representative to the Austrian authorities. It is this role, in tandem with the power base inherent in its large organizational network, that made the Gemeinde a crucial political battleground, despite its nominally non-political status.[66]

The Kultusgemeinde's self-appointed role as Jewish representative body was hotly contested by the nationalists. Following Herzl's injunction to 'conquer the communities', they set out at the turn of the century to challenge the liberal hegemony in the Gemeinde, aiming to transform it into a 'people's community', a *Volksgemeinde*.[67] 'This important Jewish instrument . . . has become an arena for the petty vanity and absurd lust for titles of unemployed philistines. . . . The symbols of this *Kultusjudentum* are the holiday frock coat and top hat, the gilt-edged prayerbook and diamond-bedecked wife', wrote Robert Stricker, expressing with his customary tact-

Century (Heb.) (Jerusalem, 1970), 9–10. On Bloch (1850–1923), see Wistrich, *The Jews of Vienna in the Age of Franz Joseph*, ch. 9; Jacob Toury, 'Josef Samuel Bloch und die jüdische Identität im österreichischen Kaiserreich', in Walter Grab (ed.), *Jüdische Integration und Identität in Deutschland und Österreich 1848–1918* (Tel Aviv, 1984), 41–64.

[66] On the structure and tasks of the Kultusgemeinde, see Klaus Lohrmann, 'Die rechtliche Lage der Juden in Wien zwischen 1848 und 1918', *Austriaca*, 31 (1990), 19–28; Wistrich, *The Jews of Vienna in the Age of Franz Joseph*, 88–9; Walter R. Weitzmann, 'The Politics of the Viennese Jewish Community 1890–1914', in Oxaal *et al.* (eds.), *Jews, Antisemitism and Culture in Vienna*, 121–4. The phrase 'an agency of government' is ibid. 122.

[67] Gaisbauer, *Davidstern und Doppeladler*, 113–15; Wistrich, *The Jews of Vienna in the Age of Franz Joseph*, 93–5; Weitzmann, 'The Politics of the Viennese Jewish Community', 140–5; Rozenblit, *The Jews of Vienna*, 185–7.

lessness a widespread Zionist disdain for what they considered the luke-warm Jewish commitment of the liberal notables.[68] To the Zionists, the Kultusgemeinde offered a ready-made infrastructure, an empty vessel that needed only to be filled with the new spirit of Jewish nationalism in order to be awakened from its torpor.

Until the war the Zionists were prevented from making inroads into liber-al control of the Gemeinde by decidedly undemocratic electoral laws. While all Jews in Vienna nominally belonged to the Kultusgemeinde, its leaders set minimum taxes at a level that ensured only a negligible minority could com-fortably afford to pay, and conditioned the right to vote in communal elec-tions upon payment of these taxes. Even as the franchise was extended in the general political arena, the Gemeinde liberals stubbornly rejected the encroachment of the less affluent into their domain, operating on the assumption that only those with sufficient means to pay taxes deserved to enjoy the privilege of voting.[69] According to the 1896 statutes, elections for one-third of the twenty-four seats on the Gemeinde's *Vorstand* (governing board) were to be held every two years. In 1900 a two-tier system was intro-duced to shore up the position of the wealthiest taxpayers. The governing board was expanded to thirty-six seats, with the additional twelve mandates elected only by the approximately 1,000 highest-paying taxpayers, who were thereby offered the chance to vote twice. No more than 15 per cent of Vien-nese Jews were eligible to vote in Gemeinde elections between 1900 and the outbreak of war. Limited eligibility was compounded by voter apathy: the number of votes cast by those eligible ranged from a peak of almost 45 per cent in 1908 to a low of approximately 10 per cent in 1912, hovering other-wise between 25 and 35 per cent. Active participation in the administration of community affairs was thus restricted to a small and unrepresentative minority. In the 1912 elections, to take the most extreme case, a mere 1,960 votes were cast—some 10 per cent of those eligible to vote and around 1 per

---

[68] Robert Stricker, 'Die Vertreter des jüdischen Volkes', in Stricker, *Der jüdische Nationalis-mus* (Vienna, n.d.), 40. On Zionist attitudes to the Kultusgemeinde, see also Ber Borochov, 'The Vienna Community and Elections to the Executive' (Heb.), in Borochov, *Writings* (Heb.), iii (Tel Aviv, 1966), 146–53; Max Rosenfeld, 'Die jüdischen Gemeinden in Österreich', *Der Jude*, 2 (1917–18), 152–62.

[69] Even Bloch shared this assumption. See Wistrich, *The Jews of Vienna in the Age of Franz Joseph*, 96 n. 141; Weitzmann, 'The Politics of the Viennese Jewish Community', 128. Further restrictions ensured that not even all taxpayers were in fact eligible to vote. For example, com-munal taxes had to be paid at least three years running; women, while they could be taxed, were denied the right to vote; and, on occasion, by-laws were arbitrarily changed to limit the pool of voters. See ibid. 146.

cent of the 180,988 Jews registered with the Kultusgemeinde.[70] The Gemeinde, then, had all the hallmarks of an oligarchy.

To the nationalists, by contrast, voting was a right, not a privilege. They calculated that many of their potential supporters among students and the poor were denied a voice in communal affairs. Even in the face of these inequities, the nationalists succeeded in making themselves a force to be reckoned with in Gemeinde elections, regularly receiving between 25 and 45 per cent of the votes. Nationalist support was not in fact confined to students and the poor, but was evident also in middle-class districts. Their respectable showing in elections was due at least in part to the fact that they drew on a more politicized and hence more easily mobilized core of support than the liberals.[71] In the 1912 elections, the last before the war, the nationalists and liberals agreed to a compromise whereby two seats on the governing board were 'reserved' for nationalist candidates running on a joint nationalist–liberal list.[72] Neither of the nationalists, however, was permitted into the Gemeinde's inner sanctum, the Vertreter Kollegium, an executive committee composed of the president, two vice-presidents, and a further eight board members (elected by the board itself). It was here that real authority resided and Gemeinde policy was made.[73] Only at the end of the war was the nationalists' battle for reform finally crowned with a measure of success. Until then the Kultusgemeinde remained the preserve of the liberals. It was, in fact, the linchpin of the liberal network. Like the leaderships of the Union, B'nai B'rith, and Allianz, the leaders of the Gemeinde were middle-class professionals and businessmen who tended to serve for long periods. Indeed, there was a good deal of personnel overlap between these leaderships. Six members of the Kultusgemeinde's 1896 governing board, for example, were still serving in 1912, as were twelve of those elected in 1900.[74]

---

[70] On the Gemeinde's electoral system and on voter participation, see Palmon, 'The Jewish Community of Vienna between the Two World Wars', 29–48; Weitzmann, 'The Politics of the Viennese Jewish Community', 123–4, 146–7; Wistrich, *The Jews of Vienna in the Age of Franz Joseph*, 90–3. The 1912 figure for the Jewish population in Vienna is in IKG Draft Report 1913–1918.

[71] See Rozenblit, *The Jews of Vienna*, 188; Freidenreich, *Jewish Politics in Vienna*, 72; Weitzmann, 'The Politics of the Viennese Jewish Community', 146–8.

[72] One of these seats was filled by Robert Stricker. See Weitzmann, 'The Politics of the Viennese Jewish Community', 145; Freidenreich, *Jewish Politics in Vienna*, 72.

[73] Weitzmann, 'The Politics of the Viennese Jewish Community', 122.

[74] *Bericht des Vorstandes der Israelitischen Kultusgemeinde in Wien über seine Tätigkeit in der Periode 1896–1897* (Vienna, 1898), 1; *Bericht des Vorstandes der Israelitischen Kultusgemeinde in*

For most of this period the dominant figure in the Gemeinde, and indeed in the liberal camp as a whole, was Alfred Stern. Stern's maternal great-grandfather, Aron Leidesdorff, had moved to Vienna from Pressburg (Bratislava) in the 1770s, when Jewish residence in the city was restricted to a few 'tolerated' families. Leidesdorff's father, Mendel ben Sabel, had been a communal leader in Pressburg and, in turn, his son achieved a measure of prominence in communal affairs in Vienna, acting on occasion as a Jewish representative to the authorities. A Viennese-born lawyer, Stern first made a name for himself in Viennese city politics, serving as a representative of the German Progressive Party on the city council (Gemeinderat) from 1888 to 1900. Even prior to this he had been active in Jewish affairs. Like so many of his liberal contemporaries, his Jewish interests crossed national borders: eastern European emigration and welfare, the struggle for Jewish rights in Romania, and legal battles against ritual murder accusations were all causes to which he devoted much time and energy. Following the 1881 pogroms in southern Russia, he played a leading role in the relief effort mounted in the Galician border town of Brody, where thousands of Jews had sought shelter. Almost simultaneously with his role in city politics Stern rose in the ranks of the Gemeinde leadership; he was a member of the governing board from 1888, its vice-president from 1889, and its president from 1904 until shortly before his death in late 1918. He brought to the Jewish community the fruits of his experience in general politics, primarily the conviction that Jewish rights must be unashamedly defended and anti-semitism vigorously combated. In this he was very much akin to Bloch, whom he readily acknowledged as a champion of Jewish issues. Not content with his pivotal role in the Gemeinde, Stern was also the instigator and long-time president of the Allgemeiner Österreichische-Israelitischer Bund (General Austrian Israelite League; the Gemeindebund, as it was commonly known). For two decades following the Gemeindebund's formation in late 1898 Stern attempted in vain to unite all of Austrian Jewry under its aegis. Even this, however, did not exhaust his ambition; he was also president of the Allianz during the war.[75]

Wien über seine Tätigkeit in den Jahren 1900 und 1901 (Vienna, 1902), 1; *Bericht der Israelitischen Kultusgemeinde Wien über seine Tätigkeit in der Periode 1912–1924* (Vienna, 1924) (hereafter *IKG Bericht 1912–1924*), 1–2. By 1914 only one member of the governing board was ennobled. The remainder were lawyers, doctors, businessmen, bankers, and industrialists. See the *Vorstand* membership lists in CAHJP, AW, 248/1; AW, 56/2; AW, 250/1.

[75] On Stern (1831–1918), see CAHJP, AW, 744/9; Freidenreich, *Jewish Politics in Vienna*, 37–8; Bloch, *Erinnerungen aus meinem Leben*, iii. 257–64; Wistrich, *The Jews of Vienna in the Age of Franz Joseph*, 198–9.

Stern came of age in the pre-emancipation period, a fact that left a deep imprint on his outlook. Autocratic and domineering, he possessed apparently limitless reserves of self-assurance and energy, and remained a formidable force in Viennese and Austrian Jewish society until a few weeks prior to his death in November 1918. His nationalist opponents derided him as the relic of a bygone era, trapped in an outmoded liberalism and still fighting past battles for emancipation. But even while pillorying him as 'despotic' and 'tyrannical', they granted him a grudging respect as a worthy opponent who towered above the 'weaklings and frauds' in the Gemeinde leadership. With his death, commented the nationalist *Jüdische Zeitung* over-optimistically, the final bastion of assimilationist, enlightenment Jewish politics had disappeared.[76] But it was not just his ideological antagonists who found him difficult. Bloch, for example, reviled Stern in his memoirs as wealthy and tight-fisted, describing him as overbearing, over-ambitious, unsentimental, obstinate, and unkind—'lacking any trace of *noblesse*'.[77] His political demise was finally brought about not by old age or infirmity but by the revolutionary 'cyclone' that swept across Europe at the war's end, 'battering also at the gates of Viennese Jewry' (as long-time Gemeinde vice-president Benjamin Rappaport put it in his oration at Stern's funeral). In the era of Franz Joseph, Stern was indeed, as Vienna's chief rabbi Tsevi Perez Chajes eulogized, the 'embodiment' of Viennese Jewry.[78]

The nationalists' portrayal of Stern as an old-fashioned assimilationist was in fact wide of the mark. Unlike most of his fellow liberals, Stern firmly believed that Jews had distinct political interests and agendas, and should act accordingly. In 1915 he noted that from his earliest days as a communal leader he had urged the Gemeinde, as the only authoritative representative of the Jews, to 'deal with those issues that to a greater or lesser degree reach into the domain of politics'.[79] Confirming this, Rappaport remarked that Stern felt that Jewish interests could simply not be confined within the official limits set by the statutes of the religious community.[80] For the nationalists, of course, Stern's conception of the nature and extent of Jewish politics was unacceptably narrow. In many respects, Stern's views on Jewish politics, and its corollary, Jewish identity, resembled those of Bloch, combining devotion to Judaism with a strong commitment to an ethnic Jewish 'peoplehood'. The boundaries between the two conceptions were not clear at the

[76] *JZ*, 6 Dec. 1918, pp. 4–5.   [77] Bloch, *Erinnerungen aus meinem Leben*, iii. 258–9.
[78] For these graveside orations and other comments, see *OW*, 13 Dec. 1918, pp. 793–9.
[79] *OW*, 22 Oct. 1915, p. 788.   [80] *OW*, 13 Dec. 1918, pp. 795, 798.

best of times, and this was never truer than during the war—both for Stern personally and for this type of politicized ethnicity in general—as the rising nationalism of the war years, along with the potentially dangerous revival of Austrian antisemitism, laid the foundation for further blurring. In 1918, for example, while negotiating with the nationalists about his possible participation in the Congress movement, Stern explicitly recognized the existence of a Jewish *Volk*; he was steadfast, however, in refusing to acknowledge this publicly, fearing negative consequences for the Jews of western and central Europe: the dark days before emancipation loomed large in his view of the world.[81]

If ethnicity came somewhat to the fore for Stern in these years, the same cannot be said of democracy. During the war Stern and the Gemeinde leadership continued in their oligarchical ways, running communal affairs with little regard for sensitivities or interests other than their own. This was consistent with developments in Austrian politics. Parliament had been prorogued in May 1914 and was not reconvened until May 1917; the government ruled by administrative fiat, aided by the introduction of emergency military rule. Similarly, the Vienna City Council functioned in truncated form for much of the war, with the mayor granted wide-ranging powers at the war's outset.[82] Kultusgemeinde elections were postponed and new members were simply co-opted upon the death or retirement of incumbents. Nine board members, a quarter of the total, died between March 1915 and June 1918. (Between the December 1912 elections, the last before the war, and the June 1920 elections, the first following the war, fully half of the board's members either died or retired.) Moreover, both board and executive committee meetings were often held in camera.[83] Indicative of Stern's approach was his invitation in late 1915 to Baron Louis von Rothschild, head of the Viennese branch of the banking family, to join the Gemeinde board in order to help maintain its 'moral credit' and 'good name'. It was the Rothschild 'prestige' that Stern desired, almost as a form of window-dressing. He made it clear to Rothschild that no active partici-

[81] On this episode, see Ch. 4.

[82] Between Oct. 1914 and Feb. 1916 regular meetings of faction leaders were held in place of full city council meetings. This practice was supported by a consensus in the council until mid-1917, when the Social Democrats began pressing for electoral reform. See Maren Seliger and Karl Ucakar, *Wien. Politische Geschichte 1740–1934* (Vienna, 1985), ii. 777–8, 981–5, 1022–7; Boyer, *Culture and Political Crisis in Vienna*, 374–6.

[83] On the postponement of elections, see Palmon, 'The Jewish Community of Vienna between the Two World Wars', 50; *OW*, 23 Oct. 1914, p. 727. On deaths and retirements, see *IKG Bericht 1912–1924*, 2–3. For a list of wartime meetings, see IKG Draft Report 1913–1918.

pation was required or even expected. A similar wish to draw notables into the communal orbit led the board to co-opt at the same time the soon-to-be-ennobled Rudolf Schwarz-Hiller, a Social Political Party city council member who, very importantly from the Gemeinde's perspective, was in charge of the government's refugee welfare effort in Vienna.[84] It was welfare work that occupied the bulk of the energies of the Gemeinde's administrative apparatus during the war years, severely straining its resources. Many of its employees were drafted, and the Gemeinde's chronic financial difficulties (it was perpetually in debt and strapped for funds) were further exacerbated by pleas for assistance from individuals and communities in all areas of the empire. Many *Kultusgemeinden* in Galicia and Bukovina, for example, were barely able to function for much of the war and turned to Vienna for assistance. The Vienna Gemeinde, though, was generally able to provide only minimal relief.[85]

The political dimension of the Gemeinde's work was made clear during the war years in the search for a new chief rabbi to preside at the Stadttempel in the Inner City, a pulpit occupied by Moritz Güdemann since the death of Adolf Jellinek in 1893.[86] In the highly visible role of chief rabbi, Güdemann, a conservative rabbi and eminent historian of Judaism, helped set the tone of 'official' Judaism in the city, as had his two predecessors, Isak Noa

[84] Stern to Baron Louis von Rothschild, 4 Nov. 1915, CAHJP, AW, 2970. For criticism of this move, see *JZ*, 26 Nov. 1915, p. 2; 11 Feb. 1916, p. 2. See also *NNZ*, 9 Apr. 1915, pp. 63–4; *JK*, 25 Nov. 1915, pp. 3–4; *WH*, 19 Nov. 1915, pp. 4–5; *OW*, 19 Nov. 1915, pp. 853–4. Stricker was at this point the only Zionist on the board; his colleague Jakob Ehrlich had been drafted soon after the outbreak of war. See Protokoll der Plenar-Sitzung, 24 Sept. 1914, CAHJP, AW, 71/15. The Social Political Party attracted considerable support among the Jewish 'liberal intelligentsia' in Vienna. See Eva Holleis, *Die Sozialpolitische Partei. Sozialliberale Bestrebungen in Wien um 1900* (Munich, 1978); Wistrich, *The Jews of Vienna in the Age of Franz Joseph*, 315–16; Cahnmann, 'Adolf Fischhof and his Jewish Followers', 122–6.

[85] Many Czernowitz Kultusgemeinde employees, for example, were in Vienna. See their Feb. 1915 letter and report, CAHJP, AW, 357/2. On the drafting of Gemeinde employees and its attempts to retain some of them for community work, see CAHJP, AW, 586/4. See also IKG Vorstand to K. und K. Reichskriegsministerium, 4 Aug. 1914; IKG circular, 11 Aug. 1914, both in CAHJP, AW, 356; and the list from 1914 in AW, 883/34. For pleas to the Gemeinde for assistance, see CAHJP, AW, 357/1–357/4. On the Gemeinde's financial situation, see Wistrich, *The Jews of Vienna in the Age of Franz Joseph*, 90; Freidenreich, *Jewish Politics in Vienna*, 20. For the effects of the war on its finances, see *IKG Bericht 1912–1924*, 9–10, 46–7; IKG Draft Report 1913–1918.

[86] Prior to his position at the Stadttempel, Güdemann had served since 1866 as rabbi of the Leopoldstadt Temple. See Marsha L. Rozenblit, 'Jewish Identity and the Modern Rabbi: The Cases of Isak Noa Mannheimer, Adolf Jellinek, and Moritz Güdemann in Nineteenth-Century Vienna', *LBIYB* 35 (1990), 119–30; Ismar Schorsch, 'Moritz Güdemann: Rabbi, Historian and Apologist', *LBIYB* 11 (1966), 42–66; Wistrich, *The Jews of Vienna in the Age of Franz Joseph*, 122–8.

Mannheimer and Jellinek. (Battles over religious reform, for example, had much to do with the public image of Viennese Jewry that the Kultusgemeinde wished to convey.) Güdemann's tenure was not free from overt political involvement. His part in the establishment of the Union and in its fight against antisemitism necessitated political engagement, as did Herzl's request for support in 1895, prior to publishing his Zionist tract *The Jewish State* the following year. After some initial enthusiasm on Güdemann's part—he saw Herzl as an ally in the struggle against antisemitism in Vienna—the chief rabbi vehemently rejected political Zionism, penning the polemical *Nationaljudenthum* in response to Herzl's pamphlet.[87] Güdemann had announced his wish to retire in March 1914; the sensitivity of the post was such that his successor was not found until 1918.[88]

In early 1915 the Gemeinde board briefly considered Simon Hevesi and Lajos (Ludwig) Venetianer, both highly respected Hungarian scholars.[89] By mid-1915 Stern's favoured candidate was the Hungarian-born and German-trained Nehemiah Anton Nobel, a prominent Frankfurt rabbi.[90] Nobel's candidature, though, met with stiff opposition. Reports of his strict Orthodoxy aroused misgivings among those who feared that he might institute changes in the Viennese rite. Further, local communal rabbis—who in any case felt aggrieved at their treatment by the Gemeinde, complaining that they were overworked and underpaid—were offended that all the candidates thus far had been from outside Vienna.[91] Surprisingly, the

[87] See Wistrich, *The Jews of Vienna in the Age of Franz Joseph*, 125, 127–8, 468–82; Rozenblit, 'Jewish Identity and the Modern Rabbi', 125–6; Moritz Güdemann, *Nationaljudenthum* (Leipzig, 1897). An earlier example was Mannheimer's forthright support of the liberal social and political agenda of the 1848 revolutions. See Wistrich, *The Jews of Vienna in the Age of Franz Joseph*, 104–6. Mannheimer was not granted the title 'rabbi' but was called instead 'religious teacher' and 'preacher'.

[88] Güdemann to IKG Vorstand, 10 Mar. 1914, CAHJP, AW, 731/3. See also his autobiographical typescript, Moritz Güdemann, 'Aus meinem Leben', LBIA, fos. 205–9.

[89] See the letters from Hevesi to Siegmund Kauders (a member of the Vertreter Kollegium), 6 Mar. 1915; Stern to Hevesi, 10 Mar. 1915; Hevesi to Stern, 16 Mar. 1915, all in CAHJP, AW, 587/1; *NNZ*, 18 June 1915, p. 103. Tsevi Perez Chajes was also considered at this stage. See the Vertreter Kollegium decisions of 30 Dec. 1914, CAHJP, AW, 587/1; *NNZ*, 23 Apr. 1915, pp. 68–9.

[90] On Nobel, see Rachel Heuberger, 'Orthodoxy versus Reform: The Case of Rabbi Nehemiah Anton Nobel of Frankfurt a. Main', *LBIYB* 37 (1992), 45–58; Yeshayahu (Oskar) Wolfsberg, *Rabbi Dr Nehemiah Tsevi Nobel* (Heb.) (Jerusalem, 1944).

[91] On the debate in the Jewish press and religious organizations, see *NNZ*, 23 Apr. 1915, pp. 68–9; 7 May 1915, pp. 76–7; 20 Aug. 1915, pp. 133–4; *WH*, 17 Dec. 1915, pp. 5–6; 14 Jan. 1916, pp. 4–5; *JK*, 20 Jan. 1916, p. 3; 4 May 1916, pp. 1–2; *OW*, 10 Mar. 1916, pp. 170–2; 17 Mar. 1916, pp. 187–8; 24 Mar. 1916, pp. 203–5; 5 May 1916, p. 300; *JZ*, 11 Feb. 1916, p. 2. See also the reports on Nobel of June 1915 and the anonymous pamphlets 'Dr. Nobel und Dr. Ziegler.

fact that Nobel had not merely been active in the Zionist movement from its early stages but had also played a role in the formation of the religious Zionist Mizrahi movement was barely mentioned in the polemics over his appointment. Stern was determined to recruit him, and in early 1916 the Gemeinde offered Nobel the post. He refused, citing the opposition he faced in Vienna and the intense pressure from Frankfurt Jewish organizations and his congregants to remain there.[92]

Following a two-year hiatus in the search, Stern turned to Tsevi Perez Chajes. Born in Brody, east Galicia, Chajes studied for the rabbinate in Vienna, taught Bible and history at the Florence rabbinical seminary from 1902, and served as chief rabbi of Trieste from 1911. A noted scholar, he was, like Nobel, an active and outspoken champion of the Zionist cause and a religious conservative in the mould of Güdemann.[93] By April 1918 a consensus had been reached that he was a suitable candidate and he was appointed with only minimal opposition, taking up the post as chief rabbi upon Güdemann's death in August 1918.[94] The undoubted strangeness of this choice did not go unnoticed. Why did the fiercely anti-nationalist Stern, whose influence was paramount in this as in most other Gemeinde affairs, opt successively for two Zionist sympathizers to fill such a pivotal communal post?[95] As already indicated, he was prepared at this stage of his career to recognize, at least in private, the existence of a Jewish *Volk*. If he could describe himself in early 1918 as an 'Oberzionist', then perhaps it was in this light that he viewed the commitment of Nobel and Chajes to a more than merely confessional Jewish identity.[96] In any event, it was not until the end

Eine Anregung', of late 1915 and early 1916, all in CAHJP, AW, 587/1; and communal rabbi Max Grunwald to Stern, 7 and 15 May 1916, CAHJP, AW, 71/16.

[92] Protokolle der Vertreter-Sitzungen, 2 and 6 Feb. 1916, CAHJP, AW, 72/15; Bericht des Dr. Elias Münz über seine Reise zu Dr. Nobel nach Frankfurt a. M., 7 Feb. 1916; Stern to Nobel, 7 Feb. and 21 Mar. 1916; Nobel to Stern, 24 Feb. and 30 Mar. 1916, all in CAHJP, AW, 587/1; Protokolle der Plenar-Sitzungen, 6 Feb. and 12 Apr. 1916, CAHJP, AW, 71/16.

[93] On Chajes (1876–1927), see Moritz Rosenfeld, *H. P. Chajes' Leben und Werk* (Vienna, 1933); Hugo Gold (ed.), *Zwi Perez Chajes* (Tel Aviv, 1971); Kuno Trau and Michael Krein, *A Man in the World: Tsevi Perez Chajes* (Heb.) (Tel Aviv, 1947); Freidenreich, *Jewish Politics in Vienna*, 123–5.

[94] Protokoll der Vertreter-Sitzung, 24 Apr. 1918, CAHJP, AW, 72/16; Protokoll der Plenar-Sitzung, 24 Apr. 1918, CAHJP, AW, 71/16. See also the reports in CAHJP, AW, 725/2; Gold (ed.), *Zwi Perez Chajes*, 11–19; *JK*, 2 May 1918, pp. 2–3; *OW*, 3 May 1918, pp. 267–8; *JZ*, 3 May 1918, p. 4. The initial appointment was as rabbi of the Stadttempel and deputy chief rabbi.

[95] That he pushed very hard for Chajes's appointment is indicated by Güdemann in his memoir. See Moritz Güdemann, 'Aus meinem Leben', LBIA, fo. 281.

[96] For Stern's description of himself as an Oberzionist, see p. 151 below.

of the war that Chajes's public support of Jewish nationalism aroused opposition within the Gemeinde. The symbolic importance and change of direction that his appointment represented was clear. Not only was he a Zionist, he was also a Galician. Galician Zionist leader Adolf Stand hailed Chajes's appointment as 'heralding a new era of reconciliation between east and west'. Jewish nationalism, he wrote, had reached the Gemeinde: 'In the Vienna Kultusgemeinde a breakthrough has occurred.'[97]

Allowing for the hyperbole in such a reaction, the installation of Chajes as successor to Güdemann, Jellinek, and Mannheimer was at the very least an indication that some of the basic assumptions of Jewish liberalism were in flux in the final years of the empire. Liberalism was an increasingly embattled force in Austrian society in the decades prior to the First World War, and was further battered by the war and its nationalist and revolutionary aftermath. Jewish liberalism certainly felt the impact of these developments, although it managed to retain its status and authority in Jewish society to a greater degree than was true of Austrian liberalism generally.[98] Jewish liberals' wartime response consisted, in the main, of sticking to their ideological guns. They were by and large content with reiterating their loyalty to Austria and expressing uncontroversial demands for greater democracy, full legal equality, and equal opportunity for all citizens regardless of religious or any other affiliation. Even Jewish liberals, though, as already seen, were forced to modify their programme to take account of the fact that discussion of political reform was increasingly proceeding along national lines.

If Austria was to be restructured as a federation of nationalities, to which nationality should (or indeed could) the Jews attach themselves? The liberal dilemma was particularly acute in Vienna, where German nationalism was offset to a degree by the city's role as imperial *Residenzstadt*, and by the dynastic patriotism of influential segments of the Social Democratic and

[97] Cited in Rosenfeld, *H. P. Chajes' Leben und Werk*, 48. For similar sentiments, see historian Majer Balaban to Chajes, 7 May 1918, CZA, A30/67.

[98] On liberalism's declining fortunes in Vienna and Austria, see Boyer, *Political Radicalism in Late Imperial Vienna*, chs. 1, 6; Felix Czeike (ed.), *Wien in der liberalen Ära* (Vienna, 1978); Pulzer, *The Rise of Political Anti-Semitism in Germany and Austria*, 122–31. For a revisionist view of liberalism's 'decline', see Judson, *Exclusive Revolutionaries*, esp. 1–10, 262–72; Harry Ritter, 'Austro-German Liberalism and the Modern Liberal Tradition', *German Studies Review*, 7 (1984), 227–48. Not surprisingly, Jewish liberalism was strongest in Vienna and many other cities of the empire. That liberalism in Germany maintained its strength in particular on the municipal level prior to the First World War has been noted by James J. Sheehan, *German Liberalism in the Nineteenth Century* (Chicago, 1978; Atlantic Heights, NJ, 1995), 229–30 and, bringing the Jews into the equation, Peter Pulzer, *Jews and the German State* (Oxford, 1992), 136–8. See also Gary B. Cohen, 'Jews in German Liberal Politics: Prague', *Jewish History*, 1 (1986), 55–74.

Christian Social movements.[99] The once powerful model of open and pluralistic Austro-German nationalism to which Vienna's Jewish liberals had enthusiastically adhered for decades had been all but supplanted by a racially based nationalism from which Jews were excluded by definition. Marxist Social Democracy and Christian Socialism were hardly attractive alternatives. The spectre of political homelessness, the absence of a party, movement, or nationality (beyond Habsburg loyalism) with which they could readily identify, loomed increasingly large. One response to this dilemma was that some Jewish liberals, such as Stern, were prepared to acknowledge the legitimacy of Jewish nationalism, not just in the far-removed eastern regions of the empire but in the capital itself. Certainly, this acknowledgement had very definite limits; it was by no means a Pauline conversion to the nationalist cause. None the less, it signified a shift in liberal attitudes to Jewish nationalism, a move from outright rejection to a somewhat begrudging accommodation on both the ideological and practical planes. This was manifested in the willingness of the liberals to co-operate with the nationalists in the welfare effort and Congress movement and, at the war's end, in the Gemeinde itself. Such co-operation was a direct consequence of developments within both Jewish and Austrian society during the war.

THE NATIONALISTS

Jewish nationalism was a long-standing presence in Vienna, first appearing formally in the early 1880s in the guise of the University of Vienna student group the Kadimah. The activists of the Kadimah and other nationalist student fraternities that grew up in its wake provided much of the local support for Herzl's World Zionist Organization, created in 1897.[100] With Herzl's death in 1904 and the move of Zionist head office from Vienna to

[99] On the Social Democrats as Habsburg loyalists, see Hans Mommsen, *Die Sozialdemokratie und die Nationalitätenfrage im habsburgischen Vielvölkerstaat* (Vienna, 1963); Anson Rabinbach, *The Crisis of Austrian Socialism: From Red Vienna to Civil War 1927–1934* (Chicago, 1983), ch. 1. On Christian Social dynastic patriotism, see Alfred Diamant, *Austrian Catholics and the First Republic* (Princeton, 1960), 80–3; Suval, *The Anschluss Question in the Weimar Era*, 190–7; Klemens von Klemperer, *Ignaz Seipel: Christian Statesman in a Time of Crisis* (Princeton, 1972), 22–5. See also Boyer, *Culture and Political Crisis in Vienna*, 439–43.

[100] On the Kadimah and pre-Herzlian Jewish nationalism in Vienna, see Julius H. Schoeps, 'Modern Heirs of the Maccabees: The Beginning of the Vienna Kadimah 1882–1897', *LBIYB* 27 (1982), 155–70; Wistrich, *The Jews of Vienna in the Age of Franz Joseph*, ch. 11; Gaisbauer, *Davidstern und Doppeladler*, 39–60, 70–81.

Cologne in 1905, the Viennese movement was taken over by its younger and more radical elements, most of them strong supporters of *Landespolitik*, who had been overshadowed by the world organization's luminaries and their strictly political agenda, exemplified by Herzl's attempts to negotiate an internationally recognized charter that would 'grant' Palestine to the Jews.[101] Reflecting developments in the world organization, the ascendance of Herzlian political Zionism in Vienna gave way in the years after Herzl's death to an approach that combined *Landespolitik* with a strong commitment to practical work in Palestine (so-called 'synthetic' Zionism).[102]

This change of orientation at the centre of the Austrian movement broadly coincided with a serious fissure in its structure. Between 1902 and 1907 Austrian Zionism was nominally unified in an organization that comprised a number of semi-autonomous districts answerable to a central authority in Vienna.[103] From the outset, ideological and organizational cohesion were at a premium; friction between the Viennese centre and the regions was endemic, with the Bohemian and Galician movements in particular pressing for decentralization.[104] This reflected not only differences between the regional Jewish political cultures, but also a characteristically Austrian political dynamic of tension between central Viennese control and strivings for regional autonomy. In both the Austrian and Jewish contexts it was the Galicians who pursued the most resolutely independent course. In 1907 Galician pressure for greater independence triggered the division of the movement into three semi-independent regional organizations: Galicia, western Austria—comprising the Czech lands and the Inner Austrian district (coterminous in territory with the inter-war Austrian republic)—and Bukovina. While nominal unity was maintained, the three regions

---

[101] On the change in the Viennese movement, see Gaisbauer, *Davidstern und Doppeladler*, 120–6. On *Landespolitik* in Austrian Zionism, see ibid. 451–523; Freidenreich, *Jewish Politics in Vienna*, 59–72.

[102] Disagreements about the degree of emphasis to be given to the twin poles of the movement's work remained a source of tension. In this, Austrian Zionism was typical of the movement in east central Europe. See Mendelsohn, *On Modern Jewish Politics*, 57–8. The most immediate manifestation of the new orientation of Austrian Zionism was the movement's involvement in the 1907 Reichsrat elections.

[103] Gaisbauer, *Davidstern und Doppeladler*, 97–110. The Austrian Landes-Organisation was formally established in 1902 (its rarely used official title was Verband Zion). The movement's executive authority was the Vienna-based Landeskomitee.

[104] Ibid. 118–30, 194–239; Nahum Michael Gelber, *The History of the Zionist Movement in Galicia 1875–1918* (Heb.) (Jerusalem, 1958), ii. 452–540; Oskar K. Rabinowicz, 'Czechoslovak Zionism: Analecta to a History', in *The Jews of Czechoslovakia*, ii (Philadelphia, 1971), 19–24.

functioned in practice as separate entities until the war. Many Viennese activists, however, remained unreconciled to the new situation and continued to agitate for a more centralized movement. For them, Vienna was the undisputed centre and the regions were the subordinate periphery, a view understandably rejected outside the capital.[105] During the war years, when many Galician Zionist leaders found themselves in Vienna and renewed efforts were made to bridge the east–west divide, these underlying tensions spilled over into open conflict.

A lengthy period of instability followed the 1907 split, in both the western Austrian region as a whole and in Vienna. The combination of unresolved strategic and tactical disagreements (concerning the relative importance of *Landespolitik* and Palestine-centred activity) and perpetual tension between the centre and the regions (reflecting organizational and ideological differences) proved debilitating. In very broad outline, the demarcation lines were between Viennese centralism and radicalism on the one hand and the more moderate and federalist inclinations of the Bohemians, Moravians, and Silesians on the other. Ideological, personal, and generational conflicts, deriving from the post-Herzl metamorphosis of the movement, led to disarray also in Vienna, where some of the most able leaders preferred the broader horizons of the western Austrian movement or the World Zionist Organization.[106]

The activist rank and file of the Viennese movement was made up in large part of youth and students, which certainly contributed to its instability. The University of Vienna was a Zionist stronghold: by 1910, faced with relentless hostility from German nationalist students, some one-third of Jewish students were prepared to declare themselves Jewish nationalists. Local Zionist support, measured by payment of membership dues to the World Zionist Organization and by voting patterns in Gemeinde elections, was strong also in the city's middle-class districts. Zionist leaders were predominantly professionals—doctors, lawyers, engineers—and were in general younger than their liberal counterparts. At the end of 1911 the Inner Austrian district claimed some 2,100 active members and supporters,

---

[105] On the events leading to the break-up, see Gaisbauer, *Davidstern und Doppeladler*, 131–5. On the post-1907 period more generally, see ibid. 250–368; Gelber, *The History of the Zionist Movement in Galicia*, ii. 541–634.

[106] On the conflicts in western Austrian Zionism between 1907 and 1914, see Gaisbauer, *Davidstern und Doppeladler*, 298–354. For Vienna, see ibid. 319–23; Weitzmann, 'The Politics of the Viennese Jewish Community', 143–4.

most of whom were in Vienna.[107] Viennese Zionism, then, as the seat of the World Zionist Organization and the Austrian movement, was always more than local in its ambience and concerns. This, in fact, was its defining characteristic and the source of much of its vitality as well as of its constant discord. For Viennese and Austrian Zionism alike, the failure of all attempts at united action, on the local, regional, or interregional levels, can be traced chiefly to the diversity of the movement's constituent parts.

For the Zionist movement in general, the war years were at one and the same time a period of internal uncertainty and a significant turning-point in the movement's fortunes, a time of unprecedented success that put Zionism on the international political map. On the local level, Zionists increasingly laid claim to being the leading Jewish force in east central Europe, the sole party capable of incorporating all elements of Jewish society within its ranks.[108] Zionism, this argument ran, had in fact been transformed from one party among many into a movement of the Jewish people as a whole, an idea popular also among Austrian Zionists during and immediately following the war.[109] While the welfare effort dominated day-to-day activity until 1917, the Austrian movement was also engaged in efforts to reorganize itself in order to be better prepared to exploit the opportunities furnished by the favourable political circumstances. At the core of these efforts was another attempt to unify the movement, this time capitalizing on the presence in Vienna of so many leading activists, particularly from Galicia and Bukovina. The instrument of this unity was the Executive Committee of United Austrian Zionists, established in Vienna in January 1915 and comprising local activists and Galician and Bukovinian leaders who had taken refuge in the city. In the absence of functioning regional alternatives, the

---

[107] On the demography of Viennese Zionism, see Freidenreich, *Jewish Politics in Vienna*, 57–9; Rozenblit, *The Jews of Vienna*, 44, 165–9; id., 'The Assertion of Identity: Jewish Student Nationalism at the University of Vienna before the First World War', *LBIYB* 27 (1982), 171–86; Gaisbauer, *Davidstern und Doppeladler*, 319, 323–6; Wistrich, *The Jews of Vienna in the Age of Franz Joseph*, 375–9. For membership figures for the Inner Austrian district, see Gaisbauer, *Davidstern und Doppeladler*, 311, 322, 334, 343.

[108] On the Zionist movement during the war, see Vital, *Zionism*, ch. 4. For examples of local Zionist political successes in this period, see Mendelsohn, *Zionism in Poland*, ch. 1; Frankel, 'The Paradoxical Politics of Marginality', 13.

[109] See e.g. Ludwig Bato, 'Das Kriegsjahr 5678', *JNK* 4 (1918–19), 3–9; Heinrich Margulies, 'Politik und Sendung', *JNK* 5 (1919–20), 22–33; Max Joseph, 'Jüdische Politik', *Hickls Wiener-jüdische Volkskalender*, 17–18 (1918–19), 27–32; *JZ*, 26 May 1916, p. 1; 22 Sept. 1916, pp. 1–2; 26 Jan. 1917, pp. 1–2; 3 May 1918, pp. 1–2; 24 May 1918, p. 1. See also Adolf Böhm, *Die zionistische Bewegung*, ii (Berlin, 1921), 341–2; D. Weinbaum, *Nationale-jüdische Zukunftsgedanken* (Zürich, 1917), 33–47, 72–4.

Executive Committee acted as the supreme council of Austrian Zionism; it was constrained in this role, however, by its provisional nature and by the fact that so many first-rank Zionist leaders were unavailable for party work. It was further hampered by personal and ideological conflicts, and by recurrent tensions between the 'easterners' and the Viennese. Moreover, there were no Czech representatives on the committee (few Jews from the Czech lands were among the refugees in the capital), which led to friction between the Bohemian party and Vienna.[110]

The push for a structural overhaul of the Austrian movement began in earnest in March 1916, when Karl Pollak, president of the Executive Committee since its inception, was drafted. Pollak was a veteran of Zionism since pre-Herzl days, a former Kadimah president, founder of a duelling fraternity in 1894, and president of the western Austrian region's Central Committee since January 1913.[111] His replacement, Rudolf Taussig, had no previous leadership experience. A senior bureaucrat in the stenographic office of the Austrian parliament (and stenographer at World Zionist Organization congresses), he devoted the bulk of his energy to welfare work and organizational matters.[112] Upon assuming office he immediately pressed for strict centralization of the movement's decision-making machinery, suggesting that all Zionist activity in the empire be subject to prior Viennese approval.[113] This approach had made very little headway by mid-1917, leading the Inner or Smaller Actions Committee (Engeres Aktionskomitee)—

[110] On the Executivkomitee der Vereinigten Österreichischen Zionisten, see *JZ*, 12 Feb. 1915, p. 1; 19 Feb. 1915, p. 1; Gaisbauer, *Davidstern und Doppeladler*, 134–5, 524; Meir Henisch, *At Home and Abroad* (Heb.) (Tel Aviv, 1961), 145, 151–5. The committee consisted of ten members, four each from Vienna and Galicia and two from Bukovina. See ZCWA to ZCO, 18 Feb. 1915, CZA, Z3/841; Protocol of the ZCWA Geschäftsführende Ausschuss meeting, 4 Feb. 1915, CZA, Z3/841. On the limited Zionist activity during the war in Galicia, see Gelber, *The History of the Zionist Movement in Galicia*, ii. 813–38; Mendelsohn, *Zionism in Poland*, 75. On the situation in Bukovina and the Czech lands, see Arie Leon Schmelzer, 'Die Juden in der Bukowina (1914–1919)', in Hugo Gold (ed.), *Geschichte der Juden in der Bukowina*, i (Tel Aviv, 1958), 67–72; Hillel J. Kieval, *The Making of Czech Jewry: National Conflict and Jewish Society in Bohemia 1870–1918* (New York, 1988), 163–82; *JZ*, 12 Nov. 1915, p. 3; 28 Sept. 1917, pp. 1–4; Gaisbauer, *Davidstern und Doppeladler*, 529.

[111] *JZ*, 25 Feb. 1916, p. 4; 3 Mar. 1916, p. 1. Taussig to Arthur Hantke, 7 Mar. 1916, CZA, Z3/844. For earlier indications of movement in this direction, see *JZ*, 21 Dec. 1915, p. 3. On Pollak, see Harald Seewann, *Zirkel und Zionsstern. Bilder und Dokumente aus der versunkenen Welt des jüdisch-nationalen Korporationswesens* (Graz, 1990), i. 134; ii. 207, 213, 277, 280; Gaisbauer, *Davidstern und Doppeladler*, 335. Henisch, a Galician colleague, described Pollak as being none too bright and a 'typical *Bursenschafiler*'. See Henisch, *At Home and Abroad*, 154.

[112] On Taussig (1862–1926), see Henisch, *At Home and Abroad*, 154; S. Wininger, *Jüdische National-Biographie* (Czernowitz, 1925–36), vi. 89.

[113] *JZ*, 3 Mar. 1916, p. 1; 5 May 1916, p. 1; ZCWA to ZCO, 27 Apr. 1916, CZA, Z3/844.

the executive council of the World Zionist Organization—to delegate Arthur Hantke, Actions Committee member and president of the German Zionist Federation, to go to Vienna to take matters in hand.[114] With open political work now possible under the new regime of Karl I, Taussig instigated an ambitious restructuring of the western Austrian branch of the movement, which, he thought, had gradually 'deteriorated' during the war, sliding into disorder. Revitalization was the goal; the means were more meetings, more recruitment, more activity throughout the city and the regions, all to be conducted under the close scrutiny and supervision of the Viennese centre.[115]

Crucial to this effort was the notion that Vienna was the Jewish capital of the empire, an idea that found expression across the board in Viennese Jewry. Nathan Birnbaum, for example, wrote that

Vienna lies on the frontier between East and West in Europe. It lies in the midst of a Jewish population numbering millions; it is the point where German and Russo-Polish, Ashkenazi and Sephardi Jewry meet and can best be united in common work; it is as if born to be the centre of Jewish national agitation.[116]

It was manifested, too, in the assumption of those leading the wartime youth movement in Vienna that theirs was an empire-wide movement. The Allianz, B'nai B'rith, and the Union, active throughout the empire, were all based in Vienna. To Alfred Stern, it was the duty of the Vienna Kultusgemeinde to provide leadership for all of Austrian Jewry.[117] Presumptions such as these did not, of course, go unchallenged by the provinces. During the war, for example, Bohemian Zionists voiced their resentment about Vienna's lack of consultation on matters affecting the whole of the western

---

[114] Protocol of the EAC meeting, 29–31 July 1917, CZA, L6/592. Hantke had already made three visits to Vienna in Feb., June, and Nov. 1916. See *JZ*, 3 Mar. 1916, p. 2; 30 June 1916, p. 3; Hantke to Taussig, 14 Apr. 1916, CZA, Z3/844; Hantke's report to Copenhagen Zionist Office, 4 Dec. 1916, CZA, Z3/640. Hantke did not actually go to Vienna until Nov. 1917, visiting again in the summer of 1918. See *JZ*, 30 Nov. 1917, p. 1; 16 Aug. 1918, p. 5. On the EAC and its difficulties in functioning effectively during the war, see Vital, *Zionism*, 129–36.

[115] On this reorganization, see the Protocol of the ZCWA meeting, 25 July 1917, CZA, Z3/847; ZCO to ZCWA, 7 and 9 Aug. 1917, CZA, Z3/848; *JZ*, 3 Aug. 1917, pp. 3–4; 31 Aug. 1917, p. 4; 21 Sept. 1917, p. 4; 12 Oct. 1917, p. 5; 9 Nov. 1917, p. 4; 30 Nov. 1917, p. 4; 14 Dec. 1917, p. 4.

[116] Quoted in Wistrich, *The Jews of Vienna in the Age of Franz Joseph*, 402. For wartime Zionist expressions of this idea, see *JZ*, 3 Mar. 1916, p. 1; 12 Apr. 1918, p. 3.

[117] See his comments to this effect in Protokoll der Plenar-Sitzung, 6 Jan. 1916, CAHJP, AW, 71/16; *WH*, 14 Jan. 1916, pp. 5–6. Similar comments by Stern in 1888 are cited in Bloch, *Erinnerungen aus meinem Leben*, iii. 258.

Austrian movement.[118] Divisions between Vienna and the Galician and Bukovinian movements also caused tensions within the Executive Committee (which, it will be remembered, had no Czech members). Adolf Stand, vice-president of the committee and a long-time Galician Zionist leader, complained that the Viennese marginalized and patronized the Galicians.[119] The uncertainty of the future status of Galicia and Bukovina reinforced the differences between the already quite distinct agendas of the various groups. For the Galicians and Bukovinians, the Executive Committee provided a valuable forum, a link with the capital, rather than a threat to their independence of action, as Taussig's plans for western Austria were to the Bohemians. It was made clear, though, upon resumption of organized Zionist work in Galicia in early 1918, that the Galicians expected Vienna to respect their autonomy.[120] In Bukovina, occupied no less than three times by the Russians before reverting to Austrian control following the Russian Revolution in March 1917, there was little Jewish political action of note prior to October 1918. The bitterly divided Bukovinian Jewish nationalist groups achieved nominal unity in Vienna in September 1917; significantly, the declaration issued to mark the occasion made no mention of a Viennese role in Bukovinian Jewish affairs.[121]

As should already be clear, ideological battles played an important role in these otherwise prosaic organizational matters. The protagonists were Robert Weltsch and Robert Stricker. Weltsch had come to Vienna in March 1918 as the Inner Actions Committee 'representative', taking up a post as secretary of an expanded Zionist administrative office. A leading figure in the intellectually inclined, neo-Romantic student circles that were influential in pre-war Prague Zionism, Weltsch proved in Vienna to be a hard-

---

[118] The Bohemians complained, for example, that they had not been consulted on a memorandum presented to the government in Mar. 1918 outlining demands for Jewish autonomy. Bohemian Zionist District Committee to ZCWA, 24, 25, and 27 Mar. 1918, CZA, Z3/848; ZCWA to ZCO, 1 May 1918, CZA, Z3/849.

[119] See Henisch, *At Home and Abroad*, 145, 152. See also Arthur Hantke's report of 4 Dec. 1916 to Copenhagen Zionist Office, CZA, Z3/640.

[120] Gelber, *The History of the Zionist Movement in Galicia*, ii. 825–31; *JZ*, 3 May 1918, pp. 3–4; 10 May 1918, pp. 4–5; Mendelsohn, *Zionism in Poland*, 78–81. The occasional voices calling for a formal reunification of Austrian Zionism went unheeded. See e.g. *JZ*, 12 Feb. 1915, p. 1; 3 Mar. 1916, p. 1; 5 May 1916, p. 1; 12 Apr. 1918, pp. 2–3; 3 May 1918, p. 2; 2 Aug. 1918, pp. 2–3.

[121] *JZ*, 28 Sept. 1917, pp. 1–2; 9 Nov. 1917, p. 2; *OW*, 3 May 1918, pp. 262–3; 5 July 1918, p. 417; Schmelzer, 'Die Juden in der Bukowina', 67–9. On the factional disputes among Bukovinian Jewish nationalists, see Gaisbauer, *Davidstern und Doppeladler*, 510–23; Manfred Reifer, *Dr. Mayer Ebner: Ein jüdisches Leben* (Tel Aviv, 1947), 51–62.

headed political functionary as well.[122] From his operational base in the Zionist office, he immediately set his sights on gaining control of the main institutional levers of the Viennese movement.[123] In doing so, he ran headlong into a brick wall of opposition erected by Robert Stricker.

Born in Brünn (Brno), Moravia, Stricker was an early convert to the Zionist cause, rising swiftly to prominence as a publicist and activist. He moved to Vienna for professional reasons soon after the turn of the century—he worked for the state railways as a surveyor—and not only became the leading figure in Viennese Zionism but was active also in the Austrian and international movements. A member of the Gemeinde board in Vienna from 1912, he was elected to the Austrian parliament in 1919, although he failed to win re-election the following year. Active as a journalist already in Brünn, he edited the *Jüdische Zeitung* in Vienna for a number of years prior to the war, and later founded and edited the first German-language Jewish daily, the *Wiener Morgenzeitung* (1919–27). His dominant position in Viennese Zionism made him the nationalist counterpart to Alfred Stern; bitter opponents, they were the principal power-brokers of Viennese Jewish society. Stricker was an uncompromising radical on the Zionist political spectrum, an early devotee of the idea of a Jewish state. As a member of the Greater Actions Committee (Grosses Aktionskomitee) from 1913 (and its vice-president from 1921 to 1924), he was a long-time opponent of the more moderate Chaim Weizmann in the World Zionist Organization, helping to form the anti-Weizmann Union of Radical Zionists in 1925. In 1931 he moved further to the right by joining Ze'ev Jabotinsky's Revisionists, rising to become one of the movement's vice-presidents. In 1933 he broke

---

[122] It had been suggested by the Berlin office in Jan. 1915 that Weltsch take up the post of secretary, but he was unable to do so until Mar. 1918. See ZCO to Pollak, 29 Jan. 1915, CZA, Z3/841; ZCO to Robert Stricker, 11 Jan. 1918, CZA, Z3/520; H[errmann] to Adolf Böhm, 14 Mar. 1918, CZA, Z3/1003. On Weltsch (1891–1984) as an exponent of *Realpolitik*, see the comments by Eva G. Reichmann, 'Wertungen und Umwertungen', in Hans Tramer and Kurt Loewenstein (eds.), *Robert Weltsch zum 70. Geburtstag* (Tel Aviv, 1961), 135. For a contrasting assessment, see Stephen M. Poppel, *Zionism in Germany 1897–1933: The Shaping of a Jewish Identity* (Philadelphia, 1977), 143–57. Weltsch and EAC secretary Leo Herrmann were friends from their days together in the Prague Zionist student group Bar Kochba. See Kieval, *The Making of Czech Jewry*, 124–30. On Prague Zionism, see ibid., chs. 4–5; Yehoshua Borman, 'The "Prague Stream" in the World Zionist Movement 1904–1914' (Heb.), *Gesher*, 15 (1969), 243–50.

[123] Weltsch's primary targets were the Central Committee for Western Austria, the Inner Austrian District Committee, and the weekly newspaper the *Jüdische Zeitung*. On the expansion of the Zionist office, see *JZ*, 12 Apr. 1918, p. 4; 26 Apr. 1918, p. 2; 3 May 1918, p. 2. That Weltsch was acting on behalf of the EAC in Vienna is indicated in Hantke to Siegmund Kaznelson, 8 May 1918; Kaznelson to Hantke, 14 May 1918, both in CZA, Z3/215.

with Revisionism to help found the Jewish State Party with Meir Grossman. At the same time Stricker was an outspoken liberal democrat and Habsburg loyalist in Austrian politics, a self-described moderate. Notorious as a master of political intrigue, his single-mindedness of purpose, imperious personality, and demagogic rhetoric made him a fearsome opponent.[124] With influential and experienced leaders such as Isidor Schalit and Adolf Böhm on the sidelines for much of the war, the consummate operator Stricker had no serious rivals on the local Zionist scene until 1917.[125]

The clash between Weltsch and Stricker was an expression of the often uneasy coexistence of several contrasting aspects of Zionist political culture. Stricker combined devotion to the idea of a Jewish state with dedication to *Landespolitik*, and had little patience for philosophical musings; Weltsch was intensely cerebral and at this stage of his career regarded *Landespolitik* instrumentally, a useful means of 'preparation' for life in Palestine but always subordinate in the Zionist hierarchy of values.[126] To Weltsch, the woeful condition of Viennese Zionism was attributable to Stricker's 'autocratic' ways and to the atmosphere of 'coffee-house politics' that reigned in the city. As a counterweight to Stricker, Weltsch tried to install Adolf Böhm, a leading theoretician and Palestine expert, in key leadership posts. For his part, Böhm (no stranger to conflict with Stricker) was reluctant to engage in party in-fighting, for which he claimed he felt no aptitude.[127]

[124] On Stricker (1879–1944), see Josef Fraenkel (ed.), *Robert Stricker* (London, 1950); Louis Lipsky, *Memoirs in Profile* (Philadelphia, 1975), 167–71; Freidenreich, *Jewish Politics in Vienna*, 61–2; Henisch, *At Home and Abroad*, 151–3; Gaisbauer, *Davidstern und Doppeladler*, 306. On Stricker's self-image as a 'moderate', see Robert Stricker, *Jüdische Politik in Österreich* (Vienna, 1920), 30.

[125] Schalit (1871–1954), an early associate of Herzl, Kadimah president, and leading advocate of *Landespolitik*, remained politically uninvolved until Nov. 1918. See Gaisbauer, *Davidstern und Doppeladler*, 51–2 n. 37; Freidenreich, *Jewish Politics in Vienna*, 60. On Böhm, see below.

[126] See Weltsch's article in *JZ*, 7 June 1918, pp. 2–3.

[127] For Weltsch's characterizations of Stricker and Viennese Zionism, see Weltsch to Herrmann, 30 June 1918, CZA, Z3/215. On the 'coffee-house politics' of Viennese Zionism, see also Henisch, *At Home and Abroad*, 146, 158; Fraenkel, *Robert Stricker*, 29, 66; Arthur Freud, 'Um Gemeinde und Organisation. Zur Haltung der Juden in Österreich', *Bulletin des Leo Baeck Instituts*, 3 (1960), 96. Weltsch wanted Böhm as president of both the Inner Austrian District Committee and the Central Committee for Western Austria. See Weltsch to Herrmann, 30 June 1918; Herrmann to Weltsch, 9 July 1918, both in CZA, Z3/849; Weltsch to Herrmann, 8 Aug. 1918, CZA, Z3/850. He was supported in his efforts by Herrmann and Siegfried Bernfeld. Taussig's plan for reorganization had been drafted by Böhm, who had been absent from the leadership since his resignation as Central Committee president in Nov. 1912. See Gaisbauer, *Davidstern und Doppeladler*, 334–6. Böhm's return—he was co-opted into the Executive Committee and the Central Committee, although he did not become president of either—was welcomed by

Notwithstanding these unresolved tensions, which cast a long shadow over all the movement's work, there were some signal political and popular successes to mark the steady improvement in nationalist fortunes. Their contribution to the welfare effort was recognized by the Austrian authorities and notably raised their political stock, both among Jews and in the eyes of the Austrian government. In the wake of the Balfour Declaration of November 1917, welcomed cautiously by the local Zionists lest they be accused of disloyalty, it was falsely rumoured that the Austrian foreign minister, Count Ottokar Czernin, had delivered a parallel declaration of Austrian support for Zionist goals in Palestine to Arthur Hantke (who visited Vienna in November 1917). Again, this was a tremendous fillip to the nationalists' morale and standing.[128] In a series of meetings with Prime Minister Ernst von Seidler and Interior Minister Count Toggenburg in December 1917 and March 1918, Stricker, Stand, and the Bukovinian Jewish nationalist Reichsrat representative Benno Straucher were given to understand that Jewish nationality might well be officially recognized in a reformed empire. The nationalists' demands included recognition of Jewish nationality, a minister for Jewish affairs, guaranteed Jewish representation in all elected bodies proportional to the Jewish percentage of the population, and the creation of Jewish electoral curias.[129] Reflecting their new-found confidence, they declared that they were now the leaders of Viennese and Austrian Jewry: 'We have pushed aside the gang of unauthorized and

Leo Herrmann, EAC secretary, who expressed his regret that 'in recent years you stood outside [the movement]' (H[errmann] to Böhm, 19 June 1917, CZA, Z3/1003). On Böhm (1873–1941), see Henisch, *At Home and Abroad*, 227–31; Gaisbauer, *Davidstern und Doppeladler*, 127–8 n. 68. On his conflicts with Stricker, see Weltsch to Herrmann, 8 Aug. 1918, CZA, Z3/850; Henisch, *At Home and Abroad*, 152, 228–9.

[128] On this episode, see Isaiah Friedman, 'The Austro-Hungarian Government and Zionism 1897–1918', *Jewish Social Studies*, 27 (1965), 160–7, 237–9; *JZ*, 30 Nov. 1917, p. 1. For local Zionist reaction to the Balfour Declaration, see *JZ*, 23 Nov. 1917, p. 1. The police were indeed monitoring the nationalists and continued to do so. See PDW, Vereins- und Versammlungswesen 1917, Report of 17 Apr. 1917, 5196/K; Vereins- und Versammlungswesen 1918, Report of 4 Mar. 1918, 5146/K; YVA, PKA/E-17 (Shmuel Weintraub); Friedman, 'Austro-Hungarian Government and Zionism', 164–5.

[129] PDW, Vereins- und Versammlungswesen 1918, Reports of 14 and 15 Mar. 1918, 5196/K. On the nationalists' memorandum to the government outlining their demands, see *JZ*, 14 Dec. 1917, p. 4; 22 Mar. 1918, p. 1; ZCWA to ZCO, 29 May 1918, CZA, Z3/849; Freidenreich, *Jewish Politics in Vienna*, 51–2. Straucher was Bukovina's leading Jewish activist, president of the Czernowitz Kultusgemeinde, member of the Czernowitz city council and the Bukovina provincial diet (Landtag), and a Reichsrat deputy from 1897. See Wininger, *Jüdische National-Biographie*, vi. 45–6; Gaisbauer, *Davidstern und Doppeladler*, 511–15, 518–20. See also Reifer, *Dr. Mayer Ebner*, 51–62, 92–6, for a very hostile view.

irresponsible "advisers" and "experts" on Jewish affairs who have hitherto
blocked our way to the Austrian peoples and government by means of cun-
ning and force. . . . Their positions are shaken to the very foundations. The
politics of the ghetto has been broken once and for all.'[130] The response of
the 'advisers' and 'experts' was orchestrated by Stern, who fervently wished
to avoid any publicity but was determined to stymie the efforts of the
'nationalist fanatics'. Stern called a meeting of the Gemeindebund, the
would-be representative body of Austrian Jewry consisting of *Kultusgemeinden* leaders and other notables, to challenge the nationalist pretensions. The
response, however, was less than overwhelming. Of the 300 invitees, gloated
the *Jüdische Zeitung*, only forty-nine attended; Stern and his colleagues were
content to rely on their time-worn practice of quiet diplomacy, submitting
anti-nationalist memorandums to the Interior Ministry and seeking an
audience with the prime minister.[131] Finally, as already noted, the appointment of Chajes to the post of chief rabbi in April 1918 was widely viewed as a
great gain for the nationalist cause.

There was progress too at the 'grass-roots' level, with a veritable boom in
nationalist activity in late 1917 and early 1918, at least in part a result of
Taussig's programme of renewal. New political, cultural, and social groups
were established, and membership of existing clubs and associations grew
by leaps and bounds; meetings and lectures were more frequent, attended
by crowds of several hundred or more. The nationalist-led youth movement began to take shape in October 1917, while the *Jüdische Zeitung*, after
experiencing several difficult years due to shortages of funds, subscribers,
and qualified personnel, regained its pre-war subscription levels in early
1918, reaching 3,500 by April 1918.[132] By this time the leadership could
happily report that 'the general atmosphere for our work has never before
been so promising'.[133]

[130] *JZ*, 22 Mar. 1918, p. 1; 24 May 1918, p. 1.
[131] See Stern to Theodor Sonnenschein, 31 Mar. 1918, CAHJP, AW, 2805/19/11; Report on
the meeting of western Austrian *Kultusgemeinden*, 7 May 1918, CAHJP, AW, 2805/19/238; *JZ*,
10 May 1918, pp. 1–2. For Orthodox disapproval of the Zionist claims, see *JK*, 13 Apr. 1918, p. 1.
[132] *JZ*, 11 Jan. 1918, p. 1; Herrmann to Hantke, 30 Apr. 1918, CZA, Z3/849. *Jüdische Zeitung*
readership was not confined to Vienna but was spread throughout the Austrian half of the
monarchy. See Henisch, *At Home and Abroad*, 147–51. Henisch edited the paper from early 1915
until he was drafted in Sept. 1916. The *Jüdische Zeitung* had been in such dire straits in the first
months of the war that serious consideration had been given to merging it for the war's duration
with the like-minded Prague *Selbstwehr*. See 19 Dec. 1914 Report of the ZCWA meeting of 13
Dec. 1914, CZA, Z3/841.
[133] *JZ*, 26 Apr. 1918, p. 2. On the upsurge in Zionist activity, see also *JZ*, 12 Oct. 1917, p. 4;
7 Dec. 1917, p. 4; 14 Dec. 1917, p. 4; 8 Feb. 1918, p. 4; 12 Apr. 1918, p. 5; 26 Apr. 1918, p. 4;

From the perspective of the balance of forces within Viennese Jewry, the cumulative effect of the nationalists' wartime ascent in the political domain, their thriving associational life, and their leading role in the Congress and youth movements was to elevate them from a clearly subordinate position in relation to the liberals to a position of near equality. It was no longer possible for the latter to regard the Zionists as a marginal, albeit vocal, element in Viennese Jewish society; the government, too, now treated nationalist leaders as serious interlocutors representing a potentially influential constituency. Although internal discord constantly threatened to undermine this new-found status, by the summer of 1918 the situation of the nationalist camp—in terms of both its internal workings and its external standing in Jewish and general politics—had been transformed when compared with August 1914. A combination, then, of propitious circumstances and their own activist *élan* placed the nationalists in a position that permitted quick and decisive action on their part when the moment of crisis arrived in October 1918.

RADICAL NATIONALISM: PO'ALEI ZION

The absence of a powerful non-nationalist Jewish Left in Vienna and Galicia did not hinder—in fact may even have encouraged—the development of Po'alei Zion (Workers of Zion), a party that attempted to synthesize Marxist socialism and Jewish nationalism. Established in Galicia in 1904, by the eve of the war the Austrian branch of Po'alei Zion claimed some 3,000 members (as well as a 1,500-strong youth organization), of whom an overwhelming majority were in Galicia. One of the first formally constituted Po'alei Zion parties, Austrian Po'alei Zion utilized the relative freedom of the Habsburg lands to act as an information conduit for the movement in Russia and, on occasion, as a haven for Russian activists. The world union of Po'alei Zion, formed in 1907, established its headquarters in Vienna; the Vienna branch itself, however, was small, consisting mostly of youths of east European origin. In addition to sharing with other Zionists the ever-present dilemma created by the conflicting demands of Palestine-centred work and *Landespolitik*, Po'alei Zion members also faced the daunting task of juggling Zionist and revolutionary commitments. Austrian Po'alei Zion, reflecting the more moderate Jewish politics of Galicia, the absence of a

10 May 1918, p. 5; 24 May 1918, p. 5; 14 June 1918, p. 5. It was reported, for example, that some 1,200 people were present at a meeting of the Nationalverein in Feb. 1918, of whom 250 subsequently joined. See *JZ*, 1 Mar. 1918, p. 3.

strong left-wing Jewish subculture in Vienna, and the influence of Austrian Marxism, was initially less doctrinaire in its Marxism than its Russian counterpart. Following the revolutionary events of 1905 in Russia, radical Marxist tendencies made some headway within the Austrian movement but did not succeed in curtailing its limited co-operation with 'bourgeois' Zionism. Like the Austrian Zionist movement in general, Po'alei Zion maintained a consistent involvement in Diaspora work. Spurred by the rise of nationalism on the one hand and the 1917 Russian Revolution on the other, factional lines within Austrian Po'alei Zion (as elsewhere) hardened during the war and post-war years, leading to the movement's split in 1920 into social democratic and communist factions.[134]

During the war Vienna became the hub of Austrian Po'alei Zion as numerous Galician members took refuge in the capital. Until early 1917 party-political work was virtually impossible, due to government restrictions and lack of experienced and available leadership (many of the movement's leaders had been drafted). The easing of political restraints by the new regime of Karl I, along with the Russian Revolution of March 1917, provided the stimulus for the party's revival. In July 1917 it relaunched in Vienna the Yiddish-language party organ formerly based in Lemberg (Lwów, Lviv), the *Yidisher Arbeter*, and in December 1917 held its first wartime conference in Kraków, at which much discussion was devoted to the future prospects of the Jewish minority in Poland. By this stage co-operation with the rest of the Zionist camp had been decisively rejected; Po'alei Zion declined to participate in the Congress and youth movements, or in joint welfare efforts. In keeping with the wartime radicalization of the movement, political separatism and a devotion to ideological purity marked the party's rhetoric and action in this period.[135]

The strike of January 1918—Austria-wide but concentrated in Vienna

---

[134] On Po'alei Zion in Austria, see Shabtai Ungar, 'Po'alei Zion in the Austrian Empire 1904–1914' (Heb.), Ph.D. diss., Tel Aviv University, 1985; Gelber, *The History of the Zionist Movement in Galicia*, ii. 737–79; Gaisbauer, *Davidstern und Doppeladler*, 396–414; Frankel, *Prophecy and Politics*, 169, 310–13. Peak membership was an estimated 4,000 in 1906. Membership figures are from Ungar, 'Po'alei Zion', 456; Gelber, *The History of the Zionist Movement in Galicia*, ii. 751, 766, 769, 774, 777. More generally, see also Shimoni, *The Zionist Ideology*, 170 ff.

[135] On Po'alei Zion during the war, see Mendel Singer, 'The Po'alei Zion Party in Austria in the First World War', in Yisrael Cohen and Dov Sadan (eds.), *Aspects of Galicia* (Heb.) (Tel Aviv, 1957), 253–62; S. Rudel, 'Poale Zion in Österreich während des Krieges', *Der Jüdische Arbeiter* (Dec. 1927), 30–3; Berl Locker, *From Kitov to Jerusalem* (Heb.) (Jerusalem, 1970), 29–32; *YA*, Sept.–Oct. 1917, pp. 11–12, 16–18; 1 Feb. 1918, p. 4; *OW*, 1 June 1917, p. 351; *JZ*, 23 Mar. 1917, p. 4. On the Dec. conference, see *YA*, 1 Feb. 1918, pp. 3–13; *JZ*, 11 Jan. 1918, p. 4.

and the surrounding areas, where over 100,000 industrial workers participated—represented the zenith of Po'alei Zion's wartime work. The party
claimed an active role in organizing the strike, estimating that between
30,000 and 40,000 Jewish workers took part.[136] Whether or not their role
was as prominent as they claimed, there is evidence that the movement's
leaders were indeed active in the unrest. With the spectre of the Bolshevik
Revolution looming large, the authorities were taking no chances; this
'success' was followed by a police crackdown, including arrests of leading
members and suppression of most Po'alei Zion activity. Pressure and sur-
veillance were maintained during the ensuing months, and it was only with
the weakening of central authority towards the end of 1918 that the movement was able to recover momentum.[137]

In the wake of the strike the small extreme-left wing of Viennese Po'alei
Zion grew ever closer to local communist groups (a Communist Party was
established in Vienna in November 1918).[138] During the war years, however, tensions between 'left' and 'right' were not particularly intense in the
Austrian party; the exigencies of the battle for the movement's survival took
precedence over questions of internal direction. However, conflict between
the left and right wings of the Viennese party emerged with a vengeance in
1919–20, when Vienna became a base for the communist-leaning sections
of the world movement. Indeed, it was the world Po'alei Zion conference of
July 1920 held in Vienna that led to the movement's split along social democratic and communist lines.[139]

Stridently left-wing, Po'alei Zion was uninterested in compromise with
'bourgeois' Zionists or anyone else, and consequently occupied a somewhat
marginal niche in Viennese Jewish society in terms of both numbers and
influence. Only at the very end of the war, and then only for a brief period,
did Po'alei Zion join in a united Zionist action—the Jewish National Council. It did, however, share the Habsburg-friendly attitude of all other Jewish

---

[136] *YA*, 1 Feb. 1918, p. 1; 15 Feb. 1918, p. 8; Mendel Singer, *Four Events with a Lesson from
the History of the Workers' Movement in Austria* (Heb.) (Haifa, 1975), 32, 35, 38, 42–5, 50–5; John
Bunzl, *Klassenkampf in der Diaspora. Zur Geschichte der jüdischen Arbeiterbewegung* (Vienna,
1975), 125–8. On the Jan. strike, see Richard Georg Plaschka, Horst Haselsteiner, and Arnold
Suppan (eds.), *Innere Front. Militärassistenz, Widerstand und Umsturz in der Donaumonarchie
1918* i. (Munich, 1974), 59–84.

[137] *YA*, 1 May 1918, p. 6; 15 July 1918, p. 1; 27 Dec. 1918, p. 7; *JZ*, 19 Apr 1918, p. 2; *FT*,
1 May 1919, p. 4; Rudel, 'Poale Zion in Österreich', 32.

[138] Bunzl, *Klassenkampf in der Diaspora*, 128–31; Hans Hautmann, *Die Anfänge der linksradikalen Bewegung und der kommunistischen Partei Deutschösterreichs 1916–1919* (Vienna, 1970),
15, 20–1, 31, 34; id., *Die verlorene Räterepublik* (Vienna, 1971), 167–8.

[139] On the split, see Mendelsohn, *Zionism in Poland*, 146–61.

parties, although this was modified by an insistence on the need for radical social as well as national transformation of the empire. In this they echoed the Austrian Marxist stance, with of course the important proviso that Po'alei Zion demanded that Jews be allotted their rightful place among the nations, something the Austrian Social Democrats were exceedingly reluctant to concede. As the *Yidisher Arbeter* stated in August 1918, in a 'free' Austria the Jews must not be the sole remaining 'slaves' ruled by their neighbours.[140] It was from Po'alei Zion, in fact, that the most comprehensive schemes for Jewish autonomy in a reformed empire emerged.[141] The primary focus of the Austrian movement was Galicia, where the 'masses' lived, not Vienna, which provided little more than a temporary base of operations. In January 1919 the *Yidisher Arbeter* returned to Lemberg, and was 'replaced' in Vienna by the German-language *Freie Tribune*, which hoped to consolidate support for the party beyond Yiddish-speaking circles.[142] The impact of Po'alei Zion in Vienna in the immediate post-war period was diminished as a consequence of the drawn-out feuding between its left and right wings. Moreover, as a centre of the communist-oriented faction of the world movement, a great deal of the energy of the party's Viennese branch was directed towards non-Jewish politics in 1919–20, in particular to the bitter conflicts between the Social Democratic Party and the insurgent communists.

THE ORTHODOX

The least politically engaged and organized of the Viennese Jews were the Orthodox, who made up some 20 per cent of the Jewish population by the inter-war period. Predominantly lower-middle-class, Viennese Orthodoxy comprised two major camps—Yiddish-speaking Galicians and German-speaking western Hungarians. In general terms, the former furnished a limited degree of support for the nationalists (although Mizrahi, the religious Zionist organization, was very weak in Vienna) and included a sizeable

---

[140] *YA*, 15 Aug. 1918, p. 2. For Po'alei Zion frustration at the Austrian Social Democratic refusal to acknowledge the existence of a Jewish nationality, see *YA*, 15 Aug. 1917, pp. 3–6; 1 Aug. 1918, pp. 2–4.

[141] See the articles by leading Po'alei Zion theoretician Max Rosenfeld, 'Die jüdischen Gemeinden in Österreich'; id., 'Zur Frage der staatlichen Anerkennung der jüdischen Nationalität in Österreich', *NJM* 1 (1916–17), 664–71; id., 'Für eine nationale Autonomie der Juden in Österreich', *Der Jude*, 1 (1916–17), 290–7. See also *YA*, 15 July 1917, pp. 12–13; 1 July 1918, pp. 1–2; 1 Aug. 1918, pp. 2–4. Dynastic patriotism was mostly absent from the increasingly communist-oriented wing of the party.   [142] *YA*, 31 Jan. 1919, p.1 ; *FT*, 31 Jan. 1919, p. 4.

hasidic component; the latter were on the whole better organized and more acculturated, and provided the base for the Vienna branch of the religious anti-Zionist organization Agudes Yisroel. Orthodox disdain for the Kultusgemeinde regime in religious affairs—in their eyes it was unforgivably lax in ritual matters and bent on assimilation—manifested itself in several attempts by the Hungarians, beginning in the 1850s, to secede from the Gemeinde and form an autonomous community, following the example set by Orthodox factions in Hungary and Germany. Neither the Austrian authorities nor the Gemeinde, however, were willing to countenance such a move, which would have fractured the unified façade of Viennese Jewry.[143] None the less, by creating a network of religious, social, and educational organizations catering to their traditionalist lifestyle, the Orthodox managed to carve out for themselves a distinctly separate public sphere, at one remove from what they saw as the lukewarm Jewishness of the liberals and the dangerous secularism of the nationalists. This aloofness was evident in welfare work, which the Orthodox, like everyone else, devotedly pursued for the first three years of the war. Theirs, however, was welfare with a spiritual bent, attempting not only to provide food and shelter but also to meet basic religious needs. To do this required the establishment of a separate Orthodox welfare network.

Orthodox separatism extended also to the political realm. A reliance on *shtadlones* and Habsburg loyalism characterized the Orthodox stance in Austrian politics until the end of the empire. It was only during the war that they first began to engage politically in the Jewish community, boosted by the presence in Vienna of many Orthodox refugees, among whom were a considerable number of prominent Galician rabbis.[144] As the nationalist star waxed in late 1917, the Orthodox overcame their habitual wariness of involvement in local Jewish politics and began to organize to defend their interests. What was at stake transcended the parochial Jewish plane: Zionist demands for Jewish autonomy were receiving an unprecedented degree of government attention and the nationalists were using the legitimacy thus conferred to claim for themselves the status of authoritative Jewish representative in both Jewish and Austrian society. It was this intersection of Jewish and general politics that sounded the alarm for the Orthodox. If Austria was indeed headed for fundamental structural reforms, then it surely

[143] On the demography of Viennese Orthodoxy and on its separatist tendencies, see Freidenreich, *Jewish Politics in Vienna*, 118–23, 138–40; Wistrich, *The Jews of Vienna in the Age of Franz Joseph*, 109–11, 272–7; Wolfgang Häusler, ' "Orthodoxie" und "Reform" im Wiener Judentum in der Epoche des Hochliberalismus', *Studia Judaica Austriaca*, 6 (1978), 29–56.

[144] See e.g. Jacob Rosenheim, *Erinnerungen 1870–1920* (Frankfurt am Main, 1970), 142.

behoved the Orthodox to make their voice heard on the issue of Jewish status in the new order; passivity would merely leave the field open to the nationalists, whose aggressive secularism was certainly more threatening to Orthodox interests than the tepid religiosity of the hitherto dominant liberals.

Local circumstances were not the only force at work in this development. Orthodox Jews, especially the younger generation, were not immune to the wartime surge of Jewish nationalist sentiment, the Jewish *Allgefühl*, as one writer described it.[145] What has been called the 'anti-Zionist Zionism' of certain German Orthodox groups, stimulated in particular by the Balfour Declaration and expressed by a commitment to Palestine work and the 'appropriation' of nationalist rhetoric, was apparent also in Austrian Orthodoxy during the war.[146] That the Jews were a distinct *Volk* was a given for the Orthodox. In their eyes, though, the foundation of the Jewish *Volk* was religion, not an ethnic Jewish nationhood in the modern, secular sense. This was the guiding principle in Orthodox pronouncements on the prospect of the introduction of Jewish autonomy in Austria: no matter what form it took, the religious basis of Jewish life must be recognized. Beyond this stipulation the Orthodox were generally loath to make concrete programmatic suggestions.[147]

The first tangible sign of Orthodox politicization was the revival in November 1917 of the Association for the Protection of the Interests of Orthodox Jewry in Vienna and Lower Austria. Members of the Adas Jisroel congregation (Community of Israel, popularly known as the *Schiffschul*), the organizational hub of Hungarian Orthodoxy in Vienna, played a prominent role in this action. Established at the turn of the century, this association now wished to don the mantle of leadership, casting itself as defender of Orthodox rights throughout the empire, with a particular focus on western Austria.[148] As its first major project, the association was instrumental in

[145] Reinhold Lewin, 'Der Krieg als jüdisches Erlebnis', *Monatsschrift für Geschichte und Wissenschaft des Judentums*, 63 (1919), 13.

[146] The expression is found in Mordechai Breuer, *Modernity within Tradition: The Social History of Orthodox Jewry in Imperial Germany*, trans. Elizabeth Petuchowski (New York, 1992), 393. See also ibid. 371, 385–94; Eva Reichmann, 'Der Bewusstseinswandel der deutschen Juden', in Mosse and Paucker (eds.), *Deutsches Judentum in Krieg und Revolution*, 570–6.

[147] For examples of Orthodox thinking on Jewish autonomy in Austria, see *JK*, 13 Apr. 1918, pp. 3–4; n. 55 above. For a polemic between the Zionists and the Orthodox over their respective understandings of Jewish nationality (and over Orthodox resentment at Zionist attempts to claim Orthodox support), see *JZ*, 25 Jan. 1918, p. 4; 15 Feb. 1918, p. 4; *JK*, 7 Feb. 1918, pp. 3–4. On nationalism and Orthodoxy in general, see Shimoni, *The Zionist Ideology*, ch. 4.

[148] On the Association for the Protection of the Interests of Orthodox Jewry in Vienna and Lower Austria (Verein zur Wahrung der Interessen des orthodoxen Judentums in Wien und Niederösterreich), see *JK*, 29 Nov. 1917, pp. 3–4, 7; *OW*, 11 Jan. 1918, p. 25.

organizing a conference of Austrian Orthodoxy, an Orthodox parallel to the Congress movement then in train. Taking their cue also from a conference held in Frankfurt of Orthodox groups from all regions of the Central Powers (including occupied Poland), the organizers hoped that the Austrian gathering would inaugurate a 'new era' in which Austrian Orthodoxy would assume a more active role in Jewish public affairs, commensurate with its position as the 'strongest element' within Jewry. The Orthodox, they said, must 'assert their rights', and the conference would serve to 'announce the existence of Orthodoxy to the broad public'. To end Orthodox isolation and powerlessness, and to ensure a voice in internal Jewish affairs as well as in the formation of the coming 'new order' in Austria, a central Orthodox representative body was envisaged. Such an organization, moreover, would help belie the claims of 'small but active' groups (i.e. the nationalists) to represent the Jews.[149]

Attended by more than 100 delegates from all parts of the empire, the conference was held in Vienna in February 1918. The state of Orthodoxy in the provinces was uniformly described as 'desolate', and high hopes were expressed that a strong representative organization could begin to remedy this situation by providing material assistance. It was agreed that the mandate of an umbrella organization would be confined to western Austria, although the co-operation of the Orthodox strongholds of Galicia and Bukovina would be welcomed. (The Galician head of Agudes Yisroel made clear his desire to unite Austrian Orthodoxy under Agude auspices.)[150] Although preparations for this organization made some progress in the following months, these efforts were overtaken by events and came to nothing; the Association for the Protection of the Interests of Orthodox Jewry reconstituted itself as the Viennese branch of Agudes Yisroel in December 1919.[151]

A key role in the planning and execution of the conference, and in

---

[149] *JK*, 10 Jan. 1918, p. 1; 14 Feb. 1918, pp. 2–4. On the Orthodox wish to play 'a leading role' in Austrian Jewry, see 'Tätigkeitsbericht der "Agudas Jisroel" für die Zeit vom September 1914 bis Oktober 1917', suppl., *JK*, 24 Jan. 1918. On the Frankfurt conference, see *OW*, 22 Feb. 1918, pp. 122–3; Friedman, 'The Austro-Hungarian Government and Zionism', 238–9.

[150] *JK*, 21 Feb. 1918, pp. 1–4; *WH*, 8 Mar. 1918, pp. 5–6; Freidenreich, *Jewish Politics in Vienna*, 126. Aside from laying the foundations for an umbrella organization, the conference resolutions focused on Orthodox demands for recognition of their special religious, social, educational, and cultural needs—all of which served to emphasize that their agenda diverged from that of the liberals and nationalists.

[151] On work towards the umbrella body, see *JK*, 7 Mar. 1918, p. 1; 25 Apr. 1918, p. 2; 16 May 1918, p. 3; 5 Sept. 1918, p. 2. On the Association's change to Agudes Yisroel, see *JK*, 19 Dec. 1919, pp. 1–2.

Austrian Orthodoxy in general, was played by the publicist and activist Jonas Kreppel. Born in 1874 in the eastern Galician town of Drohobycz, Kreppel managed his own publishing firms in Kraków and Lemberg for two decades prior to the war, producing and editing a stream of journals, newspapers, and books in Yiddish, Hebrew, and German, while also finding time to write a series of detective stories in Yiddish and a number of popular religious works. He came to Vienna as a refugee, and in August 1915 launched the *Jüdische Korrespondenz*, the first Orthodox newspaper to appear in the capital since a short-lived predecessor in 1899–1900.[152] Kreppel worked in the press department of the Foreign Ministry in Vienna during the war, rising by the mid-1920s to the rank of ministerial secretary. A pre-Herzlian supporter of Orthodox settlement in Palestine, he was an outspoken anti-Zionist and an exemplar of Orthodox Habsburg patriotism. At one point in his civil service career he aspired (unsuccessfully) to the position of Austrian consul in Palestine, and on the eve of the *Anschluss* in 1938 published a pamphlet calling for the restoration of the house of Habsburg in Austria. Active in Agudes Yisroel circles, he remained editor of the *Korrespondenz* when it became the Agude organ in Vienna in June 1919.[153] In reports written for the government in February 1918 Kreppel portrayed the Frankfurt and Vienna conferences as the beginning of Orthodox attempts to organize politically. Emphasizing Orthodox dynastic loyalty, he suggested that a central Orthodox body could act as an important source of government support in the large Jewish population now within the borders of the Central Powers, providing a counterweight to radicalism and to the 'Entente-agitation' among Jews in the wake of the Balfour Declaration.[154]

Further evidence of Orthodox politicization was the formation in Vienna of a hasidic Zionist association. Galvanized by the Balfour Declaration, a number of Galician hasidic leaders who had established their courts in Vienna following the outbreak of war set up an organization called Yishuv

---

[152] The predecessor to the *Jüdische Korrespondenz* was known first as the *Wiener Jüdische Presse* and subsequently as the *Neue Jüdische Presse*. See Toury, *Die jüdische Presse im österreichischen Kaiserreich*, 90–1.

[153] On Kreppel (1874–1940s), see Henisch, *At Home and Abroad*, 276–8; Wininger, *Jüdische National-Biographie*, iii. 537; *Jüdisches Lexikon* (Berlin, 1927–30), iii. 891; *JZ*, 31 Mar. 1916, p. 2; 15 Feb. 1918, p. 4. On his involvement with Ahavat Zion in Galicia, see Gelber, *The History of the Zionist Movement in Galicia*, i. 328, 367; ii. 472, 482, 502, 521. A good example of his patriotic writings is his *Der Weltkrieg und die Judenfrage*. After becoming the Agude organ in Vienna, the *Korrespondenz* merged in 1920 with the Bratislava Agude paper the *Jüdische Presse*. See *JK*, 13 June 1919, p. 1; Toury, *Die jüdische Presse im österreichischen Kaiserreich*, 91–2.

[154] Kreppel's reports of 3 and 19 Feb. 1918 are in the Haus-, Hof-, und Staatsarchiv, Vienna, Politisches Archiv 1, box 1051, Krieg 68.

Erets Yisrael (Settlement of the Land of Israel) in March 1918, hoping to spread the Zionist idea among the hasidim of Galicia and encourage the settlement of Orthodox Jews in Palestine. The prime movers in the formation of this group, among whom were scions of the Ruzhin hasidic dynasty, were long-time Zionist sympathizers who represented only a narrow stratum of the Galician hasidic population. Nevertheless, a number of branches were immediately established in Galicia, while the Viennese office soon claimed 150 members and a youth section.[155] Although wishing to enter the World Zionist Organization as an independent faction, the group was not prepared to relinquish autonomy in its internal affairs to the secular Zionists, a dilemma similar to that experienced by the like-minded religious Zionists of the Mizrahi movement.[156] Mizrahi had been organized in Vienna since 1912; its supporters at this stage were primarily drawn from the western-Hungarian Orthodox, who otherwise provided, as already noted, the base of support in Vienna for the anti-Zionist Agude.[157] For their part, the Zionists were willing to collaborate with the hasidim if only in order to strengthen the anti-Agude forces in Galicia.[158] Marked by mutual wariness and ambivalence, negotiations between the hasidim and the Zionist organization continued for over a year with no concrete results, and the group merged soon after with the local Mizrahi movement.[159]

The war years saw increased Orthodox willingness to engage actively in politics and to speak out more insistently when they felt their collective interests were impinged upon. If it is true that the Orthodox political style

[155] On Yishuv Erets Yisrael, see Moshe Reich, 'The Yishuv Erets Yisrael Association', in Yitzhak Raphael and Shlomo Z. Shragai (eds.), *The Book of Religious Zionism* (Heb.) (Jerusalem, 1977), i. 505–12; S. Hacohen Weingarten, 'Parallel Organizations to the Mizrahi', in Y. L. Hacohen Fishman (ed.), *The Mizrahi Book* (Heb.) (Jerusalem, 1946), 117–21; *JZ*, 22 Mar. 1918, p. 3; YVA, PKA/E-6 (Yisrael Weinstock).

[156] See the Protocol of the meeting between Yishuv Erets Yisrael and Zionist representatives (including Stricker, Stand, and Weltsch), 31 Mar. 1918, CZA, L6/342. On reluctance in the group's ranks to join the World Zionist Organization, see Reich, 'The Yishuv Erets Yisrael Association', 509–10.

[157] On the nature of Mizrahi support in Vienna, see Weingarten, 'Parallel Organizations to the Mizrahi', 121; Freidenreich, *Jewish Politics in Vienna*, 138–9. See also Rozenblit, *The Jews of Vienna*, 168. On Mizrahi in Galicia, see Gelber, *The History of the Zionist Movement in Galicia*, ii. 780–803.

[158] 'Notiz', 30 Apr. 1918, CZA, L6/342; Weltsch to ZCO, 4 May 1918, CZA, Z3/849; Weltsch to ZCO, 4 July 1918, CZA, L6/354.

[159] On the negotiations between Yishuv Erets Yisrael and the Zionists, see Yishuv Erets Yisrael to London Zionist Office, 24 Tamuz 5679 (22 July 1919); London Zionist Office to Palestine Office, Vienna, 16 July 1919; London Zionist Office to Yishuv Erets Yisrael, 27 Aug. 1919, all in CZA, Z4/2116. On the merger with Mizrahi, see Reich, 'The Yishuv Erets Yisrael Association', 512; Weingarten, 'Parallel Organizations to the Mizrahi', 121.

was somewhat tame and passive by comparison with that of the nationalists, this was by design, intending to convey an image of sobriety and patriotism.[160] Underpinning Orthodox strategy was the fairly modest wish that its voice be heard in the debate about Jewish status in the empire. Reluctant to venture beyond the Jewish domain—their focus was at all times Torah and the preservation of Jewish religious life—the Orthodox were stalwart advocates of the political *status quo*, closer in this respect to the liberals than to the nationalists.

[160] See Freidenreich, *Jewish Politics in Vienna*, 123, on the war as an 'important turning point' for Orthodox attitudes to Kultusgemeinde politics. On the similarly reactive and moderate nature of Orthodox politics in Poland during the war, see Bacon, *The Politics of Tradition*, 37–46, 68–9.

TWO

THE REFUGEES

R EFUGEES, sadly, have a permanent place in the history of modern Europe. The phenomenon of mass refugee flight began during the First World War, as millions of civilians were cast adrift, fleeing the Russian army's advance into Habsburg Galicia or displaced by Russian military rule in the western territory of the tsarist empire. In the enormous areas designated as a theatre of military operations, Nicholas II gave his military authorities a free hand, which quickly assumed the nature of an iron fist. Military rule was uncompromisingly harsh, intruding, as one historian has written, into 'virtually every facet of life'. For the civilian population, military administration was a 'disaster . . . marked by arbitrariness, confusion, administrative abuses, and outright atrocities'.[1] In the initial weeks of the war hundreds of thousands fled the fighting in the Polish lands and Galicia, while the army engaged in massive expulsions into the Russian interior of locals whose patriotism it regarded as suspect. These traumas pale in relation to the horrors unleashed by the Russian army as it retreated in the first part of 1915, perpetrating wholesale massacres and civilian expulsions, and in general acting in accordance with the view expressed by one of its commanders that 'war proceeds by fire and the sword, and whoever happens to get in the way must suffer'.[2] Although precise figures do not exist, estimates of the number of refugees by the end of 1915 range up to several million. Worse was to come. Political transformations in the wake of the war led to an estimated 9.5 million refugees in Europe by 1926.[3]

Jews were among the hardest-hit by this whirlwind. In Russia's western borderlands the army took advantage of the *carte blanche* it had received

---

[1] Daniel W. Graf, 'Military Rule behind the Russian Front 1914–1917: The Political Ramifications', *Jahrbücher für Geschichte Osteuropas*, 22 (1974), 392, 395.

[2] The quotation is attributed to General Yanushkevich, chief of staff of the military commander-in-chief Grand Duke Nikolay Nikolaevich. See ibid. 401.

[3] For estimates of refugee numbers, see ibid. 402; Marrus, *The Unwanted*, 51, 54.

from the tsar to implement a wide range of anti-Jewish measures, including large-scale expulsions (20,000 from Polish cities during late January 1915, for example), random violence and looting, and widespread hostage-taking on the grounds that Jews were surely sympathetic to the Central Powers, if not actively engaged in anti-Russian espionage.[4] Executions and massacres were widely reported, if difficult to confirm. Sixty-seven Jews were said to have been killed in Horodenka in eastern Galicia; seven executed in Sochaczew; five hanged in Zamość.[5] All this, though, was a mere prelude to subsequent Russian actions.

Persecution of Jews intensified in the early months of 1915, with mass expulsions from Polish territory, from Galicia, and from the north-western provinces of Kovno and Courland. Expulsions were generally carried out at extremely short notice, often between twenty-four and forty-eight hours. The American Jewish Committee's report on the situation of the Jews in the war zone conservatively estimated that in June 1915 at least 600,000 Jews were 'homeless' and 'ruined' in the Polish lands and the north-western districts of Russia.[6] Brutality was a hallmark of the Russian treatment of the Jews. Speaking in the Duma (Russian parliament), one deputy described what he had witnessed:

I . . . can testify with what incredible cruelty the expulsion of the Jews from the Province of Radom took place. The whole population was driven out within a few hours during the night. At 11 o'clock the people were informed that they had to leave, with a threat that any one found at daybreak would be hanged. And so in the darkness of the night began the exodus of the Jews. . . .

The police and the gendarmes treat the Jewish refugees . . . like criminals. At one station, for instance, the Jewish [aid] Commission . . . was not even allowed to approach the trains to render aid to the refugees or to give them food and water. In one case a train which was conveying the victims was completely sealed and when finally opened most of the inmates were found half dead, sixteen down with scarlet fever and one with typhus.[7]

Such scenes were commonplace, and were multiplied as the Russian army retreated in confusion and haste throughout the summer of 1915.

---

[4] See e.g. Graf, 'Military Rule behind the Russian Front', 398.
[5] S. An-ski, *The Destruction of Galicia: The Jewish Catastrophe in Poland, Galicia, and Bukovina*, in An-ski, *Collected Writings* (Yid.), vi (New York, 1921), 78–9; Abraham G. Duker, 'Jews in the World War', *Contemporary Jewish Record*, 2 (Sept.–Oct. 1939), 10.
[6] *The Jews in the Eastern War Zone* (New York, 1916), 64. This report provided a basis for subsequent accounts and estimates, such as those of Abraham Duker and Salo Baron. See Baron, *The Russian Jew under Tsars and Soviets*, 157–60.   [7] *The Jews in the Eastern War Zone*, 62–3.

The situation of Galician Jewry during this period was similarly dire. By the middle of September 1914 the Russian offensive on the eastern front led to the occupation of nearly all of eastern Galicia and part of Bukovina; by mid-November Russian forces were closing in on the west Galician capital, Kraków.[8] In these areas of densely concentrated Jewish settlement, Russian troops indulged in an orgy of anti-Jewish violence and rape. In countless towns and cities the arrival of the Russians signalled the outbreak of pogroms. In Husiatyn, for example, near the Russian border, Russian troops reportedly began looting and burning Jewish homes immediately upon entering the town in early August. The house-to-house rampage, in which peasants from the surrounding villages joined, left hundreds of Jewish families destitute and homeless. Many Jews fled, many others were driven out. Within a few days, commented the writer S. An-ski, the contemporary chronicler of Galician Jewry's wartime devastation, Husiatyn had been reduced to ruins.[9] Extensive expulsions occurred in many locations. An estimated 15,000 Jews were expelled from Przemyśl; 8,000 were forced to leave Zaleszczyki; thousands were forcibly removed from Śniatyn, Buczacz, and elsewhere in eastern Galicia. An-ski reported tales of Cossacks playing with the corpses of Jewish babies, of Jews being forced to ride naked on pigs, of Jews being shot. 'In every corner', he wrote, 'reigned the fear of death.'[10] According to the account of one soldier, the front was soon 'almost *judenrein*'.[11] Jews, of course, were not the only ones to suffer at the hands of the Russian military. Whereas in the Baltics and in the Volga regions the German minority was singled out for abuse and expulsion, in Galicia, and particularly in eastern Galicia, Ukrainians bore the brunt of Russian rule along with the Jews. Aiming at thorough Russification, the occupiers closed Ukrainian educational and cultural institutions, and

---

[8] On the progress of the war in Galicia and Russian Poland from Aug. 1914 to early 1915, see Norman Stone, *The Eastern Front 1914–1917* (New York, 1975), chs. 4–5; Holger H. Herwig, *The First World War: Germany and Austria-Hungary 1914–1918* (London, 1997), 87–96; *Österreich-Ungarns letzter Krieg*, i (Vienna, 1930), suppls. 14, 20, 26. Czernowitz was taken by the Russians at the end of Aug. and by the middle of Dec. they occupied large parts of Bukovina. See ibid. ii, drafts 1 and 2; Schmelzer, 'Die Juden in der Bukowina', 67–8.

[9] An-ski, *The Destruction of Galicia*, vi. 66–8. An-ski travelled extensively in Galicia during the war, organizing relief work and keeping a diary.

[10] Ibid. 62. For the tales of Russian cruelty, see ibid. 104–13. On expulsions, see Duker, 'Jews in the World War', 13–14; *Jews in the Eastern War Zone*, 84–6.

[11] Quoted in Walter Mentzel, 'Weltkriegsflüchtlinge in Cisleithanien 1914–1918', in Gernot Heiss and Oliver Rathkolb (eds.), *Asylland wider Willen. Flüchtlinge in Österreich im europäischen Kontext seit 1914* (Vienna, 1995), 22. I wish to thank Paul Weindling for this reference.

attempted to forcibly convert the Uniate population to Russian Orthodoxy.[12]

The Austrian record in Galicia was similarly marred by atrocities,
although to a lesser degree. During its retreat, for example, the Austrian
army conducted a scorched-earth policy, razing hundreds of villages. Jews
were expelled *en masse*, their houses plundered by troops and hostile locals.
Hundreds of Ukrainians were executed for allegedly aiding the Russians,
while thousands were interned in concentration camps.[13] The consequences of this prolonged period of ruinous violence were devastating, particularly for eastern Galicia. An Austrian official, describing the 'terrible
ravages' in December 1915, calculated that upwards of 7 million people had
been 'severely affected' economically, with several million made destitute.[14] Within the context of this general desolation, Galician Jewry experienced economic ruin, social and political dislocation, and a general
'collapse of the religious and moral order'.[15] Put simply, this was a catastrophe of unprecedented proportions.

It should already be clear that refugees were a feature of the wartime
landscape in the Habsburg lands, even if in somewhat lesser numbers than
in Russia. During the course of the war hundreds of thousands of people
took flight from places as diverse as Galicia and Bukovina, South Tyrol, the
Trentino, Bosnia-Herzegovina, Dalmatia, and Istria. The great majority
(some half a million, according to contemporary estimates) headed west
from Galicia and Bukovina as the Russian army occupied these areas in the
first months of the war. Large-scale evacuations and flight also occurred in
the wake of Italy's entry into the war on the side of the Entente in May
1915, and yet another tidal wave of refugees was set in motion by the Russian offensive at the beginning of 1916, this time particularly affecting the
already devastated north-eastern regions of the monarchy.[16]

In Austria, as in Russia, Jews figured in disproportionate numbers among
the refugees. Evidently well aware of the dangers posed by Russian military

---

[12] On the Germans, see Graf, 'Military Rule behind the Russian Front', 400–1; Marrus, *The
Unwanted*, 53–4. On the Ukrainians, see Paul Robert Magocsi, *Galicia: A Historical Survey and
Bibliographical Guide* (Toronto, 1983), 167–73; Orest Subtelny, *Ukraine: A History* (Toronto,
1988), 340–3.

[13] Magocsi, *Galicia*, 167; Subtelny, *Ukraine*, 341; Mentzel, 'Weltkriegsflüchtlinge in Cisleithanien', 19–23.   [14] Quoted in Mentzel, 'Weltkriegsflüchtlinge in Cisleithanien', 22.

[15] Roskies, *Against the Apocalypse*, 117. See also ibid. 115–18, 134–8.

[16] Mentzel, 'Weltkriegsflüchtlinge in Cisleithanien', 17. See ibid. 22 for the figure of half a
million.

occupation, Jews responded to news of the Russian advance into eastern Galicia by mass flight, with perhaps as many as 400,000 making for the empire's western provinces or Hungary. The speed of the Russian campaign left little time for preparation. The vast majority simply abandoned their homes and property, fleeing by foot or in crowded trains and cattle-wagons.[17] Given the haste of departure, the destination was often uncertain; the primary objective was simply to put oneself out of reach of the Russians. Many of those from small villages headed for the closest town or city, hoping to continue their journey westward by train. The rapidity and extent of the Russian advance quickly turned the refugee stream into a torrent, causing widespread chaos. Roads were clogged and trains were packed to capacity, as tens of thousands of Jews clamoured to leave the area in what one contemporary called a 'veritable mass migration'.[18] The writer Abraham Schwadron described the 'frenzied' scenes as the 'last train' left Lemberg with fifty to sixty carriages crammed with anxious, screaming, and fainting people.[19] With the Russians moving so fast and so far, to stay in Galicia at all soon came to be seen as an increasingly risky proposition for Jews. Vienna became the preferred destination of many. The journey to the safety of the capital, however, sometimes took weeks of enervating travel in the most difficult conditions—often destitute, always lacking in material comfort, hungry, and reliant on the charity of strangers for food and shelter.[20]

Vienna was an obvious choice for the refugees, who hoped to find help there from relatives or friends among the city's large Galician Jewish community. Beyond their expectations of fraternal assistance, the *Residenzstadt* also exerted a powerful attraction for many Galician Jews as an almost mythical place of beauty and limitless opportunity, governed by a benevolent monarch. Much quoted by Jews during the war was the emperor's

[17] Precise statistics were not compiled. An Austrian Interior Ministry report from late 1915 estimated a peak of approximately 600,000 'destitute' refugees, a figure excluding both those in Hungary and those not registered as refugees with the Austrian government. See *Staatliche Flüchtlingsfürsorge im Kriege 1914–1915* (Vienna, 1915), 46–7. Jonas Kreppel, *Juden und Judentum von Heute* (Vienna, 1925), 66–7, speculated that as many as 450,000 Jews either fled or were forcibly evacuated by the Austrian authorities. See also Arieh Tartakower, 'Jewish Migratory Movements in Austria in Recent Generations', in Fraenkel (ed.), *The Jews of Austria*, 289–90.

[18] Kreppel, *Juden und Judentum von Heute*, 66.

[19] *OW*, 18 Sept. 1914, pp. 652–4. David Horowitz (*My Yesterday* (Heb.) (Tel Aviv, 1970), 34–6) was apparently also on this 'last train' from Lemberg.

[20] For descriptions of the journey, see also Helen Hilsenrad, *Brown was the Danube* (London, 1966), 75–80; Henisch, *At Home and Abroad*, 142–4; Minni Lachs, *Warum schaust du zurück? Erinnerungen 1907–1941* (Vienna, 1986), 34–45; *JZ*, 18 Sept. 1914, p. 2; Beatrix Hoffmann-Holter, *'Abreisendmachung'. Jüdische Kriegsflüchtlinge in Wien 1914 bis 1923* (Vienna, 1995), 26–9.

purported response to the complaint in late 1914 by the Christian Social mayor, Richard Weiskirchner, about lack of accommodation in the capital due to the refugee influx. Franz Joseph reportedly—and comfortingly, from the Jewish point of view—replied that if necessary he would place the Hofburg and Schönbrunn palaces at the refugees' disposal.[21] The sudden arrival and very visible presence of over 100,000 Galician Jews precipitated an eruption of virulent antisemitism, initially targeting the refugees but later directed at Viennese Jews in general. (Indeed, one Jewish newspaper commented in September 1917 that antisemitism had become a 'national sport'.[22]) The Viennese treatment of the refugees, a rude awakening for those who had cherished idealistic fantasies about the city, has recently been described as 'the prologue to the darkest chapter in Austrian history'.[23] Without going quite so far, it was certainly an acutely unhappy moment in the history of Austrian–Jewish relations. Never before had the Viennese been faced in their own backyard with quite so many Jews from the far reaches of the empire. If quantitatively different, it was qualitatively familiar, and Viennese responses were drawn from the by then standard repertoire of anti-Jewish rhetoric and action.

It was not just the Viennese who were disturbed by the refugees. Predictably, Jewish responses were also mixed, revealing a degree of nervousness about Jewish status and identity. Both the Jewish press and the Viennese police noted local Jewish ambivalence towards the refugees, whether on the part of established Jews who feared being identified with the Galicians or poorer Jews who were unhappy at the prospect of economic competition. Admonitions about ostentation in fashion and lifestyle (aimed in particular at refugee women) were frequent until early 1915.[24] Patronizing attitudes towards the *Ostjuden* surfaced at regular intervals. To B'nai B'rith, for example, the refugees had emerged from the darkness of their

[21] See e.g. *OW*, 14 Dec. 1917, p. 789; *NNZ*, 30 Oct. 1914, p. 1; Kreppel, *Juden und Judentum von Heute*, 70. For examples of Galician Jewish images of Vienna, see Hilsenrad, *Brown was the Danube*, 83–5; Manes Sperber, *Die Wasserträger Gottes* (Vienna, 1974), 126–7; *NNZ*, 25 Dec. 1914, p. 2; Hoffmann-Holter, *'Abreisendmachung'*, 12. Idealization of Vienna coexisted with a marked degree of cultural Polonization among middle-class Galician Jewry. See Ezra Mendelsohn, 'From Assimilation to Zionism in Lvov: The Case of Alfred Nossig', *Slavonic and East European Review*, 49 (1971), 521–34; id., 'Jewish Assimilation in Lvov: The Case of Wilhelm Feldman', *Slavic Review*, 28 (1969), 577–90.

[22] *OW*, 14 Sept. 1917, p. 582.   [23] Hoffmann-Holter, *'Abreisendmachung'*, 14.

[24] *JZ*, 25 Dec. 1914, p. 1; *OW*, 18 Sept. 1914, p. 644; 28 Sept. 1914, p. 665; 5 Mar. 1915, pp. 174–5; 12 Mar. 1915, pp. 196–7; 30 Nov. 1917, pp. 149–50; *JK*, 19 Aug. 1915, pp. 2–3; *NNZ*, 18 Sept. 1914, p. 6; 2 Oct. 1914, p. 6; 26 Mar. 1915, pp. 50–2; PDW, SB 1914/15, 25 Feb. 1915.

ghetto into the 'bright light of the west' and needed to be 'educated' to adopt a west European lifestyle. Poor, unfamiliar, and *déclassé*, they were still at the cultural level of western Jewry's great-grandparents. The Austrian Israelite Union, too, was unimpressed by the cultural level of the refugees and recommended forestalling further immigration by improving living conditions in Galicia.[25] Samuel Krauss, later rector of the Vienna Israelitisch-Theologische Lehranstalt, saw a 'true and authentic Jewish heart' beating beneath the 'raw and sometimes repulsive' exterior of the 'childlike' *Ostjude*.[26] In Budapest and Prague, where refugees gathered in lesser numbers than Vienna, they evoked similar reactions. A familiar pattern emerged: on the one hand, embarrassment on the part of acculturated Jews (in Budapest local Jewish leaders reportedly went so far as to request the refugees' expulsion) and, on the other, Zionist enthusiasm for the 'authentic' Jewish culture of the refugees.[27] The refugee influx into the monarchy's major cities was a vivid illustration of the mix of east and west that was a defining characteristic of Habsburg Jewry, demonstrating the cultural and social abyss that still separated east and west European Jews, while at the same time making plain their uncomfortably interdependent relationship.

Both antisemitism and the Jewish east–west divide were evident in the refugee welfare effort, the single most daunting task confronting Viennese Jewry in the first two years of the war. The politics of welfare bulked large for Viennese Jewry during the war, driving and reflecting the changing power relations within Jewish society. As refugee welfare developed into a highly charged issue in Viennese politics, so too it became an important arena of Jewish politics. Success in the provision of welfare was central to the nationalists' striking achievements in both general and Jewish political spheres, contributing in the process to the increasing prestige of ideologies

[25] For B'nai B'rith, see *ZBB* 18 (1915), 119; 19 (1916), 103. For the Union, see *MOIU* 28 (Jan.–Mar. 1916), 1–2; (Apr.–May 1916), 12–13.

[26] Krauss, *Die Krise der Wiener Judenschaft*, 2, 15. See also Nathan Birnbaum, 'Wir und die Flüchtlinge', *JNK* 1 (1915–16), 101–8. For a series of sympathetic impressionistic sketches of the refugees by a Zionist writer, see Otto Abeles, *Jüdische Flüchtlinge. Szenen und Gestalten* (Vienna, 1918).

[27] On Budapest, see Avigdor Löwenheim, 'The Leadership of the Neolog Jewish Congregation of Pest in the Years 1914–1919: Its Status and Activity in the Jewish Community' (Heb.), Ph.D. diss., Hebrew University of Jerusalem, 1991, 137, 142–5; *OW*, 7 May 1915, p. 346; *JZ*, 30 Apr. 1915, p. 2; 21 Jan. 1916, p. 1; Bloch, *Erinnerungen aus meinem Leben*, iii. 244–9. On Prague, see Kieval, *The Making of Czech Jewry*, 174–8; Moses Wiesenfeld, 'Begegnung mit Ostjuden', in Felix Weltsch (ed.), *Dichter, Denker, Helfer. Max Brod zum 50. Geburtstag* (Mährisch-Ostrau, 1934), 54–7.

of nationalism and ethnic self-determination. The refugee episode, then, was significant for a number of reasons: the clash between Jewish east and west, the upsurge of antisemitism, the shift in political culture. It was the final, often unhappy, meeting of the empire's magnetic Jewish poles, simultaneously attracting and repelling one another.

The refugees began to arrive in late August 1914. In mid-September the *Neue Freie Presse* commented that Vienna was already 'overflowing' with refugees, while the *Österreichische Wochenschrift* estimated that there were between 50,000 and 70,000 in the city.[28] Incorporating only those registered with the police and receiving assistance, government statistics lagged behind actual numbers, as many refugees avoided registration. The police had recorded 53,500 arrivals from Galicia and Bukovina by early October; in the course of November the official tally of welfare recipients rose to 70,000, and then to nearly 80,000 by the end of the first week of December.[29] The sheer volume and speed of the influx overwhelmed any efforts to accurately keep track of numbers. In May 1915 the Israelitische Allianz zu Wien calculated that at its peak the 'mighty stream' of Jewish refugees in Vienna had reached nearly 150,000, comprising mostly women, children, and the elderly. A government report in October 1915 put the high point of 'destitute' refugees at 125,000 early in that year, but at least 50,000–60,000 who did not qualify as destitute may be added to this.[30] Numbers remained at this level until July 1915, when, in the wake of the Austrian reconquest of much of Galicia in the preceding two months, the government instituted a programme of refugee repatriation.[31]

[28] Hoffmann-Holter, *'Abreisendmachung'*, 35. See also ibid. 35–7; *OW*, 18 Sept. 1914, p. 649.

[29] Hoffmann-Holter, *'Abreisendmachung'*, 35; *OW*, 6 Nov. 1914, p. 765; 27 Nov. 1914, p. 823; *Die Tätigkeit der Wiener Gemeindeverwaltung in der Obmänner-Konferenz während des Weltkrieges* (Vienna, 1917), 17; AVA/MI, no. 4608/15, 19/1.

[30] *BIAW* 42 (1914), 10; *Staatliche Flüchtlingsfürsorge im Kriege*, 6, 29. This figure of 125,000 was incorporated into subsequent government reports. See e.g. *Zentralstelle der Fürsorge für Kriegsflüchtlinge* (Vienna, 1917), 45; *Die Gemeinde-Verwaltung der Stadt Wien vom 1 Jänner 1914 bis 30 Juni 1919* (Vienna, 1923), 168. On the gender and age breakdown of the refugees, see Marsha L. Rozenblit, 'For Fatherland and Jewish People: Jewish Women in Austria during the First World War', in Frans Coetzee and Marilyn Shevin-Coetzee (eds.), *Authority, Identity and the Social History of the Great War* (Providence, RI, 1995), 207.

[31] The Austrian offensive in Galicia began in early May 1915. By 22 June, when they re-entered Lemberg, the Austrians had succeeded in recapturing all of western Galicia and most of eastern Galicia; Czernowitz had been reoccupied in Feb. 1915. See *Österreich-Ungarns letzter Krieg*, ii. 315–504, and suppls. 32, 36. See also Stone, *The Eastern Front*, 136 ff. The situation on the eastern front remained fairly static from Sept. 1915 until the Russian army's June 1916 offensive.

While overall responsibility for dealing with the refugees was the province of the Interior Ministry, local authorities and the police took charge of day-to-day administration outside Vienna, sharing the burden with welfare organizations.[32] For the Austrian authorities, refugee welfare had an ideological dimension over and above the practical task of co-ordinating a huge relief system. It offered the government an opportunity to demonstrate the unity of the empire's population in the war effort, thereby, it was hoped, counteracting centrifugal nationalist tendencies. Official pronouncements and publications about the refugees emphasized the *Gesamtösterreich* idea and co-operation between the nationalities.[33] Success in providing aid for the refugees, it was maintained, was due to a 'deep and intuitive understanding of the community of fate that binds together all of the empire's peoples'.[34] The welfare effort was presented as a project that could promote the stability of the state. The many vocational and retraining courses offered to the Galician refugees—such as embroidery, shoemaking, horticulture, plumbing, and poultry farming—would contribute after the war to the economic and cultural development of that notoriously 'backward' region. Of more immediate practical use was the refugees' role as a large and loyal substitute workforce in munitions and supply factories and in agriculture.[35] From the Jewish side, meanwhile, the very flight of the refugees from the Russians was portrayed as a patriotic affirmation of Austrian identity.[36]

By far the greatest concentration of refugees was in the capital. In early September 1914, at the prompting of Rudolf Schwarz-Hiller, a Viennese-born lawyer and liberal city councillor since 1910, the government created the Central Office for the Welfare of Refugees from Galicia and Bukovina to co-ordinate refugee care in the city, with Schwarz-Hiller as its director.[37]

[32] *Staatliche Flüchtlingsfürsorge im Kriege*, 5.
[33] See e.g. *WH*, 1 Jan. 1915, pp. 3–4; *MOIU* 27 (May–June 1915), 4; *OW*, 23 Apr. 1915, pp. 317–18; Redlich, *Austrian War Government*, ch. 4; *Neue Freie Presse*, 15 Dec. 1915 (a.m.), p. 13. See also Mentzel, 'Weltkriegsflüchtlinge in Cisleithanien', 28–9.
[34] *Staatliche Flüchtlingsfürsorge im Kriege*, 9.
[35] See Friedrich von Wiser, *Staatliche Kulturarbeit für Flüchtlinge* (Vienna, 1916); *Staatliche Flüchtlingsfürsorge im Kriege*, 16, 20, 22; *OW*, 30 Sept. 1916, pp. 436–7; Mentzel, 'Weltkriegsflüchtlinge in Cisleithanien', 34–6. On Galician 'backwardness', see Raphael Mahler, 'The Economic Background of Jewish Emigration from Galicia to the United States', *YIVO Annual*, 7 (1952), 255–67; Magocsi, *Galicia*, 136–42.
[36] See e.g. *OW*, 20 Apr. 1917, p. 238; 20 July 1917, p. 453; *JZ*, 9 Oct. 1914, p. 1.
[37] For Schwarz-Hiller's account of his initiative in founding the Zentralstelle der Fürsorge für die Flüchtlingen aus Galizien und der Bukowina, see *ASW* 25/36 (5 May 1916), 933–4. See also *Staatliche Flüchtlingsfürsorge im Kriege*, 6. Schwarz-Hiller was co-opted onto the Kultusgemeinde

The Central Office in Leopoldstadt soon became the hub of a vast welfare network, functioning as the primary point of contact between refugees and the state authorities. With some 80 per cent of all refugees availing themselves of its services, the Central Office was supporting an estimated 125,000 people by early 1915. For the less numerous refugees from the professional and middle classes, two smaller committees were created with government backing in late September. All these bodies, it should be noted, were nominally non-confessional.[38] Funded by the Interior Ministry, the Central Office provided a comprehensive range of services, including advice and assistance upon arrival at Vienna's railway stations, financial aid, subsidized food and accommodation, free medical care and legal assistance, child care, transport, clothing, an employment bureau, occupational courses, cultural and recreational activities, and, eventually, free repatriation. From fourteen departments with 140 mostly voluntary staff in early November 1914, it grew to sixty-eight departments with 500 employees by early 1917.[39]

Although initially overwhelmed by the magnitude and speed of the mass flight, the authorities attempted to exercise a degree of control over its direction. Military needs were paramount; railways were needed for troop transport, for example. To assist in the co-ordination of the welfare effort, the government appealed to private voluntary organizations.[40] Concerned about Vienna's capacity to absorb such an influx, the Interior Ministry turned in early September 1914 to the Allianz for help in setting up a number of camps in Moravia to house refugees. While eager to do its part in what it called 'patriotic aid', the Allianz was wary of a potential blurring of the distinction between government and private welfare. Moreover, ever

board in Nov. 1915 and was elevated to the nobility in Sept. 1917, assuming the title of Dr Rudolf Ritter Schwarz-Hiller von Jiskor. See Hanns Jäger-Sunstenau, 'Der Wiener Gemeinderat Rudolf Schwarz-Hiller. Kämpfer für Humanität und Recht', *Zeitschrift für die Geschichte der Juden*, 10 (1973), 9–16; Holleis, *Die Sozialpolitische Partei*, 103.

[38] The Wiener Hilfskomitee, headed by the Galician politician and academic Leon von Bilinski, handled some 20% of the refugees (perhaps *c.*15,000), while the Ukrainische Hilfskomitee supported between 1,500 and 3,000. There was also a committee for 'German' refugees. See Hoffmann-Holter, *'Abreisendmachung'*, 45; *Staatliche Flüchtlingsfürsorge im Kriege*, 6; *NNZ*, 25 Sept. 1914, p. 7; 16 Oct. 1914, p. 6; *OW*, 20 Apr. 1917, p. 238; *Reichspost*, 29 Sept. 1915 (a.m.), pp. 8–9; excerpt from *Die Zeit*, 24 Nov. 1914, CAHJP, AW, 357/1.

[39] *OW*, 6 Nov. 1914, p. 765; 1 Jan. 1916, pp. 17–19; *Zentralstelle der Fürsorge für Kriegsflüchtlinge*, 10–25; *Die Gemeinde-Verwaltung der Stadt Wien*, 167–8; *Staatliche Flüchtlingsfürsorge im Kriege*, 6; PDW, Vereins- und Versammlungswesen 1916, no. 3725/K.

[40] *Staatliche Flüchtlingsfürsorge im Kriege*, 7–8; *MOIU* 27 (May–June 1915), 2–3; Redlich, *Austrian War Government*, 104–6.

sensitive to possible accusations of parochialism, the Allianz was initially determined to maintain the fiction of non-denominational help, preferring a joint venture with the authorities on both practical and ideological grounds. In response to the ministry's request, the Allianz, while declining to assume responsibility publicly, and thus set a precedent for open confessionally based relief, provided many of the basic provisions for the hastily erected camps in Moravia and later contributed to the establishment of schools in the camps. It also undertook a series of intensive fund-raising drives among its members. One such drive was carried out in the columns of the *Neue Freie Presse*, a common practice in the war; the Allianz, however, refused to give its public imprimatur to this effort.[41]

Kultusgemeinde leaders and other welfare bodies voiced similar concerns, arguing that refugee welfare was primarily the government's responsibility and that Jewish groups should avoid shouldering too much of the burden as this would allow or encourage the government to reduce its role. Further, the task was in any case too enormous for Jewish organizations to handle.[42] But it was precisely the extent of the problem that overwhelmed the government and led it to request assistance, as only a co-operative effort could begin to cope with it. Although the Allianz continued to prefer a minimum of publicity, it relaxed its strictures when faced with the government's use of nationality as a convenient organizing principle in relief work. Not only were the refugee camps organized along national lines, but the government's welfare statistics categorized the refugees according to nationality—Germans, Poles, Ruthenians, Romanians, Slovenes, Croats, Italians, and Jews—despite the fact that the Jews did not enjoy legal status as one of the monarchy's constitutionally recognized nations.[43]

It was not long before protests were heard about the refugee influx into Vienna. In early September 1914 Mayor Weiskirchner asked the Interior

---

[41] *BIAW* 42 (1914), 7–9; 43 (1915), 8. The Allianz made frequent representations to the Interior Ministry regarding living conditions in the camps, and was successful in persuading the government to assume the costs of basic provisions for further camps. See *BIAW* 42 (1914), 10.

[42] See Protokoll der Plenar-Sitzung, 30 Dec. 1914, CAHJP, AW, 71/15; *OW*, 4 Sept. 1914, pp. 609–10; *ZBB* 17 (1914), 183; *NNZ*, 25 Sept. 1914, pp. 5–6.

[43] The categorization of Jews as a nationality did not go unnoticed. See *JZ*, 10 Aug. 1917, p. 3. On the continued Allianz preference for behind-the-scenes activity, see *BIAW* 45 (1917), 7. For the government's use of national categories in its statistics, see *Staatliche Flüchtlingsfürsorge im Kriege*, 29 ff.; AVA/MI, no. 59736/15, 19; no. 56166/16, 19. On a 'national' camp, see Maria Ostheim-Dzerowycz, 'Gmünd. Ein Lager ukrainischer Flüchtlinge in Österreich während des Ersten Weltkrieges', in Ilona Slawinski and Joseph P. Strelka (eds.), *Die Bukowina. Vergangenheit und Gegenwart* (Bern, 1997), 73–89.

Ministry to divert the flow of refugees from the capital, claiming that they posed a threat to public hygiene. City council representatives complained at the beginning of October to the prime minister, Karl Stürgkh, that the city was 'bursting' and requested a halt to the admission of refugees. In mid-October leading Christian Social activist Leopold Steiner called for their immediate forced repatriation; they were not only a public health risk, he maintained, but also a drain on already scarce provisions.[44] The Interior Ministry's response was to steer refugees to the camps: Jewish refugees were sent to Moravia, while Italians, Ruthenians, and Poles were sent to camps in Lower Austria, Carinthia, and Bohemia respectively. In early December the ministry decreed that no further refugees would be admitted to Vienna; they would instead be housed in the camps and in Moravian and Bohemian towns and villages. None the less, at least some of those with means to support themselves were able to enter and remain. In the communities that took in the refugees, the government worked in close co-operation with the Allianz to set up local welfare committees, often identical with the local *Kultusgemeinden*, which enjoyed quasi-official status as intermediaries between the refugees and the authorities.[45]

The camps proved an unsatisfactory solution to the problem of refugee accommodation, at no point holding more than 20 per cent of all refugees. From a peak of over 12,000 in April 1915, Jewish numbers in the camps fell to under 6,000 by June 1917, a decline that was only temporarily interrupted by refugees fleeing the Russian offensive in the summer of 1916. Of a total camp population of 73,000 in October 1915, some 10,500 were Jewish.[46] Conditions were brutal, with the camps run by unsympathetic, often cruel, administrators, and with epidemics—striking disproportionately at children—common. Articles in the Jewish press regularly complained of overcrowding, poor hygiene, and insensitivity to the refugees'

[44] See *Die Tätigkeit der Wiener Gemeindeverwaltung in der Obmänner-Konferenz während des Weltkrieges*, 12, 16, and *NNZ*, 16 Oct. 1914, p. 1, for Weiskirchner's and Steiner's requests. See also Hoffmann-Holter, '*Abreisendmachung*', 39–40. On Weiskirchner, see Boyer, *Culture and Political Crisis in Vienna*, 278–84, 429–31.

[45] On refugee distribution, see *Staatliche Flüchtlingsfürsorge im Kriege*, 30 ff. For the 10 Dec. order to close Vienna to refugees, see *Die Gemeinde-Verwaltung der Stadt Wien*, 168. Rumours of a pending closure had been circulating since late Oct. See *JZ*, 30 Oct. 1914, p. 1; 13 Nov. 1914, p. 2. On the less than hermetic nature of the closure, see Hoffmann-Holter, '*Abreisendmachung*', 40–1. Police reports also indicate further arrivals in the city. See PDW, SB 1914/15, 23 Dec. 1915. On government co-operation with the Allianz in the provinces, see *BIAW* 42 (1914), 15; Wiser, *Staatliche Kulturarbeit für Flüchtlinge*, 2–3.

[46] *BIAW* 42 (1914), 17–19; 44 (1916), 13–14; 45 (1917), 12; *Staatliche Flüchtlingsfürsorge im Kriege*, 30, 44, 46.

social and religious needs (such as maintaining kosher kitchens), while Jewish groups lobbied the Interior Ministry to improve conditions.[47] Until November 1914 it was mostly destitute east Galicians who were sent to the camps; subsequently the government opted, after consultation with the Allianz, to disperse the many west Galician and Bukovinian arrivals among communities in Moravia and Bohemia. Both government and Jewish organizations came to view the camps as inadequate, and the overwhelming majority of refugees in the summer of 1916 were distributed among towns and villages in the Czech lands, in Lower and Upper Austria, and in Hungary.[48]

The first statistical survey of the refugees was published by the Interior Ministry in late 1915. Of 390,000 refugees dispersed throughout the Austrian half of the monarchy (i.e. excluding Hungary) in October 1915, 157,000 (40 per cent) were Jews. In Vienna the 77,000 Jewish refugees represented some 55 per cent of the 137,000 refugees in the city. Thus, half of all Jewish refugees were concentrated in the capital. In Bohemia 57,000 Jews comprised 60 per cent of 97,000 refugees, while in Moravia 18,500 Jewish refugees made up 30 per cent of the 57,500 total.[49] In early July 1915, following the Austrian reconquest of most of Galicia, the government had instituted a programme of refugee repatriation.[50] By the beginning of November an estimated 250,000 refugees had returned home, including 70,000 from Vienna.[51] While government sources put the number of Jewish refugees receiving support in Vienna in December 1915 at 32,000 (of a total of

---

[47] On Jewish efforts to bring these problems to the government's attention, see *BIAW* 42 (1914), 8–10; *JZ*, 30 Oct. 1914, p. 2; *NNZ*, 8 Jan. 1915, pp. 5–6. On conditions in the camps, see *OW*, 20 Nov. 1914, pp. 803, 811; 4 Dec. 1914, pp. 846–7; 30 July 1915, pp. 582–3; *JZ*, 30 Oct. 1914, p. 1; 27 Nov. 1914, p. 3; 1 Jan. 1915, p. 2; *NNZ*, 16 Oct. 1914, p. 2; 27 Nov. 1914, p. 2; 8 Jan. 1915, pp. 5–6. See also Mentzel, 'Weltkriegsflüchtlinge in Cisleithanien', 29–33.

[48] *Staatliche Flüchtlingsfürsorge im Kriege*, 10–13; *BIAW* 42 (1914), 15; 43 (1915), 9; 44 (1916), 12–15; 45 (1917), 10; *ZBB* 19 (1916), 184.

[49] *Staatliche Flüchtlingsfürsorge im Kriege*, 29 ff. As government statistics were estimates, numbers are rounded to the nearest 500; percentages are also approximations. An indication of the concentration of Jewish refugees in Vienna is the fact that of 49,000 refugees in Lower Austria only 4,000 were Jewish, and 3,000 of these were housed in a camp.

[50] Ibid. 24. Some refugees had already begun making their way home in June. See PDW, SB 1915, 10, 17, 18, 24 June 1915. While the passage of returning refugees was subsidized, those remaining in Vienna faced the loss of their government allowance. As it became clear that many regions of Galicia (particularly in the east) were close to uninhabitable, the government decided to continue supporting those who stayed in the capital. See *Staatliche Flüchtlingsfürsorge im Kriege*, 24; *JZ*, 23 July 1915, p. 1; Kreppel, *Juden und Judentum von Heute*, 150; *ZBB* 18 (1915), 144–5. See also Hoffmann-Holter, *'Abreisendmachung'*, 52–60.

[51] *Staatliche Flüchtlingsfürsorge im Kriege*, 24, 29, 46–7. Schwarz-Hiller estimated that 50,000 refugees had left the capital by 1 Sept. See *Reichspost*, 29 Sept. 1915 (a.m.), pp. 8–9.

56,000), Jewish sources estimated that some 40,000–50,000 were still in the city in June 1916, when the Russian offensive triggered a new wave of approximately 200,000 refugees.[52] Few, however, were admitted into Vienna and any new arrivals were balanced by a resumption of repatriation; some 12,000 returned to Galicia in the latter part of the year. By the end of 1916 an estimated 40,000 Jewish refugees remained in the capital.[53] In July 1917 the Interior Ministry was supporting 423,500 refugees in the Austrian half of the monarchy; 177,000 (just over 40 per cent) were Jewish, of whom some 41,000 were in Vienna. By this time, then, nearly 90 per cent of refugees in the city were Jewish. Many of the refugees of the previous summer had been settled in Bohemia and Moravia; in the former there were 71,000 Jewish refugees (60 per cent of a total of 114,500) and in the latter 29,000 (just over half of a total of 55,000).[54]

Vienna was not alone among the monarchy's major cities in receiving refugees, although it was host to by far the largest number. By April 1915 the Allianz estimated that 30,000 Jewish refugees were in the Hungarian half of the monarchy, of whom some 20,000 were in Budapest (the Hungarian government put the figure at 12,000–13,000 in the capital).[55] As the refugees were Austrian citizens, the Austrian government and local Jewish groups provided support, grudgingly assisted by the Hungarian authorities, who preferred to view the refugees as a purely Austrian problem.[56] From the outset, the Hungarians were intent on moving as many Galicians as possible through Hungarian territory into Austria, if necessary in sealed

[52] *BIAW* 44 (1916), 10, 16. The new refugees were described in the Allianz report as 'mostly without means and unfit for work'. For the Dec. 1915 figure, see Hoffmann-Holter, *'Abreisendmachung'*, 57. The Russian offensive was launched on 4 June 1916. By the end of July they occupied nearly all of Bukovina and had made significant advances in eastern Galicia. See *Österreich-Ungarns letzter Krieg*, iv (1933), 359–664, and suppls. 21, 27; v (1934), 190, and suppl. 5. See also Stone, *The Eastern Front*, ch. 11; Herwig, *The First World War*, 208–17.

[53] *Die Tätigkeit der Wiener Gemeindeverwaltung in der Obmänner-Konferenz während des Weltkrieges*, 68; Hoffmann-Holter, *'Abreisendmachung'*, 60–71; *BIAW* 44 (1916), 15.

[54] AVA/MI, no. 46578/17, 19; *BIAW* 45 (1917), 11–12. There were also 89,000 Ruthenians, 82,000 Italians, 37,500 Poles, 20,000 Slovenes, 9,000 Croats, and 7,000 ethnic Germans. Of 67,000 refugees in Lower Austria, only 350 were Jewish.

[55] *BIAW* 42 (1914), 19–20. *JZ*, 1 Jan. 1915, p. 1, reported 30,000 in Budapest alone. For the Hungarian government estimate, see Löwenheim, 'The Leadership of the Neolog Jewish Congregation of Pest', 140.

[56] On the organization of refugee welfare in Hungary, and on the government's reluctance to shoulder the financial burden, see *NNZ*, 25 Sept. 1914, pp. 7–8; 22 Jan. 1915, p. 17; *OW*, 18 Sept. 1914, p. 650; 25 Dec. 1914, pp. 901–2; 5 Feb. 1915, pp. 99–100; Löwenheim, 'The Leadership of the Neolog Jewish Congregation of Pest', 37–9, 145, 147; Kreppel, *Juden und Judentum von Heute*, 70–1.

trains.[57] In April 1915 the government ordered the expulsion of all destitute refugees from Budapest and the provinces. Despite protests from Jewish organizations and the Austrian government, the majority of the refugees had been expelled to Austrian territory by mid-May 1915. In late September the authorities decreed the expulsion of the remaining 2,500–3,000 refugees in Budapest.[58] Thousands, however, flowed through the city, either returning to Galicia after the Austrian reconquest in summer 1915 or fleeing once more in the summer of 1916 from the Russian offensive and the Romanian invasion of Transylvania. Some of these new arrivals inevitably remained. By the end of 1916 the Allianz estimated 20,000 Jewish refugees in the provinces and the capital.[59]

In September 1917 the government again ordered the immediate repatriation of all Galician refugees in Budapest, citing shortages of accommodation and food supply.[60] The Hungarian interior minister announced in November that 9,000 refugees, of an estimated 25,000, had already been 'removed', and promised quick action to remove the rest.[61] Attempts to expel the refugees continued throughout 1918 and 1919, and were foiled primarily by the Austrian government's repeated interventions with the Hungarian authorities.[62] Hungarian complaints about the refugees echoed those heard in Vienna: profiteering, shirking military service, lack of hygiene and culture, exacerbation of housing and food shortages.[63]

The third major urban destination for the refugees was Prague, where some 15,000 had arrived by early 1915.[64] Soon after, the city was closed

---

[57] *OW*, 8 Oct. 1914, pp. 688–9; *NNZ*, 2 Oct. 1914, p. 6; 16 Oct. 1914, p. 6; Löwenheim, 'The Leadership of the Neolog Jewish Congregation of Pest', 7–38, 144–5; *BIAW* 42 (1914), 20.

[58] *OW*, 16 Apr. 1915, p. 291; 7 May 1915, pp. 345–6; *NNZ*, 23 Apr. 1915, p. 67; 7 May 1915, pp. 77–8; Löwenheim, 'The Leadership of the Neolog Jewish Congregation of Pest', 40–3; *BIAW* 43 (1915), 7; *JZ*, 15 Oct. 1915, p. 3.

[59] Löwenheim, 'The Leadership of the Neolog Jewish Congregation of Pest', 143–6; *BIAW* 44 (1916), 10–12, 15.

[60] *JZ*, 7 Sept. 1917, p. 2; 5 Oct. 1917, p. 2; *OW*, 12 Oct. 1917, p. 637; *SPOR*, annexe 1917, 787/1 (25 Sept. 1917); Löwenheim, 'The Leadership of the Neolog Jewish Congregation of Pest', 146.

[61] *OW*, 16 Nov. 1917, p. 725; Kreppel, *Juden und Judentum von Heute*, 155.

[62] See *OW*, 16 Apr. 1915, p. 291; 26 Apr. 1918, p. 251; Kreppel, *Juden und Judentum von Heute*, 155–6; *JK*, 25 Oct. 1917, p. 3; Löwenheim, 'The Leadership of the Neolog Jewish Congregation of Pest', 137, 147.

[63] Löwenheim, 'The Leadership of the Neolog Jewish Congregation of Pest', 137, 140, 144, 153, 156–7; *OW*, 16 Apr. 1915, p. 291; 26 Apr. 1918, p. 251; *NNZ*, 7 May 1915, pp. 77–8; Kreppel, *Juden und Judentum von Heute*, 156.

[64] *ZBB* 18 (1915), 64, calculated 14,000 in mid-March. Heinrich Rosenbaum, director of

to refugees and towards the end of 1915 many returned to the Austrian-occupied sections of Galicia. By mid-1916 B'nai B'rith estimated that 5,000 remained.[65] Although many of the estimated 200,000 refugees from Russia's summer 1916 offensive settled in Bohemia and Moravia, only 6,000 non-Jewish refugees were permitted into Prague. The number of Jewish refugees in the city continued to decline, and in early 1918 B'nai B'rith reported that most had left.[66] In the immediate post-war months several thousand arrived, this time fleeing war in Poland and Ukraine.[67]

Refugee numbers in Vienna dwindled gradually. There was little incentive for the destitute to return to the devastated regions of east Galicia, while others had by now established themselves and were perhaps reluctant to return to an area that seemed increasingly likely to become part of a newly independent Polish state.[68] By the beginning of 1918 nearly 39,000 Jewish refugees (of a total of 45,500) were still receiving government support. In early August the Central Office reported that it was supporting 26,000 refugees, and by mid-September this had fallen to 20,600 as repatriation quickened.[69] While the number of refugees receiving support remained at more or less this level until February 1919, thousands arrived from Galicia in the wake of pogroms in November 1918 and from Budapest

Allianz welfare work in Prague during the war, counted 15,000 in mid-January. See his 'Die Prager Flüchtlingsfürsorge', in *Das jüdische Prag. Eine Sammelschrift* (Prague, 1917; Kronberg/Ts., 1978), 55–6. *BIAW* 42 (1914), 18, estimated 13,000 in mid-Apr. 1915. See also Jiri Kudela, 'Die Emigration galizischer und osteuropäischer Juden nach Böhmen und Prag zwischen 1914–1916/1917', *Studia Rosenthaliana*, suppl., 23 (1989), 125, who estimates 30,000 'at the beginning' of 1915.

[65] Rosenbaum, 'Die Prager Flüchtlingsfürsorge', 55, gives mid-Jan. 1915 as the closure date. An Interior Ministry report of 3 Nov. 1915 indicates only that Prague was closed sometime prior to Nov. See AVA/MI, no. 59736/15, 19. For 1916, see *ZBB* 19 (1916), 109. According to Rosenbaum, 'Die Prager Flüchtlingsfürsorge', 56, 3,600 were left in mid-1916.

[66] *ZBB* 21 (1918), 46. On the non-Jewish refugees and the authorities' insistence on keeping Prague closed to Jewish refugees, see Rosenbaum, 'Die Prager Flüchtlingsfürsorge', 55–6.

[67] *OW*, 15 Nov. 1918, p. 729, and *JZ*, 29 Nov. 1918, p. 5, reported 10,000 Jewish refugees in Bohemia and 7,000 in Moravia. The *Prager Tagblatt* of 21 Nov. 1918 estimated 7,000 in Bohemia: see the excerpt in CZA, L6/366. *WM*, 2 Mar. 1919, p. 7, reported 15,000 in the new republic. See also Ladislav Lipscher, 'Die Lage der Juden in der Tschechoslowakei nach deren Gründung 1918 bis zu den Parlamentswahlen 1920', *East Central Europe*, 16 (1989), 8 n. 18.

[68] Kreppel, *Juden und Judentum von Heute*, 156; *BIAW* 45 (1917), 6; *ZBB* 20 (1917), 163.

[69] For figures from May 1917 to Sept. 1918, see Hoffmann-Holter, '*Abreisendmachung*', 65. See also Kreppel, *Juden und Judentum von Heute*, 154. By Apr. 1918 Jewish refugee numbers in Bohemia and Moravia had dropped to 41,500 (of a total of 65,000) and 18,500 (of 35,500). For the Central Office figures, see Sitzung des Stadtrates, 8 Aug. 1918, *ASW* 27/67 (20 Aug. 1918); Sitzung des Stadtrates, 12 Sept. 1918, *ASW* 27/76 (20 Sept. 1918).

in March 1919 after the Béla Kun regime took power.[70] By January 1920 there were perhaps as many as 25,000 refugees still in Vienna.[71]

THE POLITICS OF WELFARE

For Viennese Jewry, mounting a relief effort on such a large scale required an unprecedented mobilization of resources, yet the actual contours of the task were familiar. Aiding their less fortunate east European co-religionists had always constituted an important part of the work of both the Allianz and B'nai B'rith, and neither organization, as we have seen, was free of the ambivalent attitudes common among acculturated western Jews towards the *Ostjuden*.[72] To the nationalists, the refugees were a potential reservoir of support rather than supplicants in need of cultural elevation. As Galicia came to Vienna in the war years, the welfare effort dominated the Jewish agenda until 1917, becoming a site of sharply contested political turf battles. The nationalists' prominence in relief work contributed significantly to their increased influence in both Jewish and Austrian government circles during the war. Welfare work was thus an important element in the wartime realignment of the balance of power within Jewish society, in particular the emergence of Jewish nationalism as a major force. Similar developments took place in Poland and Russia. Zionist welfare work in Congress Poland

---

[70] Estimates of refugee numbers varied. *JZ*, 29 Nov. 1918, p. 5, reported 17,275; AR, Staatskanzlei, no. 313, gives 20,000 on 1 Dec. 1918; AR, Staatsamt des Innern, no. 8456/19, 19, gives 19,832 for 1 Jan. 1919, and 19,723 for 1 Feb. 1919. On pogrom refugees, see Polizeidirektion Wien to Staatsamt des Innern, 17 Nov. 1918, AR, Bundeskanzleramt-Inneres, no. 633/18, 25/1; Polizeidirektion Wien to Staatsamt des Innern, 17 Dec. 1918, AR, Staatsamt des Innern, no. 4101/18, 20/1. The Jewish National Council claimed there were 44,000 refugees in Vienna in mid-Dec. 1918, of whom 40,000 were destitute. See Report of Jewish National Council for German-Austria, 13 Dec. 1918, JDCA, Austria, file 19. In May 1919 the Jewish National Council's press service noted the recent influx from Budapest, estimating 40,000 refugees in Vienna. See Jüdisches Pressbüro to ZCO, 3 May 1919, CZA, Z4/2116. Rudolf Schwarz-Hiller calculated that 20,000 remained in July 1919, while in Oct. Interior Secretary Matthias Eldersch spoke of some 30,000. See *WM*, 12 July 1919, 4–5; 10 Oct. 1919, p. 3. Joint Distribution Committee representatives in Vienna set higher figures: 60,000–70,000 in Aug. and 75,000 in Oct. See the Aug. 1919 report by Meyer Gillis and the Oct. 1919 report by the Vienna Branch of the Joint, both in JDCA, Austria, General, 1919–Mar. 1920.

[71] *Jüdische Rundschau*, 20 Jan. 1920, pp. 29–30. Precise figures are elusive. For estimates of between 25,000 and 40,000, see Hoffmann-Holter, '*Abreisendmachung*', 145; Leopold Spira, *Feindbild 'Jud'. 100 Jahre politischer Antisemitismus in Österreich* (Vienna, 1981), 73; Frances L. Carsten, *The First Austrian Republic 1918–1938* (Aldershot, 1986), 35 n. 75; Palmon, 'The Jewish Community of Vienna between the Two World Wars', 97, 318 n. 7.

[72] On the Allianz attitude to Galician Jews, see Wistrich, *The Jews of Vienna in the Age of Franz Joseph*, 74–83. For B'nai B'rith, see *ZBB* 18 (1915), 117–24; 19 (1916), 102–4.

during the war, for example, has been described as contributing to 'the transformation of Zionism into a movement of great popular appeal'.[73]

Fragmentation marked the Jewish welfare effort from the outset, with separate relief drives launched simultaneously by the nationalists, the Allianz, and B'nai B'rith. The Gemeinde, immediately inundated with entreaties for assistance from individuals and organizations alike, proceeded on a case-by-case basis, shying away from any attempt either to undertake systematic relief or to assume a co-ordinating role in welfare work. Its leaders argued that, despite the Gemeinde's statutory obligation to provide welfare services for Viennese Jewry, in this instance it was the government's duty to care for the refugees, given the magnitude and provenance of the task (the war was, after all, a state rather than a Jewish affair). In mid-August 1914 Gemeinde vice-president Gustav Kohn argued against confessionally based welfare at a meeting of Jewish welfare groups, while Heinrich Schreiber, a member of the governing board, wrote in September that the task was overwhelming, beyond the Gemeinde's capacities. In the Gemeinde budget for 1915 no special allocations were made for refugee welfare, despite the efforts of the nationalist Robert Stricker, who suggested a voluntary 'war tax' to raise additional funds. This remained the Gemeinde's attitude throughout.[74] Although the Allianz, B'nai B'rith, and nationalist leaderships, like the Gemeinde leaders, agreed in principle that the government was ultimately responsible for the refugees, all chose nevertheless to set up extensive welfare networks of their own.[75] Competition for the kudos that flowed from welfare work was evident also in Prague, where Jewish organizations co-operated somewhat better than in Vienna, and in Budapest; in all three cities disputes arose over who was the leading welfare provider.[76]

[73] Mendelsohn, *Zionism in Poland*, 46. See also Steven J. Zipperstein, 'The Politics of Relief: The Transformation of Russian Jewish Communal Life during the First World War', in Frankel (ed.), *Studies in Contemporary Jewry*, iv. 22–40; Samuel Kassow, 'Jewish Communal Politics in Transition: The Vilna *Kehile* 1919–1920', *YIVO Annual*, 20 (1991), 69.

[74] For Kohn, see CAHJP, AW, 356; for Schreiber, see *NNZ*, 25 Sept. 1914, pp. 5–6. On the budget, see Protokoll der Plenar-Sitzung, 30 Dec. 1914, CAHJP, AW, 71/15; *OW*, 8 Jan. 1915, pp. 28–30; *NNZ*, 8 Jan. 1915, pp. 4–5. For examples of appeals to the Gemeinde for help, see CAHJP, AW, 357/1–357/2. For Stricker, see Stricker to Vorstand Präsidium, 19 Nov. 1914, CAHJP, AW, 357/1; *JZ*, 9 Oct. 1914, p. 1. See also Heinrich Schreiber, 'Die Wiener Kultusgemeinde und die Fürsorge für die jüdische Flüchtlinge', *Hickls Wienerjüdische Volkskalender*, 14 (1916–17), 66–9; *OW*, 18 Sept. 1914, pp. 648–9.

[75] *ZBB* 17 (1914), 183; *BIAW* 42 (1914), 7–9; *JZ*, 9 Oct. 1914, p. 1.

[76] On welfare co-operation in Prague, see Rosenbaum, 'Die Prager Flüchtlingsfürsorge', 55; *ZBB* 20 (1917), 16, 31; *BIAW* 43 (1915), 9–10. On competing claims for the leading role in

The Jewish groups offered a wide array of services, often paralleling those of the Central Office. Food and shelter, medical help, financial and legal aid, education and child care, representation before the authorities—all were available.[77] A central figure in this work was the 24-year-old Anitta Müller, who organized a large and impressive welfare network devoted primarily to the needs of women and children. With little experience to draw on, Müller established a home for abandoned and orphaned children, a nursery and kindergarten, maternity and infant clinics, a soup kitchen, and a vocational school for girls and women, providing invaluable assistance and sustenance for thousands of refugees. From a well-to-do family—her father was a well-established businessman, her husband was similarly comfortable—Müller rapidly became a luminary in Jewish society, building on this success to achieve prominence in general Viennese welfare circles. Her work soon attracted the attention and praise of the government, which saw fit to give her some responsibility for state-sponsored welfare institutions also.[78]

Welfare, in fact, was the sole public Jewish arena in which women were expected to participate and permitted to lead. Welfare work, as Marion Kaplan has remarked, was 'women's political involvement', and this is borne out by the experience in Vienna.[79] Müller, for example, was active in the Zionist movement, but her party work focused almost entirely on social welfare issues; in this she was not untypical. Despite lip-service to the contrary, women 'tended to engage in the cultural and humanitarian aspects' of the movement's work.[80] During the war the traditional Jewish philanthropic impulse was partially transmuted into modern and professionalized social work, while women gained administrative and political experience hitherto

refugee welfare, see ZCO to ZCWA, 28 Dec. 1914, CZA, Z3/841; Leo Herrmann to Leo Motzkin, 24 Dec. 1914, CZA, L6/598; *ZBB* 20 (1917), 31; Rudel, 'Poale Zion in Österreich während des Krieges', 31; Löwenheim, 'The Leadership of the Neolog Jewish Congregation of Pest', 138.

[77] *JZ*, 19 Feb. 1915, pp. 1–2; 14 Apr. 1916, pp. 7–9; *NNZ*, 22 Sept. 1915, pp. 148–9; *BIAW* 42 (1914), 7–20. There were numerous private Jewish initiatives also, concentrating mainly on food distribution. See *OW*, 12 Mar. 1915, pp. 196–7; *BIAW* 42 (1914), 12–13.

[78] On Müller, see Nanny Margulies-Auerbach, 'Anitta Müller', *NJM* 4 (1919–20), 203–8; Wininger, *Jüdische National-Biographie*, iv. 468–70. On her organizations, see Anitta Müller, 'Mein Beistand für die Flüchtlinge', *Hickls Wienerjüdische Volkskalender*, 14 (1916–17), 70–5; *Ein Jahr Flüchtlingsfürsorge der Frau Anitta Müller 1914–1915* (Vienna, 1916); *Zweiter Tätigkeits- und Rechenschafts-Bericht der Wohlfahrtsinstitutionen der Frau Anitta Müller 1915–1916* (Vienna, 1917); *Dritter Tätigkeits- und Rechenschafts-Bericht der Wohlfahrtsinstitutionen der Frau Anitta Müller für Flüchtlinge aus Galizien und der Bukowina* (Vienna, 1918).

[79] Marion A. Kaplan, *The Making of the Jewish Middle Class: Women, Family, and Identity in Imperial Germany* (New York, 1991), 226.   [80] Freidenreich, *Jewish Politics in Vienna*, 59.

denied them, both in the Jewish community and in Viennese society generally. The fruits of this experience, part of the nexus between welfare and politics, were reflected in the immediate post-war period in the partially
successful battles to achieve women's suffrage in both the general and the
Jewish political domains.[81]

Efforts on behalf of the refugees extended beyond material assistance.
Galician and Viennese Zionists, for example, sponsored lectures and publications in an attempt to counter anti-refugee sentiment and inform a wider
public about the culture and history of east European Jews. The bulk of this
activity, it should be said, was undertaken by Galicians.[82] From the Orthodox side, Agudes Yisroel played a prominent role in the provision of welfare
with what it called a 'spiritual' emphasis, providing religious education,
kosher food distribution, and strictly supervised accommodation for children. Claiming that it was 'at the very centre of refugee life in Vienna', the
Agude described the refugees as turning naturally in their distress to the
organization as 'children would come to their mother'.[83]

Casting a wider net was the Austrian Central Committee for the Protection of the Civil Rights of the Jewish Population in the Northern War Zones,
the Austrian counterpart to the German Jewish Committee for the East and
the German Association for the Interests of East European Jews. Formed in
response to a Committee for the East initiative, the Austrian committee
included Jewish parliamentarians, nobles, and leading figures from the
Allianz, B'nai B'rith, the Union, the Gemeinde, and Zionists. Focusing on
the treatment of Jews in the Austrian military occupation zone in Poland, the
many eminent members of the committee enjoyed access to the highest levels of the Austrian administration; its good contacts notwithstanding, the
committee was denied permission to function as the Interior Ministry's
'official' Jewish advisory body on this issue. Protection of Jewish rights in

[81] Kaplan, *The Making of the Jewish Middle Class*, 219–27; Rozenblit, 'For Fatherland and
Jewish People', 210. See also Harriet Anderson, *Utopian Feminism: Women's Movements in fin-
de-siècle Vienna* (New Haven, 1992), ch. 6; Birgitta Zaar, 'Dem Mann die Politik, der Frau die
Familie—die Gegner des politischen Frauenstimmrechts in Österreich 1848–1918', *Öster-
reichische Zeitschrift für Politikwissenschaft*, 16 (1987), 357–9; Birgitta Bader-Zaar, 'Women in
Austrian Politics 1890–1934: Goals and Visions', in David F. Good, Margarete Grandner,
and Mary Jo Maynes (eds.), *Austrian Women in the Nineteenth and Twentieth Centuries:
Cross-Disciplinary Perspectives* (Providence, RI, 1996), 59–90.

[82] On the Komitee zur Aufklärung über ostjüdische Fragen (Committee for Information on
East European Jewish Issues), see *OW*, 29 Oct. 1915, pp. 805–6; 7 Jan. 1916, p. 29; 26 Jan. 1917,
p. 57; Henisch, *At Home and Abroad*, 156–7, 260.

[83] 'Tätigkeitsbericht der "Agudas Jisroel" für die Zeit vom September 1914 bis Oktober
1917', suppl., *JK*, 24 Jan. 1918. See also *JK*, 21 Dec. 1916, p. 2.

the Austrian-occupied areas was one of the rare matters on which all shades of Jewish opinion managed to co-operate.[84]

Co-ordination between all these groups was in fact minimal. Zionist offers of co-operation, for example, to the Gemeinde, the Central Office, and B'nai B'rith were either rebuffed or ignored, while Central Office director Rudolf Schwarz-Hiller apparently attempted to undermine the nationalists by playing on the authorities' fears of their political agenda.[85] The Allianz, as the largest and most powerful of the welfare agencies, was chosen by the American Joint Distribution Committee to be the conduit for the vitally important American Jewish relief funds.[86] Although prepared to work with the Zionists in distributing funds in Galicia, it was only in response to direct Joint pressure that in late 1916 the Allianz requested Zionist (and Orthodox and B'nai B'rith) participation at the administrative level. Even so, Maximilian Paul Schiff, the Joint representative in Vienna, expressed his reservations about working with the nationalists to the American Zionist leader Judah Magnes. The Zionists, Schiff complained, 'never lose sight of their political aspirations'.[87] For their part, the Zionists resented the Allianz monopoly on the distribution of American Jewish funds (with its attendant political benefits), and the issue remained a source of

[84] On the Österreichische Zentralkomitee zur Wahrung der staatsbürgerlichen Interessen der jüdischen Bevölkerung im nördlichen Kriegsgebiete, see ZBB 19 (1916), 6, 71; 21 (1918), 88; OW, 24 Mar. 1916, p. 208; Report by Siegfried Fleischer (a member of the Gemeinde board), PDW, St/22, Staats- und Sicherheitspolizei Agenden 1917, Politisch: Jüdische Bewegung. For the Interior Ministry's attitude to the committee, see the note of 24 Feb. 1916, AVA/MI, no. 65208/15, 28. For an example of co-operation on the issue of protection of Jewish rights, see the memorandum of 28 Sept. 1915 from various Jewish groups to the Austrian Army High Command, CZA, Z3/155. On the German Komitee für den Osten and Deutsche Vereinigung für die Interessen des osteuropäischen Juden, see Egmont Zechlin, Die deutsche Politik und die Juden im Ersten Weltkrieg (Göttingen, 1969), 126–38; Steven E. Aschheim, 'Eastern Jews, German Jews and Germany's Ostpolitik in the First World War', LBIYB 28 (1983), 351–65.

[85] The Zionists assailed the Gemeinde for its 'utterly passive' stance. See JZ, 25 Dec. 1914, p. 1. Dissatisfied by what they saw as the bureaucratic and exclusionary tendencies of the Central Office (see JZ, 27 Nov. 1914, p. 1; 19 Feb. 1915, p. 1), the Zionists turned to B'nai B'rith but received no response. See Zionist Central Office for Western Austria to ZCO, 19 Sept. 1914 and 10 Oct. 1914, CZA, Z3/840; ZCWA circulars to regional Zionist organizations, 27 Nov. 1914 and n.d. (probably Jan. 1915), CZA, Z3/841. On Schwarz-Hiller, see Hoffmann-Holter, 'Abreisendmachung', 112–13.

[86] American Jewish Relief Committee to Allianz, 21 Jan. 1915, JDCA, Austria, file 19; Boris D. Bogen, 'Activities of the Joint Distribution Committee in Austria', JDCA, Austria, General, Apr. 1920–1, 8.

[87] Schiff to Magnes, 15 Apr. 1916, JDCA, Austria, file 19; JZ, 8 Dec. 1916, p. 4; Report on the ECUAZ meeting of 23 Nov. 1916, CZA, L6/313. On the issue of distribution of American Jewish relief funds, see Zosa Szajkowski, 'Jewish Relief in Eastern Europe 1914–1917', LBIYB 10 (1965), 24–51; id., 'Concord and Discord in American Jewish Overseas Relief 1914–1924', YIVO Annual, 14 (1969), 99–158.

friction. The political potential of welfare work was an important consideration for the Zionists; government recognition of their prominent role—the authorities praised and supported their medical clinic, legal rights office, and welcome service at railway stations—was a gratifying confirmation of its significance.[88] This politicization of welfare work led, as already noted, to all groups at one time or another claiming to be the dominant agency of relief work.[89]

By the end of the war it was the Zionists who had emerged as victors in this competition. The most active Jewish welfare body at this point was the nationalist-oriented Anitta Müller Social Relief Society (Soziale Hilfsgemeinschaft Anitta Müller), the successor to Müller's earlier organizations. (The Central Office closed its doors in early 1919.[90]) With the Gemeinde's financial resources severely depleted by inflation, the communal welfare infrastructure was stretched to breaking-point, while government assistance was similarly inadequate. One nationalist source noted in December 1918 that, with food and clothing scarce, prices high, and tuberculosis raging, the Gemeinde was simply unable to provide sufficient help to cover 'even the barest necessities'.[91] Only a large-scale aid operation mounted by the Joint made it possible to meet the needs of the tens of thousands of Jewish unemployed, demobilized soldiers, and pogrom refugees. Estimating in early 1919 that 60,000–70,000 Jews required aid, a Joint representative in Vienna wrote that the war and pogrom refugees

are in direst need and misery. No human being can paint a complete picture of the bitter and horrible condition of the places they occupy. By no stretch of the imagi-

[88] On Zionist resentment at being excluded from the distribution of American Jewish money, see Leo Herrmann to Leo Motzkin, 21 Jan. 1915; unsigned letter of 18 Feb. 1915 to the Relief Committee of Austro-Hungarian Zionists, New York, both in CZA, L6/598; *JZ*, 28 Sept. 1917, p. 4. On Zionist recognition of the political value of welfare work, see ZCWA to ZCO, 10 Oct. 1914, CZA, Z3/840. On government recognition, see *JZ*, 12 Feb. 1915, p. 1; 14 Apr. 1916, pp. 7–9; AVA/MI, no. 31922/16, 19.

[89] See e.g. ZCWA circular of 27 Nov. 1914, CZA, Z3/840; *JZ*, 13 Nov. 1914, p. 2; 25 Dec. 1914, p. 1; 19 Feb. 1915, pp. 1–2; *ZBB* 17 (1914), 204–5; *BIAW* 42 (1914), 10; 44 (1916), 12.

[90] See 'Zehn Jahre Arbeit des Vereines Soziale Hilfsgemeinschaft Anitta Müller', CAHJP, AW, 2317; *Dritter Tätigkeits- und Rechenschafts-Bericht der Wohlfahrtsinstitutionen*, 10–19. On the Central Office, see Schwarz-Hiller's letter of 30 Aug. 1919, Haus-, Hof-, und Staatsarchiv, Vienna, Administrativ Registratur, F36/341, Krieg 1914–1918, 58A, no. 128797; Hoffmann-Holter, '*Abreisendmachung*', 159; *OW*, 4 Apr. 1919, p. 219; Kreppel, *Juden und Judentum von Heute*, 255.

[91] Jewish National Council report of 13 Dec. 1918. See also the undated (1919) Jewish National Council report, both in JDCA, JDC Representative Committee Overseas, Austria, file 19.

nation can they be thought to be fit for human habitation. . . . [Living in] dark and pestilential surroundings . . . it is . . . no wonder that most of them have become consumptive and look like skeletons.[92]

When the Joint established a committee in June 1919 to co-ordinate all relief work in Vienna, its representatives treated the Zionists as equal partners with the Allianz. Hoping to democratize and broaden the social and political base of welfare, the Joint regarded Zionist co-operation as essential.[93] The Allianz, weakened by the rising nationalist tide and the loss of its empire-wide network, was reluctant to treat the Zionists as equals but was in no position to dictate terms.[94] In the course of the war, then, the relative status of the Zionists and their ideological opponents had been virtually inverted in the welfare sphere.

What accounts for the emergence of the Jewish nationalists into such a prominent position in the welfare effort and, given the links between successful welfare provision and improvement of political status, in the hierarchy of Viennese Jewry as a whole? Certainly, they built a strong welfare organization, but so too did the Allianz and (to a lesser extent) B'nai B'rith. The Zionists, however, focused the bulk of their attention and resources on the refugees in Vienna (whereas their rivals expended greater energy and funds on welfare projects in Galicia and elsewhere) and provided a more comprehensive range of services, in a sense offering themselves as an alternative to the Central Office. The success of Anitta Müller's organizations also contributed to the nationalists' prestige, as Müller became publicly identified with their cause. It was, though, external factors that gave the

[92] Report by Meyer Gillis, one of the two Joint representatives sent to Vienna in early 1919, in JDCA, Austria, General, 1919 – Mar. 1920. See also the report by the 'Vienna Branch of the JDC', Oct. 1919, JDCA, Austria, General, 1919 – Mar. 1920. On Jewish poverty in the post-war period, see Freidenreich, *Jewish Politics in Vienna*, 20, 153–5; *IKG Bericht 1912–1924*, 9–10, 46–7. The first major study of Viennese Jewish poverty, published in 1920, was subsidized by the nationalists. See Bruno Frei, *Jüdisches Elend in Wien. Bilder und Daten* (Vienna, 1920).

[93] Boris D. Bogen, 'Activities of the Joint Distribution Committee in Austria', JDCA, Austria, General, Apr. 1920–1, 14. See also the report by Meyer Gillis; *JZ*, 16 May 1919, p. 4; *WM*, 16 Aug. 1919, p. 5.

[94] On the precarious situation of the Allianz, see *BIAW* 46 (1925), 4–6; Report (in Yiddish) by Max Pine, the second Joint representative in Vienna, JDCA, Austria, General, 1919 – Mar. 1920. On the Allianz reluctance to treat the Zionists as equals, see Jewish National Council to Netherlands Relief Committee and Stockholm Jüdische Hilfsverein, 4 Jan. 1919, CZA, L6/87. On the situation of B'nai B'rith, affected in much the same way as the Allianz by the rise of Jewish nationalism and loss of empire-wide connections, see Wilhelm Jerusalem, *U.O.B.B. Humanitätsverein Wien. Festschrift zur Feier des fünfundzwanzigjährigen Bestandes 1895–1920* (Vienna, 1920), 70–6; *ZBB* 21 (1918), 198–203; 22 (1919), 30–4, 50–9, 154–64.

Zionists certain crucial advantages. Increasing international political support for Zionism during the war, the democratic and nationalist upsurge within the empire, and the identification of the nationalists as the primary Jewish democratic force all helped pave the way for powerful outside agencies to endorse the Zionists in Vienna. Thus, the Joint Distribution Committee and the Austrian authorities, both with an interest in democratic reforms, granted the Zionists respect and recognition. B'nai B'rith and the Allianz were obliged to extend grudging co-operation, acquiescing to the wishes of these outside actors. As Viennese Jewry grew progressively more dependent on external aid, the nationalists' good standing in the eyes of the Joint and the Austrian government was an important source of influence and power within Jewish society.

THE VIENNESE RESPONSE

The refugees were by no means a homogeneous population. Rather, they comprised a cross-section of Galician and Bukovinian Jewry, from a small middle class to the more numerous poverty-stricken, from the strictly Orthodox to the acculturated and secularized. Common to most, however, was the experience of flight and uprootedness, a contingent status as outsiders and visitors of uncertain duration in the capital, and an awareness of increasing hostility aimed explicitly at them. Common too, for the majority who had abandoned home and hearth to seek refuge in Vienna, was a precarious economic situation. While they could be found across the economic spectrum, from white-collar professions and business to industrial and seasonal agricultural work, the refugees were for the most part mired in poverty, working in petty trade, in cottage industry, and as middlemen. Moreover, some restrictions were placed on their right to work. Galician lawyers, for example, were prohibited from practising in Vienna from February 1915, while small businesses, traders, and artisans often experienced difficulty in obtaining work permits from local authorities.[95]

---

[95] On refugee poverty and the obstacles faced by lawyers, small businesses, traders, and artisans, see Hoffmann-Holter, 'Abreisendmachung', ch. 3, esp. 85–90; OW, 14 Sept. 1917, p. 582; NNZ, 25 Dec. 1914, pp. 2–3; Protokolle der Plenar-Sitzungen, suppl., 26 Apr. 1915, CAHJP, AW, 71/16; Jüdisches Archiv, Aug. 1915, pp. 22–5; Kreppel, Juden und Judentum von Heute, 70. On the concentration of refugees in petty trade, see Hoffmann-Holter, 'Abreisendmachung', 90–1; PDW, SB 1914/15, 21 Jan. 1915, 11 Feb. 1915, 5 Oct. 1916. Some 3,000 women were trained and employed in domestic industry, manufacturing household items and military undergarments. See Ein Jahr Flüchtlingsfürsorge der Frau Anitta Müller, 12–14, 49–53; Zweiter

The impact of the refugees on Viennese Jewish life was palpable. In short order they created a variety of social, cultural, religious, and political organizations, thereby at least partially compensating for the loss of community and the intensive Jewish environment to which many had been accustomed. (Numerous accounts attest to a preference on the part of the refugees for socializing with one another.[96]) Refugees, for example, provided both the leadership and the bulk of the rank and file for the youth movement that flourished between late 1917 and early 1919. They established two libraries, a Zionist association, and a Yiddish theatre, and published a considerable amount of Hebrew and Yiddish literature, as well as several Polish-language journals produced by the youth movement.[97] The brief efflorescence of Yiddish culture in Vienna in the early 1920s owed much to the foundations laid by the refugees.[98]

An expansion of the local Jewish press was one immediate manifestation of their presence. Jonas Kreppel's Yiddish daily *Der Tog* appeared fleetingly in Vienna while Lemberg was under Russian occupation.[99] An entirely new venture was the nationalist-oriented *Wiener Morgen-Zaytung*, a Yiddish daily launched in January 1915 that pronounced itself an organ for the entire Jewish people in its hour of distress, open to all shades of opinion. Clearly with an eye on its potential audience, though, it promised to pay particular attention to matters of interest to the refugees.[100] Stopped without explanation by the Austrian censor in September 1915, the *Morgen-*

Tätigkeits- und Rechenschafts-Bericht der Wohlfahrtsinstitutionen, 37–49; *Dritter Tätigkeits- und Rechenschafts-Bericht der Wohlfahrtsinstitutionen*, 35–7; *ZBB* 17 (1914), 194–5; 18 (1915), 40, 173–6; 21 (1918), 55–8.

[96] See e.g. Henisch, *At Home and Abroad*, 145; PDW, SB 1914/15, 8 Oct., 12 Nov. 1914; Kreppel, *Juden und Judentum von Heute*, 69–70; Abeles, *Jüdische Flüchtlinge*, 60, 68.

[97] *JZ*, 29 Jan. 1915, pp. 1–2; *OW*, 25 Feb. 1916, pp. 142–3; 12 July 1918, p. 436; Henisch, *At Home and Abroad*, 169, 275; id., 'Galician Jews in Vienna', in Fraenkel, *The Jews of Austria*, 369; id., 'Galician Jews in Vienna', in Yisrael Cohen and Dov Sadan (eds.), *Aspects of Galicia* (Heb.) (Tel Aviv, 1957), 405; Gelber, *The History of the Zionist Movement in Galicia*, ii. 692–3; CZA, A188, CM 179/7/79; *JZ*, 27 Mar. 1918, pp. 5–6.

[98] Brigitte Dalinger, *'Verloschene Sterne'. Geschichte des jüdischen Theaters in Wien* (Vienna, 1998), 173–83; Gabriele Kohlbauer-Fritz, 'Jiddische Subkultur in Wien', in Peter Bettelheim and Michael Ley (eds.), *Ist jetzt hier die 'wahre' Heimat? Ostjüdische Einwanderung nach Wien* (Vienna, 1993), 96, 99.

[99] *OW*, 8 Oct. 1914, p. 695; Henisch, 'Galician Jews in Vienna', in Cohen and Sadan, *Aspects of Galicia*, 405. Published by Kreppel from 1909 to 1914, *Der Tog* appeared in both Lemberg and Kraków. See Toury, *Die jüdische Presse im österreichischen Kaiserreich*, 127, 128–9 n. 52.

[100] *Wiener Morgen-Zaytung*, 1 Jan. 1915, pp. 1–3; 'Notiz' from Arthur Hantke to Leo Herrmann, 30 Apr. 1918, CZA, Z3/849.

Zaytung only resumed publication in January 1918.[101] Further bolstering the nationalist cause, Po'alei Zion's *Yidisher Arbeter*, which, as already noted, had ceased publication in Lemberg at the outbreak of war, appeared in the capital from July 1917 to January 1919.

Nationalism did not, of course, go unchallenged. The presence of so many traditionally minded refugees contributed greatly to the wartime expansion of institutional Orthodoxy in Vienna. The *Jüdische Korrespondenz*, established by Jonas Kreppel in August 1915 as a forum for religious viewpoints more orthodox than those generally aired in the *Österreichische Wochenschrift* or *Die Wahrheit*, has already been mentioned. The war years saw the first signs, too, of an organized Agudes Yisroel presence in Vienna. Initially, Agude activity focused primarily on welfare, but towards the end of the war it expanded into the political arena also. Hasidim appeared in Vienna for the first time in significant numbers during these years, with several hasidic leaders (including the *rebbes* of Czortków, Husiatyn, Sadagora, Brody, and Drohobycz) setting up courts in the city. Divested of their property and livelihood, the economic base of these hasidic courts was fragile, and the proximity to both western culture and less traditional modes of Jewish life was not without influence, particularly among the younger generation.[102] Finally, refugees furnished both the leadership and membership for the (admittedly modest) wartime growth of religious Zionism in Vienna, manifested most obviously by the formation of the hasidic Zionist group Yishuv Erets Yisrael.

It is clear, then, that the refugees were a distinct and highly visible presence in the city. Many locals resented them (despite official protestations to the contrary), complaining, among other things, that the refugees were dirty and noisy, pushed up food prices, congregated in the streets and coffeehouses, bought up businesses and residential properties, received overly gen-

---

[101] Henisch, *At Home and Abroad*, 146; *SPÖR* (1917), i, annexe 1917, 283/1 (26 June 1917); *JZ*, 13 July 1917, p. 2. The *Morgen-Zaytung* was edited and published by Galician Zionists Aharon Leib Shossheim (a leading Po'alei Zion activist and former chief editor of the party's newspaper, the *Yidisher Arbeter*) and Naphtali M. Racker. In Jan. 1919 it changed its name to *Yidishe Morgenpost*. See the Jan. 1919 circulars to this effect in CZA, L6/87 and L6/88; *Yidishe Morgenpost*, 23 Jan. 1919, p. 4; Jens Budischowsky, 'Assimilation, Zionismus und Orthodoxie in Österreich 1918–1938: Jüdisch-politische Organisationen in der Ersten Republik', Ph.D. diss., University of Vienna, 1990, 169–70. For a slightly different account, see Toury, *Die Jüdische Presse im österreichischen Kaiserreich*, 109–10. On Shossheim, see Anshel Reiss, *The Beginnings of the Jewish Workers' Movement in Galicia* (Heb.) (Tel Aviv, 1973), 202–3.

[102] J. Heshel, 'The History of Hassidism in Austria', in Fraenkel (ed.), *The Jews of Austria*, 354–5. For accounts of the wartime hasidic courts in the city, see YVA, PKA/E-6; PKA/E-38.

erous welfare payments, engaged in profiteering, and shirked military duty.[103] Mayor Weiskirchner set the tone by remarking that the refugees were incapable of adapting to Viennese mores and that their presence posed a threat to the city's character.[104] These themes remained the staples of anti-refugee agitation throughout the war years. Police agents in Leopoldstadt, which together with Brigittenau received the majority of the refugees, reported that the locals felt 'invaded' and that the newcomers received 'no sympathy'.[105] Antagonism and hostility were so widespread, in fact, that the police on occasion feared for the refugees' safety, and reported great joy at the departure of many refugees in the summer of 1915.[106] While government publications initially stressed the compassion of the local population towards the new arrivals, Jewish sources only rarely, and then only in the very early stages of the war, echoed this.[107] Clearly aware of the mounting frictions, the government was at pains to encourage increased tolerance.[108]

Viennese antisemitism thus found a new lease on life by focusing on the refugees. Muted at first by censorship and the restrictions imposed by military rule, antisemitic voices grew in volume and intensity as the war dragged on and living conditions deteriorated, and, in particular, as a measure of democracy was reinstituted in 1917 by the new emperor Karl.[109] Daily life in the city grew progressively more severe, with rising prices, shortages of basic foodstuffs, fuel, and consumer goods, controls on gas and

[103] See e.g. PDW, SB 1914/15, 5, 12, and 26 Nov., 17 Dec. 1914, 7 Jan., 18 Mar., 8 Apr., 13 May 1915; PDW, SB Jan.–Dec. 1915, 8 Feb. 1915; Hoffmann-Holter, '*Abreisendmachung*', ch. 6; Edmund Daniek, *Das Judentum im Kriege* (Vienna, 1919).

[104] Quoted in Mentzel, 'Weltkriegsflüchtlinge in Cisleithanien', 36.

[105] PDW, SB 1914/15, 1 and 8 Oct. 1914. On the distribution of the refugees in the city, see John and Lichtblau (eds.), *Schmelztiegel Wien*, 117; 'Brigittenauer israelitischer Frauen-Wohltätigkeits-Verein. Bericht über seine Tätigkeit 1914', CAHJP, AW, 247/4. Animosity was greatest in Leopoldstadt and Brigittenau. See PDW, SB 1914/15, 20 May, 14 Oct. 1915. Favoriten, a working-class area with relatively few Jews, also received many refugees. See *OW*, 30 Oct. 1914, p. 752; *NNZ*, 30 Oct. 1914, p. 1.

[106] On the threat of anti-refugee violence, see PDW, SB 1914/15, 25 Mar. 1915; SB July–Dec. 1916, 5 Oct. 1916. On the widespread joy greeting the refugees' departure, see PDW, SB 1914/15, 24 June, 28 July, 26 Aug. 1915.

[107] See *Staatliche Flüchtlingsfürsorge im Kriege*, 4, 9–10; Wiser, *Staatliche Kulturarbeit für Flüchtlinge*, 1; *OW*, 28 Sept. 1914, p. 668; 30 Oct. 1914, p. 749; *WH*, 16 Oct. 1914, pp. 4–5; *JZ*, 15 Jan. 1915, p. 1.

[108] See e.g. the text of the Interior Ministry's decree of Apr. 1915, in *MOIU* 27 (May–June 1915), 2–5; Hoffmann-Holter, '*Abreisendmachung*', 41–3; *Staatliche Flüchtlingsfürsorge im Kriege*, 3.

[109] On wartime censorship in Austria, see Kurt Paupie, *Handbuch der österreichischen Pressgeschichte 1848–1959*, ii (Vienna, 1966), 142–7, 161–2; Mark Cornwall, 'News, Rumour and the Control of Information in Austria-Hungary, 1914–1918', *History*, 77 (1992), 50–64.

electricity consumption, restricted public transport, and increased levels of crime. Disease and hunger became the everyday experience of many.[110] In such dire circumstances the refugees were an obvious scapegoat, and already in early 1915 Christian Socials and German nationalists in the city council called for their expulsion or internment.[111]

In keeping with the notion of *Burgfriede*, a truce in the empire's internal conflicts, Jewish responses were initially kept out of the public sphere, and were confined mostly to private appeals to government officials.[112] As antisemitic articles began to appear with increasing frequency in the Viennese press from early 1915, attempts to respond in the Jewish press were often censored.[113] From the Jewish point of view, government reluctance either to act decisively against expressions of antisemitism or to allow a public Jewish response denoted a breakdown of the bargain implicit in the *Burgfriede*. Antisemitism, it was argued, was divisive and chauvinistic, threatening not only the Jews but also the democratic reforms vital to the empire's survival: antisemitism was thus anti-Austrian.[114] Jewish disappointment was all the more keen as the euphoric national unity of the first weeks of the war had seemed finally to promise acceptance as truly equal citizens—the quid pro

---

[110] On conditions in Vienna, see Boyer, *Culture and Political Crisis in Vienna*, 419–28; Reinhard J. Sieder, 'Behind the Lines: Working-Class Family Life in Wartime Vienna', in Richard Wall and Jay Winter (eds.), *The Upheaval of War: Family, Work and Welfare in Europe 1914–1918* (Cambridge, 1988), 109–38; Arthur J. May, *The Passing of the Hapsburg Monarchy 1914–1918* (Philadelphia, 1966), i. 329–35; ii. 662–9; Herwig, *The First World War*, 272–83.

[111] *OW*, 22 Jan. 1915, p. 64; *JZ*, 15 Jan. 1915, pp. 1–2. The term 'German nationalist' will be used here to refer to the various nationalist and pan-German parties associated with the Deutscher Nationalverband (German National Association) and like-minded groups. See Boyer, *Culture and Political Crisis in Vienna*, 502 n. 62.

[112] See e.g *MOIU* 27 (Jan.–Feb. 1915), 11–12; *JZ*, 30 Oct. 1914, p. 2; 13 Nov. 1914, p. 2; 14 Apr. 1916, pp. 7–8; Protokoll der Plenar-Sitzung, 26 Apr. 1915, CAHJP, AW, 71/16; *NNZ*, 22 Sept. 1915, pp. 148–9. On Jewish fidelity to the *Burgfriede*, see *OW*, 21 July 1916, 477–8; 10 Nov. 1916, pp. 731–2; *WH*, 12 May 1916, p. 5; 25 Aug. 1916, pp. 3–4; *JZ*, 12 Mar. 1915, p. 2; *MOIU* 29 (June–Sept. 1917), 1–2.

[113] See *JZ*, 12 Mar. 1915, p. 2; 16 Apr. 1915, p. 1; 10 Mar. 1916, p. 2; 14 July 1916, p. 1; 12 Dec. 1916, p. 1; *NNZ*, 22 Jan. 1915, pp. 12–14; 5 Feb. 1915, p. 25; *OW*, 5 Mar. 1915, pp. 174–5; 21 July 1916, pp. 478–9; *WH*, 25 Aug. 1916, p. 3; *MOIU* 30 (Jan.–Feb. 1918), 18; *YA*, 1 May 1918, p. 6. On the haphazard practices of the Austrian censors, see Henisch, *At Home and Abroad*, 148–50; Cornwall, 'News, Rumour and the Control of Information in Austria-Hungary', 60–1; *SPÖR* (1917–18), iii, annexe 1918, 3008/1. The Christian Social *Reichspost* and the German nationalist *Ostdeutsche Rundschau* were the most consistently antisemitic of the Viennese papers. See Hoffmann-Holter, *'Abreisendmachung'*, ch. 8; *OW*, 28 July 1916, p. 495; 8 Sept. 1916, p. 595; 2 Nov. 1917, p. 685; *JZ*, 8 Dec. 1916, p. 1; *MOIU* 29 (June–Sept. 1917), 1–2.

[114] See *OW*, 22 June 1917, pp. 389–91; 2 Nov. 1917, pp. 685–6; 10 May 1918, pp. 278–9; 21 June 1918, pp. 375–6; 19 July 1918, pp. 441–2; 30 Aug. 1918, pp. 541–3; *JZ*, 8 Dec. 1916, p. 1; 21 June 1918, p. 1; *MOIU* 29 (Oct.–Dec. 1917), 3–7.

quo for unconditional loyalty and a proven readiness to offer the ultimate sacrifice for the fatherland. This prospect dimmed with the rise of increasingly vitriolic and unchecked antisemitism.[115] The initial Jewish reluctance to protest publicly—the *Österreichische Wochenschrift*, for example, practised self-censorship in order to preserve the *Burgfriede*—gradually gave way to spirited defence (when permitted by the censor) and, after the May 1917 reconvening of parliament, to open discussion and even criticism of the authorities' handling of the refugees and tolerance of antisemitism.[116] The recall of parliament provided a platform for a series of verbal assaults on the refugees by Christian Social and German nationalist deputies, in which the by now familiar themes were rehashed.[117] On the initiative of Heinrich Reizes, an east Galician deputy with Jewish nationalist sympathies, a parliamentary subcommittee was formed in June 1917 to investigate the refugee situation in the empire as a whole. The committee's work resulted in a law regulating the status of the refugees. Passed by the Reichsrat in July, but taking effect only in January 1918, the new law nominally ensured their legal and economic protection, and freedom of movement.[118]

Spearheaded by the German nationalists, with the Christian Social Party in a supporting role, antisemitic agitation in parliament, the city council, the press, and at university and public meetings intensified in the latter half of 1917 and 1918, reaching a peak in the summer of 1918.[119] Perhaps the most

[115] See *MOIU* 29 (Oct.–Dec. 1917), 5–6; *OW*, 22 June 1917, pp. 389–91; 29 June 1917, pp. 405–7; *JZ*, 22 June 1917, p. 3; 3 Aug. 1917, pp. 1–3; 21 June 1918, p. 1; *Festschrift zur Feier des 50-jährigen Bestandes der Union Österreichischer Juden*, 9–10. On a similar trajectory of hope and disillusionment for German Jews, see Reichmann, 'Der Bewusstseinswandel der deutschen Juden', 513–20; Werner Jochmann, 'Die Ausbreitung des Antisemitismus', in Mosse and Paucker (eds.), *Deutsches Judentum in Krieg und Revolution*, 409–510.

[116] For Jewish self-censorship, see *OW*, 30 Oct. 1914, p. 755; 6 Nov. 1914, p. 772; 19 Mar. 1915, p. 231. For rebuttals of antisemitic attacks, see *OW*, 22 June 1917, pp. 389–91; 29 June 1917, pp. 405–7; 20 July 1917, pp. 453–5; 2 Nov. 1917, pp. 685–6; 30 Nov. 1917, pp. 749–50; 21 Dec. 1917, pp. 797–9. For criticism of the government, see *OW*, 26 Oct. 1917, pp. 669–72; 30 Nov. 1917, pp. 749–50; 2 Aug. 1918, pp. 473–4; *JZ*, 23 Nov. 1917, pp. 1–2; 9 Aug. 1918, p. 1; *MOIU* 29 (Oct.–Dec. 1917), 5–7; 30 (Jan.–Feb. 1918), 11–15.

[117] See *OW*, 15 June 1917, p. 381; 29 June 1917, pp. 389–91; 20 July 1917, pp. 453–5; 19 Oct. 1917, pp. 654–5; *SPOR*, annexe 1917, 29/1 (5 June 1917); 1313/1 (13 Nov. 1917).

[118] *SPOR* (1917), i. 105–6 (6 June 1917); *OW*, 6 July 1917, p. 430; *JZ*, 15 June 1917, p. 2; 6 July 1917, p. 3; 20 July 1917, pp. 2–3; 3 Aug. 1917, p. 3; 7 Sept. 1917, p. 2; 18 Jan. 1918, p. 2; Kreppel, *Juden und Judentum von Heute*, 150–2. Reizes and the Bukovinian Zionist Benno Straucher were vocal defenders of the refugees in parliament. See *SPOR*, annexe 1917, 1744/1 (5 Dec. 1917); *OW*, 19 Oct. 1917, pp. 654–5; *JZ*, 22 June 1917, pp. 1–3; 20 July 1917, pp. 2–3; 19 Oct. 1917, p. 2. On Reizes, see Gelber, *The History of the Zionist Movement in Galicia*, ii. 596, 604; Gaisbauer, *Davidstern und Doppeladler*, 493.

[119] For various examples, see Jonny Moser, 'Die Katastrophe der Juden in Österreich

common of the accusations levelled against the refugees was that they
engaged in various forms of economic crime, primarily smuggling, profiteering, and black-market trading.[120] That there was some truth to this was
acknowledged in many Jewish responses. Apologists generally emphasized
the extreme social and economic dislocation of the refugees in their defence:
desperate to survive, they often circumvented the law. Moreover, it was
argued, antisemites passed over in silence the widespread profiteering and
hoarding of food perpetrated by others, most prominently the landowners
and peasantry. It was even claimed that Jewish smuggling played a vital role
in maintaining Vienna's food supply, and that smugglers had in fact helped
ward off starvation for many in the city.[121] Jewish reactions to the rising antisemitic tide in 1918 were unanimously indignant. While the Jewish press
denounced the 'pogrom threats' and the 'sadistic' and 'bloodthirsty' attacks,
Central Office director Schwarz-Hiller expressed dismay at the authorities'
apparent apathy. The Union, meanwhile, complained to the Justice Ministry
that the Austrian authorities were apparently adopting the former tsarist
regime's tolerance and even encouragement of anti-Jewish activity.[122] If the
refugees provided the initial catalyst, the target was soon broadened to

1938–1945. Ihre Voraussetzungen und ihre Überwindung', *Studia Judaica Austriaca*, 5 (1977),
70–1; *SPOR*, annexe 1918, 2617/1 (12 Mar. 1918); annexe 1918, 2767/1 (16 July 1918); *ASW*
27/76 (20 Sept. 1918), 1896; 27/83 (15 Oct. 1918), 2012; *JZ*, 7 Sept. 1917, p. 2; 23 Nov. 1917,
pp. 1–2; 14 Dec. 1917, p. 3; 27 June 1918, p. 6; 19 July 1918, p. 4; *OW*, 1 Mar. 1918, pp. 129–31;
10 May 1918, pp. 278–9; 19 July 1918, pp. 441–2; 30 Aug. 1918, pp. 541–3. On attempts to intro-
duce a *numerus clausus* aimed at Galician students in the medical faculty at the University of
Vienna, see *JZ*, 23 Aug. 1918, pp. 1–2; 30 Aug. 1918, p. 1; Kreppel, *Juden und Judentum von
Heute*, 147–8. See also John Haag, 'Students at the University of Vienna in the First World War',
Central European History, 17 (1984), 299–309. On Christian Social antisemitism in the decade
preceding the war, see Boyer, *Culture and Political Crisis in Vienna*, 63–9. On the party during the
war years more generally, see ibid., ch. 7.

[120] See e.g. Hoffmann-Holter, *'Abreisendmachung'*, 91–4; PDW, SB 1914/15, 21 Jan. 1915;
SB Jan.–Dec. 1915, 8 Feb. 1915; Daniek, *Das Judentum im Kriege*, ch. 3; Kreppel, *Juden und
Judentum von Heute*, 147; Hans Tietze, *Die Juden Wiens* (Vienna, 1933, 1987), 276–7. On
wartime economic crime in general, and on the refugees' role in it, see Franz Exner, *Krieg und
Kriminalität in Österreich* (Vienna, 1927), 17, 45–59.

[121] See Protokolle der Plenar-Sitzungen, suppl., 26 Dec. 1915, CAHJP, AW 71/16; *OW*,
1 Dec. 1916, p. 787; *JZ*, 27 Sept. 1918, p. 1; *WH*, 21 Sept. 1917, p. 5; *MOIU* 27 (Mar.–Apr.
1915), 1; *Festschrift zur Feier des 50-jährigen Bestandes der Union Österreichischer Juden*, 11, 13,
73–4.

[122] See *JZ*, 21 June 1918, p. 1; *OW*, 3 May 1918, pp. 261–2, 278–9; 21 June 1918, pp. 375–6;
19 July 1918, pp. 441–2; 2 Aug. 1918, pp. 473–4; 30 Aug. 1918, pp. 541–3; 27 Sept. 1918,
pp. 609–10. For Schwarz-Hiller's comments, see *OW*, 16 Aug. 1918, pp. 505–6. Schwarz-Hiller
had complained already in May 1916 to Mayor Weiskirchner of a campaign to discredit his work
in the Central Office. See *ASW* 25/36 (5 May 1916), 933–4. For the Union complaints to the
Justice Ministry, see *MOIU* 30 (Jan.–Feb. 1918), 11–15.

encompass all Viennese Jews. At the June 1918 Deutsche Volkstag (German People's Assembly), attended by government officials and chaired by Mayor Weiskirchner, it was not just the refugees but the Jews in general who were denounced as profiteers, black-marketeers, smugglers, military-service shirkers, and aliens in a German Austria.[123]

In the face of this barrage, Gemeinde leaders felt compelled for the first time during the war to issue a public protest, calling in July 1918 for government action to restrain the antisemites. The protest resolution made clear that only with the greatest reluctance had the Gemeinde gone public, refraining from such a step for as long as possible in order not to inflict damage on Austria's international reputation. Initiated by the Vienna Gemeinde, and approved by some 440 communities in the Austrian half of the monarchy, the resolution stressed Jewish patriotism and the great suffering endured by the Jews in the war. It ended with a veiled threat of dire consequences should the authorities fail to act, and warned that, if necessary, Jews would organize their own defence.[124] To have even broached the notion of Jewish self-defence was a remarkable departure from previous Gemeinde practice, which scrupulously avoided any action liable to be interpreted as an intimation of anything less than total faith in the state's goodwill towards the Jews. That the Gemeinde would make such a statement, and that it was able to persuade over 400 other communities to endorse it, indicates both the intensity of the antisemitism and a pragmatic recognition on their part that the government was either unable or unwilling to control it. The truth of this latter assumption was borne out by the fact that the protest went unheeded by the authorities, who were indeed losing their ability to control the flow of events in September and October 1918. The Zionists remained ambivalent about the whole affair; they acknowledged the protest as a significant first step, but criticized it as outmoded and inadequate in its moderation.[125]

Immediately following the establishment of the republic at the end of the war, the refugees again became the target of verbal and mild physical

---

[123] *OW*, 21 June 1918, pp. 375–6; *JZ*, 21 June 1918, p. 1. See also Boyer, *Culture and Political Crisis in Vienna*, 416.

[124] See *OW*, 2 Aug. 1918, pp. 474–5, and *JZ*, 2 Aug. 1918, pp. 1–2, for the text of the protest. The Prague Kultusgemeinde objected to the final point as ambiguous and overly aggressive, suggesting a more moderate wording to emphasize that the Jews demanded only the protection due to them by law. The Vienna Gemeinde was not swayed and Prague refused to support the resolution. See Prague IKG to Vienna IKG, 30 July 1918, and the 19 Aug. 1918 reply from the Vienna IKG, CAHJP, AW, 325.   [125] *JZ*, 2 Aug. 1918, p. 1; 9 Aug. 1918, p. 1.

abuse on the streets and in the press and parliament.[126] The new government coalition of Christian Social and Social Democratic parties was intent on expelling them, citing as justification housing and food shortages and local anti-refugee sentiment. In early November 1918 Interior Secretary Heinrich Mataja promised expulsion as soon as arrangements could be made with the successor states, and ordered that no more refugees (from the Polish–Ukrainian war in Galicia) be admitted.[127] In December Mayor Weiskirchner wrote to Chancellor Karl Renner requesting a stop to further refugee intake and stricter controls on those already in Vienna.[128] Throughout the first half of 1919 Christian Social and German nationalist deputies in national and regional parliaments and in the Vienna city council demanded either expulsion or internment of the refugees. The government, meanwhile, continued to urge refugees to return 'home', and acted to limit its support of those remaining.[129] When the authorities finally moved to expel the refugees in July and September 1919, however, they were thwarted in their efforts by Zionist-led opposition.[130] None the less, some 10,300 refugees left Vienna between July and October 1919.[131] A further

---

[126] Moser, 'Die Katastrophe der Juden in Österreich', 82–4, 93–5; Anton Staudinger, 'Christlichsoziale Judenpolitik in der Gründungsphase der österreichischen Republik', in *Jahrbuch für Zeitgeschichte* (Vienna, 1978), 29–33; Kreppel, *Juden und Judentum von Heute*, 252–4; Spira, *Feindbild 'Jud'*, 75–80.

[127] AVA/MI, no. 63533/18, 19 (4 Nov. 1918); no. 63914/18, 19 (9 Nov. 1918); Report of 19 Nov. 1918 meeting in Staatsamt des Innern, AR, Bundeskanzleramt-Inneres, Mataja, 1918/19, 79/18; *JZ*, 29 Nov. 1918, p. 5. Police chief Johann Schober warned of increased antisemitism should more Jewish refugees be admitted. See Schober to Mataja, 17 Nov. 1918, AR, Bundeskanzleramt-Inneres, no. 633/18, 25/1.

[128] Weiskirchner to Renner, 23 Dec. 1918, AR, Staatskanzler, no. 313.

[129] See *WM*, 15 Feb. 1919, p. 2; 28 Feb. 1919, p. 5; 2 Mar. 1919, p. 7; 17 Apr. 1919, pp. 4–5; 18 Apr. 1919, pp. 4–5; 19 Apr. 1919, p. 1; 12 July 1919, pp. 4–5; Petition of 'Verband der östlichen Juden' to Karl Renner, 23 Apr. 1919, and Renner's 18 June 1919 reply, AR, Staatsamt des Innern, no. 15857/19, 19; Kreppel, *Juden und Judentum von Heute*, 254–7; Spira, *Feindbild 'Jud'*, 76–80.

[130] On expulsion attempts and Jewish opposition, see *WM*, 29 July 1919, p. 3; 31 July 1919, p. 3; 1 Aug. 1919, pp. 3, 5; 11 Sept. 1919, p. 3; 12 Sept. 1919, pp. 2, 4; 18 Sept. 1919, p. 2; 20 Sept. 1919, p. 3; 24 Sept. 1919, p. 1; 25 Nov. 1919, p. 3; 6 Dec. 1919, p. 1; Robert Stricker to Karl Renner, 27 Sept. 1919; Stricker to Schober, 15 Nov. 1919; Report of 19 Oct. 1919; Report of 28 Nov. 1919 meeting, all in AR, Staatsamt des Innern, no. 42242/19; Moser, 'Die Katastrophe der Juden in Österreich', 89–92; Hoffmann-Holter, *'Abreisendmachung'*, 190–204. East European Jewish refugees were also threatened with expulsion from Germany, Czechoslovakia, and Hungary in the immediate post-war period. See Trude Maurer, *Ostjuden in Deutschland 1918–1933* (Hamburg, 1986), 274–85, 355–416; Kreppel, *Juden und Judentum von Heute*, 244–5; Jochmann, 'Die Ausbreitung des Antisemitismus', 503–7; *JZ*, 29 Nov. 1918, p. 5; *WM*, 8 Oct. 1919, p. 2.

[131] Polizeidirektion Wien to Niederösterreichische Landesregierung, 9 Dec. 1919, AR, Bundeskanzleramt-Inneres, no. 119041/1, 25/1; Schober to Staatsamt für Inneres und Unterricht, 19 Nov. 1919, AR, Staatsamt des Innern, no. 15770/1. See also *WM*, 10 Oct. 1919, p. 3.

expulsion attempt in 1920 brought League of Nations intervention on behalf of the refugees.[132] Thereafter, the Austrian authorities did not actively pursue expulsion and the issue gradually faded from the public limelight, although anti-refugee agitation continued sporadically until early 1923.[133]

In the main, Viennese Jewish responses to antisemitism during the war followed familiar paths; tactical adjustments were made, but underlying strategies remained constant. All Jews, of course, were bitterly disappointed by the intense upsurge of anti-Jewish hostility that dashed initial hopes of unity achieved through shared sacrifice and bloodshed. That the war was a radicalizing and nationalizing experience for many Jews, both on the home front and in battle, and that the confrontation with antisemitism loomed large in these responses, is clear. Sensing the impotence of their traditional modes of quiet diplomacy (*shtadlones*), Jewish liberals eventually took a public stand on the issue, stressing the need for Jewish dignity and honour. The brutalization of the war years, coming after decades of Viennese antisemitism, led to their readiness to take tougher and more overt defensive action.[134] With the advent of the republic, however, *shtadlones* returned to favour, although the Gemeinde hedged its bets somewhat, subsidizing a Zionist-led defence force and co-operating with the nationalists in occasional public protests.[135] For their part, Zionists tended to see in wartime antisemitism a confirmation of their long-held beliefs about the role of Jews in European society; the most worthwhile and logical response, they argued, was to continue striving for a society made up of separate but equal nations, a conviction they carried over into the post-war years. Even with the partial convergence of the ideological poles of Jewish society that

---

[132] See Hoffmann-Holter, '*Abreisendmachung*', 240–4; *Festschrift zur Feier des 50-jährigen Bestandes der Union Österreichischer Juden*, 90–5. On government attempts to deny refugees citizenship, see Edward Timms, 'Citizenship and "Heimatrecht" after the Treaty of St. Germain', in Ritchie Robertson and Edward Timms, *The Habsburg Legacy: National Identity in Historical Perspective*, Austrian Studies, v (Edinburgh, 1994), 158–68; Margarete Grandner, 'Staatsbürger und Ausländer. Zum Umgang Österreichs mit den jüdischen Flüchtlingen nach 1918', in Gernot Heiss and Oliver Rathkolb (eds.), *Asylland wider Willen. Flüchtlinge in Österreich im europäischen Kontext seit 1914* (Vienna, 1995), 60–85.

[133] See Francis L. Carsten, *Fascist Movements in Austria: From Schönerer to Hitler* (London, 1977), 97–102; Hoffmann-Holter, '*Abreisendmachung*', chs. 7–8.

[134] See e.g. *OW*, 29 June 1917, pp. 405–7; 20 July 1917, pp. 453–5; 19 Oct. 1917, pp. 653–4; 7 Dec. 1917, pp. 764–5; 3 May 1918, pp. 261–2, 278–9; 21 June 1918, pp. 375–6; 2 Aug. 1918, pp. 473–4; 30 Aug. 1918, pp. 541–3. The Gemeinde resolution of July 1918 is further evidence of this.

[135] Freidenreich, *Jewish Politics in Vienna*, 181–6.

took place in the crisis atmosphere of the war years, differences remained too entrenched to permit durable and effective co-operation either in the welfare effort or in combating antisemitism. Despite a constant chorus of rhetorical appeals for unity, a great deal of energy was frittered away in internecine argument.

In the negotiations about refugee expulsion between 1919 and 1921 the government was as ready to deal with the Jewish nationalists as with the Jewish establishment in the Gemeinde or the Union. Although this was in part a result of the government's own situation as an inexperienced administration feeling its way forward in extremely trying conditions, equally important in establishing the Zionists' increased access to power was their successful welfare work during the war. That the refugees constituted a highly sensitive welfare and political problem in Vienna was crucial in translating the nationalists' prominence in the welfare effort into political influence.

The experience of the refugees is illustrative not only of the nexus between welfare and politics but also of the striking 'nationalization' of ethnic and minority politics in east central Europe during this period, a process whereby the boundaries between ethnicity and nationality grew increasingly blurred. If the refugees' impact was evident in the political arena, it was clear too in the economic, cultural, and religious domains. Beyond a sudden infusion of dynamism into local Jewish society, the presence of the refugees touched on a number of major themes of Viennese and Austrian Jewish history: the relationship between 'eastern' and 'western' Jews of the empire, antisemitism, and, most broadly, the very notion of Austrian Jewry as a cohesive (or otherwise) entity. On all counts, the final Habsburg legacy was ambiguous: problematic at best, a dismal failure at worst.

THREE

WARRING YOUTH

A s never before, the war years presented opportunities to youth for radical change. The evident collapse of civilized society, along with the
unprecedented horrors visited upon young men of military age, led to a
powerful demand for catharsis. If they were old enough to fight and die, or to
assume the burdens of family and welfare on the home front, young people
were surely ready also for greater responsibility and influence in a society
clearly in urgent need of purge and renewal. Such notions were widespread
among Jewish youth in Austria, where they were most clearly expressed by a
nationalist youth movement that emerged in Vienna in late 1917, its ranks in
the main comprising young refugees. Jewish politics of the inter-war period
in eastern and central Europe have been described as sometimes resembling
a 'children's crusade', and Vienna in the latter part of the war certainly fits
this description at least in part.[1] This youth subculture existed at one
remove from the world of adult politics, in this context represented by the
Zionist organization. Their mutual antipathy was driven from the one side
by the Zionist leadership's distaste for what it regarded as the impractical
and overly spiritual nature of the youth movement, and from the other by a
desire not to be sullied by too intimate an involvement with the corrupt
world of bourgeois adulthood and politics. It was an estrangement, however,
that fatally undermined the youth movement.

   Among the refugees streaming into Vienna in late 1914 were members
of the nationalist youth movements Tse'irei Zion (Youth of Zion) and
Hashomer (the Guard). Tse'irei Zion in Galicia was a loose collection of
youth groups devoted to the study of Jewish history and culture; Hashomer
looked for inspiration to the Polish and English scouting movements, fostering Jewish identity by means of physical exercise and a 'return to nature'.
The membership of both comprised predominantly middle-class, Polish-

---

[1] Ezra Mendelsohn, 'Reflections on East European Jewish Politics in the Twentieth Century', *YIVO Annual*, 20 (1991), 31.

speaking high-school students.[2] Towards the end of 1914 the two movements began to reconstitute themselves in Vienna, joining with the local
Jewish scouting-oriented Blau-Weiss movement for expeditions in the
Vienna woods, and even collaborating fleetingly with the Austrian scouting
movement.[3] This remained an isolated instance of contact between Jewish
youth movements and their non-Jewish counterparts. Even where such contact was feasible—in the socialist movement, for example—the striking success of the youth movements in creating all-enveloping subcultures for their
members seems to have inhibited the crossing of ethnic boundaries.[4]
Despite considerable mutual ambivalence, Tse'irei Zion and Hashomer set
out to join forces in Vienna in late 1915, planning also to unite in Galicia if
co-operation succeeded in the capital. The Shomer regarded its intellectually inclined partners as passive and bookish, while its own enthusiasm for
communing with nature and for military-like discipline was decidedly alien
to Tse'irei Zion sensibilities; none the less, the union held firm.[5] The new
movement, which came to be known as Hashomer Hatsa'ir (The Young
Guard), became a leading left-wing force in Jewish society in Europe and
Palestine in the next decades. Vienna remained the movement's centre until
mid-1918, with the bulk of the leadership and the largest groups located
there. At its peak, membership in the city reached approximately 1,000. As
the refugees went home, however, the movement's centre of gravity shifted
to Galicia, and by May 1918 there were some 400 members in Vienna compared with 2,500 in Galicia.[6]

  [2] Matityahu Mintz, *Pangs of Youth: Hashomer Hatsa'ir 1911–1921* (Heb.) (Jerusalem, 1995),
ch. 1; Elkana Margalit, *Hashomer Hatsa'ir: From a Youth Group to Revolutionary Marxism
1913–1936* (Heb.) (Tel Aviv, 1971), 20; Mendelsohn, *Zionism in Poland*, 81–2.
  [3] *Dr Shemariyahu Ellenberg: In Memoriam* (Heb.) (Tel Aviv, n.d.), 19–20; Moshe Chizik, *The
Unification of Hashomer and Tse'irei Zion* (Heb.) (Haifa, 1984), 34–7; Ephraim Waschitz, 'Die
"Schomrim"', *JNK* 1 (1915–16), 110–11; Ehud Nahir, *The Story of the Viennese Troop* (Heb.)
(Givat Havivah, 1984), 8–9. On Austrian Blau-Weiss, see Arthur Engländer, 'Die österreichische Wanderbewegung', in Joseph Marcus (ed.), *Tagebuch für jüdische Wanderer 1916–1917*
(Vienna, 1916), 194–6; Reuven Kalisch and Arieh Stein, *Blau-Weiss Austria: The First Zionist
Youth Movement in Austria 1911–1914* (Heb.) (Hadera, 1987).
  [4] On the socialist youth movement during the war, see Wolfgang Neugebauer, *Bauvolk der
kommenden Welt. Geschichte der sozialistischen Jugendbewegung in Österreich* (Vienna, 1975),
92–107; Friedrich Scheu, *Ein Band der Freundschaft. Schwarzwald-Kreis und Entstehung der
Vereinigung Sozialistischer Mittelschüler* (Vienna, 1985), 46–77.
  [5] For their perceptions of one another, see Mendelsohn, *Zionism in Poland*, 81. On the process
of unifying the two organizations, see Mintz, *Pangs of Youth*, ch. 3; Chizik, *The Unification of
Hashomer and Tse'irei Zion*, 37–47; Levi Dror and Yisrael Rosenzweig (eds.), *The Hashomer Hatsa'ir Book* (Heb.) (Merhavia, 1956), i. 30–1, 37–40; S. Horowitz, 'Wie aus zwei Organisationen
eine Bewegung ward', *BJJ* (May 1918), 10–13; Margalit, *Hashomer Hatsa'ir*, 22–4.
  [6] Margalit, *Hashomer Hatsa'ir*, 22, 25; Horowitz, 'Wie aus zwei Organisationen eine

A rebellious and bourgeois group searching for new forms of community and identity, Hashomer (as the new movement was commonly known at this point) synthesized an eclectic range of ideas to form its own powerful, if inchoate, ideology. Prominent in this synthesis were Martin Buber's mix of universalism and Jewish particularism, Gustav Wyneken's neo-Romantic cult of youth, the ideas of the German youth movement Wandervogel (mediated through Wyneken's Viennese disciple Siegfried Bernfeld), and an idealization of the pioneering Jewish settlers in Palestine.[7] The Shomer aspired to no less than the creation of 'a new type of Jewish youth, "with strong muscles, a strong will, a healthy and normal intellect without sophistry and casuistry, a disciplined person . . . who possesses an idealistic world view with love for everything which is beautiful and sublime"'.[8] Similar lofty aspirations and a comparable *mélange* of ideologies characterized the movement that took shape in Vienna, in which Hashomer played an important part. Militating against its wholehearted involvement, however, was a more explicitly activist turn in its development during 1917–18, involving a growing emphasis on pioneering and preparation for emigration to Palestine (*aliyah*). Only in the immediate post-war period, though, did it become a predominantly *aliyah*-oriented movement.[9] Already flourishing by 1917, Hashomer exerted considerable influence on the new Jewish youth movement as a role model, although the extent of this influence was limited by its resolute focus on Galicia and Palestine. In this sense, Hashomer was in, but not of, Vienna.

Outside the refugee milieu, youth groups maintained a low profile during the first years of the war. Many of their members had been drafted, and the government imposed stringent restrictions on political activity. Throughout 1916–17 a variety of associations (Hebrew, sport, literary) held regular meetings, their agendas emphasizing culture rather than politics. As prohibitions on overt political action eased during 1917 under the new regime of

Bewegung ward', 13. See also Mintz, *Pangs of Youth*, ch. 5; Angelika Jensen, *Sei stark und mutig! Chasak we'emaz! 40 Jahre jüdische Jugend in Österreich am Beispiel der Bewegung 'Haschomer Hazair' 1903 bis 1943* (Vienna, 1995), ch. 5; Horowitz, *My Yesterday*, 46–7; Sperber, *Die Wasserträger Gottes*, 217–20.

[7] Margalit, *Hashomer Hatsa'ir*, 20–48; Mintz, *Pangs of Youth*, 66–74. On Wyneken and the German Wandervogel, see Walter Z. Laqueur, *Young Germany: A History of the German Youth Movement* (London, 1962); Peter D. Stachura, *The German Youth Movement 1900–1945* (New York, 1981). On the Austrian Wandervogel, see Gerhard Seewann, *Österreichische Jugendbewegung 1900 bis 1938* (Frankfurt am Main, 1971), i. 59–90.

[8] Quoted in Mendelsohn, *Zionism in Poland*, 82–3.

[9] Margalit, *Hashomer Hatsa'ir*, 37–43; Mendelsohn, *Zionism in Poland*, 84–5.

Karl I, nationalist groups gradually intensified their work.[10] Even prior to
the war the nationalists had encouraged independent associational life
among youth as an integral component of their movement, unlike most liberal and religious organizations. Although the latter, such as B'nai B'rith
(and the Austrian Israelite Union in the post-war period), did on occasion
maintain youth sections, these were little more than appendages of their parent bodies, and were generally wary of conspicuous political activity.
Gemeinde president Alfred Stern, for example, whose definition of permissible Jewish political action was more elastic than that of many of his colleagues, believed that the first priority of youth groups should be to promote
Jewish solidarity in order better to equip young Jews in the fight against antisemitism, and viewed reform of religious education as the best means of
ensuring the Jewish consciousness of the younger generation.[11] Politics, of
course, was the nationalists' *raison d'être*, and it is therefore no surprise that
in the summer of 1917 they set out to establish an organizational framework
for the increasingly active youth scene in Vienna.[12]

The new movement was launched at a mass meeting in October 1917.
Estimating an attendance of almost 1,000, the organizers described the gathering as 'a powerful demonstration of the new Jewish youth spirit'. What
emerged most clearly from this assembly, however, were the serious divisions of opinion among the various groups, 'between the goals and methods
of eastern and western Jews, duelling student fraternities and Blau-Weiss,
the unconditionally Palestinocentric Hashomer and the Diaspora-affirming
Po'alei Zion'. The often stormy arguments presaged the later dissent within
the movement, indicating at the outset that unity was at a premium.
Expressing his faith that 'the divisions that exist today among Jewish youth
are reconcilable, [that] the will to *Judentum* binds all groups within Jewish
youth with equal force, and it is necessary only to find the means to help this
will break through', the meeting's opening speaker spoke of the 'special
obligations and tasks' awaiting youth in the post-war order. These fine sentiments notwithstanding, discussion at the meeting ran along familiar party

[10] Seewann, *Zirkel und Zionsstern*, i. 250–1; *BJJ* (Apr. 1918), 7; (May 1918), 14–15. See also,
for the German nationalists, Paul Molisch, *Politische Geschichte der deutschen Hochschulen in
Österreich von 1848 bis 1918*, 2nd edn. (Vienna, 1939), 237.

[11] *OW*, 27 Sept. 1918, p. 617. On the importance of youth groups for nationalist movements,
see Raymond Pearson, *National Minorities in Eastern Europe 1848–1945* (New York, 1983), 40–1.

[12] In 1913–14 Jewish nationalists made an effort to co-ordinate the growing number of their
youth groups in Austria, holding a Western Austrian Youth Conference in Vienna in Sept. 1913.
Before anything substantial was achieved, however, war broke out and the majority of those
involved were drafted. See Gaisbauer, *Davidstern und Doppeladler*, 434–8; *JZ*, 19 Apr. 1918, p. 5.

lines. Po'alei Zion supporters declared that the only concern of Jewish youth was the physical and spiritual health of the Jewish masses; Hebraists emphasized the centrality of Hebrew language and culture; Hashomer and Blau-Weiss stressed the importance of Palestine and the need for new forms of community; the student corporations called for a Jewish representative authority.[13] No overtures were made, either now or later, to non-nationalist youth to participate in the movement. If they could agree on little else, this much at least was certain: the renewal of Jewish youth was to take national forms only. The emerging movement was provided with a concrete focus at this point by an ambitious plan to hold a massive rally of Jewish youth, a *Jugendtag*, in the spring of 1918.

The *Jugendtag* was the brainchild of Siegfried Bernfeld, already at this stage a key figure in the nascent movement. Born in Lemberg to a middle-class family, Bernfeld was raised in Vienna and immediately prior to the war had been a leading figure in a Wyneken-inspired youth movement devoted to educational reform, editing its journal, *Der Anfang* ('The Beginning').[14] Combining Wyneken's ideas on the autonomy and uniqueness of youth with his own interests in psychology and libertarian socialism, Bernfeld developed a philosophy of youth that focused on education and the primacy of *Geist* and community. Previously uninvolved in organized Jewish life, Bernfeld's interest was sparked by the presence in Vienna of the refugees, and in particular by the plight of the children among them. Here was an opportunity to join philanthropy, Jewish nationalism, and modern educational techniques. New forms of national Jewish education were necessary, he wrote, in order to prevent the overwhelming majority of the refugee children from becoming pedlars, beggars, proletarians, or emigrants, alienated from both Jewish and general society.[15] Increasing antisemitism in the Austrian and

---

[13] For reports on the meeting, see *JZ*, 19 Oct. 1917, p. 4; 2 Nov. 1917, p. 4. The meeting was called by a nationalist student association on behalf of the Preparatory Committee for the Creation of a Co-ordinating Office of Jewish Youth Groups. For protocols of this committee's meetings from July to Dec. 1917, see SBP, folder 40, nos. 155785–155800.

[14] On *Der Anfang* and Wyneken's influence on Bernfeld (1892–1953), see Willi Hoffer, 'Siegfried Bernfeld and "Jerubbaal": An Episode in the Jewish Youth Movement', *LBIYB* 10 (1965), 152–3; Scheu, *Ein Band der Freundschaft*, 20–7; Peter Paret, Preface to Siegfried Bernfeld, *Sisyphus; or, The Limits of Education*, trans. Frederic Lilge (Berkeley, 1973), pp. x–xiii; Laqueur, *Young Germany*, 59–65; Philip L. Utley, 'Siegfried Bernfeld's Jewish Order of Youth 1914–1922', *LBIYB* 24 (1979), 356.

[15] Siegfried Bernfeld, 'Die Kriegswaisen', *Der Jude*, 1 (1916–17), 269–71; Hoffer, 'Siegfried Bernfeld and "Jerubbaal" ', 154–5. Bernfeld later wrote that it was in June 1914 that he had decided to devote himself to Jewish work. See Siegfried Bernfeld, *Kinderheim Baumgarten* (Berlin, 1921), 9. On Wyneken's ideas, see Laqueur, *Young Germany*, 53–5.

German pre-war youth movements, symbolized by widespread demands for exclusion of Jews from their ranks, may also have contributed to his turn to Jewish nationalism.[16] As part of the general revamping of Austrian Zionism in the summer of 1917, Bernfeld—who spent almost the entire war in Vienna, doing office work for the military—had been recruited to take charge of education and youth work.[17] By taking him on board, the Zionist organization made clear its wish to play an active role in shaping what promised to be a popular movement. But the relationship between official Zionism and the youth movement, with Bernfeld as the primary link between the two, was to prove extremely problematic.

At the October 1917 meeting Bernfeld set out for the first time in public his vision of the new Jewish youth community, a vision that was to guide his activity over the next two years. Youth, he declared, was inherently aesthetic, moral, and spiritual, rebelling against imposed patterns of thought and action, filled with the knowledge of its material and spiritual singularity, in search of its own means of expression. In a rhetorical invocation that no doubt sounded familiar to the members of Hashomer in his audience, Bernfeld cited a biblical episode of rebellion, and summoned Jewish youth to fulfil what he called the Jerubbaal mission: 'filled with deepest dissatisfaction with the present state of the world and humanity, it is the task of youth to create a new model of humankind, to become a complete person and a complete youth'.[18] Early in 1918 Bernfeld embarked upon the task of giving this mission concrete form by gathering a group of his closest associates in the Order of Jerubbaal, a secret coterie replete with masonic-like oaths and symbols. Outside this inner sanctum was the Circle of Jerubbaal, a forum for the non-initiated and less committed supporters of his ideas.[19] The Jerubbaal groups were components of a grand political structure of youth communities conceived by Bernfeld just before the war, the Order of Youth. A hierarchical edifice designed to unite youth and catalyse political change, the Order of Youth had no Jewish content at the time of its

[16] Utley, 'Siegfried Bernfeld's Jewish Order of Youth', 356–7. On antisemitism in the Austrian and German youth movements, see Seewann, *Österreichische Jugendbewegung*, i. 90–5; Laqueur, *Young Germany*, 47–83.

[17] *JZ*, 31 Aug. 1917, p. 5; 12 Oct. 1917, p. 5. See also Hoffer, 'Siegfried Bernfeld and "Jerubbaal"', 155; Paret, Preface, p. xiv. For early discussions about the *Jugendtag*, see SBP, folder 40, nos. 155786–155787 (29 July and 1 Aug. 1917); 155789–155792 (1 and 9 Sept. 1917).

[18] *JZ*, 2 Nov. 1917, p. 4. The biblical reference is to the story of Gideon's destruction of the temple of Baal in Judges 6: 25–32.

[19] Utley, 'Siegfried Bernfeld's Jewish Order of Youth', 351; Hoffer, 'Siegfried Bernfeld and "Jerubbaal"', 156–9.

conception. At its highest level were small revolutionary cells, such as the *Zielgemeinde* formed by Bernfeld early in the war. Propounding socialism and youth autonomy, these cells failed to attract much support. The Order of Jerubbaal was a Jewish version of these *Zielgemeinde*, i.e. the revolutionary vanguard of the Order of Youth transposed to a Jewish setting. Élite youth groups dedicated to constructing new models of 'community' were to provide the underpinning for this vanguard. During the war Hashomer and Blau-Weiss seemed to Bernfeld to fit this bill. A 'mass' base would be provided by institutions in which education and intellectual exchange would draw in previously uninvolved young people; this would facilitate the formation of a 'community of ideas'. With the help of the Zionist organization he established the Circle of Jerubbaal; a Jewish studies Teacher Training Institute (Pädagogium); and a Jewish Youth Centre (Jugendheim).[20] To Bernfeld, then, the presence in Vienna of thousands of uprooted east European Jewish youngsters offered an opportunity to put his philosophy into practice. From the youngsters' point of view, even if they did not necessarily subscribe to (or even fully understand) his ideas, Bernfeld was a proven leader with a seemingly impressive philosophical scheme that offered both plans for immediate action and the prospect of an important role for youth in the future.

One of the first substantial realizations of Bernfeld's plans was the opening of the 'Jewish pedagogical courses' (*jüdisch-pädagogische Kurse*) in November 1917. He rather grandly conceived of these as a first step in the reinvigoration and redefinition not just of Jewish education but also of general education, although his emphasis was on the former. Recasting what he saw as the woefully inadequate models for teachers in general and religious instruction teachers in particular (since these would be responsible for Jewish education in government schools), he wanted to train teachers not for positions in schools, but rather for 'the freer forms of education, for children's homes and nurseries, orphanages, for the diverse groups and institutions of the youth movement'. The school, in fact, would no longer be seen as the focal point of education. Rather, 'a whole complex of institutions'— kindergartens, nurseries, youth and sport groups, libraries, and Hebrew courses—would constitute the building-blocks of Jewish education. To be successful, a system of this type required educators well schooled in both

---

[20] Utley, 'Siegfried Bernfeld's Jewish Order of Youth', 351–4; Hoffer, 'Siegfried Bernfeld and "Jerubbaal"', 156–9; Mintz, *Pangs of Youth*, 74–80; Siegfried Bernfeld, 'Jugendbewegung', *Der Jude*, 5 (1920–1), 351–3; id., *Die neue Jugend und die Frauen* (Vienna, 1914), 57–71.

Jewish and general knowledge and modern educational theory. It would be the task of a Jewish Teacher Training Institute, envisaged as an expanded version of the pedagogical courses, to train such teachers.[21] Some 150 teachers, civil servants, and students enrolled for the courses—which were conducted in rooms provided by Anitta Müller's welfare organization—on Jewish and general educational techniques, philosophy, psychology, religion, Jewish history, the Jewish Question, Bible, Talmud, and Hebrew language and literature.[22] The impressive roster of instructors included Bernfeld himself; Samuel Krauss, later the head of Vienna's Israelitisch-Theologische Lehranstalt; Wilhelm Jerusalem, professor of education and philosophy at the University of Vienna; Harry Torczyner, a lecturer in semitic languages at the university (later known as Naphtali Herz Tur-Sinai, professor of Hebrew at the Hebrew University of Jerusalem); Adolf Böhm, historian of the Zionist movement; and Abraham Sonne, a noted Hebrew writer.[23] The expanded Teacher Training Institute formally opened in October 1918. Courses continued until mid-1919, by which point 120 students were registered (in addition to some 300 enrolled in 'youth courses') and the Zionist organization had recognized the Teacher Training Institute as its official educational agency.[24]

During late 1917 and the first months of 1918 youth groups of all sorts were busy. The Zionist organization ran a lecture series on Jewish education; Po'alei Zion held lectures on education and politics, while its youth section published a modest periodical; the women's association Moriah held regular lectures and seminars, organized Hebrew courses, and under-

[21] *JZ*, 22 Feb. 1918, pp. 3–4. On the courses and the Pädagogium, see SBP, folders 22–6. Bernfeld further developed his educational philosophy in his book *Das jüdische Volk und seine Jugend* (Berlin, 1919). He was given an opportunity to implement his ideas when he was appointed director of a Jewish orphanage in Vienna in Oct. 1919. He organized this institution as a radically experimental and democratic community; it survived in this form until mid-1920, but Bernfeld's direct involvement was limited after he fell seriously ill in Dec. 1919. See Bernfeld, *Kinderheim Baumgarten*; Hoffer, 'Siegfried Bernfeld and "Jerubbaal"', 159–67; Utley, 'Siegfried Bernfeld's Jewish Order of Youth', 362–5.

[22] *JZ*, 9 Nov. 1917, p. 5; 22 Feb. 1918, pp. 3–4; 6 Sept. 1918, p. 5; 25 Oct. 1918, p. 5; 17 Jan. 1919, p. 6; *OW*, 29 Mar. 1918, p. 205; 20 Sept. 1918, p. 604. On similar courses run by the Zionist organization in May 1914, see Gaisbauer, *Davidstern und Doppeladler*, 346–7.

[23] *OW*, 29 Mar. 1918, p. 203.

[24] *WM*, 19 Aug. 1919, pp. 1–2. In Nov. 1919, by which time Bernfeld was no longer actively involved, the Teacher Training Institute was incorporated into the Zionist organization and reconstituted with somewhat different emphases and personnel. See *JZ*, 4 Nov. 1919, pp. 5–6. The Teacher Training Institute was an indirect progenitor of the Chajes Gymnasium, the Jewish nationalist day school that opened its doors in Oct. 1919. See Binyamin Shimron, *Das Chajes-realgymnasium in Wien 1919–1938* (Tel Aviv, 1989); Freidenreich, *Jewish Politics in Vienna*, 156.

took political 'propaganda work'; student groups held popular 'discussion evenings' and sponsored lectures on Zionism; sports and gymnastics associations resumed activity; the student Hebrew-language association Hatchijah held weekly meetings and sponsored Hebrew readings and excursions; Bukovinian youngsters socialized in their own *Landsmannschaften*.[25] At the beginning of 1918 there were approximately forty nationalist youth groups in Vienna, claiming a combined membership of over 2,000.[26] The range and extent of this activity indicates the support potentially available to Bernfeld and his associates should they manage to bring it under one roof.

Attempting to document and guide all this bustle was the movement's newsletter, *Blätter aus der jüdischen Jugendbewegung*. The fragmentation of the youth scene, asserted the first issue in January 1918, was its greatest weakness. As the great majority of youth groups in Vienna possessed only meagre resources, the most pressing task was to establish a unified organization. A central co-ordinating body would be able to create resources— libraries, reading-rooms, theatres, a youth centre, a career advice bureau —and offer financial support and direction to smaller groups.[27] Remaining true to its self-image as a newsletter, the *Blätter* concentrated on reporting the activities of the different groups in Vienna and Austria, paying particular attention to preparations for the *Jugendtag*, now scheduled for May 1918.[28] Already at the time of the first appearance of the *Blätter*, plans were afoot for a second journal that would be less prosaic in content. Targeted at 16- to 25-year-olds 'who take themselves and their *Judentum* seriously', the new journal, *Jerubbaal*, first appeared in April 1918, aiming not to 'entertain' but to stimulate 'discussion of the tasks of youth and of the forms and goals of the youth movement'. Edited by Bernfeld, *Jerubbaal* aspired to be the 'voice' of youth, a forum that would enable 'a larger circle of Jewish

---

[25] On the Zionist organization's activity, see *JZ*, 4 May 1917, p. 5. On Po'alei Zion, see *YA*, 15 Aug. 1917, pp. 13–14; Sept.–Oct. 1917, p. 18; *JZ*, 30 Nov. 1917, p. 4; 8 Feb. 1918, p. 4. On Moriah, see *JZ*, 28 Sept. 1917, p. 5; 12 Oct. 1917, p. 5; 19 Oct. 1917, p. 4; 9 Nov. 1917, p. 6; 7 Dec. 1917, pp. 4–5; *BJJ* (Feb. 1918), 4–5. On student groups, see *JZ*, 12 Oct. 1917, p. 5; 21 Dec. 1917, p. 4; 26 Apr. 1918, p. 4. On sports and gymnastics groups, see *JZ*, 13 July 1917, p. 5; 17 Aug. 1917, p. 4; 22 Feb. 1918, p. 4. On Hatchijah, see *JZ*, 7 Dec. 1917, p. 5; 22 Mar. 1918, p. 4; 27 Mar. 1918, pp. 5–6. On the Bukovinians, see *JZ*, 19 Apr. 1918, p. 4; Seewann, *Zirkel und Zionsstern*, i. 251. [26] *BJJ* (Jan. 1918), 1.

[27] Ibid. Regular exhortations were published on the necessity of establishing a central body. See e.g. *BJJ* (Mar. 1918), 2–4; (Apr. 1918), 1–3. The *Blätter*'s editor was the socialist Zionist Robert Weiss, later known as Moshe Livni. See CZA, A383/60.

[28] The *Blätter* continued publication throughout 1918. In Jan. 1919 it changed its name (but little else) to *Jüdische Jugendblätter*, surviving in this form until May 1919. On the change of name, see *WM*, 23 Jan. 1919, p. 6.

youth to become aware of that which is alive within themselves'.[29] It did indeed provide a literary outlet for aspiring writers, many of whom indulged in the rhetorical excesses characteristic of certain sections of the movement. In a not untypical example, Eugen Höflich (later known as the Hebrew writer Moshe Ben-Gavriel) wrote of the role of Hashomer in the

concentration of all the absolute primordial values of Jewry in the land of its blood and its innermost history, the concentration of all pure Jewish forces on the goal of the re-entry of a worthy Jewry into the stream of world events, and the . . . overcoming of . . . barbarism through the self-knowledge of a new Jewish *Volk*, in order to provide an opportunity for wretched tormented humanity to become at last truly human, through the teaching that goes forth from Zion.[30]

Theirs was a sensibility at times almost obsessively fixated on the primacy of *Geist* in youth affairs, and often dismissive of the mundane tasks necessary to the functioning of a political movement. Mutual hostility between 'idealists' and 'pragmatists' (which in practice amounted to pro-Buber and contra-Buber factions) plagued the movement, ultimately playing a considerable role in its demise. Neither the pragmatic *Blätter* nor the more florid *Jerubbaal* survived past 1919.[31]

The journals served a growing and varied constituency. A new gymnastics association was formed in December 1917, for example, with the express purpose of bringing together nationally minded youth of the fourth, fifth, and tenth districts of the city, not traditionally areas of intensive Jewish life.[32] Reflecting the increasing orientation of Hashomer towards Palestine, a *hakhsharah* group (for agricultural training in preparation for emigration to Palestine) was formed in Vienna in January 1918, immediately attracting some sixty recruits.[33] In April 1918 an estimated 750 nationalist students formed an association that proposed itself as the representative

[29] *OW*, 25 Jan. 1918, p. 63; *Jerubbaal*, 1 (1918–19), 2.

[30] *Jerubbaal*, 1 (1918–19), 200. See also Höflich's articles, ibid. 245–7; 331–4. See also ibid. 179–84, 359–72. On Höflich, see Armin A. Wallas, 'Der Pförtner des Ostens. Eugen Hoeflich—Panasiast und Expressionist', in Mark H. Gelber, Hans Otto Horch, and Sigurd Paul Scheichl (eds.), *Von Franzos zu Canetti. Jüdische Autoren aus Österreich* (Tübingen, 1996), 305–44. On the Nietzschean overtones evident in youth movement rhetoric, see Steven E. Aschheim, 'Nietzsche and the Nietzschean Moment in Jewish Life 1890–1939', *LBIYB* 37 (1992), 205.

[31] Both publications received funds collected in 1913–14 by the pre-war youth movement to finance a journal, *Aus der Jugendbewegung*, which appeared only once. A copy can be found in CAHJP, AW, 248/5. Subsidies were also received from external sources. See *JZ*, 19 Apr. 1918, p. 5. On the youth movement's journals, see the material in SBP, folders 52–8.

[32] *BJJ* (Apr. 1918), 5.   [33] *JZ*, 18 Jan. 1918, p. 4; *OW*, 8 Feb. 1918, p. 89.

of all tertiary-level Jewish students in Austria. The war, the new group declared, had clearly demonstrated the need for Jewish unity.[34] All this did not go unnoticed. The *Reichspost* was moved to comment that secretive Zionist activity was surely corrupting Jewish students. If so many young Jews were now active in youth groups, this merely furnished further proof that they were shirking their military service, in obedience to the injunctions of the Talmud.[35] By April 1918 a Central Office of Viennese Jewish youth groups was functioning, with its headquarters in the newly inaugurated Youth Centre in Leopoldstadt. The Central Office and Youth Centre were henceforth the nerve centre of the burgeoning movement.[36] With these promising beginnings of an institutional and popular base—Central Office, Youth Centre, educational courses, two journals, flourishing associational life, and a link to the Zionist organization—the stage was set for the pivotal event in the brief history of the youth movement, Bernfeld's long-planned *Jugendtag*.

THE *JUGENDTAG*

Expectations were high for the three-day gathering. Two days were to be devoted to debate about the movement and its goals, culminating in the establishment of an Austria-wide federation (*Verband*) of Jewish youth associations. A final day would be spent hiking in the Vienna woods, reinforcing the importance of contact with nature. The mission of the *Jugendtag*, announced the programme, was to 'end the divisive isolation of our youth in innumerable small groups'.[37] It would be, so the organizers hoped, a 'powerful, impressive rally that would demonstrate the strength of the Zionist idea and the will of youth'. Jewish life, stagnating in the 'swamp' of Gemeinde institutions, must be revolutionized, and this revolution was the task of youth, 'whose idealism rebels against the irresolution of decrepit and frail conventionality'. Each individual must make the sacrifices necessary to enrich the Jewish collective, to ensure 'the reconstruction of the community'. It was Bernfeld's hope that the collective transformative

---

[34] *BJJ* (Apr. 1918), 5; Seewann, *Zirkel und Zionsstern*, i. 251. A similar effort had been made in early 1914 to form an umbrella organization of Jewish students in Vienna. See Seewann, *Zirkel und Zionsstern*, ii. 321–2. See also Rozenblit, 'The Assertion of Identity'.

[35] Cited in *BJJ* (Apr. 1918), 6–7.

[36] *JZ*, 12 Apr. 1918, p. 5. On the Central Office (Zentralstelle), see the Protocols of its 'Leitungssitzungen', Feb.–Sept. 1918, SBP, folder 40, nos. 155802–155819.

[37] *BJJ* (Mar. 1918), 1. On preparations for the *Jugendtag*, see SBP, folder 36.

experience of the *Jugendtag* would catalyse the individual and national redemptive processes that he regarded as crucial for the moral and physical renewal of Jewish youth.[38] Others, however, had somewhat more prosaic hopes, and dissatisfaction with Bernfeld's rarefied visions was immediately apparent. The *Jugendtag* was to be, in many respects, the movement's definitive episode.

The two days of discussion were held at the Musikvereinssaal, a spacious auditorium in the city centre. Considering that many on active military duty were unable to attend, the capacity audience of an estimated 2,000 was impressive. Some 200 youth group delegates were present, along with more than 300 'guests' from various areas of the empire.[39] The keynote speaker of the opening evening was Martin Buber, whose speech on Zion and youth became, along with Bernfeld's address the following day, the centrepiece around which most subsequent discussion revolved. At this time 'the reigning spiritual leader of the German Zionist youth movement', Buber exhorted the assembled youth to prepare for their role in the construction of a new and just society in Palestine by first reconstructing their 'inner self'. Consistent with his emphasis on Zionism as 'a vehicle for Jewish spiritual rebirth', he evoked the 'craving for life and death in and for the community [that has been] . . . awakened in the youth of our time', calling upon them to fulfil the national, social, and religious mission of liberation struggle, revolution, and apostleship.[40]

A lengthy and often acrimonious debate ensued. Hashomer leader Eliezer Rieger explained that while the Shomer might agree with the fundamental principles of Bernfeld's ideas on Jewish education and moral renewal, it

[38] Bernfeld conceived of the Federation as a Jewish version of his pre-war Order of Youth. See his remarks in *JZ*, 17 May 1918, pp. 1–2; Utley, 'Siegfried Bernfeld's Jewish Order of Youth', 354. See *JZ*, 17 May 1918, p. 1, for the preceding quotations.

[39] Willi Hoffer, for example, comments that he was unable to attend owing to his military service. See Hoffer, 'Siegfried Bernfeld and "Jerubbaal"', 151. The presence of hundreds of delegates from outside the capital further testifies to the expectations aroused by the *Jugendtag*. Travel from Galicia to Vienna, for example, was extremely difficult. See Horowitz, *My Yesterday*, 60–1.

[40] Buber's address, 'Zion und die Jugend', was later reprinted in *Der Jude*, 3 (1918–19), 99–106. For the characterizations of Buber, see David Biale, *Gershom Scholem: Kabbalah and Counter-History* (Cambridge, Mass., 1979), 56. On Buber's influence on central European Jewish youth, see also Kieval, *The Making of Czech Jewry*, 127–38; George L. Mosse, *Germans and Jews* (New York, 1970), 85–94; Chaim Schatzker, 'Martin Buber's Influence on the Jewish Youth Movement in Germany', *LBIYB* 23 (1978), 151–71. Paraphrasing and quotations from the *Jugendtag*, here and below, are from the report in *JZ*, 24 May 1918, pp. 2–4, unless otherwise indicated. An abridged version of this report is in *OW*, 31 May 1918, pp. 332–3.

insisted on bringing to Palestine not only Jewish *Geist* but also Jewish physical strength. Further, he argued, the first priority of Jewish youth must be to deal with the Jewish Question, not the general problems of humanity. The Shomer demanded action, he declared, not merely discussion.[41] Rieger's preference for action over rhetoric was emblematic of a debate that focused primarily on the relative merits of idealism and materialism as guiding intellectual principles for the movement. Idealism in this context was construed by its opponents as excessive concentration on the *geistig* or spiritual realm (moral renewal, re-creation of self) to the point where the 'material' realm (concrete political action) was marginalized. Harsh criticism of 'Bubermania', as one opponent later called it, was voiced by a former Buber acolyte, Heinrich Margulies.[42] During the war years Margulies turned away from what he called 'a kind of [élitist] moral Zionism' that drew its inspiration from German metaphysics, producing a 'German Jewish *Kulturchaos*' and a 'dogma of anti-politics'.[43] To Margulies, Buber worked with 'such intangible concepts and terminology that hopeless ambiguity and confusion are unavoidable'.[44] 'Back to reality' must instead be the Jewish slogan.[45] The point of departure for Zionism must be the sorry plight of Jewish youth rather than a universalist concern with the general human predicament. Buber and Bernfeld's lack of intellectual clarity was a severe hindrance to effective action; their 'dictatorship of *Geist*' paid too little attention altogether to quotidian reality.[46] Margulies argued for a 'synthetic' approach in which both the material and spiritual realms would receive their due weight.[47]

Supporting Margulies, and in fact going much further in its rejectionism, was Po'alei Zion, whose attitude was unrelentingly negative. Railing against the 'new Torah from the west', Buber's 'religious mysticism', Bernfeld's 'German Hebrew' bourgeois educational philosophy, and the 'Polish

---

[41] On the impression made by Rieger, a student at the Vienna Israelitisch-Theologische Lehranstalt and later professor of education at the Hebrew University of Jerusalem, see Hoffer, 'Siegfried Bernfeld and "Jerubbaal"', 151 n. 2; Horowitz, *My Yesterday*, 61. His speech was in Hebrew and Yiddish.

[42] On Margulies (1890–1989), a political economist, see the material in CZA, A392. On his initial support of Buber's enthusiastic response to the war as a 'mystical experience', see Biale, *Gershom Scholem*, 59–61. On Shlomo Horowitz's term 'Bubermania', see Margalit, *Hashomer Hatsa'ir*, 29.

[43] Heinrich Margulies, 'Wege und Irrwege', *NJM* 2 (1917–18), 274–5, 281.

[44] *JZ*, 7 June 1918, p. 5.   [45] Margulies, 'Wege und Irrwege', 277.

[46] *JZ*, 24 May 1918, p. 4.

[47] He developed this idea further in 'Wege und Irrwege', 276–81. See also his 'Kritik des Zionismus', *NJM* 4 (1919–20), 17–21.

Hebrew' ideas of Hashomer, Po'alei Zion's representatives declined to join the proposed federation, demanding instead political activism and 'Jewish-proletarian, socialist education'. Buber's utopian rhetoric was largely incomprehensible to the audience, and the discussion was accordingly conducted at a 'frightfully low level' (in this, at least, they were in agreement with Bernfeld, who described the debate as 'for the most part rhetorically poor, and inconsequential with regard to content'[48]). Rieger was attacked not only for his use of Hebrew but also for his 'empty phraseology' and his 'odious and mutilated' Yiddish. That the 'Buber–Wyneken hotchpotch' and Bernfeld's 'florid German-style rhetoric' could attract support was merely a reflection of Jewish youth's 'spiritual poverty and emptiness', of which the entire *Jugendtag* was convincing evidence.[49] This harsh assessment was of a piece with Po'alei Zion's attitude to the youth movement in the preceding months. Bernfeld's repeated calls for suprapolitical unity among Jewish youth had little resonance for Po'alei Zion activists, who rejected the very notion of co-operation with the class enemy within Jewish society.[50]

Po'alei Zion's separatist stance was akin to that of the Orthodox, who were similarly less than impressed with the proceedings of the *Jugendtag*. That it began on the religious holiday of Shavuot, that organ music was used, that women sat on the platform—all this was bad enough. More dangerous, though, was that Jewish youth could be seduced away from religious observance by Buber's fine speechifying. 'We Orthodox Jews are all Zionists', proclaimed one observer, but only the Almighty can 'hasten our return to Palestine'. From a meeting 'which begins with the desecration of the Sabbath, Jewish youth cannot prosper'.[51] Another cautioned that it was not possible, as the Zionists would have it, to identify with only one component of Jewish identity, be it culture, history, religion, or nationality. For Jews, it is all or nothing: religion and nationality are inseparable. Thus, a truly Jewish youth movement would encompass all aspects of Jewry, paying particular attention, of course, to its essential foundation, religion. Clearly, the Orthodox—represented in this instance by the Verein Jeschurun, formed in June 1917 and devoted to the 'cultivation of Jewish

---

[48] Siegfried Bernfeld, 'Der österreichisch-jüdische Jugendtag in Wien', *Jerubbaal*, 1 (1918–19), 119.

[49] *YA*, 1 June 1918, pp. 9–10. The primary Po'alei Zion representative at the *Jugendtag* was Mendel Singer.   [50] See *BJJ* (July–Aug. 1918), 6.

[51] See the comments in *Jeschurun*, the organ of the Organisation für die Thoratreue Jugend, 18, suppl., *JK*, 23 May 1918. The *Jugendtag* commenced on Saturday evening, 18 May 1918.

knowledge and spirit among Torah-faithful youth'—were intent on keeping their distance from the dangerous secularists.[52]

If the Orthodox and Po'alei Zion remained aloof, Bernfeld still managed to attract sufficient support to form his cherished Federation of Austrian Jewish Youth. This act of 'decisive significance', it was announced, would 'inaugurate a new epoch for the Jewish youth movement in Austria'. Once more stressing its suprapolitical and inclusive nature, Bernfeld saw the Federation as a 'vessel' in which Jewish youth could 'quarrel and struggle'. Unlike at the *Jugendtag*, however, with its political 'squabbles and disputes', in the Federation there must be only 'work, persuasion, and development'.[53] Bernfeld and Buber's leading defender, both at the *Jugendtag* and during the following year of polemics, was Robert Weltsch. Responding to Margulies, Weltsch tried to bridge the gap between the two camps, asserting that the dichotomy between the 'primacy of [either] *Geist* or reality' was false. 'Power cannot exist in the abstract; it can be productive only with the guidance of *Geist*. . . . *Geist* is not aestheticism or frivolity, but the compelling power of the Idea, that which creates all human action.'[54] If the dichotomy was false, Weltsch's own preference for the subordination of mundane politics to the dictates of the 'Idea' was clear. This exchange marked the beginning of an extended and often caustic debate between Margulies and Weltsch that continued until the summer of 1919. Weltsch had already been an enthusiastic advocate of Buber's ideas for several years. Prior to the war he had been involved in an intellectual battle over these ideas in the Prague Zionist group Bar Kochba, a battle that bore a striking resemblance to the argument now unfolding in Vienna. Whereas in Prague Weltsch and his allies prevailed, in the harsher social and political conditions of wartime Vienna (and in that city's markedly different Zionist political culture) the result would be different.[55] For his part, Bernfeld admonished Margulies for distortion of his ideas and the 'unacceptable style of his polemic'. Expressing disdain for Margulies's intellectual dilettantism, he recommended that Margulies 'make the effort to prepare his ideas a little more thoroughly than heretofore' in order to present a programme 'some-

[52] 'Jeschurun', 19, *JK*, 30 May 1918. On the formation of the Verein Jeschurun, see *WH*, 6 Apr. 1917, p. 8; 29 June 1917, p. 8.

[53] On the Verband der jüdischen Jugend Österreichs, see Bernfeld, 'Der österreichisch-jüdische Jugendtag in Wien', 119–20; *JZ*, 24 May 1918, p. 4.   [54] *JZ*, 24 May 1918, p. 4.

[55] On Weltsch, Buber, and Bar Kochba in Prague, see Kieval, *The Making of Czech Jewry*, 145–7.

what more concrete, practical, and scientific . . . and somewhat less certain and apodictic'.[56]

The acrimony of these disagreements was at least temporarily suspended on the meeting's final day. 'All ideological antagonisms vanished due to the binding force of youthful *Lebensgefühl* and Jewish consciousness. . . . In the clearest spring weather, the colourful [multitude] . . . scouting, playing, and singing . . . in the Vienna woods . . . presented a truly festive spectacle.' A 'stirring' address by Buber capped the afternoon.[57] The day in nature made a strong impression on Bernfeld. On the final day, he wrote,

we experienced it clearly, even the sceptics, the ideological opponents, the young and the older. There in the Vienna woods on the heath—that was something! A powerful feeling of joy, a feeling of surprise: all who were there with us in the fields singing and playing, walking, camping, talking, they all belonged to us, to me, we are One, one saw us: Youth, Jewish. We all want one thing, a more beautiful present; more lively, richer, more intimate, more youthful than hitherto; [and] a more earnest future. And one thing gives our lives a sustaining sense: that for the sake of our *Volk* we live and grow more beautiful, freer, nobler, more Jewish. This feeling, even if experienced for only one minute, is something; it is a great deal. And it was there at our *Jugendtag*.

Reiterating his priorities, Bernfeld stressed that education was the key to the 'birth of a new Jewish type, whose arrival signifies the renewal of Jewry in a more important sense than the political'.[58]

The culmination of months of intensive preparation, the *Jugendtag* provided a focus for the energies of those striving to fuse a loose assortment of groups into a cohesive movement. But the desire for such a movement, especially one organized along the lines proposed by Bernfeld and Buber, was neither widespread nor strong enough to overcome the ideological resistance that its advocates engendered. A wide gulf separated the political orientation of Margulies's programme from Bernfeld's almost messianic vision of the movement's potentialities. Each approach had its supporters in the Zionist organization: Margulies was backed by Stricker, Bernfeld by Weltsch. Like the Congress movement, the youth movement became part of the power struggle within the Zionist leadership between the Weltsch and Stricker camps, and although Bernfeld held high hopes for the

---

[56] *JZ*, 7 June 1918, p. 5. See also Bernfeld to Margulies, 31 May 1918; Margulies to Bernfeld, 2 June 1918, both in CZA, A392/16; Weltsch to Margulies, 7 June and 5 July 1918; Margulies to Weltsch, 10 Sept. 1918, all in CZA, A392/17.   [57] *JZ*, 24 May 1918, p. 4.

[58] Bernfeld, 'Der österreichisch-jüdische Jugendtag in Wien', 120.

Federation, the difficulties it faced were manifest. While nominally empire-wide in its embrace, the bulk of its membership and activity was in Vienna. Even those willing to belong pulled in numerous and often contradictory directions. The political and cultural agenda of Margulies, for example, hardly chimed with that of the increasingly pioneering and Palestine-oriented Hashomer, while the student groups were more concerned with threats of antisemitism at their institutions than with moral and spiritual renewal.

These considerable hurdles notwithstanding, the infrastructure for a potentially successful movement was now in place. The *Jugendtag* had attracted some 2,000 participants from all parts of the empire, and was widely considered to have been a resounding success. It was, after all, a significant and unprecedented event, analogous in its function for the Jewish youth movement to the German youth movement's Hohe Meissner gathering of October 1913. (That, too, was a talkfest that promised much, 'meant different things to different people', and had few tangible long-term results.[59]) A central administrative body had been set up, and the youth scene in Vienna—and, to a lesser degree, in the provinces—was flourishing as never before. The problem, then, was not lack of potential interest or membership but rather of co-ordination and direction; what was sorely needed was harmonious and effective leadership invested with a sufficient measure of authority, whether from above by the Zionist organization or from below by the rank and file, to guide the movement.

Immediately following the meeting Bernfeld proposed to the Zionist organization that it create a Youth Office to take charge of all youth work conducted under Zionist auspices. Bernfeld had been responsible for Zionist youth affairs since the summer of 1917; he suggested now a more formal structure that would allow the Zionist organization to consolidate its position as the leading force in the youth movement. For Bernfeld, appointed to head the Youth Office, this step represented a formalization of his position in the Zionist hierarchy, providing him with an important operational base. For the youth movement, it provided a closer and more direct link with the

<hr />

[59] On the Hohe Meissner, see Laqueur, *Young Germany*, 32–8; Scheu, *Ein Band der Freundschaft*, 16–19. The quotation is from Laqueur, *Young Germany*, 38. The *Jugendtag* also had much in common with the three-day festival (*Bundestag*) organized by the German Blau-Weiss at Lockwitz in Aug. 1916. See Glenn Richard Sharfman, 'The Jewish Youth Movement in Germany 1900–1936: A Study in Ideology and Organization', Ph.D. diss., University of North Carolina, Chapel Hill, 1989, 144–7.

Zionist organization, an invaluable financial and material resource.[60] From
the Zionist leadership's point of view, this relationship offered the prospect
of a leading role in a movement that promised much in the way of support.
Zionist activists in the youth movement, while not engaged in 'party activity in the narrowest sense, would nevertheless fulfil an exceedingly important function [for the Zionist organization]'.[61] This was by no means a
hidden agenda. One of the declared tasks of the Youth Office, in addition to
education, youth welfare, and liaison between the youth movement and the
Zionist organization, was 'regular supervision . . . [and] deliberate guidance
of [youth] groups according to the policies laid down by the Zionist organization'.[62] But of what exactly did this supervision and guidance consist?
Given the unresolved differences in viewpoints between the Stricker and
Weltsch camps over the nature and purpose of youth work, the Zionist
organization at this stage was able to offer only the most general guidelines.
(It was the task of the Youth Office, for example, to provide for 'Zionist
education of youth'.[63]) Until a more definitive policy was set, something of
which there was no prospect in the immediate future, Bernfeld was free to
follow his inclinations. His success in working his way into powerful positions as head of the Youth Office, created at his instigation, and as head of
the Federation (also essentially his creation) belies Margulies's claims that
he deprecated or neglected the political realm. Bernfeld was clearly no
political novice.

There now ensued a temporary hiatus in the movement's internal conflicts, at least as far as public airing of tensions went. Practical work in the
summer of 1918 was limited in the main to consolidation. A new sports and
gymnastics journal, *Hagibor* ('The Hero'), appeared; a library and youth
archive were planned; Robert Weltsch's previously floated idea that each
individual should devote a year of work to the Zionist cause, an *Arbeitsjahr*,
was now taken up for serious consideration.[64] Noteworthy was the com-
mencement in mid-October of the already mentioned 'youth courses' under
the auspices of the Teacher Training Institute. Despite a delayed start due to

---

[60] *JZ*, 7 June 1918, p. 5; 14 June 1918, p. 4. As part of the restructuring of the Zionist organization, Bernfeld was slated to take over the reconstituted secretariat of the Inner Austrian District Committee, firmly ensconcing him in the party's higher echelons.

[61] *JZ*, 14 June 1918, p. 2.   [62] Ibid. 4.   [63] Ibid.

[64] On *Hagibor*, see *JZ*, 26 July 1918, p. 4. On the library, see *BJJ* (July–Aug.), 10. On the youth
archive, see *JZ*, 14 June 1918, p. 4; *BJJ* (Feb. 1918), 5. The *Arbeitsjahr* was originally elaborated
by Robert Weltsch in the winter of 1916–17 and was vigorously supported by Hashomer, who
viewed it as appropriate preparation for *aliyah*. See *JZ*, 12 July 1918, pp. 2–3; 'Schomrim–Zeire

the political upheavals in Vienna of October and November 1918, by mid-January 1919 there were some 300 12- to 24-year-olds enrolled.[65]

Hashomer, meanwhile, still an important part of the movement, increasingly turned its attention in the months following the *Jugendtag* to activism and *aliyah*.[66] At the same time, with fewer refugees now left in the capital, the Shomer focused more intently on its work in Galicia. An important turning-point was its conference in late July 1918 in the remote Carpathian town of Tarnawa Wyżna, attended by a reported 600 delegates. Here Rieger and others intensified their polemic against Bernfeld's vision of an introspective and 'passive' youth movement, urging instead activism, discipline, and 'heroic Zionism'.[67] Although no binding decisions were taken, from the point of view of the relationship to the Bernfeld-led movement the conference was a significant signpost for future developments. The growing influence of activist and *aliyah* ideologies, and the increasing likelihood that Galicia would become part of a Polish state, both contributed to the gradual dissolution of Hashomer's ties with the Vienna-centred movement of Bernfeld.

The *Jugendtag*, it turned out, was the first, last, and only great moment of the wartime youth movement. Before any of its internal conflicts could be resolved, it was overtaken by the events of October and November 1918. The end of empire deprived it of a primary source of ideological sustenance and potential membership, Galician Jewry; a Federation of Austrian Jewish Youth suddenly became a far more modest concept. Paradoxically, it was precisely at this moment of enforced narrowing of horizons that the youth movement in Vienna experienced a surge of dynamic growth, catalysed by the political uncertainty of the post-war months. In this highly charged atmosphere all political and social options, it seemed, were open. More concretely, the renewed influx into Vienna of thousands of young east European Jews intent on emigration to Palestine, many of whom were fleeing pogroms in Galicia, helped create a minor eruption of youth activism.

Zion' to EAC, 8 Jan. 1918, CZA, Z3/848; Arthur Ruppin to Aktionskomitee, 11 Mar. 1918, CZA, Z3/849.

[65] *JZ*, 4 Oct. 1918, p. 5; 17 Jan. 1919, p. 5; *OW*, 17 Jan. 1919, pp. 41–2; *JJ*, 1 Mar. 1919, p. 17; 15 Apr. 1919, n.p.   [66] Mendelsohn, *Zionism in Poland*, 85.

[67] Margalit, *Hashomer Hatsa'ir*, 38–9. See also Chizik, *The Unification of Hashomer and Tse'ire Zion*, 74–83; Jensen, *Sei stark und mutig!*, 78–9.

EUROPE OR PALESTINE

A distinct bifurcation occurred on the Jewish youth scene in the immediate post-war months. Shorn of its empire-wide pretensions, Bernfeld's Federation continued its work, reinforced by a revitalized student movement; at the same time, Vienna became a way station for young Palestine-bound east Europeans, who then generally proceeded to the port of Trieste. That Vienna played an important role in the early stages of what became known in the Zionist movement as the 'third *aliyah*' (1919–23) owes more to its location than to any internal Jewish dynamic of the city.[68] In the first half of 1919 Zionist sources noted the 'importance of Vienna as a transit point for emigration' and reported 10,500 people registered for departure. The prospective emigrants were overwhelmingly young, middle-class Poles; many of lesser means remained unregistered.[69] To deal with the influx of Palestine-bound youths, local Zionists set up a Palestine Office in late November 1918. Explaining its genesis, the Vienna Palestine Office reflected that the presence of so many refugees clamouring to leave for Palestine, and the prospect of expulsions of east European Jews from the Habsburg successor states, had caused 'panic' in Viennese Zionist circles. It was the job of the Palestine Office to take matters in hand.[70] Directed by Emil Stein (with the active assistance of Adolf Böhm and long-time head of the Austrian branch of the Jewish National Fund Egon Zweig), its self-proclaimed task was the co-ordination of all Palestine-related work in the territories of the former Habsburg monarchy.[71] This rather overweening ambition was far beyond its capabilities, and similar bodies were established soon after in Galicia and somewhat later in other former Habsburg lands.[72]

To assist the emigrants the Vienna Office established a transport company

[68] On Vienna's role in the third *aliyah*, see Meir Henisch, 'Vienna on the Threshold of the Third *Aliyah*', in Yehuda Erez (ed.), *The Third Aliyah Book* (Heb.) (Tel Aviv, 1964), 193–5.

[69] Emil Stein, *Auf dem Wege nach Palästina* (Vienna, 1919), 20–1, 24; Palestine Office, Vienna, to Copenhagen Zionist Office, 27 Mar. 1919, CZA, L6/94. One eyewitness in early 1919 reported 'six thousand Polish refugees waiting in Vienna to leave for Palestine'. See the letters of Rudolf G. Sonneborn, 15 and 18 Feb. 1919, CZA, K11/297.

[70] Palestine Office, Vienna, to ZCO, 3 Jan. 1919, CZA, L6/87.

[71] Jewish National Fund, Vienna, to ZCO, 20 Nov. 1918, CZA, Z3/850; Palestine Office, Vienna, to ZCO, 12 Jan. 1919, CZA, Z3/851; Stein, *Auf dem Wege nach Palästina*, 2–4. Although a Zionist body, the Palestine Office also received financial support from the Viennese branches of B'nai B'rith and the American Joint Distribution Committee.

[72] Mendelsohn, *Zionism in Poland*, 111–12; Harriet Pass Freidenreich, *The Jews of Yugoslavia: A Quest for Community* (Philadelphia, 1979), 161; Rabinowicz, 'Czechoslovak Zionism', 36.

and bank, developed a comprehensive 'propaganda and information' network, and organized professional and agricultural training geared to facilitate absorption in Palestine.[73] The World Zionist Organization was at this
point endeavouring to restrict emigration to Palestine to an élite of the 'productive' and well-prepared. This was necessary, so the Zionist organization
reasoned, in order to avoid antagonizing the new British authorities there
and because the Zionists themselves believed that the land was too resource-
poor and undeveloped to cope with a mass influx of poor and unskilled
immigrants.[74] The Vienna Palestine Office acted in accord with the policy of
its parent body by stressing the need for patience and thorough preparation.
Organizing the potential emigrants in time-consuming preparations for
aliyah was in effect a delaying tactic designed to forestall their precipitate
departure.[75] It was seen precisely in this light by a number of disgruntled
activists, who set up an Aliyah Committee to subvert the intentions of the
Palestine Office and provide practical assistance to those hoping to emigrate.
The Aliyah Committee functioned as an alternative Palestine Office; its aim,
however, was to facilitate emigration rather than to act as a brake on it.[76]

From among the same circles came moves to form a Viennese branch of
Hapo'el Hatsa'ir (The Young Worker), a non-Marxist workers' organization
based in Palestine. The idea was first broached in late December 1918 by
Eugen Höflich, who sought moral support from Hapo'el Hatsa'ir leader
Chaim Arlosoroff in Berlin. He was assisted locally by Robert Weiss, editor of
the youth movement's newsletter *Blätter aus der jüdischen Jugendbewegung*,
who in September 1917 had himself attempted to form a Jewish socialist
youth group.[77] Active by March 1919, the Vienna Hapo'el Hatsa'ir initially
lacked clear ideological direction, providing a home for a cross-section of
Palestinianists, general Zionists, and Hebraists. Its founders included the

---

[73] See Stein, *Auf dem Wege nach Palästina*, 6–32.

[74] Mendelsohn, *Zionism in Poland*, 111–20.

[75] Stein, *Auf dem Wege nach Palästina*, 22–3; Jewish National Fund, Vienna, to Jewish
National Fund Central Office, The Hague, 5 Dec. 1918, CZA, L6/371; Palestine Office, Vienna,
to Copenhagen Zionist Office, 31 Jan. 1919, CZA, L6/88. For one would-be emigrant's
encounter with the Vienna Palestine Office, see Moshe Shoshani, 'Group 105', in Yehuda Erez
(ed.), *The Third Aliyah Book* (Heb.) (Tel Aviv, 1964), 117–18.

[76] Among the Aliyah Committee's founders were Adolf Böhm, who now found himself in disagreement with his colleagues in the Palestine Office. See Henisch, *At Home and Abroad*, 173–4,
305.

[77] Chaim Arlosoroff to Höflich, 11 Jan. 1919, CZA, A197/3. Arlosoroff wrote that Bernfeld
had also indicated interest in the group. Weiss's group was to be called the Jüdische-Sozialistische
Vereinigung Junger Juden (Jewish Socialist Alliance of Young Jews). In a flyer announcing its formation, radicalism was rejected in favour of 'sensitivity to social issues'. See CZA, A383/60.

new Hashomer leader in Vienna, Meir Wald (Ya'ari), the writer Abraham Schwadron, and Robert Weltsch. Along with a pronounced emphasis on Hebrew language and culture, it developed in time a slightly more activist and *aliyah*-oriented agenda but remained primarily a forum for discussion and lectures.[78] The activist impulse of those involved with Hapo'el Hatsa'ir found an outlet with the emergence of a reinvigorated *hakhsharah* movement and the Pioneer (Hehaluts) groups that were established to co-ordinate it in the winter of 1918–19.[79] The Pioneer—at this time in east central Europe a moderately popular, left-leaning youth organization devoted to agricultural and physical training in preparation for *aliyah*—attained a modicum of short-lived popularity in Vienna. By April 1919 some 200 mostly east European pioneers were engaged in intensive agricultural training in and near the city, often living, working, and studying together.[80] In August 1919 the Viennese Pioneer claimed 400 members and a small library; by the end of 1920, however, some 180 of the most active members had left for Palestine, leaving the local pioneers bereft of leadership.[81]

The role of Hashomer in this wave of fervour for Palestine was surprisingly limited. Its Vienna branch was by now a pale reflection of its dynamic wartime incarnation. While it retained a sizeable membership (estimates range from 400 to 700), its adherents were older and more diverse in socioeconomic status, and were drawn mostly from the local, rather than the refugee, population. The repatriation of the bulk of the Galician refugees led to the loss of the Vienna group's most prominent leaders, as well as much of its rank and file. Somewhat isolated from the movement's Galician

[78] *JZ*, 14 Mar. 1919, p. 5; Henisch, *At Home and Abroad*, 172–3; Robert Weiss, 'Jugendbewegung und Hapoel Hazair', *JJ*, 20 May 1919, pp. 119–25; Eugen Höflich, 'Der Volkssozialismus des Hapoel Hazair', *JJ*, 1 Apr. 1919, pp. 45–7.

[79] As already noted, a *hakhsharah* movement first took shape in Vienna in early 1918, when both Simon Federbusch (later a prominent rabbi, writer, Polish parliamentarian, and Mizrahi leader) and Hashomer had called for a Pioneer movement in Austria. On the Pioneer, see *OW*, 8 Feb. 1918, p. 89; *JZ*, 22 Feb. 1918, p. 3; 26 Apr. 1918, pp. 3–4. See also *JZ*, 13 Dec. 1918, p. 7; 20 Dec. 1918, p. 8; 3 Jan. 1919, p. 4; 24 Jan. 1919, p. 5; 31 Jan. 1919, p. 6; *BJJ* (Nov.–Dec. 1918), 1–3, 9. A detailed circular on *hakhsharah* plans, dated 13 Feb. 1919, is in CZA, A130/70.

[80] Palestine Office, Vienna, to ZCO, 17 Mar. 1919, CZA, Z3/852; Egon Zweig, 'Von unseren Chaluzim', *JJ*, 1 Apr. 1919, pp. 48–50. See also 'Die Landarbeiterschaft', *JJ*, 15 Mar. 1919, pp. 38–9; Emanuel Fiscus, 'Aus dem Tagebuch eines Wiener Chaluz', *JJ*, 15 Apr. 1919, pp. 76–8; Stein, *Auf dem Wege nach Palästina*, 26–30. On the Pioneer movement more generally, see Mendelsohn, *Zionism in Poland*, 120–30.

[81] See *JZ*, 29 Aug. 1919, pp. 3–4; *Baderekh*, 1 (31 Dec. 1920), 36–7. *Baderekh* ('On the Path') succeeded the Pioneer's monthly *Ha'avodah* ('Labour'), which was edited by Chaim Tartakower (a founding member of Hapo'el Hatsa'ir) and published from Apr. to Nov. 1920. See Henisch, *At Home and Abroad*, 173.

centre, the group was to a large degree held together by the strong leadership of Meir Ya'ari, a Galician who arrived in Vienna as a refugee early in
the war, spent over two years in the Austrian army, and then returned to the
city at the war's end. Upon his departure for Palestine in early 1920, the
Viennese Hashomer subsided into inactivity.[82]

Despite some overlap in personnel between these Palestine-centred
groups—the Palestine Office, the Aliyah Committee, Hapo'el Hatsa'ir, the
Pioneer, Hashomer—and Bernfeld's Federation, the relationship between
them was tenuous at best. (Robert Weiss, for example, played a central role
in both the Federation and Hapo'el Hatsa'ir.) In the first six months of 1919
national-minded Jewish youth in Vienna operated on two distinct but related tracks, whose divergent orientations reflected a common internal Zionist
divide: while the first directed its energies towards a future in Palestine, the
second concentrated on local conditions in the here and now.

Galvanized by an influx of demobilized soldiers, the local movement
flourished, consisting now of Bernfeld's Federation, which had merged (in
reality if not in name) with the Central Office in Vienna, and a large and
fractious student organization, formed in February 1919.[83] But just as in
the months following the *Jugendtag* internal frictions had hindered further
expansion, so too now renewed bickering between the rival ideological poles
of Bernfeld–Weltsch and Margulies proved debilitating. Their conflict was
part of the continuing battle between the Weltsch and Stricker camps for
control of Viennese Zionism. In a time of economic collapse communal
resources were limited, and the youth movement was dependent for its viability on the generosity of the Zionist organization. Here, Bernfeld maintained his foothold as co-ordinator of youth affairs, but found himself in
constant confrontation with Stricker and Margulies.

The movement's most incisive internal critic from the Buber camp was
Robert Weiss. To Weiss, the Zionist organization was a 'graveyard' for youth,

[82] See Mintz, *Pangs of Youth*, ch. 14; Chizik, *The Unification of Hashomer and Tse'irei Zion*,
88–90; Nahir, *The Story of the Viennese Troop*, 19–20; David Zayit and Yosef Shamir (eds.), *Portrait of a Leader as a Young Man: Meir Ya'ari, Chapters from Life 1897–1929* (Heb.) (Givat
Havivah, 1992), 35–40. The Vienna group reappeared in a different guise a few years later.

[83] On the Central Office at this stage, see *OW*, 17 Jan. 1919, pp. 41–2; *JZ*, 17 Jan. 1919, p. 7;
JJ, 1 Mar. 1919, p. 21; 15 Mar. 1919, pp. 39–40; Seewann, *Zirkel und Zionsstern*, i. 252; ii. 328.
On the students, see *JZ*, 31 Jan. 1919, p. 4; 28 Feb. 1919, pp. 2–3; *OW*, 28 Feb. 1919, p. 139;
Heinrich Margulies in 'Aus der Jugendbewegung', *JJ*, 1 Mar. 1919, pp. 16–17; A. Freud, 'Zum
jüdischen Studententag', *JJ*, 15 Mar. 1919, pp. 27–30. Estimates of Jewish tertiary student num-
bers in Mar. and Apr. 1919 ranged from 2,000 to 4,800. See *JZ*, 4 Apr. 1919, p. 5; Jüdischer
Nationalrat Bukowina to Nathan Birnbaum, 20 Mar. 1919, CZA, A188, CM 179/8/172.

where 'idealist' and 'Kulturzionist' were terms of abuse, where squabbles, superficiality, and an obsession with joining clubs and associations were the order of the day.[84] The situation was little better outside the Zionist movement. The majority of Viennese Jewish youth came from assimilated families where *Judentum* was seen as repulsive and contemptible; they were raised as 'Jewish antisemites', alienated from all forms of Jewish life. Outmoded liberalism with its devotion to *Deutschtum* was no longer viable for a new Jewish generation. Echoing Buber, Weiss declared that youth's greatest wish was to be 'authentically' Jewish: 'a truly Jewish life is more necessary for the welfare of Jewish youth than food, drink, and shelter'. And while such a life was only possible in Palestine, one could at least begin the process in Europe.[85] The instrument for this transformation was the youth movement. Unfortunately, though, it had proved unequal to the task. After the peak of the *Jugendtag*, wrote Weiss, the movement had fallen into 'decay' and 'stagnation'. Despite impressive membership statistics, it was disorganized and factionalized, its work 'dilettantish and unsystematic'. Idealism was all very well, but if not harnessed to action it degenerated into 'sterility'. 'Action' in this context for Weiss meant *aliyah*. In sum, he lamented, 'Nothing has happened in Vienna which can with justification bear the name "Jewish youth movement".' Reflecting on the year's events, he remarked on 'the rise of a harrowing sensation of terrible emptiness'.[86]

Weiss, for all the hyperbole of his indictment and the utopian nature of his demands and expectations, was not alone in his dissatisfaction. In fact, its leading activists concurred, the movement was in a state of disarray, unable to turn to its advantage the considerable ferment among Jewish youth.[87] Moreover, the Zionist leadership, all agreed, was antipathetic, providing the movement with only negligible material support.[88] Within the Zionist organization, Margulies now enjoyed the decisive support of Robert Stricker, whose election to the new Austrian parliament in February

---

[84] *JZ*, 11 Apr. 1919, p. 2. Weiss wrote of *Gezänke*, *Tanzkränzchenseligkeit*, and *Vereinsmeiertum*.

[85] *OW*, 30 May 1919, pp. 330–2.

[86] Robert Weiss, 'Jugendbewegung?', *JJ*, 1 Apr. 1919, pp. 41–3; id., 'Jugendbewegung und Hapoel Hazair', *JJ*, 20 May 1919, pp. 119–25.

[87] Margulies, for example, complained of widespread apathy. See his 'Der zionistische Parteitag', *JJ*, 15 Apr. 1919, pp. 80–2. See also Freud, 'Zum jüdischen Studententag'; and Robert Weltsch's criticism in *JZ*, 4 July 1919, p. 2. Many student groups remained aloof, while Hashomer opted out altogether. See *JZ*, 25 July 1919, p. 4; Weiss, 'Jugendbewegung?', 42.

[88] The reasons for this, however, were disputed, with Margulies and his opponents engaging in mutual recriminations. See the polemics in 'Aus der Bewegung', *JJ*, 15 Apr. 1919, n.p., 80–2;

1919 made him all but unassailable in the party. This odd alliance between the convinced socialist Margulies and the more conservative Stricker made tactical sense: they shared a strong conviction that political activism was a Zionist's paramount duty. For his part, Bernfeld rejected Margulies's contention that Zionist youth was too concerned with 'spiritual' matters, objecting also to the notion that youth should be educated to 'party Zionism'. While he admitted that 'part of the youth movement (and by no means the worst part) is hostile or ambivalent' to the Zionist organization, the distrust was mutual. Whereas many in the youth movement considered themselves socialists, the Zionist organization was thoroughly bourgeois-democratic and anti-socialist, even if some of its leading personalities happened to consider themselves socialists. And, said Bernfeld, youth indeed ought to keep its distance from the 'senseless meddling and parochialism' of party politics: its 'right and mission is to sacrifice itself for an idea . . . to place itself completely in the service of its *Volk*'. Youth was unstable and unruly and therefore needed guidance, but the Zionist organization was not the appropriate instrument to provide that guidance.[89]

If party politics was anathema to Bernfeld, for Margulies the party was a microcosm of a Jewish 'society' in the process of creation. It offered youth a home, an identity, and a future. Youth, he declared, 'must be politicized'. By this, he understood that 'one must bring our youth to the realization that it must not stand aside from the party, removed from politics, occupied solely with itself, but rather must consider its primary mission to be entrance into society, i.e. the party, and activity (whether in a bourgeois or socialist sense) within it'. Bernfeld and Weiss's *Kulturzionismus* remained merely 'a chaos of nebulous mysticism'; their *Geistigkeit* had degenerated into separation from, and renunciation of, 'reality'. The pernicious influence of such ideas, complained Margulies, was the 'ruin' of Viennese Jewish youth. The rejection of Europe and the concomitant utopian obsession with Palestine were not, as Bernfeld would have it, revolutionary self-recreation but a sign of 'other-worldly' nihilism and '*ressentiment*' of the sort that 'drives weak and impotent men to the monastery' (i.e. away from

---

1 May 1919, n.p.; *JZ*, 11 Apr. 1919, p. 2. In mid-May, citing the Central Office's 'desperate' financial straits, Bernfeld proposed an indefinite suspension of all its activities and withdrew 'temporarily' from any participation in the organization, pleading too many other commitments. It was decided, rather than suspending the Central Office, to attempt to revive it from its 'desolate' state. See *JJ*, 20 May 1919, p. 142.

[89] *JZ*, 9 May 1919, pp. 3–4.

political engagement).[90] Bernfeld and Margulies agreed, then, that youth needed above all guidance and a spiritual 'home'. But they were diametrically opposed in their conception of what that home should be and who should provide the guidance. For Bernfeld, it was the youth movement itself, an autonomous entity guided by experienced and enlightened educators, and unsullied by the mundane world of party politics. For Margulies, the home should be the party, a microcosm of a future autonomous Jewish society in either Europe or Palestine, guided by unapologetically political principles but not, he stressed, to the exclusion of *Geist*.

Matters came to a head in June 1919, when Bernfeld, strongly backed by Weltsch, requested further financial support for youth work from the Zionist organization. His appeal fell on deaf ears.[91] To the Strickerite pragmatists who now held the upper hand, the Zionist movement should have no further truck with 'a youth movement founded on a superabundance of puberty', in which the ideas of Nietzsche and Wyneken outweighed those of Jewish thinkers. The movement, they charged, had been hijacked: 'It is one of the deplorable consequences of the war that . . . while the old comrades were at the front, new members with quite different [ideological] orientations took over the youth movement.' This was in fact the crux of the Zionist leadership's objections to Bernfeld and, as one critic expressed it, 'his fifty followers'.[92] This decisive rejection made it clear to Bernfeld that he could expect neither support nor co-operation from Zionist sources. He quickly resigned his post in the Zionist leadership, and turned his full attention to the orphanage project Kinderheim Baumgarten, which opened

[90] *JZ*, 16 May 1919, pp. 3–4. See also Heinrich Margulies, 'Kritik am Deutschtum', *JJ*, 15 Mar. 1919, pp. 23–7; id., 'Bernfeld und Arlosoroff', *JJ*, 20 May 1919, pp. 111–16. For comments highly critical of Margulies, see Rudolf Glanz, 'Unsere Stellung am Parteitage', *JJ*, 1 May 1919, n.p. See also the article by Robert Weiss, *JZ*, 11 Apr. 1919, p. 2.

[91] See *JZ*, 26 June 1919, p. 6; 11 July 1919, p. 7. For Weltsch's criticism of Margulies's 'Prussian educational methods', 'sterile nationalist abstractions', and 'nationalist chauvinism', see *JZ*, 4 July 1919, pp. 2–3. Margulies responded in kind in *JZ*, 1 Aug. 1919, pp. 4–5, blasting Weltsch's 'ethical pathos and conceptual muddle'.

[92] *JZ*, 25 July 1919, pp. 4–5. See *JZ*, 22 Aug. 1919, p. 6, for the Central Office's indignant response, demanding 'satisfaction' for the insults it had suffered. Bernfeld agreed that the wartime movement was the creation of 'new and revolutionary' elements who had taken the place of those drafted. See his 'Jugendbewegung'. See also *JZ*, 31 Oct. 1919, pp. 4–5, where Blau-Weiss founder Isidor Klaber complains of the 'outside' influences—such as the German youth movements—that had penetrated Blau-Weiss during the war as a result of the absence at the front of the regular leaders. He, for example, had spent the entire war away from Vienna. See Kalisch and Stein, *Blau-Weiss Austria*, 11–12.

in October.[93] Bernfeld's withdrawal represented a significant victory for Stricker's camp. Writing some months later, Robert Weltsch commented that this 'wretched dispute, that for half a year filled Viennese Zionist party life, led to Bernfeld's resignation', thereby rendering Viennese Jewish youth leaderless.[94]

By the summer of 1919 Bernfeld's youth movement no longer existed in any recognizable form. The loose coalition of forces united in his Federation had dissolved: Margulies was now responsible for Zionist youth affairs; the journals had ceased publication in late May due to lack of funds; Po'alei Zion had severed its tenuous links with the 'bourgeois liars' of the Central Office and student groups in June; Hashomer and Blau-Weiss had already turned away. The 'old guard' had returned from the war and reentered the movement, decisively altering its political and ideological make-up.[95] Politics, as conceived by Margulies and Stricker, had triumphed over *Geist*. If youth was still marked by 'inner strife' and the search for guidance, wrote Margulies in December 1919, this was a reflection of the 'general atmosphere of conflict and lack of direction prevailing in our public Jewish life', rather than, as was previously the case, a result of the youth movement's confused and misguided leadership.[96] With new leaders and a new direction, this was now a revamped and fundamentally different enterprise from Bernfeld's movement.

The popularity of Jewish youth movements in inter-war east central Europe has been attributed to a widespread sentiment among young Jews that they faced a crisis of almost existential proportions: a miserable present of economic impoverishment and antisemitism, and a future that afforded little in the way of hope.[97] All these ingredients were present in abundance in wartime Vienna. The war itself, of course, and the challenges it posed to the norms of civilized society were the omnipresent backdrop. For many, involvement in the youth movement offered a temporary respite from the sense of loss and uncertainty permeating daily life in these years. The

[93] *JZ*, 8 Aug. 1919, p. 6; Utley, 'Siegfried Bernfeld's Jewish Order of Youth', 361; Hoffer, 'Siegfried Bernfeld and "Jerubbaal"', 162 ff.; Bernfeld, *Kinderheim Baumgarten*, 23–9. Bernfeld resigned from the Zionist Landeskomitee, the organization's executive council.

[94] *Jüdische Rundschau*, 31 Oct. 1919, p. 596.

[95] *JZ*, 25 July 1919, p. 5; *FT*, 7 June 1919, p. 4. On the movement's restructuring following Bernfeld's departure, see *JZ*, 8 Aug. 1919, p. 4; 24 Sept. 1919, p. 10; 4 Nov. 1919, pp. 5–6.

[96] *JZ*, 12 Dec. 1919, p. 1. See also Jakob Weiner's comments in *JZ*, 19 Dec. 1919, p. 7, where he stresses the need for better organization and for strong, experienced, and pragmatic leadership.   [97] Mendelsohn, *On Modern Jewish Politics*, 120–2.

prodigious optimism and energy of the youthful activists testifies to the strength and resilience of an idealism given precious few other opportunities for release. Although relatively short-lived, the movement left an indelible imprint on many who took part in it by virtue of the intensity of their experience.[98]

Echoing the splits and feuds that sometimes vitiated the Jewish welfare effort, the youth movement found unity of purpose frustratingly elusive. It was not co-operation between nationalists, liberals, and the Orthodox that was at issue, since that was virtually non-existent; in this instance it proved impossible for the nationalists to find common ground among themselves. The movement's troubled course underscores the difficulties involved in any effort to forge unity among the disparate elements of Viennese or Austrian Jewry. Moreover, it again demonstrates that Vienna's claim to be the empire's Jewish capital was at best a half-truth. While the youth leaders considered themselves to be at the centre of an empire-wide movement, their reach was confined in practice mostly to Vienna itself. The interminable wrangling that immobilized and ultimately sank the movement was not merely indicative of youthful immaturity; it was also of a piece with the endemic divisiveness of the parent Jewish society in Vienna, and of Jewish political culture in central and eastern Europe as a whole. Conflict of this sort was, of course, not unique to Viennese or Jewish youth. The history of the German youth movement, for example, which provided so much of the impetus for its Viennese counterpart, has been summarized as one of 'splits and temporary reunions [and] . . . unending squabbles', a not inappropriate epitaph also for the Viennese movement.[99]

[98] See e.g. Sperber, *Die Wasserträger Gottes*, 22–3; Horowitz, *My Yesterday*, 43–8; Nahir, *The Story of the Viennese Troop*, 9–10; Margalit, *Hashomer Hatsa'ir*, 21–5.

[99] Laqueur, *Young Germany*, 37.

FOUR

IN PURSUIT OF UNITY

BOTH the welfare effort and the youth movement suffered from near-debilitating discord, yet in both cases enough common ground was found to achieve a measure of success. The same cannot be said of Austrian Jewish efforts during the war to form a united front, initially by establishing a central representative body and subsequently by convening a Congress. These efforts were a response, on the one hand, to uncertainties about Jewish status should the empire undergo structural reform and, on the other, to increasingly threatening antisemitism. Underlying the drive for unity was a widely felt desire to project a Jewish voice in the public debates on these issues. The conflicts engendered by these ideas derived from disagreements over fundamental questions of identity. Were the Jews a religious community only or were they to be considered one of the empire's constituent nations? Or were they perhaps both, with western Jews 'Austrians of the Mosaic faith' and eastern Jews a distinct nation? To what degree, if at all, could it be admitted that uniquely Jewish interests existed in Austria? These were, of course, not new questions for Austrian Jews, but the turmoil generated by the war brought them into sharper focus and demanded a renewed reckoning.

THE GEMEINDEBUND

While the existence of *Kultusgemeinden* was provisionally mandated in 1852 and given further legal definition with full Jewish emancipation in 1867, only in 1890 did the government formally regulate the legal status of Jewish communities in Austria.[1] Following the promise of emancipation in the short-lived March 1849 constitution (a by-product of the 1848 Revolution), Austrian Jews attempted periodically to set up regional representative bodies. In 1850, for example, the government suggested the formation

---

[1] See Lohrmann, 'Die rechtliche Lage der Juden in Wien'; Wistrich, *The Jews of Vienna in the Age of Franz Joseph*, 43, 88–9, 108.

of an organization to represent Bohemian Jews, as did the Bohemian communities themselves in 1862. Both attempts failed due to disagreements between rabbis and lay representatives over the aims and scope of such a body.[2] Similar plans were mooted in Galicia in the 1870s, while in 1885 the authorities considered a plan to establish a consistory system on the French model.[3] Nothing, however, came of these efforts.

The first concrete step towards establishing an Austria-wide relationship between communities came in December 1898 with the creation of the Allgemeiner Österreichische-Israelitischer Bund. Instigated by the Vienna Gemeinde, with Alfred Stern as the prime mover, the Gemeindebund (as it was initially known) was conceived of as a form of 'super-Gemeinde', coordinating collective defence against antisemitism and dealing with administrative, educational, and welfare matters that would overtax the resources of any individual community. It was to be a liaison between government and Jews, aspiring to official recognition from both sides as Austrian Jewry's representative institution. All this, though, would be within strictly circumscribed limits. The treatment of religious and political issues was explicitly proscribed, reflecting not only the objections of many communities to any infringement of their autonomy but also the reluctance of Orthodox groups to co-operate with non-Orthodox and lay leaders, whom they perceived as a threat to traditional Jewish values.[4] Orthodox separatism and the coveted autonomy of regional communities (particularly in Galicia) remained serious obstacles to Austrian Jewish unity.[5]

[2] Memorandum of 27 Nov. 1915 from Verband der Schlesischen israelitischen Kultusgemeinden to the Ministerium für Kultus und Unterricht, CAHJP, AW, 2805/16/149a (hereafter Silesian Memorandum); Rudolf M. Wlaschek, *Juden in Böhmen* (Munich, 1990), 13; Salo Baron, 'Aspects of the Jewish Communal Crisis in 1848', *Jewish Social Studies*, 14 (1952), 140–2. In 1849 and 1869 similar discussions took place in Vienna. See Protokoll über die Verhandlungen des vom 'Allgemeinen Österr. Israel. Bund' einberufenen Allgemeinen Österreichisch-Israelitischen Gemeindetages, 4 May 1909 (hereafter Gemeindetag Protokoll, May 1909), CAHJP, AW, 2805/12/135.

[3] On Galicia, see Oswald Byk, *Dr. Emil Byk. Ein Lebensbild* (Vienna, 1907), 14. A member of the Lemberg Gemeinde from 1879, its president from 1898 until his death in 1906, and a member of the Polish Club in the Austrian parliament from 1891 until 1906, the anti-Zionist Byk was instrumental in these efforts. For the consistory idea, see Silesian Memorandum; *OW*, 16 Oct. 1885, pp. 1–2. Attempts at organizational unity were also in train in the Hungarian half of the monarchy in the late 1860s. See Jacob Katz, *A House Divided: Orthodoxy and Schism in Nineteenth-Century Central European Jewry* (Hanover, NH, 1998), esp. pts. 3–4.

[4] Establishing the Gemeindebund took nearly two years. Material on its formation, including its records and negotiations between the Vienna Gemeinde and the authorities, can be found in CAHJP, AW, 2805/2 and 2805/3.

[5] German Jews encountered similar problems in their efforts to form a central body at this

From the outset Galician reluctance to join presented a serious problem, although membership gradually increased from 150 communities in October 1899 to 200 at the end of 1902, reaching 'over 200' communities and sixty-four 'notables' as individual members by mid-1905.[6] The large measure of autonomy enjoyed by Galicia, particularly after 1867 in the context of the *Ausgleich* and the formation of the Dual Monarchy, had led to increased Polonization among the Jewish middle classes, most notably in urban centres.[7] By the late nineteenth century the strong Polish orientation of many Jewish leaders made them unwilling to join a Vienna-based organization. Orthodox leaders, a powerful force in Galician Jewry, were united in their rejection of co-operation with the non-Orthodox and lay leaders who dominated the Gemeindebund. Despite repeated assurances that the Gemeindebund would scrupulously respect both the autonomy of local communities and Orthodox sensibilities, Galician participation remained minimal.[8]

In its first years the Gemeindebund occupied itself with routine legal and welfare matters, and campaigns against antisemitism. Quiet diplomacy was its preferred strategy; to avoid 'misunderstandings and suspicions', discretion and tact were essential.[9] In April 1908 Gemeinde, Zionist, B'nai B'rith,

time. See Jacob Toury, 'Organizational Problems of German Jewry: Steps towards the Establishment of a Central Organization 1893–1920', *LBIYB* 13 (1968), 57–90; Marjorie Lamberti, 'The Attempt to Form a Jewish Bloc: Jewish Notables and Politics in Wilhelmian Germany', *Central European History*, 3 (1970), 73–93.

[6] There were a total of some 540–50 *Kultusgemeinden* in the Austrian half of the monarchy. By Oct. 1899 thirty Galician communities had joined, compared with fifty-two from Bohemia. See the Protocol of the Allgemeiner Österreichische-Israelitischer Bund meeting of 31 Oct. 1899, CAHJP, AW, 2805/4/73, which provides a regional breakdown of membership; Resolution of 31 Oct. 1899, CAHJP, AW, 2805/4/71; AOIB Annual Report, Dec. 1903, CAHJP, AW, 2805/8/107 (hereafter AOIB Report, 1903).

[7] Mendelsohn, *Zionism in Poland*, 17–18. See also id., 'From Assimilation to Zionism in Lvov' and 'Jewish Assimilation in Lvov'. On Galician autonomy, see Norman Davies, *God's Playground: A History of Poland* (Oxford, 1981), ii. 149–55.

[8] See AOIB Annual Report, July 1902, CAHJP, AW, 2805/7 (hereafter AOIB Report, 1902); AOIB Report, 1903, for attempts to assuage Galician anxieties. See also Wistrich, *The Jews of Vienna in the Age of Franz Joseph*, 275–6; Hödl, *Als Bettler in die Leopoldstadt*, 249–54.

[9] The provision of religious education, the establishment of a training school for rabbis, the delicate issue of Galician white-slave trade, proposed ritual slaughter taxes in Lower Austria, Galicia, and Bukovina, and the threatened razing of part of the Prague Jewish cemetery to make room for a new school building were all concerns of the Gemeindebund. Regular efforts were made both to expand the existing membership and to solicit government recognition as Austrian Jewry's representative body. See AOIB Reports, 1902 and 1903; Resolution of 31 Oct. 1899, CAHJP, AW, 2805/4/71; AOIB Circular, Feb. 1900, CAHJP, AW, 2805/5/83; Protocol of the AOIB meeting of 15 May 1905, CAHJP, AW, 2805/10/110a; Silesian Memorandum. The quotation is from AOIB Report, 1902.

and Orthodox leaders, along with Galician Reichsrat representatives—the 'élite' of Austrian Jewry, as Stern described them—joined together in a concerted effort to expand the Gemeindebund further into a truly Austria-wide umbrella body. They could not, however, arrive at a consensus on either the organization's spheres of competence or the degree to which Orthodox interests should be represented.[10] During the following year Galician communities (save for the Zionists, who were in favour of a 'democratic and progressive' organization) attempted to torpedo the project, while Stern tried to persuade government officials of its viability.[11] In May 1909 it was resolved to proceed if necessary without Galician participation. The Galicians, commented Brünn Gemeinde president Hermann Fialla, were welcome to remain mired in mass poverty and *Unkultur* but ought in future to refrain from requesting material aid from their western brethren.[12] The plan's proponents argued that it was surely in the interest of efficient administration for the state to regulate the Jewish community's corporate status, as it had already done for the empire's other religious minorities.[13]

Galician and Orthodox opposition proved effective in blocking government approval. For the next three years Stern tried in vain to overcome government reluctance to move ahead with a project that clearly did not enjoy majority support among Jews.[14] Narrowing its horizons, the Gemeindebund decided in February 1912 to form regional associations, again without the Galicians or the Orthodox, as a first step towards a larger umbrella body.

[10] See Gemeindetag Protokoll, 27–8 Apr. 1908, CAHJP, AW, 2805/11/115; Silesian Memorandum. They proposed a pyramidal structure, with individual communities forming the base, *Landesverbände* (regional associations of communities) making up the middle level, and a supreme council comprising delegates from the *Landesverbände* at the peak. This remained the model until 1918. Behind this initiative was Theodor Sonnenschein, president of the Troppau (Opava) Gemeinde in Silesia and a leader of both the Gemeindebund and B'nai B'rith.

[11] Gemeindetag Protokoll, May 1909; Stern Circular to Austrian *Kultusgemeinden*, Apr. 1909, CAHJP, AW, 2805/12.

[12] See Gemeindetag Protokoll, May 1909; Bericht und Antrag zur Schaffung einer Organisation für die Juden in Österreich, CAHJP, AW, 2805/11/119. Of some ninety delegates at the May 1909 meeting, thirty-seven were from Vienna.

[13] See the Dec. 1909 Motivenbericht zu dem Gesetzentwurfe betreffend den Ausbau der äusseren Rechtsverhältnisse der israelitischen Religions-Gesellschaft, CAHJP, AW, 2805/12/129a; Gemeindetag Protokoll, May 1909; Silesian Memorandum.

[14] Stern raised the issue with both Prime Minister Stürgkh and Kultus und Unterricht Minister Hussarek (later to be the monarchy's penultimate prime minister). See Stern to AOIB members, 4 Feb. 1912, CAHJP, AW, 2805/14/141a/12; Circular letter from Stern to *Kultusgemeinden Vorstände*, 30 Mar. 1914, CAHJP, AW, 2805/15/143 (hereafter Stern to *Vorstände*, Mar. 1914).

Even this, however, aroused protests from the Galician Orthodox (led this time by the hasidic court at Belz), who feared that establishment of these regional bodies could set a precedent for a similar organization in Galicia. By the time the war broke out, only the Silesian Federation had been officially constituted (in early 1914), although negotiations with the government over the formation of a Federation for Inner Austria—an area virtually identical with the territory of the post-war Austrian republic— were well advanced.[15]

The new circumstances brought about by the war revived Stern's determination to strive for an all-inclusive umbrella organization. He began negotiations with what he called the 'leading personalities' of Galician Jewry, now in Vienna as refugees, focusing his attention in particular on rabbinical leaders.[16] Stern's campaign received considerable support. To Heinrich Schreiber, a loyal Stern ally in Vienna, Jewish unity would prove that the Jews were equal to the demands of 'this fateful hour'.[17] Alois Kulka, editor of *Die Wahrheit*, issued a rousing call for unity, emphasizing that the Jews must organize politically to ensure that their voice be clearly heard in the coming *Völkerdämmerung*.[18] In these appeals the traditional liberal conception of collective Jewish interests was expanded beyond the confines of welfare and religion to incorporate an explicitly political agenda, in direct response to the challenges posed by the war. As Schreiber commented, 'the inspiration for this new Jewish political strategy certainly derives from the war and its experiences'.[19] In the Orthodox camp, too, Stern's proposals found qualified support. In its first issues in the summer of 1915 the *Jüdische Korrespondenz* noted that the lack of a representative

[15] On the decision to form *Landesverbände*, see the 5 Mar. 1912 Report of AOIB *Vorstand* meeting of 20 Feb. 1912, CAHJP, AW, 2809/16. Five were planned: Lower Austria and the Alpine lands (Inner Austria), Bohemia, Moravia, Silesia, and Bukovina. On Galician opposition, see the Report of the AOIB *Vorstand* meeting of 14 Apr. 1913, CAHJP, AW, 2805/14/141b/1; Stern to *Vorstände*, Mar. 1914. The authorities preferred a voluntary association of *Kultusgemeinden*. See Lower Austrian *Statthalter* to Stern, 23 Mar. 1914, CAHJP, AW, 2805/15/142; Sonnenschein to Stern, 28 Feb. 1914, CAHJP, AW, 2809/18. On the Silesian and Inner Austrian federations, see *ZBB* 19 (1916), 170; *WH*, 21 Aug. 1914, p. 6; Stern to *Vorstände*, Mar. 1914. Copies of the statutes of the proposed Inner Austrian Federation are in CAHJP, AW, 2805/15/148.

[16] See Bericht des Präsidiums, AOIB meeting of 28 Dec. 1915, CAHJP, AW, 2809/20/150.

[17] See *OW*, 16 July 1915, pp. 540–1; 23 July 1915, pp. 549–50; 6 Aug. 1915, p. 593; 20 Aug. 1915, pp. 629–30.

[18] *WH*, 17 Dec. 1915, pp. 3–5. Stern's plan was greeted, too, at the annual general meeting of the Allianz in May 1915. See *OW*, 28 May 1915, pp. 398–9.

[19] *OW*, 23 July 1915, p. 550.

organization had been felt particularly keenly during the first year of war. Such a body, said the paper, was necessary to undertake the social and economic reconstruction of Galician Jewry; it must, however, be strictly non-political, as Austrian Jewry had no separate Jewish political interests, only patriotic Austrian interests. Avoid politics and unite on a minimal programme of economic and welfare issues, counselled Jonas Kreppel.[20] Similar calls for the creation of a strong central organization to protect and represent Austrian Jewry were made frequently in the Yiddish and Zionist press.[21]

This renewed impetus to unity derived much of its urgency from resurgent antisemitism. Early on in the war it became clear that government restraints on antisemitism were limited at best—hence the appeal of a central organization to co-ordinate Jewish defence. Further, as already noted, ideas about restructuring the empire along more democratic, federal, or national lines were widespread, especially following the accession of the reform-minded emperor Karl I in November 1916. Many thought that the Jews needed a voice in this process in order to guarantee their rights, however defined.[22] While many could agree, then, that a united Jewish organization was needed, there was little or no agreement on its nature, the definition of Jewish interests, and how and by whom they should be presented.

Galician and Orthodox rejectionism continued to frustrate Stern's plans. He pressed on regardless, hoping to persuade the government to utilize the executive powers at its disposal under emergency military rule simply to summon the desired organization into existence. (As previously mentioned, parliament had been prorogued in May 1914 and the government ruled by administrative fiat under Count Stürgkh.) In this way, it would be possible to skirt the difficulties of obtaining bureaucratic and parliamentary approval, something he could not be sure would be forthcoming given the strong Galician and Orthodox opposition. In any case, Stern reasoned, when parliament resumed, it would surely have more pressing matters to attend to than a Jewish representative body. Convinced that antisemitism posed a serious

[20] *JK*, 12 Aug. 1915, p. 3; 19 Aug. 1915, p. 1; 26 Aug. 1915, p. 1; 23 Sept. 1915, pp. 1–3. Along the same lines was the booklet written by the Galician rabbi Moshe Leiter, *Between Hope and Despair* (Heb.) (Vienna, 1916), the proceeds of which the author donated to Agudes Yisroel.

[21] See e.g. *Wiener Morgen-Zaytung*, 3 Feb. 1915, p. 2; 8 Feb. 1915, p. 2; 9 Feb. 1915, p. 2; *JZ*, 5 Mar. 1915, p. 1; 12 Mar. 1915, p. 1.

[22] On the various plans for reform of the empire during the war, see Robert A. Kann, *The Multinational Empire* (New York, 1950), vol. ii, ch. 24.

threat, and anticipating post-war chaos in which the Jews would be a prime scapegoat, he believed that only an officially sanctioned organization would be capable of effective defence. Both Minister for Public Worship and Education Max von Hussarek and the new interior minister, Prince Konrad von Hohenlohe (who took office in December 1915), were prepared, so Stern reported, to consider the possibility of using their emergency powers to create the organization; they were, though, concerned about Galician opposition. Stern was prepared to forgo Galician participation, expressing the hope that in due course they would join. In accordance with his plan, the Gemeindebund decided in December 1915 to move ahead with the creation of this truncated organization.[23]

While response was generally positive, Orthodox and Galician resistance was unbending.[24] At this stage Galician reluctance was compounded by uncertainty regarding the future status of Galicia—i.e. whether it would be within the German orbit, part of Austria, or part of an independent Poland. Whatever its final disposition, it seemed increasingly likely that Galicia would be linked at the very least with Congress Poland.[25] The Zionists expressed reserved approval. For them, the proposed organization offered an opportunity for later expansion into a more nationalist-oriented body, in much the same way that they hoped to transform the *Kultusgemeinden* into *Volksgemeinden*.[26] Circumstances converged to foil Stern's plan for an

[23] Stern's reasoning is outlined in Bericht des Präsidiums, AOIB meeting of 28 Dec. 1915, CAHJP, AW, 2809/20/150. On the decision to proceed without Galicia, see Protocol of the AOIB meeting, 28 Dec. 1915, CAHJP, AW, 2805/16/150; draft letter from AOIB to Hohenlohe, 16 Jan. 1916, CAHJP, AW, 2805/17/151; Ministerium für Kultus und Unterricht to AOIB, 16 May 1916, CAHJP, AW, 2805/17/154.

[24] For response, see *OW*, 11 Aug. 1916, pp. 525–6; 22 Sept. 1916, pp. 621–3; 29 Sept. 1916, p. 639; 17 Oct. 1916, pp. 679–82; *WH*, 25 Aug. 1916, pp. 3–4; 1 Dec. 1916, pp. 5–6; *JK*, 18 Aug. 1916, pp. 1–2; *SW*, 8 Sept. 1916, pp. 1–2; *ZBB* 19 (1916), 173–4; and the material in CAHJP, AW, 2805/17.

[25] Making Galician participation even less likely was the proclamation by Germany and the Austrians in Nov. 1916 of an 'independent' Poland. See Heinz Lemke, *Allianz und Rivalität. Die Mittelmächte und Polen im ersten Weltkrieg* (Vienna, 1977), 321–73. The Orthodox attempted soon after to set up an all-party organization of Galician Jewry. See *JK*, 11 Jan. 1917, p. 1; 8 Feb. 1917, pp. 1–2; 15 Feb. 1917, p. 3. The effect of this continuing uncertainty on Galician participation in a central Austrian Jewish organization is remarked upon in *OW*, 26 Oct. 1917, p. 684. On conditions set by Galician *Kultusgemeinden*, aimed at increasing Orthodox representation and excluding the planned body from any role in religious affairs, see *OW*, 17 Nov. 1916, pp. 753–4; *JZ*, 15 Dec. 1916, p. 3.

[26] See ZCWA to ZCO, 4 Oct. 1916, CZA, Z3/845; *JZ*, 25 Aug. 1916, p. 1; 1 Sept. 1916, p. 1; *SW*, 8 Sept. 1916, pp. 2–3; Otto Abeles, 'Ein Reichsverband der österreichischen Judengemeinden', *NJM* 1 (1916–17), 294–5. Although it was hardly a priority, pre-war Zionist programmes did sometimes call for the creation of an Austria-wide Jewish organization (*Reichsverband*). See

imposed solution. Prime Minister Stürgkh, who according to Stern had been favourably disposed towards the idea, was assassinated in mid-October 1916.[27] Most importantly, any use of emergency powers was unlikely after the accession of Karl I and the reintroduction of parliamentary rule in May 1917. In light of the new political situation and the failure to achieve a Jewish consensus, it was resolved yet again to form regional associations as a first step towards a now indefinitely postponed central organization. By May 1918 these had been established in Inner Austria and Bohemia, but were still awaiting government approval when the monarchy's disintegration rendered them anachronistic.[28]

These efforts to establish a central organization in 1917–18 were subsumed in the campaign to convene a Jewish Congress, an alternative substantially different in form but similar in intent, aspiring to unite Austrian Jewry in a broad representative body.[29] Siegmund Kaznelson, who first raised the idea of an Austrian Jewish Congress and became the Congress movement's central figure, indirectly acknowledged that Stern's work had formed an important part of the immediate ideological and political background to his work. For Kaznelson, though, Stern's proposed organization was entirely inadequate for the tasks he envisaged.[30]

JZ, 25 Aug. 1916, p. 1; 12 Oct. 1917, pp. 1–3; Gaisbauer, *Davidstern und Doppeladler*, 113–14, 313, 406–7; *SW*, 8 Sept. 1916, p. 2. During the war they continued to support this idea. In Feb. 1915, for example, the Zionists considered the possibility of approaching other parties with a view to forming an all-party committee. See ZCWA to ZCO, 1 Mar. 1915, CZA, Z3/842. See also *JZ*, 3 Mar. 1916, p. 1; 5 May 1916, p. 1; 30 June 1916, p. 1; 29 June 1917, pp. 1–2.

   [27] For Stern's claim of Stürgkh's support, see *Jüdische Gemeinschaft*, 3–6 Oct. 1918, p. 1.

   [28] Protokoll der konstituierenden Sitzung des Verbands der israel. Kultusgemeinden von Niederösterreich und den Alpenländern, 7 May 1918, CAHJP, AW, 2805/19/219; Report of the 7 May 1918 meeting of representatives of western Austrian *Kultusgemeinden*, CAHJP, AW, 2805/19/238; *ZBB* 20 (1917), 80–1. See also *OW*, 26 Oct. 1917, p. 684; 21 June 1918, p. 384; *JK*, 16 May 1918, p. 11; *JZ*, 7 June 1918, p. 4. Similar bodies were set up in Bukovina and Galicia. See *JZ*, 28 Sept. 1917, p. 1; 25 Jan. 1918, p. 3; *JK*, 10 Jan. 1918, pp. 6–7. A Silesian Federation was already functioning; a Moravian Federation was formed in Nov. 1918. On the latter, see Gustav Fleischmann, 'The Religious Congregation 1918–1938', in *The Jews of Czechoslovakia*, i (Philadelphia, 1968), 270, 296–7.

   [29] The idea of a central organization received sporadic attention until the end of the war. See *OW*, 8 June 1917, pp. 356–7; 13 July 1917, pp. 437–8; 26 Oct. 1917, p. 684; 26 July 1918, pp. 458–9; 2 Aug. 1918, pp. 482–3; *JK*, 21 June 1917, p. 2; 12 July 1917, p. 1; *JZ*, 1 June 1917, pp. 2–3; 29 June 1917, pp. 1–2; Protocol of the AOIB meeting, 16 Oct. 1917, CAHJP, AW, 2805/18/210. Attempts at organizational unity in post-war Austria were plagued by similar problems of regional and Orthodox rejectionism. See Freidenreich, *Jewish Politics in Vienna*, 163–4. In Czechoslovakia the existing *Landesverbände* formed the basis for a national federation of Jewish communities.

   [30] *SW*, 15 Dec. 1916, p. 1. A Congress-like scheme had been proposed in May 1916 by

THE AUSTRIAN JEWISH CONGRESS

December 1916 – July 1917

Born in Warsaw and raised in Gablonz (Jablonec), Bohemia, Kaznelson was in his final year of law studies in Prague at the outbreak of war; during the war years he managed with only minimal assistance to edit and publish the Zionist-oriented weekly *Selbstwehr*.[31] In December 1916 Kaznelson suggested that an Austrian Jewish Congress, modelled on the American Jewish Congress movement (in which the diverse parties within American Jewry had apparently united to create a representative organization), might be a viable alternative to Stern's moribund organization. He proposed a democratically elected assembly that would decide on a minimal programme to which all Austrian Jews could subscribe, regardless of party or religious affiliation. Only a united representative body, Kaznelson believed, could provide both effective defence against antisemitism and a powerful political voice; only in this way could Austrian Jewry realize its political potential and become a 'Machtfaktor'. American Jewry, thought Kaznelson, was a potentially powerful influence in American politics because of the unity achieved by the Congress movement. If similarly united, Austrian Jewry could exert its influence in Austrian politics and perhaps even at a post-war peace conference. Kaznelson's insistence on a broad-based Congress, and on political flexibility and moderation as prerequisites for its success, remained characteristic of his approach throughout the course of the Congress movement over the next year and a half.[32]

Salomon Kassner, who later described the Congress movement as a 'continuation' of his own efforts, which found little public echo. See *JZ*, 12 May 1916, p. 1, for Kassner's unsigned article. He claims to be the author in Salomon Kassner, *Die Juden in der Bukowina* (Vienna, 1917), 40–1 n. 45. See also *SW*, 6 July 1917, pp. 2–3. Kassner, a leading Jewish activist in Czernowitz, spent the war years in Vienna. See Gaisbauer, *Davidstern und Doppeladler*, 357–8 n. 187.

[31] The editor of *Selbstwehr* since 1913, Kaznelson (1893–1959) later became editor and publisher of the Berlin periodical *Der Jude* and the *Jüdisches Lexikon*, and director of the publishing firm (first in Berlin, subsequently in Jerusalem) Jüdischer Verlag. See Robert Weltsch's introduction to *Das jüdische Prag*, pp. v–vi; Kieval, *The Making of Czech Jewry*, 126, 163–4, 170.

[32] *SW*, 15 Dec. 1916, p. 1. Writing later under the pseudonym Albrecht Hellmann, Kaznelson emphasized that the Congress initiative had been his alone. See Albrecht Hellmann, 'Erinnerungen an gemeinsame Kampfjahre', in Weltsch (ed.), *Dichter, Denker, Helfer*, 51. On the American Jewish Congress, see Jonathan Frankel, 'The Jewish Socialists and the American Jewish Congress Movement', *YIVO Annual*, 16 (1976), 202–341; Melvin I. Urofsky, *American Zionism from Herzl to the Holocaust* (New York, 1976), 153–81; Janowsky, *The Jews and Minority Rights*, 161–90.

Early in 1917 Kaznelson sent a circular to 'prominent personalities' of Austrian Jewry, requesting their response to a series of questions on a proposed Congress. Was closer co-operation and better organization necessary for Austrian Jewry and, if so, was the American Jewish Congress an appropriate model? What ought to be the tasks and programme of a Congress, and when should it be held? From March to November 1917 Kaznelson published in *Selbstwehr* the generally (but not uniformly) positive responses, representing a broad spectrum of opinion and interests in Austrian Jewish society. There was consensus that Austrian Jews were indeed faced with severe and critical problems; most often mentioned were antisemitism and Jewish status in a reformed empire. While ideas concerning the timing, scope, programme, and composition of a Congress varied, the fact that Kaznelson's proposal had elicited such broad interest was in itself encouraging. With progress towards expanding the Gemeindebund at a standstill, his timing had been auspicious.[33]

A strikingly negative response to Kaznelson's initiative came from a perhaps surprising source: his nationalist compatriots. Deriding the notion that such an important venture could be launched by a provincial newspaper, Zionist organization president Rudolf Taussig scornfully pronounced the idea stillborn, given Kaznelson's failure to consult with the Zionists in either Prague or Vienna. The damage, he declared, was 'simply irreparable'. He suggested, with Robert Stricker's support, that the Zionists instead convene their own 'people's assembly'; otherwise, Austrian Jewry's inability to unite in its own defence would be exposed for all to see.[34] Local Zionist disapproval was soon addressed by the movement's higher authorities. In June 1917 EAC member Arthur Hantke urged Taussig and Stricker to put aside their misgivings and take a leading role in the Congress. Focusing on tactics rather than principles, Hantke argued that while Kaznelson's initiative was inopportune and contrary to party discipline, the Congress was none the less a potentially important vehicle for Zionism. The Con-

[33] It was suggested that a Congress might function as an adjunct to, or preparation for, an expanded Gemeindebund. See e.g. the responses of Schwarz-Hiller, *SW*, 12 Apr. 1917, p. 2; and Simon Rendi, president of the Graz Kultusgemeinde, *SW*, 31 Aug. 1917, p. 2. Gemeindebund stalwart Theodor Sonnenschein and Siegfried Fleischer (secretary of the Union) thought unity a chimera not worth pursuing, and the democratic and public forum of a Congress unwieldy and undesirable. For Sonnenschein, see *SW*, 12 Apr. 1917, pp. 2–3; for Fleischer, *SW*, 29 June 1917, pp. 1–2. For objections to a Congress convening in wartime, see *SW*, 8 June 1917, p. 4.

[34] See Taussig to Kaznelson, 10 May 1917; ZCWA to ZCO, 11 May 1917, both in CZA, Z3/846. The 11 May letter also contains the text of a resolution expressing the party's disapproval of Kaznelson's initiative.

gress idea appeared to be gaining momentum, drawing support from the increasingly influential democratic and nationalist tendencies in Austrian society, and it was vital that the Zionist organization be identified with precisely these notions. It was therefore necessary not only to be involved with the Congress at an early stage but to take a dominant role, or else face the 'great danger' of being marginalized. The Congress movement, Hantke added, was international in scope, encompassing the United States, Russia, and Germany.[35]

As noted, it was the American Jewish Congress that was promoted as a model for emulation by those favouring a broad-based Congress. Unity among the warring American Jewish parties had been at least temporarily achieved by December 1916, when the Austrian initiative was launched. By June 1917 elections for the American Jewish Congress had produced a 'clear-cut and decisive victory for the nationalist camp'.[36] The potential political capital of an Austrian Jewish Congress thus seemed clear, notwithstanding the differences between the Austrian and American Jewish situations. The Inner Actions Committee felt the issue important enough to warrant the dispatch of an emissary to Vienna to examine the situation more closely.[37] Taussig and Stricker remained sceptical, predicting a 'fiasco'. A formal decision on a Zionist stance regarding the Congress was left to the Austrian movement's highest authority, the Executive Committee of United Austrian Zionists (of which Taussig was president). Should a pro-Congress position be adopted there, Taussig and Stricker promised, they would raise no further objections.[38]

Led by the veteran Galician activist Adolf Stand, a majority of the Executive Committee felt that a Congress was 'necessary, desirable, and feasible'. But Stricker and Taussig held fast in their opposition, arguing that non-nationalist Jewish groups would agree to a Congress only if its pro-

[35] ZCO to ZCWA, 14 June 1917, CZA, Z3/846; Hantke to Taussig and Stricker, 26 June 1917, CZA, Z3/847 (also in Z3/520).

[36] Frankel, 'The Jewish Socialists and the American Jewish Congress Movement', 271–302. See ibid. 300–2 for the June elections. The quotation is from p. 302.

[37] EAC secretary Leo Herrmann wrote to Robert Weltsch (then stationed on military duty in southern Bohemia) requesting that Weltsch spend a few days in Vienna for this purpose. See Herrmann to Weltsch, 26 June 1917, CZA, Z3/847. In early June Herrmann had appealed to Adolf Böhm to mediate between the two sides, recommending that the Zionist organization take the Congress movement in hand to avoid the potential damage of a public display of discord. See ZCO to Böhm, 5 June 1917, CZA, Z3/1003.

[38] ZCWA to ZCO, 18 June 1917, CZA, Z3/847. Hantke saw fit to remind Taussig and Stricker that passivity was not enough; if the Executive Committee adopted a positive stand, they were obliged to take an active role. See Hantke to Taussig and Stricker, 26 June 1917, CZA, Z3/847.

gramme was limited to defence against antisemitism. Politics would be rigorously excluded, and it could only damage Zionist credibility to assent to the role of junior partner in a non-political Congress, where Zionism's minority status in Austrian Jewry would be made plain. Any real cooperation, they argued, was therefore both undesirable and impractical; better by far to hold a purely nationalist gathering. Hantke, for his part, thought this inadvisable as it would be, in effect, preaching to the converted. In view of these divergent opinions, it was decided to attempt to achieve consensus by putting the issue to a wider assembly of Zionist representatives in mid-July 1917.[39]

Pro-Congress forces quickly recognized that one of the keys to the success of the Congress movement was Stricker's attitude.[40] In response to Hantke's cajoling, Stricker began to work for the Congress, though he acted characteristically with little or no regard for his nominal partners in the enterprise. He remained committed throughout to a maximal nationalist programme and was at all times prepared—indeed he preferred—to act without co-operation from non-nationalists. If a 'people's assembly' was not a viable option, he wanted to ensure that a Congress would adopt the recognition of Jewish nationality in Austria as one of its fundamental premisses, or at the very least include in its programme a demand that the government make provision for recognition of Jewish nationality in any reform of the empire. The debate at the mid-July meeting highlighted the division between the moderate and cautious approach of Kaznelson, supported by both Stand and the Prague writer and Zionist activist Max Brod, and the radical line taken by Stricker and his associates. This division was most clearly expressed in disagreements about the degree of emphasis to be placed on Jewish nationality in the Congress programme. Should acknowledgement of the existence of a Jewish nationality be required of those participating in the Congress? Should the demand for government recognition of Jewish nationality be incorporated into the Congress programme? For Stricker, these were the minimal requirements; save for Austria and Germany, he believed, all of Jewry was now 'nationalized and Zionized'. The American Jewish Congress movement represented a nationalist triumph, and even the leadership of British Jewry ('Rothschild und die Kahile in

[39] ZCWA to ZCO, 22 June 1917; ECUAZ to EAC, 28 June 1917, both in CZA, Z3/847. Some Executive Committee members felt that although a Congress posed almost insurmountable difficulties in execution, it nevertheless afforded a good opportunity for Zionist agitation and propaganda work. For Hantke's view, see Hantke to Stricker, 3 July 1917, CZA, Z3/847.

[40] See Leo Herrmann to Robert Weltsch, 26 June 1917, CZA, Z3/847.

England') had been won over to the cause. The non-nationalists, said Stricker, should not even be considered 'equal partners' in Jewish affairs. For Kaznelson, in contrast, too pronounced an emphasis on Jewish nationality at such an early stage was bound to be rejected by important groups whom he wished to draw into the Congress—for example, B'nai B'rith, the Austrian Israelite Union, the Allianz, and the *Kultusgemeinden*. Better, thought Kaznelson, to downplay the contentious national issue while the Congress movement developed; only when the basic infrastructure was in place should it be tackled.[41]

Beyond this tactical disagreement was a deeper ideological conflict regarding the nature of Jewish autonomy. Insisting on the cultural and political divide between east and west European Jews, Kaznelson envisaged a limited cultural autonomy restricted almost exclusively to the realm of education, buttressed by state recognition of the existence of a Jewish nationality. Each individual must be free to declare him- or herself a 'Jewish national' without any consequent infringement of civic equality. Nobody, however, should be forced to do so. For Jews in the Czech lands, and by implication in Vienna, political (as opposed to cultural) autonomy could lead to re-ghettoization; the introduction of national quotas (Czech, German, and Jewish) could only redound to the Jews' social and economic disadvantage, forcibly reducing their numbers in the professions and in government service. In this Kaznelson echoed, as he was fully aware, the arguments of non-Zionists.[42] To Stricker, the admission of any split between eastern and western Jewry, and the differentiation of treatment and policy that this implied, was anathema. That the Jews were an indivisible people was for him the inviolable essence of Zionism. Further, the abstract theoretical nuances that Kaznelson wished to translate into a concrete political programme were inappropriate to the harsh realities of national politics in the empire. Clear, sharply defined principles were more effective.

A compromise was eventually struck, represented by the first point of a programme—'recognition of the Jewish *Volk* and guarantee of its rights in the new Austrian constitution'—to be later presented by the nationalists as a

---

[41] Protocol of 15 July 1917 Vertrauensmännerversammlung, CZA, L6/328.

[42] Albrecht Hellmann, 'Die Geschichte der österreichisch-jüdischen Kongressbewegung', *Der Jude*, 5 (1920–1), 389–95, 634–45, 685–96; id., 'Ein jüdischer Kongress in Österreich', *Der Jude*, 2 (1917–18), 269–70. Some thirty years later Kaznelson felt much the same way, writing in 1946, 'On the whole, my scepticism regarding national autonomy and national minority rights was justified from a general as well as from the specific Jewish point of view.' See Siegmund Kaznelson, *The Palestine Problem and its Solution* (Jerusalem, 1946), 83.

basis for discussion with other parties. Stricker's concession lay in his acquiescence in the use of the (slightly) less charged term *Volk*, rather than *Nation*. Elections to the Congress were to be democratic and open to all, irrespective of party affiliation. Relying once more on the American Jewish experience, the nationalists calculated that the broader the voting participation, the stronger their representation would be. The 'masses', they hoped, were with them.[43] Kaznelson regarded his concession as a 'great sacrifice'; he would have preferred no mention of *Volk* or *Nation* at this stage, and was only persuaded to agree by the persistent mediation efforts of Max Brod. The conceptual differences between the two camps, he wrote, had merely been 'patched up'.[44] In this he was correct: point 1 of the Congress programme later became the lightning-rod for his conflict with Stricker. The remainder of the proposed programme found broad agreement: the Congress would deal with economic reconstruction of war-ravaged Jewish communities, welfare problems, emigration, and antisemitism. This was a minimal programme on which the nationalists could agree. The next step, convincing non-nationalists to accept the explicit recognition of a Jewish *Volk*, posed a problem that bothered Kaznelson enormously but Stricker not at all.

August 1917 – January 1918

Stricker's first action on the Congress front following the July meeting clearly indicated that he did not consider himself bound by the compromise achieved there. In a circular to regional Zionist organizations Stricker, Taussig, and Stand declared themselves to be provisionally in charge of Congress preparations. They substituted *Nation* for *Volk* in point 1, adding also that participation in the Congress would be contingent on acceptance in full of the proposed programme. Attracting support for the Congress in the current pro-Zionist atmosphere in Austrian Jewry, they wrote, would not be difficult.[45] Kaznelson was furious, accusing Stricker and his colleagues of a 'blatant breach' of the July compromise. The provisional Congress committee (set up following the July meeting) included himself, Brod, and the

---

[43] Protocol of 15 July 1917 Vertrauensmännerversammlung, CZA, L6/328; Hellmann, 'Erinnerungen an gemeinsame Kampfjahre', 52; id., 'Die Geschichte der österreichisch-jüdischen Kongressbewegung', 207–9.

[44] Kaznelson to Stricker, 28 Aug. 1917, CZA, Z3/215; Kaznelson to Hantke, 15 Nov. 1917, CZA, Z3/215.

[45] See e.g. Stricker etc. to Zionist District Committee for Bohemia, 15 Aug. 1917, CZA, Z3/215.

Prague Zionist leader Ludwig Singer, none of whom had been informed about the circular. Further, it had been agreed to avoid any official Zionist involvement in the Congress until the movement's success appeared more certain. Finally, the alteration of the all-important first point of the programme, along with the demand for full acceptance of the programme in this form as a prerequisite for Congress participation, not only represented a formal breach of the agreement but was also a move sure to alienate non-nationalist Jews. The Zionists, Kaznelson believed, were not strong enough to withstand concerted opposition from the *Kultusgemeinden*, the Union, B'nai B'rith, and the Allianz, who together had a better claim than the nationalists to be representative of Austrian Jewry, both internally and in the eyes of the government and the public at large. From the Zionist movement's point of view, he wrote, the Congress could help to attract support among the Jewish 'masses', but if hobbled at the outset by false radicalism it would turn instead into a deplorable fiasco, inflicting in the process a 'humiliation' on the movement. Patience and painstaking hard work were required, not empty rhetorical flourishes.[46]

During a visit to Prague and Vienna in September 1917 EAC secretary Leo Herrmann endeavoured to mediate between Kaznelson and Stricker. Raising the possibility that it might be necessary for Arthur Hantke to travel to Vienna in order to effect a settlement, Herrmann stressed that without real agreement between the two protagonists the Congress movement would fail at the outset.[47] In the event, though, only a formal settlement was achieved. As Kaznelson prepared to go to Vienna to resolve the conflict, Stricker quickly convened an Executive Committee meeting at which the July compromise was reinstated as the Congress programme. Although the main thrust of the Prague contingent's complaints was thereby neutralized, Stricker made clear to Herrmann that he felt no regret about his action: he did not 'trust' the Prague tactics. Taussig, meanwhile, was scornful of the 'paranoia' of the Prague Zionists, blithely dismissing the breach of compromise as 'changes that the Executive Committee considered necessary'. He paid little heed to Hantke's repeated pleas to take an active role

---

[46] Kaznelson to ECUAZ and Jüdische Nationalverein, 29 Aug. 1917, CZA, Z3/215.

[47] For Herrmann's comments, see Herrmann to ZCO, 9 and 20 Sept. 1917, both in CZA, Z3/1693. Stand, Adolf Böhm, and Herrmann all agreed that Stricker was in the wrong, but were reluctant to oppose him openly. Herrmann considered Stand 'intellectually inferior to Stricker' and 'lacking in political insight', while Böhm considered himself 'not enough of a politician' to oppose Stricker. See Herrmann to ZCO, 20 and 28 Sept. 1917, both in CZA, Z3/1693.

in the Congress movement, remaining dubious about the whole project.[48] The legacy of this episode was Kaznelson's lingering mistrust of Stricker. Over and above personal differences, their conflict also reflected ideological and regional fault lines in Austrian Zionism: on the one hand, Viennese political intransigence and a commitment to strong central control of the movement; on the other, the by and large more moderate and flexible Zionists of the Czech lands, strongly resistant to Viennese centralism and always aware of their delicate position between Czechs and Germans.[49]

From the perspective of the EAC, the Congress movement in Austria was potentially a rich source of Zionist support, an important link in a movement now embracing the United States, Russia, Austria, Poland, Germany, and Switzerland.[50] Herrmann and Hantke feared, however, that the Austrian Zionists would be unable to cope with the demands of a successful Congress. Stressing Vienna's future role as a post-war Zionist centre for central and eastern Europe, Hantke wrote that Austrian Zionism must 'draw in new forces' to take advantage of the favourable circumstances for Zionist work.[51] The EAC attitude was illustrated by its support for German Zionist involvement in the Congress-like body set up by German Jewish organizations in January 1918, the Union of German Jewish Organizations for the Protection of the Rights of the Jews of the East. Responding to Viennese criticism, led by Stricker, that the Zionists would gain nothing by joining this apolitical, non-nationalist body, Hantke argued that as the organization was a *fait accompli*, it was surely better for the Zionists to participate than to face the danger of irrelevancy outside its ranks.

[48] Hantke to Taussig, 16 Sept. 1917, CZA, Z3/847; Taussig to Hantke, 24 Sept. 1917, CZA, Z3/215. For Stricker's comments to Herrmann, see Herrmann to ZCO, 20 Sept. 1917, CZA, Z3/1693.

[49] In the Congress movement Galician and Bukovinian Zionists generally supported Stricker but rejected Viennese centralism. See Kaznelson's introductory remarks to his series of articles (Hellmann), 'Die Geschichte der österreichisch-judischen Kongressbewegung'; Albrecht Hellmann, 'Nationale Minderheitsrechte der Juden', *Der Jude*, 4 (1919–20), 482; id., 'Erinnerungen an gemeinsame Kampfjahre', 52–3.

[50] Herrmann wrote that the Congress was potentially of 'enormous significance' for Austrian Zionism. See Herrmann to ZCO, 28 Sept. 1917, CZA, Z3/1693. See also Hantke to Taussig and Stricker, 16 Sept. 1917, CZA, Z3/215. On Congress plans in other countries, see Janowsky, *The Jews and Minority Rights*, 192–4, 199; Mordechai Altshuler, 'The Attempt to Organize an All-Jewish Conference in Russia after the Revolution' (Heb.), *He'avar*, 12 (1965), 75–89; Zvi Y. Gitelman, *Jewish Nationality and Soviet Politics: The Jewish Sections of the CPSU 1917–1930* (Princeton, 1972), 77–80; Mendelsohn, *Zionism in Poland*, 62; Herrmann to ZCO, 20 Sept. 1917, CZA, Z3/1693; *JZ*, 7 Sept. 1917, p. 4; 30 Nov. 1917, p. 1.

[51] Hantke to Taussig, 24 Oct. 1917; Hantke to Kaznelson, 27 Nov. 1917, both in CZA, Z3/215; Herrmann to ZCO, 28 Sept. 1917, CZA, Z3/1693.

The Austrian Congress, thought Hantke, offered even greater opportunities than the new German organization.[52]

Kaznelson now set to work on establishing as wide a base of support as possible prior to the convening of the Congress Committee in Vienna, at which a definitive programme would be determined. At this stage he and Stricker worked for the most part separately, with Kaznelson active in Prague and Stricker (much less intensively) in Vienna. Kaznelson planned to relocate to Vienna once the movement had gained momentum, at which point the Congress Committee could begin its deliberations in earnest. His move, however, was delayed by difficulties in obtaining permission to settle in the capital. Without at least the nominal protection afforded by legal residence in Vienna, Kaznelson was reluctant to take a public role in a movement that might well involve him in disagreements with the authorities.[53]

Kaznelson's most visible success in this period reflected the disparity between his and Stricker's respective conceptions of a Congress. At a meeting in Prague in November 1917, attended by some fifty of the 'leading Jewish personalities of the city', the Congress idea, Kaznelson wrote to Hantke, was 'unanimously and enthusiastically' greeted. There was much opposition, however, to the wording of the first point of the July programme—the subject of Kaznelson's strife with Stricker. Objections to the phrase 'recognition of the rights of the Jewish *Volk*' came not only from non-nationalists but also from Bohemian Zionists, whose leader, Ludwig Singer, commented that such a demand was inappropriate for Bohemian ('western') Jews. In order to win the meeting's declaration of support, Kaznelson jettisoned his own compromise formula from July, substituting for 'recognition of the rights of the Jewish *Volk*' the somewhat less provocative 'the question of recognition of the rights of the Jewish *Volk*'. Kaznelson anticipated a furious reaction from Stricker, but his rival maintained an indifferent silence, apparently paying little attention to Kaznelson's efforts in Prague.[54] It was Hantke who reprimanded him, insisting that Zionist interests could be served only if the Congress programme included an

[52] See Hantke to Stricker, 14 Dec. 1917; Hantke to Kaznelson, 20 Dec. 1917; Hantke and Herrmann to Zionist Office, Vienna, 28 Jan. 1918; Hantke to ECUAZ, 14 Feb. 1918, all in CZA, Z3/215. For Austrian Zionist criticism, see Kaznelson to Hantke, 4 Feb. 1918, CZA, Z3/215; ZCWA to ZCO, 19 Feb. 1918, CZA, Z3/848; *JZ*, 22 Feb. 1918, p. 3. On the Vereinigung jüdischer Organisationen Deutschlands zur Wahrung der Rechte der Juden des Ostens, see Toury, 'Organizational Problems of German Jewry', 81–4.

[53] Kaznelson to Hantke, 17 Nov. 1917, CZA, Z3/215.

[54] This was certainly Kaznelson's impression. See Kaznelson to Hantke, 5 Dec. 1917, CZA, Z3/215.

explicit recognition of the existence of Jewish nationality. Kaznelson, in defence, responded that all such 'agreements' were in any case provisional and non-binding, as only the not-yet-functioning Congress Committee could make Congress policy.[55]

Stricker was also active in the latter half of 1917 on behalf of the Congress, although for him this was merely one of his many activities rather than (as for Kaznelson) the almost exclusive focus of his work. At a meeting in October, for example, he was successful in inducing Vienna Gemeinde employees to declare their support for the Congress. In early November he spoke out strongly for the Congress at a Prague Zionist meeting. On both these occasions Stricker maintained his uncompromising stance on the national issue. The Congress must be a powerful *Volksorganisation*, he proclaimed, whose task was to bring about the recognition of a Jewish *Volk* in Austria.[56] In a newspaper article in January 1918 Stricker attacked in the sharpest terms those who purported to be Jewish leaders but had attained their positions only by dint of their fawning, greed, and wealth, profiting handsomely from the '*Protektions- und Schutzjuden* system'. They served foreign masters and therefore had no place in a Congress that must serve only the Jewish cause.[57] Such stridency, which seemed designed to subvert any possible co-operation across party lines, was the antithesis of Kaznelson's careful bridge-building. Stricker also held crucial discussions in the summer of 1917 with Alfred Stern, who remained non-committal: if over the next few months the Congress appeared likely to succeed, he would consider giving it his backing. The pro-Congress forces were thus spared the formidable Stern's active opposition, at least temporarily.[58]

Echoing Stricker's hard line but unconstrained by any agreements or compromises, Po'alei Zion—the 'spearhead' of the American Congress movement—was vehement in its advocacy of a national and democratic Congress, unfettered and unsullied by the participation of the 'plutocratic assimilationists'. The Jews of Austria, wrote Max Rosenfeld (the chief theoretician of Austrian Po'alei Zion), were disorganized, isolated, and

[55] Kaznelson to Hantke, 15 Nov. and 5 Dec. 1917; Hantke to Kaznelson, 27 Nov. 1917, all in CZA, Z3/215. These tensions were further discussed in a series of joint meetings of the Executive Committee and the Zionist Central Committee for Western Austria in late 1917 and early 1918, with no concrete results. See *JZ*, 30 Nov. 1917, p. 4; 14 Dec. 1917, p. 4; 25 Jan. 1918, p. 4.

[56] *JZ*, 9 Nov. 1917, p. 3; *OW*, 16 Nov. 1917, p. 726; Taussig to Hantke, 24 Sept. 1917, CZA, Z3/215.   [57] *JZ*, 18 Jan. 1918, p. 1.

[58] Herrmann to ZCO, 28 Sept. 1917, CZA, Z3/1693; Hellmann, 'Die Geschichte der österreichisch-jüdischen Kongressbewegung', 209.

defenceless, devoid of allies; a nationalist-led Congress movement would wake the masses from their lethargy. Unlike in the United States, where co-operation with the 'money and assimilationist Jews' had proven useful and necessary, in Austria such a partnership was neither possible nor desirable. The Jewish leadership, claimed Po'alei Zion, had corrupted the greater part of Austrian Jewry, reducing it to a state of political and moral degrada-tion. It was rumoured that the bourgeois Zionist leaders were negotiating in secret with this leadership—even with Rothschild! A Congress, how-ever, must represent the Jewish 'masses' or it would be of no value whatso-ever. Its focus should be on internal Austrian Jewish affairs: lobbying for Jewish rights in a reformed empire, the democratization of Jewish institu-tional life, and promotion of the economic and social reconstruction of war-devastated Galician Jewry. Matters of international import such as Palestine or emigration were to be left to other branches of the Congress movement, primarily the American Jewish Congress. In contrast to its leading role in the American movement, Po'alei Zion was at best a marginal player in Austria, its activity confined in the main to relentless and unre-strained criticism, which went mostly unheeded.[59]

Indications of a willingness to explore the Congress idea came from a vari-ety of sources. Kaznelson managed, for example, to attract the interest of a number of prominent religious personalities, including David Feuchtwang and Israel Taglicht, future chief rabbis of Vienna, and Max Grunwald (active in Palestine aid and Jewish ethnography). Further, Joseph Samuel Bloch, Armand Kaminka, secretary of the Allianz, and Salomon Ehrmann, president of B'nai B'rith, all expressed a degree of support.[60] From Kaznel-son's point of view, Allianz and B'nai B'rith backing was invaluable, as both represented an Austria-wide, non-nationalist constituency with strong links to both government and influential Jewish circles. Some in the Orthodox camp also expressed interest, proposing a compromise Congress pro-gramme between the 'nationalist' and 'assimilationist' positions. That the Jews constituted a *Volk* (a concept that the Orthodox tied to religion and

---

[59] *YA*, 15 July 1917, pp. 8–10; Sept.–Oct. 1917, pp. 11–12. On the Po'alei Zion role in the American movement, see Frankel, 'The Jewish Socialists and the American Jewish Congress Movement', 208. More generally on the Po'alei Zion stance, see Leo Chasanowitsch, 'Der jüd-ische Kongress', *Der Jude*, 2 (1917–18), 3–16.

[60] Herrmann to ZCO, 28 Sept. 1917, CZA, Z3/1693. On B'nai B'rith interest, see *ZBB* 20 (1917), 162. The American B'nai B'rith maintained a scrupulous neutrality in the American Jew-ish Congress movement. See Frankel, 'The Jewish Socialists and the American Jewish Congress Movement', 227, 247.

Torah rather than modern nationalism) was a given. Gemeinde work should accordingly be expanded to incorporate the 'complete spiritual and economic interests and needs of the Jews'. By emphasizing a religious framework for Jewish demands in order to protect Jews from the 'poison' of western culture, this Orthodox programme hoped to find acceptance from 'all good Jews'.[61] Other proposals called for a Congress based on reformed and expanded *Kultusgemeinden* (but excluding women from active participation, as they would be mere 'ballast') and, conversely, a Congress from an explicitly women's perspective. Women, it was argued in this case, remained aloof from party strife and were thus able to see the larger picture.[62] The variety of these proposals indicates not only that the Congress idea was attracting a good deal of interest, but also that conceptions of what shape it ought to take diverged widely.

Outside the Jewish domain Congress activists made important contacts on the political level. Government approval would clearly be necessary to hold a Congress—the eleventh Zionist Congress in Vienna in 1913, for example, had been 'tolerated' rather than officially sanctioned by the authorities. Moreover, governmental support would provide a counterweight to the expected opposition of Galician Jewish 'assimilationists' (the same elements that had so strenuously objected to the Gemeindebund). Kaznelson also feared the spectre of a parallel Congress initiated by Galician Jewish leaders and their allies in the Polish Club of the Reichsrat. Such a Congress, which would, of course, be fervently anti-Zionist, had the potential to attract precisely those non-nationalist Jewish groups whose support he was working so assiduously to win. Kaznelson hoped that government sanction of *his* Congress could also neutralize this threat.[63] To this end, Hantke discussed the Congress idea with government officials on a visit to Vienna in November 1917, extracting expressions of support and co-operation from the Interior Ministry, the police, and, most importantly, from the Austrian foreign minister, Ottokar Czernin.[64]

Congress advocates looked to the parliamentary representatives of other national groups for further political backing. A united front of support

---

[61] *JK*, 24 Jan. 1918, pp. 1–3. See also *JK*, 10 Jan. 1918, p. 1.

[62] On the first proposal, see *WH*, 6 Sept. 1917, p. 3; 21 Sept. 1917, pp. 5–6; 16 Nov. 1917, pp. 4–5. On the second, see *OW*, 24 Aug. 1917, pp. 537–8.

[63] Kaznelson to Hantke, 15 Nov. 1917, CZA, Z3/215; Herrmann to ZCO, 28 Sept. 1917, CZA, Z3/1693. *WH*, 24 Aug. 1917, pp. 4–5, hints at the possibility of this anti-nationalist Congress. See also *YA*, Sept.–Oct. 1917, pp. 11–12.

[64] On Czernin's support, and on Hantke's discussions with government officials, see

from the various nationalities offered the prospect of a degree of protection, whether from possible government disapproval if overly radical nationalist demands or vigorous protests about the authorities' poor record in controlling antisemitism were voiced, or from the Polish Club and its Galician Jewish supporters. Contact was made with Czech, Romanian, Ukrainian, and Italian representatives, and even (by Stricker) with German nationalists, in order to shore up potential support for Jewish demands for some form of autonomy. Herrmann and Kaznelson had meanwhile persuaded the prominent Jewish writer Felix Salten of the value of the Congress idea, and through him hoped to reach wider circles, Jewish and non-Jewish, in the literary and journalistic worlds.[65]

With this promising basis of potential support on a variety of fronts, Kaznelson moved to Vienna in January 1918 in order to set up a Congress bureau to co-ordinate the movement.[66] The notion underlying the Congress—that a forthright public display of Jewish will and solidarity was worthwhile—had the potential to unite, if only temporarily, the disparate Jewish factions in Austria. Many felt that the stakes were high: a time of unprecedented crisis demanded unusual and innovative action. The common denominator was a powerful desire for Jewish unity, or at the very least a voice that could both express Jewish wishes in the looming reorganization of the empire and demand protection from antisemitism. Clearly, the broader the support such a voice enjoyed, the greater its potential influence. Congress supporters hoped that the customary disunity among Austrian Jews could be overcome in the light of the external pressures

Herrmann to ZCO, 20 Sept. 1917, CZA, Z3/1693; Hantke to Arthur Rosenberg, 22 Nov. 1917, CZA, Z3/215; Hantke to Kaznelson, 27 Nov. 1917, CZA, Z3/215. Czernin's goodwill was apparently supplied through the good offices of his confidant, Bukovinian Jewish businessman Nathan Eidinger. Eidinger was credited by the nationalists with great influence due to his reputedly close relationship with Czernin. He helped to arrange the meeting between Hantke and Czernin in Vienna, and was expected to expedite Kaznelson's permit to settle in the capital. Czernin was referred to only obliquely in Zionist correspondence (as 'Chef der Wiener Firma', 'Eidinger's boss', 'Cz.'), presumably to avoid censorship. On Eidinger, see Markus Kraemer, 'Am Rande der Geschichte. Aus der Lebens-Chronik von Nathan Eidinger', *Mitteilungsblatt Irgun Olej Merkas Europa*, 17 Oct. 1962, p. 7; Friedman, 'The Austro-Hungarian Government and Zionism', 160–1; Hantke to Taussig, 24 Oct. 1917; Hantke to Kaznelson, 27 Nov. 1917; Kaznelson to Hantke, 5 Dec. 1917, all in CZA, Z3/215.

[65] Herrmann to ZCO, 28 Sept. 1917, CZA, Z3/1693; Hellmann, 'Erinnerungen an gemeinsame Kampfjahre', 52.

[66] Kaznelson to Hantke, 21 Dec. 1917 and 4 Feb. 1918; Hantke to Kaznelson, 16 Jan. 1918, all in CZA, Z3/215. Kaznelson had already begun to raise money for the Congress in Prague. See Kaznelson to Hantke, 5 Dec. 1917, CZA, Z3/215.

bearing down upon all of them, regardless of party or religious affiliation.[67] The challenge was now to translate vague expressions of possible support or non-interference into more substantial collaboration. This would be the first and most pressing task of the Congress Committee, where negotiations between the parties were to take place.

February – May 1918

The first meeting of the Congress Committee, attended by some fifty delegates representing a cross-section of Austrian Jewry, took place in Vienna on 21 February 1918.[68] For the Congress proponents, a central aim of this meeting was to elicit a public declaration of support from Alfred Stern. To this end, Stricker met with Stern on several occasions prior to the meeting. Admitting to Stricker that he was generally in agreement with the Congress programme, Stern none the less asked to attend as a 'guest' and observer rather than as a full participant. Disregarding Kaznelson's wish to play down the implications of legal recognition of Jewish nationality (the controversial point 1 of the programme), Stricker opened the meeting with a speech that emphasized the far-reaching nature and consequences of such recognition, including demands for a Jewish affairs minister and a separate Jewish voting curia. Stern, ostensibly attending as a non-participating guest, reacted sharply to Stricker's provocative formulation, speaking out against the introduction of a Jewish curia as a voluntary return to the ghetto. Although he did not deny the existence of a Jewish *Volk* in Austria, he noted that 'one could not publicly admit to this, as it would result in the greatest calamity for Austrian Jewry'. Stern's outspoken opposition served to dissuade a number of liberal and Orthodox participants from wholehearted commitment to the Congress.[69]

Two days later, however, Stern had a change of heart. Informing Max Grunwald that he had erred by adopting a rejectionist stance, he asserted

---

[67] See e.g. *WH*, 24 Aug. 1917, pp. 4–5; 6 Sept. 1917, p. 3; *OW*, 24 Aug. 1917, pp. 537–8; 19 Oct. 1917, pp. 653–4. This was in effect the same impulse that had driven the movement for an expanded Gemeindebund. See *ZBB* 21 (1918), 133–4, where Theodor Sonnenschein makes this clear. See also Hellmann, 'Ein jüdischer Kongress in Österreich', and the Nationalverein resolution in *JZ*, 9 Nov. 1917, p. 3.

[68] Its full title was the Wiener provisorische Arbeitsausschusses des österreichisch-jüdischen Kongress-komitees. See Kaznelson to Kaminka, 14 Feb. 1918, CZA, A147/17/19.

[69] Kaznelson to Hantke, 25 Feb. 1918, CZA, Z3/215; Stern to Sonnenschein, 31 Mar. 1918, CAHJP, AW, 2805/19/211; *JK*, 14 Mar. 1918, pp. 2–3; Hellmann, 'Die Geschichte der österreichisch-jüdischen Kongressbewegung', 210. Despite what Kaznelson called the 'exceptionally great failure' of the meeting, a provisional Steering Committee was formed, comprising Reichsrat

that he now accepted the Congress programme and would welcome the opportunity to participate. Having long since retreated from his anti-Zionist stance of the Herzlian era, he was now, he affirmed, an 'Oberzionist', though he retained grave doubts about the implications of a Jewish voting curia. Kaznelson, Grunwald, and Stricker immediately drafted a statement designed to allay his misgivings on this score: recognition of Jewish nationality in Austria would not oblige any individual Jew to identify as a 'Jewish national', and measures would be taken to protect Jews in western Austria from the introduction of any form of *numerus clausus*. For Kaznelson, this was consistent with his beliefs in any case; for Stricker, or so he explained to Kaznelson, point 1 was a framework that allowed for various interpretations. Only later would a more definitive version of Jewish autonomy need to be elaborated.

Once more, however, Stern reversed himself, complaining that the issue was causing him sleepless nights. He did not deny the existence of a Jewish *Volk*, he averred, but he *was* against any constitutional recognition of Jewish nationality. In other words, while there was indeed a Jewish *Volk* in Austria, he would not admit to this in any public forum. It would be a misfortune, he said, should Jewish nationality be recognized by law (a sentiment with which Kaznelson, an advocate of a strictly voluntary Jewish autonomy confined to the cultural sphere, could well empathize).[70] Despite the dichotomy between his private and public stances, Stern's admission of the existence of a Jewish *Volk* (if not nation) was important. It was a concrete expression of his broad conception of Jewish political interests, a vision clearly extending beyond the traditional Gemeinde realms of welfare, religion, and education. As the leading representative of Austrian Jewish liberalism—the 'embodiment' of a half-century of Austrian Jewish history, as Kaznelson described him—Stern's agonizing over this issue suggests that during the war years the barriers between the liberal and nationalist poles of Jewish society in Austria had become more fluid.[71] And it was precisely

deputies Straucher and Reizes, Rabbis Grunwald, Feuchtwang, and Taglicht, Stricker, Eidinger, Stand, Salten, and the executive secretaries of the Vienna Gemeinde and the Gemeindebund. See Kaznelson to Hantke, 25 Feb. 1918, CZA, Z3/215. A list of members of the Steering Committee is in Kaznelson to Ziegler, 1 Mar. 1918, CZA, Z3/215. The committee's membership indicated that support for the Congress was strongest among the nationalist-minded.

[70] See Kaznelson to Hantke, 25 Feb. 1918; Kaznelson to Ignaz Ziegler, 1 Mar. 1918, both in CZA, Z3/215; Hellmann, 'Die Geschichte der österreichisch-jüdischen Kongressbewegung', 209–10.

[71] Hellmann, 'Die Geschichte der österreichisch-jüdischen Kongressbewegung', 210.

this fluidity that allowed for at least the possibility of pan-Jewish co-
operation in the Congress movement.

Stricker's intransigence not only disturbed Stern but also ran the risk of
alienating other vitally needed allies, such as Ehrmann of B'nai B'rith,
Kaminka of the Allianz, and Siegfried Fleischer of the Union. Orthodox
representatives stressed that a 'general Jewish Congress' could indeed be
'of some real value', but wanted no part in a nationalist 'rump Congress'.[72]
Thus, Stricker's maximalism threatened to drive away the very support
that Kaznelson was wooing, in addition to contributing to ideological and
personal intranationalist tensions that debilitated the movement. These
tensions were not merely surface phenomena; rather, they reflected real
ideological and political differences within the nationalist camp. Still at
issue was the interpretation of point 1 of the programme, with its demand
for 'guarantee of the rights of the Jewish *Volk* in Austria'. What guarantees
should be demanded? How were these rights to be defined? And if there
were a Jewish *Volk*, who belonged to it? Previously, Austrian Zionists had
needed no definitive elaboration of the extent and content of Jewish autonomy, as constitutional reform had not been on the Austrian political agenda. They had been content with a loose commitment to some form of
Jewish autonomy along the lines of the models put forward by Simon
Dubnow and the Austrian Marxists Karl Renner and Otto Bauer.[73] Now,
however, they needed to agree on a more precise definition in order to be
able to voice a concrete demand, both to the Austrian authorities in the case
of constitutional reform and to the non-nationalist Jewish parties for the
purposes of the Congress programme.[74]

There was potentially more at stake here than internecine ideological
conflicts: the government invited the nationalists to present their views and
demands on Jewish status in a reformed empire in December 1917 and
March 1918. Their lack of consensus, Kaznelson feared, could enfeeble the

---

[72] Stricker's Jan. article in the *Jüdische Zeitung* (*JZ*, 18 Jan. 1918, p. 1) had infuriated Flei-
scher, for example, who expressed support for the 'fruitful idea' of a broad-based Congress. See
MOIU 30 (Jan.–Feb. 1918), 1–4; Kaznelson to Hantke, 25 and 27 Feb. 1918, both in CZA,
Z3/215. On the Orthodox, see *JK*, 14 Mar. 1918, pp. 2–3.

[73] The most serious attempt to examine the implications of Jewish autonomy in Austria was
made by Po'alei Zion theoretician Max Rosenfeld. See the works cited in Ch. 1 n. 141. In Hellmann, 'Die Geschichte der österreichisch-jüdischen Kongressbewegung', Kaznelson presented
his own theoretical exposition of the problem, intended as part of a larger study in which he
planned to take issue with Renner's rejection of the principle of Jewish national autonomy.

[74] This point is made, for example, by O(tto) A(beles), 'Ein Kongress der Juden Österreichs',
NJM 2 (1917–18), 287–8. See also *JZ*, 27 Mar. 1918, 4.

Zionist movement and the Congress both internally and in its relations with the government. He thus pushed for the Zionist Executive Committee to adopt an 'authoritative interpretation' of point 1. He proposed to append to it a qualification almost identical to the one that he (along with Stricker and Grunwald) had suggested to Stern, that is, a formula stressing the voluntary nature of Jewish national identification and conditioning acceptance of Jewish autonomy on the promise of legal safeguards that would preclude any infringement of Jewish rights. This proposal was modelled on the compromise adopted by the American Jewish Congress in its battles over a formula to express recognition of Jewish nationality. Common to both was the element of voluntarism.[75]

Kaznelson now believed that political autonomy for western Jews in Austria would signal disaster. He wrote to Hantke: 'In November [1917] I had already come to the perhaps somewhat pessimistic conclusion that constitutional recognition of Jewish nationality would lead to the almost total ruin of Austrian Jewry.'[76] Following the meeting of the Congress Committee and Stern's outburst, Stricker had indicated to Kaznelson his belief that flexibility might, after all, be called for: point 1 should perhaps be regarded, for tactical purposes, as merely a broad statement of intent with no binding consequences (such as a Jewish voting curia). Kaznelson felt that a *Parteitag*, the highest decision-making forum in western Austrian Zionism, might be necessary to decide the issue once and for all, writing to Hantke that 'The co-operation of the non-Zionist Jews of the west depends on the interpretation of point 1.'[77] A victory for the 'Jewish-national chauvinists', he predicted, would lead to 'complete defeat' for Austrian Jewry. 'Unfortunately, the conditions of Austrian Jewish existence do not permit maximalist politics in the style of the radical German, Polish, and Czech nationalists, or the Russian Bolsheviks.'[78] In the event, the Executive Committee, meeting at the

[75] Kaznelson to Hantke, 15 Nov. 1917; 25, 26, 27 Feb. 1918; Kaznelson to Ziegler, 1 Mar. 1918, all in CZA, Z3/215; Janowsky, *The Jews and Minority Rights*, 272–3; Frankel, 'The Jewish Socialists and the American Jewish Congress Movement', 280. The compromise proposal was similar in intent to the Copenhagen Manifesto issued by the World Zionist Organization in Oct. 1918. See Leon Chasanowitsch and Leo Motzkin (eds.), *Die Judenfrage der Gegenwart* (Stockholm, 1919), 68–9.

[76] Kaznelson to Hantke, 27 Feb. 1918, CZA, Z3/215. Kaznelson claimed that he was supported in this unorthodox viewpoint by Böhm.

[77] Kaznelson to Hantke, 26 Feb. 1918. See also Kaznelson to Hantke, 25 and 27 Feb. 1918; Kaznelson to Bohemian Zionist District Committee, 28 Feb. 1918; Kaznelson to Ziegler, 1 Mar. 1918, all in CZA, Z3/215. What Kaznelson referred to as a *Parteitag* was formally called the Westösterreichische Zionistentag. See Gaisbauer, *Davidstern und Doppeladler*, 302–3.

[78] Kaznelson to Ziegler, 1 Mar. 1918, CZA, Z3/215.

end of February, adopted Kaznelson's proposal. Whether this would have the desired effect from Kaznelson's point of view depended primarily on how Stricker interpreted this decision.

Stricker's attitude became clear soon after the second Congress Committee meeting in Vienna in early March 1918, at which it was decided to form a twenty-member Programme Commission whose task was to prepare within one month as precise a programme as possible to put before the Congress Committee. In the interim no official programmatic or policy statements were to be issued. The Programme Commission was suggested by Po'alei Zion representatives, led by Max Rosenfeld, who were dissatisfied with the current (insufficiently radical) programme, particularly the diluted version of point 1 advocated by Kaznelson. To Kaznelson, the Commission's establishment amounted to a 'burial' of the existing programme. If unity was unattainable in the Congress Committee, the same would prove true, he was certain, of the new body. Indeed, with the Commission providing a focus for disagreements, the conflict between Stricker and Kaznelson and their respective camps intensified. In a series of meetings during March the Commission was unable to arrive at any agreement. 'The ideological differences', wrote Kaznelson, 'were too great.'[79]

In early March Kaznelson for the first time started to entertain serious doubts about the viability of the Congress project. Impressed by Zionist successes outside Austria, Po'alei Zion and the 'Strickerites' laboured under the delusion that Zionism was sweeping all before it, that no opposition existed, that the 'masses' were behind them. Their 'mindless party demagogy' and 'hullabaloo politics', he believed, were bound to antagonize their supposed partners. Attacked by Po'alei Zion as 'a representative of western Jewish capitalist interests', Kaznelson regarded the politics of 'mood and sentiment' as a poor substitute for 'hard work'. Alienated from Stricker, Kaznelson was becoming increasingly disillusioned. 'It is only with difficulty that I can work with Stricker. . . . his dictatorial politics . . . poor tactics and tactless actions will surely bring about a grand coalition against us.'[80] This, he feared, would only serve to highlight the nationalists' minority status in Austrian Jewry, leading to a 'colossal humiliation' for Austrian Zionism and destroying in the process its prospects for the fore-

---

[79] Hellmann, 'Die Geschichte der österreichisch-jüdischen Kongressbewegung', 211–12; Kaznelson to Herrmann, 6 and 24 Mar.; 3 Apr. 1918, all in CZA, Z3/215. Stricker and Rosenfeld, for example, continued to press for a Jewish People's Assembly or National Congress.

[80] Kaznelson to Herrmann, 6 Mar. 1918, CZA, Z3/215.

seeable future. The situation, he wrote to Herrmann in late March, had become critical.[81]

Kaznelson and Stricker were by now working almost entirely separately, and generally at cross-purposes. With neither able to win majority support within nationalist ranks, Kaznelson turned in desperation to the EAC for assistance. In early April he wrote despondently to Herrmann, 'I can do absolutely nothing here.'[82] Help, though, was not forthcoming. Committed to the autonomy of regional organizations, the EAC lacked the requisite authority to dictate policy, and although he wished he were in a position to intervene more forcefully, wrote Hantke to Kaznelson, he was in fact able only to counsel patience.[83] While the Programme Commission deliberated, Kaznelson planned a meeting of *Kultusgemeinden* and other 'large Jewish corporations' to try once more to arrive at an agreement. He was prepared to accept, as an 'absolute minimum', an even more diluted version of the compromise formula presented to Stern, this time merely demanding national minority rights for eastern Jews and guarantees of legal equality for western Jews. The constitutional recognition of Jewish nationality, a prerequisite for national rights in Galicia and Bukovina, would have no political consequences for Jews in western Austria. This, he declared, was as far as he could go.[84]

His interlocutors, however, were wary. Kaznelson presented his 'absolute minimum demand' to B'nai B'rith's Ehrmann, who (according to Kaznelson) was 'fully in agreement' but reluctant to commit B'nai B'rith, a non-political body, to public support for a political venture. Ehrmann suggested instead that B'nai B'rith members of the Congress Committee should strive to forge a compromise combining Kaznelson's formula and B'nai B'rith's own formulation of point 1, which was not unlike Kaznelson's but replaced recognition of Jewish nationality with a proposal for a

[81] Kaznelson to Herrmann, 6 and 24 Mar. 1918, both in CZA, Z3/215.

[82] Kaznelson to Herrmann, 3 Apr. 1918, CZA, Z3/215. In early Mar. Kaznelson had suggested forming a directorate consisting of himself, Weltsch, and Bernfeld to take over the whole enterprise, and had toyed (not for the first time) with the idea of toppling Stricker in the Executive Committee, if possible with EAC assistance. While much of the Zionist apparatus in Vienna, along with Po'alei Zion, backed Stricker, some important local figures none the less sided with Kaznelson, including Weltsch, Bernfeld, Böhm, and Anitta Müller. Outside the capital, too, nationalist opinion was split, with both camps enjoying considerable support. See Kaznelson to Herrmann, 6 and 24 Mar.; 3 Apr. 1918; Kaznelson to Ziegler, 22 Mar. 1918; Kaznelson to Hantke, 14 May 1918, all in CZA Z3/215; *JZ*, 1 Mar. 1918, p. 3.

[83] Hantke to Kaznelson, 8 May 1918, CZA, Z3/215.

[84] Kaznelson to Ziegler, 22 Mar. 1918; Kaznelson to Ehrmann, 10 Apr. 1918, both in CZA, Z3/215.

government department for Jewish religious affairs (*Kultusangelegenhei-ten*).[85] Kaznelson explained to Ehrmann that without unqualified B'nai B'rith support he would be unable to sell any compromise to his own nationalist opposition. B'nai B'rith was Kaznelson's final hope at this stage. Faced with caution and passivity from Stern, the *Kultusgemeinden*, and the Allianz, outright opposition from the Union and the Orthodox, and a continuing fissure in nationalist ranks, the Congress project was poised at a delicate juncture. The initiative for further compromise had to come from the nationalist side; the liberals had staked out their position and would respond accordingly.[86]

As noted, Kaznelson felt that the most effective means of clarifying Zionist policy was for a full party conference (what he called a *Parteitag*) to make a definitive decision; this would hopefully unify the nationalists and bring Stricker to heel, forcing him to obey party discipline. At such a meeting, attended if possible by an EAC member, the Stricker-inspired Viennese hard line would be balanced, so Kaznelson hoped, by the more moderate approach of the Bohemian and Moravian Zionists.[87] In early April 1918 a Bohemian Zionist conference declared its unanimous support for a broad-based, inclusive Congress, adopted Kaznelson's minimal version of point 1, and called for a *Parteitag* to resolve differences over the issue.[88] For technical reasons, it proved impossible to convene a full *Parteitag*; there would instead be a 'conference of delegates' confined in essence to discussion and recommendation, without the authority to determine policy.[89] Meeting on 27 and 28 April and attended by 106 delegates, this was the largest assembly of Austrian Zionists during the war.

Two days prior to the conference Kaznelson fell seriously ill. Very weak,

---

[85] *ZBB* 21 (1918), 103–5, 108–9; Kaznelson to Ehrmann, CZA, Z3/215; Hellmann, 'Die Geschichte der österreichisch-jüdischen Kongressbewegung', 213. Prominent Jewish Reichsrat members Julius Ofner and Camillo Kuranda, thought Ehrmann, would object even to a Congress based on the B'nai B'rith formula. See Kaznelson's note to Herrmann, in Kaznelson to Ehrmann, 10 Apr. 1918, CZA, Z3/215. Theodor Sonnenschein had meanwhile reversed his opposition, and now saw the Congress (so long as it proceeded quietly and in a dignified fashion) as a stepping-stone to his long-sought-after expanded Gemeindebund. See *ZBB* 21 (1918), 134; ECUAZ to ZCO, 1 May 1918, CZA, Z3/849.

[86] Kaznelson and Ehrmann both made this clear. See *ZBB* 21 (1918), 103–5, 108–9; Kaznelson to Hantke, 14 May 1918, CZA, Z3/215.

[87] Kaznelson to Ziegler, 22 Mar. 1918, CZA, Z3/215.

[88] Circular of the Bohemian Zionist District Committee, 8 Apr. 1918, CZA, Z3/215; Hellmann, 'Die Geschichte der österreichisch-jüdischen Kongressbewegung', 212.

[89] ZCWA to ZCO, 2 Apr. 1918, CZA, Z3/849. The Congress was not the sole issue on the conference agenda.

with a high fever, he broke down completely and was hospitalized.[90] In a pre-conference agreement reached with Bohemian leader Ludwig Singer, Stricker committed himself to accepting the Bohemian (and thus Kaznelson's) formula of early April. In addition, the assembly called for a Congress that would attract the widest possible Jewish participation. If accepted by the Galician and Bukovinian branches, this programme was to form the basis for future action.[91] On the face of it, this was a victory for Kaznelson's moderation. But in the absence of a binding policy set by the Zionist movement, any compromise agreed to by Stricker was hardly a guarantee of his future co-operation.[92]

Kaznelson, by now 'thoroughly disgusted', described the conference as a 'comedy', arguing that Stricker had deceived the Bohemians and would pay no more than lip-service to any agreement. Indicative of Stricker's attitude, feared Kaznelson, was the former's warning to Adolf Böhm, who had assumed Kaznelson's role as Stricker's opposition at the conference. Cautioning Böhm against taking on the Congress project, Stricker predicted that Kaznelson, now in hospital, would soon be in the asylum, while Böhm could end up 'dead and buried'.[93] Indeed, very little had actually changed. Stricker had not been bound by official party policy; he had merely agreed to abide by what was in essence a milder version of existing policy, to which in any case he paid little or no attention. Disagreements about the implications for western Jews of recognition of Jewish nationality were too great, the issue too complex, for the conference to decide. The matter was thus referred back to the EAC for further clarification.[94]

Nationalist policy on the Congress, while formally set, was in practice suspended in limbo between two irreconcilable ideological positions. And with this, the Congress movement reached the end of the road. Under

[90] Robert Weltsch to ZCO, 1 May 1918, CZA, Z3/849.

[91] ECUAZ to ZCO, 1 May 1918; ZCWA to ZCO, 1 May 1918, both in CZA, Z3/849. The conference decisions are referred to in veiled form in *JZ*, 3 May 1918, pp. 1–2. See also the conference report in *YA*, 1 June 1918, pp. 7–8, where the 'bourgeois Zionists' are attacked by Po'alei Zion for 'betraying the national cause'.

[92] As Stricker had already admitted, tactical freedom of manœuvre was as important to him as any nominal compromise. Kaznelson recalled that Stricker had broken their July 1917 agreement about the Congress programme, had reinstated the programme following Kaznelson's protests, and had then proceeded for the most part to ignore it. See Kaznelson to Hantke, 14 May 1918, CZA, Z3/215.

[93] Robert Weltsch to ZCO, 1 May 1918, CZA, Z3/849; Kaznelson to Hantke, 14 May 1918, CZA, Z3/215.

[94] ECUAZ to ZCO, 1 May 1918, CZA, Z3/849. See also Hellmann, 'Die Geschichte der österreichisch-jüdischen Kongressbewegung', 214.

doctor's orders to refrain from any activity liable to upset or excite him, Kaznelson withdrew from Congress work at the end of April.[95] Deprived of its prime mover, the Congress movement came to an abrupt halt and rapidly disintegrated. That Kaznelson's absence could be fatal to the movement indicates that the Congress idea had not penetrated beyond a limited stratum of leadership élites; it had by no means become a 'mass' movement as its proponents had hoped. No one was prepared to assume Kaznelson's mantle, and the liberals had no interest in Stricker and Po'alei Zion's 'people's assembly'. By mid-May the Congress movement had virtually collapsed.[96]

Despite the failure to achieve its stated goals, the Congress movement left traces in the Jewish political landscape of the empire's successor states and beyond. Kaznelson, for example, believed that the movement's inclusive tendencies (at least in the Czech lands), and the practical political experience it had provided for the nationalists, laid the basis for the 'all-Jewish' politics of the Jewish National Councils that emerged at the end of the war in east central Europe.[97] The Councils, as already discussed, were a revolutionary departure from the prevailing norms of Jewish political culture in this region, enjoying brief success as a guiding force of Jewish society in the immediate post-war period. As Kaznelson noted, the Congress movement played a central role in preparing the ideological and political ground for this success. Beyond this, the search for an acceptable formula—in Congress movements in Austria and elsewhere—to express demands for Jewish minority rights formed part of the background to the work of the Committee of Jewish Delegations at the Paris Peace Conference and to the minori-

---

[95] Kaznelson to Hantke, 30 Apr. 1918; 14 May 1918, both in CZA, Z3/215. Kaznelson had also been ill in early March. See Kaznelson to Ziegler, 22 Mar. 1918, CZA, Z3/215. He seems to have suffered something akin to a nervous breakdown in late April. See the comments to that effect in Robert Weltsch to ZCO, 1 May 1918, CZA, Z3/849; Hantke to Kaznelson, 8 May 1918; Kaznelson to Hantke, 14 May 1918, both in CZA, Z3/215.

[96] Kaznelson to Hantke, 14 May 1918; Hantke to ZCWA, 16 May 1918, both in CZA, Z3/215; Hellmann, 'Die Geschichte der österreichisch-jüdischen Kongressbewegung', 214. Faint echoes reverberated through the summer of 1918, but these focused on convening a Galician, rather than Austrian, Congress. See e.g. *JZ*, 31 May 1918, pp. 1–2; *YA*, 1 June 1918, pp. 2–4, 11; 15 June 1918, pp. 2–4; 1 July 1918, pp. 3–4; 15 Aug. 1918, p. 3. In Dec. 1918 the Zionist Federation of Germany launched a German Jewish Congress movement, which reached considerable proportions (if only briefly) in Germany but elicited no response in Vienna. See Toury, 'Organizational Problems of German Jewry', 84–8; *Volk und Land*, 13 Feb. 1919, pp. 211–14; 6–13 Mar. 1919, pp. 329–32. On his efforts to revive the Congress movement in Vienna, see Leo Herrmann, 'Bericht über meine Reise', Dec. 1918 – Jan. 1919, CZA, Z3/1696.

[97] See Hellmann, 'Die Geschichte der österreichisch-jüdischen Kongressbewegung', 214; id., 'Erinnerungen an gemeinsame Kampfjahre', 53.

ties treaties drafted there.[98] Finally, the Congress movements were the ideological precursors of the World Jewish Congress, established in 1936.[99]

While the forces animating the Congress movement—the desire for active defence against antisemitism and for a corporate voice in Austrian society—were familiar in Austrian Jewish history, the war and its attendant crises gave these impulses to unity renewed urgency. If Austria's future was unclear in many respects, the consensus among Jewish activists was that antisemitism would be a prominent part of the post-war social and political scene. The Congress, and the Gemeindebund before it, represented the possibility of pan-Jewish co-operation in tackling these problems. Their failure was due in large measure to the intractable fragmentation that beset Austrian Jewish life.[100]

Paradoxically, despite the incessant discord that eventually overwhelmed it, the Congress movement was an example of the partial dissolving of barriers between the various ideological camps. A large-scale undertaking, the Congress necessitated at least some measure of co-operation, and in fact revealed a good deal of common ground between nationalists, liberals, and the Orthodox. The limits to this co-operation, however, were clearly circumscribed, and no side was able to muster sufficient strength or conviction to carry out such a project alone. The Congress campaign was evidence, too, of the increasing strength of Austrian Jewish nationalism during the war years. It was the nationalists, after all, who created, propelled, and ultimately destroyed the Congress movement. Underlying the seemingly interminable squabbles over the Congress programme were important, and related, issues: the nature and definition of collective Jewish interests in Austria and the contours of Jewish autonomy and identity in a restructured empire. To be sure, there was more than a hint of optimism (if not outright suspension of disbelief) involved here; all plans regarding Jewish autonomy were predicated on the assumption that a reformed Austria

[98] See Stillschweig, *Die Juden Osteuropas in den Minderheitenverträgen*, 21–38; Janowsky, *The Jews and Minority Rights*, 309–83.

[99] See e.g. *Volk und Land*, 23 Jan. 1919, p. 108; 6–13 Mar. 1919, p. 327. See also *Unity in Dispersion: A History of the World Jewish Congress* (New York, 1948), 17–25, where this connection is made explicit.

[100] For a similar reading of the difficulties involved in Jewish efforts from late 1917 'to create an effective organ of Jewish representation to the Ukrainian government', see Henry Abramson, *A Prayer for the Government: Ukrainians and Jews in Revolutionary Times 1917–1920* (Cambridge, Mass., 1999), ch. 3. The quotation is from p. 101.

would be democratic, pluralist, and multinational.[101] This optimism perhaps derived from the fierce Habsburg patriotism that was one of the few
unifying forces of Austrian Jewry. The Congress movement, a valiant attempt to embrace the entirety of Austrian Jewish society, is testimony to this
enduring faith in the empire. It was, in fact, as Kaznelson wrote, the 'last
major act' of Austrian Jewry.[102]

[101] On the conditions needed for successful Jewish autonomy, i.e. 'consolidation of parlia-
mentary democracy [and] a high degree of order, stability and liberalism', see Jonathan Frankel,
'The Dilemmas of Jewish National Autonomism: The Case of Ukraine 1917–1920', in Peter J.
Potichnyj and Howard Aster (eds.), *Ukrainian–Jewish Relations in Historical Perspective*
(Edmonton, 1988), 275. See also Paul Radensky, 'The Ministry for Jewish Affairs and Jewish
Autonomy in Lithuania' (Yid.), *YIVO Bleter*, NS 2 (1994), 127–46.

[102] Hellmann, 'Die Geschichte der österreichisch-jüdischen Kongressbewegung', 207.

FIVE

A JEWISH REVOLUTION

B Y early October 1918, with the Czechs and South Slavs striving for national independence and the incorporation of Galicia in a reconstituted Poland increasingly likely, it was evident that dissolution of the monarchy was a distinct possibility. Notwithstanding last-minute dynastic attempts at federal reform, the general contours of a new political order were emerging. On 21 October Reichsrat delegates from the German-speaking regions that formed the historical core of the Habsburg lands convened as the Provisional National Assembly of the Independent German-Austrian State, a body dominated by German nationalists, Christian Socials, and Social Democrats. Until the proclamation of the German-Austrian republic on 12 November this assembly functioned as the executive authority of the nascent state, parallel to the imperial administration. The last Habsburg government was installed on 27 October; its primary role was to oversee the transfer of power to the new authorities.[1] Political and popular responses to the new republic were ambivalent. Established almost by default as a result of the monarchy's disintegration and military defeat, the new state's founding declaration was accompanied by a demand for immediate *Anschluss* to Germany. Merging with the new German republic was a notion that received broad popular support in the immediate post-war months.[2] Widely regarded as incapable of independent existence,

---

[1] Owing to the existence of German-speaking enclaves in areas claimed by the Habsburg successor states, the borders of 'German-Austria' remained temporarily undefined. The Provisional Assembly 'governed' through an executive council, later called the Staatsrat. On the final dissolution of the monarchy, see Zeman, *The Break-Up of the Habsburg Empire*, ch. 8; Walter Goldinger, *Geschichte der Republik Österreich* (Vienna, 1962), 9–19; Karl R. Stadler, 'Die Gründung der Republik', in Erika Weinzierl and Kurt Skalnik (eds.), *Österreich 1918–1938* (Graz, 1983), i. 66–73.

[2] This was prohibited by the Entente powers. On the *Anschluss* movement, see Alfred D. Low, *The Anschluss Movement 1918–1919 and the Paris Peace Conference* (Philadelphia, 1974); Karl R. Stadler, *The Birth of the Austrian Republic 1918–1921* (Leiden, 1966), ch. 3.

German–Austria was seen as the 'remains' of the dismembered monarchy, a 'state without a nation, a republic without republicans'.[3]

This was a period, then, of revolutionary turmoil, a culmination of four years of war and privation. Compounding the political chaos was the near-total collapse of Vienna's socio-economic infrastructure. If during the war the city had suffered from chronic shortages of food and raw materials, the immediate post-war winter months saw a drastic deterioration of the already grim living conditions. Inundated by hundreds of thousands of returning soldiers and cut off from sources of raw materials by the successor states' economic blockade, the Viennese population endured extreme hardship. Hunger was endemic, poverty and unemployment widespread. As Julius Braunthal, a leading Social Democrat, described it:

> the transport services in Vienna had to be suspended for weeks; electric light in the homes, shops and on the streets had to be restricted to one or two hours a day for want of electric power. And of course there was no heating whatever in the houses. During that grim winter of 1918–1919, in blacked-out Vienna, we had to work and to live in icy rooms, underfed and in worn-out clothes.

'In Austria', wrote a Viennese woman in March 1919, 'we live on hopes, expectations and promises. The war years were times of wanton luxury in comparison with this hopeless spring.'[4]

In this atmosphere of upheaval and crisis, the foundations of Jewish society were similarly shaken by the abrupt disappearance of central authority and the loss of familiar signposts by which all had navigated. The break-up of the monarchy was greeted with expressions of dismay and regret. Austrian politicians had failed to grasp the historic Austrian 'mission' of facilitat-

---

    [3] Klemens von Klemperer, 'Das nachimperiale Österreich 1918–1938: Politik und Geist', in Heinrich Lutz and Helmut Rumpler (eds.), *Österreich und die deutsche Frage im 19. und 20. Jahrhundert* (Vienna, 1982), 301; Bruce Pauley, 'The Social and Economic Background of Austria's *Lebensunfähigkeit*', in Anson Rabinbach (ed.), *The Austrian Social Experiment: Social Democracy and Austromarxism 1918–1934* (Boulder, Colo., 1985), 21–37. Shaping a coherent Austrian identity out of the chaos created by the empire's dissolution remained a formidable problem throughout the inter-war years. See e.g. William T. Bluhm, *Building an Austrian Nation* (New Haven, 1973), ch. 1; Kurt Skalnik, 'Auf der Suche nach der Identität', in Erika Weinzierl and Kurt Skalnik (eds.), *Österreich 1918–1938* (Graz, 1983) i. 11–24; Klemperer, 'Das nachimperiale Österreich'.

    [4] Julius Braunthal, *In Search of the Millennium* (London, 1945), 221; Anna Eisenmenger, *Blockade: The Diary of an Austrian Middle-Class Woman 1914–1924* (London, 1932), 196. On conditions in Vienna in these months, see also David F. Strong, *Austria (October 1918 – March 1919): Transition from Empire to Republic* (New York, 1939), chs. 3–4, 6; Henry Noel Brailsford, *Across the Blockade* (New York, 1919), 37–58.

ing co-operation between peoples, wrote Robert Weltsch in early October; the Jews, he later commented, had been enthusiastic bearers of this mission.[5] Liberal Gemeinde leader Heinrich Schreiber mourned the fall of the Habsburgs:

We Jews were without exception and regardless of party affiliation true and authentic Austrians, body and soul; we were and are Austrian, loyal and reliable to the core. . . . We bid farewell to the united fatherland with grief-stricken . . . and anxious hearts, and we stand shaken at the grave. . . . Only one thought consoles us: We Jews are blameless in this![6]

Jewish fealty to the idea of a large multinational state was slow to die. In the immediate post-war years, for example, Zionists regularly expressed support for the establishment of a federation of the successor states. In the new states, they argued, Jews were a negligible minority, lacking influence; strength was in numbers and the closer the links between the successor states, the better the Jews would be able to defend their rights.[7]

The collapse of the empire and the establishment of the ethnically homogeneous German-Austrian republic, whose only numerically significant minorities were Viennese Czechs and Jews, left Jews in a quandary. A simple transfer of allegiance, an option available to the empire's national-territorial minorities, was problematic for the many Jews who prided themselves on their broader Austrian loyalties. Rudolf Schwarz-Hiller, for example, director of the government's wartime refugee effort, felt the war had utterly destroyed all dreams of 'cosmopolitanism' and international co-operation. Sadly, he wrote, only the national idea had survived.[8] The liberal *Wahrheit*, stressing that Jews had always been devoted citizens of the empire and lamenting the 'brusque disavowal' by the successor states of any commonality of interests, expressed what it claimed was a widespread sense

---

[5] *JZ*, 4 Oct. 1918, pp. 1–2; Robert Weltsch, 'Österreichische Revolutionschronik', *Der Jude*, 3 (1918–19), 350–1. See also Robert Stricker's comments, *JZ*, 18 Oct. 1918, p. 2.

[6] *OW*, 25 Oct. 1918, p. 673. For similar sentiments from the Orthodox, see *JK*, 3 Oct. 1918, p. 1; 1 Nov. 1918, pp. 1–2.

[7] See Hermann Kadisch, 'Das mitteleuropäische Chaos und die Juden', *Volk und Land*, 1 (12 June 1919), 735–6; Heinrich Margulies, 'Wiener Brief', *Volk und Land*, 1 (28 Aug. 1919), 1098–1102; Stricker's articles in *WM*, 28 June 1919, p. 1; 10 Aug. 1919, p. 1. See also *WM*, 28 Nov. 1919, p. 1; 22 Dec. 1919, p. 1; 28 Nov. 1920, p. 1. On the idea of a post-war federation, see Rudolf Wierer, *Der Föderalismus im Donauraum* (Graz, 1960), ch. 9; Stadler, *The Birth of the Austrian Republic*, ch. 13. Mintz, 'Jewish Nationalism in the Context of Multi-National States', 203, 222–3, advances a similar argument, although primarily in the context of the Russian empire, regarding strength in numbers and the nationalist preference for large, multinational states. [8] *OW*, 18 Oct. 1918, pp. 657–8.

of Jewish bewilderment: 'in this chaos of immense public, political, and social change the worrying question arises for Jews: how shall we prepare for our future?'[9] The writer Arthur Schnitzler, arguing with Zionist friends in early November, declared himself 'an Austrian citizen of Jewish race and German culture'. Succinctly expressing the Jewish dilemma, Schnitzler asked '*Who* shall decide where I belong?'[10] In addition, the possibility of *Anschluss* to Germany further complicated, in the short term at least, the difficult issue of Jewish identification.[11]

For the nationalists, the transition from empire to nation-state involved a renewed reckoning with the perennial problem of reconciling potentially conflicting loyalties. Whereas in the multinational empire Jewish nationalism did not of necessity conflict with Austrian patriotism, the political atmosphere in the German–Austrian republic was rather less amenable to pluralistic identities. The Zionist solution was to insist that the concepts of nation and state ought not to be conflated, and that in the post-empire settlement national minorities would be a prominent feature of the landscape (this was true, as it turned out, of almost everywhere but German-Austria); adherence to Jewish nationalism, they argued, was perfectly consistent with patriotism and good citizenship. Moreover, only on the basis of constitutionally anchored equality between peoples, i.e. collective or group equality as well as individual legal equality, could tensions between Jews and others be resolved. If antisemitism was in part a product of the Jewish drive to assimilate into areas of society where they were not welcome, as the Zionists believed, then a certain degree of Jewish separation and autonomy was surely desirable. This separation, they emphasized, must be voluntary—an option, not an obligation—and should entail no negative consequences for Jewish rights. Such reasoning was predicated on the optimistic assumption that the new regime would practise a pluralistic and tolerant form of nationalism.[12]

[9] *WH*, 1 Nov. 1918, p. 3.

[10] Schnitzler, *Tagebuch 1917–1919*, 196, 204. More generally on these dilemmas, see Marsha L. Rozenblit, 'Jewish Ethnicity in a New Nation-State: The Crisis of Identity in the Austrian Republic', in Michael Brenner and Derek J. Penslar (eds.), *In Search of Jewish Community: Jewish Identities in Germany and Austria 1918–1933* (Bloomington, Ind., 1998), 134–53.

[11] For the generally ambivalent Zionist discussions on the possibility of *Anschluss*, see Stricker, *Jüdische Politik in Österreich*, 20–3; id., *Wege der jüdischen Politik. Aufsätze und Reden* (Vienna, 1929), 189–93; *JZ*, 28 Feb. 1919, pp. 1–2; *WM*, 7 Feb. 1919, p. 1; 11 Feb. 1919, p. 1; 19 Feb. 1919, p. 1; 19 Mar. 1919, p. 1.

[12] See e.g. *JZ*, 1 Nov. 1918, p. 2; Hermann Kadisch, 'Das Donaureich und seine Juden', *NJM* 3 (1918–19), 41–3; Heinrich Margulies, 'Jüdische und europäische Politik', *NJM* 3 (1918–19), 502; Weltsch, 'Österreichische Revolutionschronik'.

Any form of separatism was anathema to Jewish liberals. As they never tired of pointing out, Zionist demands for recognition of Jewish nationality were supported by the antisemites. Fearing the imposition of quotas in the civil service and judiciary, in schools and higher education—in short, a forced return to the ghetto—they saw no logic in providing anti-Jewish forces with the means to push Jews out of public life. More than the nationalists or the Orthodox, who had strong extra-Austrian allegiances beyond their Habsburg patriotism, the liberals had abruptly been deprived of their *only* homeland. Acutely aware of the danger of provoking antisemitism, they were by and large passive in this crucial period, preferring to maintain a low collective profile. Their attitude amounted, in fact, to 'wait and see'.[13] The Orthodox, too, were reluctant to act forthrightly, guided by the principle of non-interference in the political affairs of the host society at such an unsettled time.[14] To the liberals and the Orthodox, the situation was fraught with risk; to the nationalists, while not blind to the potential dangers for Jews inherent in the breakdown of central authority, it seemed also to offer great opportunities.

Activist by nature, the nationalists rushed in to fill the vacuum created by the temporary paralysis of their opponents. From October 1918 to early 1919 Jewish politics in Vienna was radical, mobilized, and nationalist—characteristics more commonly associated with east European Jewish political culture than with the sober and correct style of the Vienna Gemeinde. Mass rallies and rowdy street demonstrations replaced quiet diplomacy in the corridors of power. Jewish liberal hegemony was challenged by the appearance of a Jewish National Council, a Jewish Soldiers' Committee, and a Jewish militia. Following the success of their welfare work and their leading role in the youth and Congress movements, this period represented the denouement of the wartime transformation of nationalist fortunes. Clearly subordinate in August 1914, they now assumed the leading role in Viennese Jewish society. And while the liberals soon regained the upper hand, their pre-war dominance was never fully restored; in the 1920s, as the Austrian republic gradually attained a semblance of stability, power in the Jewish community was more evenly distributed than previously.

Participants described this decisive shift in the balance of power, both at the time and in retrospect, as a 'revolution'. What happened in Austrian

---

[13] See e.g. *WH*, 1 Nov. 1918, pp. 3–4; *OW*, 25 Oct. 1918, pp. 673–5; 22 Nov. 1918, p. 737.
[14] See *JK*, 7 Nov. 1918, pp. 1–2; 5 Dec. 1918, p. 1.

Jewry in 'those November days', wrote Weltsch, 'was a genuine revolution'.[15] He breathlessly described to Leo Herrmann in Berlin the reigning 'chaos and confusion', the sensation of events moving too fast to control. In a similar vein, Isidor Schalit wrote of the 'frenzied' atmosphere in Vienna in the days after the war.[16] In January 1919 a lead article in the nationalist *Jüdische Zeitung* wrote that 'In the days of the revolution, we had a little revolution in the Jewish world.'[17] On the other side of the political fence, Heinrich Schreiber called it a 'revolution in the Kultusgemeinde'. The Gemeinde, he wrote, was under threat from the 'violent advancing battalions' of the nationalists; a 'revolutionary directorate' had taken control of Viennese Jewry.[18] The primary instrument of this 'revolution' was the Jewish National Council (Jüdischer Nationalrat).

THE JEWISH NATIONAL COUNCIL

'Ever more forcefully and urgently the vital question arises for the Jews . . . of whether and in what manner they will participate as a community in the reorganization of the monarchy.'[19] From early October, as signs of impending change multiplied, calls for united action were heard from all sections of Jewish society. For Jews, a crucial issue was the nature of the relationship between the successor states. A numerically significant minority of over 1,300,000 spread throughout the Austrian half of the monarchy (4.6 per cent of the total population), their political leverage would be greatly diminished in sovereign nation-states in which they constituted a much smaller minority.[20] Regardless of what form the new political order took, the prerequisite for an effective assertion of Jewish rights was a modicum of unity and broadly acknowledged leadership. Unity and leadership, though, were precisely what was lacking as a consequence of the failure of the Congress movement. The 'criminal indifference' of Jewish leaders to the needs of the hour, thundered a lead article in the *Österreichische Wochenschrift*, was tantamount to 'moral, social, and economic suicide'. For the peoples of

---

[15] Robert Weltsch, 'Die nationale Revolution im österreichischen Judentum und die jüdischen Nationalräte', *JNK* 5 (1919–20), 58. See also Weltsch's comments in 'Österreichische Revolutionschronik', and in 'Jüdischer Nationalrat für Deutschösterreich 1918', *Michael: On the History of the Jews in the Diaspora*, 2 (1973), 205–11.

[16] Weltsch to Herrmann, 16 Oct. 1918, CZA, Z3/850; 16 Nov. 1918, CZA, L6/212. For Schalit, see CZA, A196/28.

[17] *JZ*, 24 Jan. 1919, p. 1.   [18] *OW*, 8 Nov. 1918, pp. 706–7; 15 Nov. 1918, pp. 724–5.

[19] *OW*, 11 Oct. 1918, p. 641.   [20] For population figures, see Bihl, 'Die Juden', 882–3.

Austria, the writer continued, it was no longer a question of if, but of how, self-determination should be exercised; they were therefore striving for unity. The Jews, however, were gripped by an 'unnatural, inexplicable timidity', still unable to move beyond debates about whether self-determination was an appropriate solution.[21]

Underlying these rallying-calls was the recognition that a forceful Jewish voice was needed in order to ensure that Jews played a role in determining their status in the post-empire world. True to form, however, co-ordination proved impossible and the piecemeal attempts to stake out a Jewish position led only to discord within Jewish ranks. As the emperor met national representatives from among Reichsrat members, for example, he was confronted first with the *de facto* Jewish nationalist representative Heinrich Reizes (elected as a member of the Galician Radical Democratic Party) and subsequently with the Polish Club member and nationalist *bête noire* Nathan von Löwenstein, who assured him that Galician Jews were devoted Poles.[22] In an audience with the emperor in early October Chief Rabbi Chajes, far from confining himself to religious matters, expressed his support for Jewish national minority rights and the Zionist agenda in Palestine. For his temerity in doing so, he was roundly criticized by Gemeinde liberals and reprimanded by Stern.[23]

Stern, meanwhile, convened a meeting at the end of October of the virtually defunct Gemeindebund, now limited to delegates from German-Austrian territory. Reviewing the situation, he urged caution above all, citing the negative repercussions of overly prominent Jewish involvement in the 1848 Revolution which he had experienced at first hand. Keep calm and remain at one remove from the vortex of this new revolution, Stern counselled. Reichsrat member Camillo Kuranda, too, recommended that Jews avoid pursuing a separate political or religious agenda in the emerging state. The Gemeindebund opted to refrain from any public action or declaration of intent.[24] An

---

[21] *OW*, 11 Oct. 1918, p. 641. On calls for Jewish unity and action, see *OW*, 4 Oct. 1918, pp. 625–6; 18 Oct. 1918, pp. 657–9; 1 Nov. 1918, pp. 689–90; 8 Nov. 1918, p. 706; *JK*, 22 Oct. 1918, p. 1; *WH*, 1 Nov. 1918, pp. 3–4; 15 Nov. 1918, pp. 3–4; *YA*, 18 Oct. 1918, pp. 3–4; 1 Nov. 1918, pp. 1–3.

[22] For the furious nationalist reaction to Löwenstein's comments, see *JZ*, 18 Oct. 1918, pp. 2–3.

[23] *OW*, 11 Oct. 1918, p. 650; *JZ*, 11 Oct. 1918, p. 2; Rosenfeld, *H. P. Chajes' Leben und Werk*, 83–5; Trau and Krein, *A Man in the World*, 75–6. This marked the beginning of a lengthy period of tension between Chajes and the Gemeinde leadership. See Rosenfeld, *H. P. Chajes' Leben und Werk*, 127–33; Gold (ed.), *Zwi Perez Chajes*, 30–9; *JZ*, 25 Oct. 1918, p. 4.

[24] The Gemeindebund was called together in response to entreaties from the Linz Kultusgemeinde for guidance from Vienna. Protocols of the meeting are in CAHJP, AW, 2805/19/239.

unwillingness to commit to any binding course of action and a reluctance to act publicly were the defining characteristics of liberal behaviour from early October to mid-November. Underpinning this passivity was a deeply ingrained defensive prudence that aimed at minimizing the very real risks to which Jews were likely to be exposed in a time of revolutionary convulsion.[25]

The nationalists, by contrast, were ready to leap into the fray. Keeping all options open and casting as wide a political net as possible, Viennese Zionist leaders made contact with both those still in power and those that looked likely to be the new leaders. As Weltsch complained to his Prague colleagues, events were moving so fast that it was difficult to know with whom to speak.[26] In one case at least they guessed correctly. Weltsch, Stricker, and Böhm met Heinrich Lammasch, a prominent jurist and peace advocate who in late October became the monarchy's last prime minister. Noteworthy in this meeting was the Zionists' attempt to exploit stereotypes of international Jewish wealth and influence: political support and economic aid to Austria might be forthcoming, they suggested, if the administration were to recognize Jewish nationality and remain vigilant about suppressing anti-semitic outbreaks. This recourse to the threat of international Jewish pressure was to be a recurring tactic.[27]

By early October Weltsch had devised the plans that would form the

[25] B'nai B'rith held a number of combined meetings of its two Viennese lodges in the second half of November. Despite some 'lively debate', the tone in these meetings remained 'dignified'. See Ascher, '25 Jahre Eintracht', 34–5. In the immediate post-war months, disagreements between nationalist-minded members and others were felt also in the lodge 'Wien'. See Jerusalem, *U.O.B.B. Humanitätsverein Wien*, 71–2; *ZBB* 21 (1918), 198–203, 208; 22 (1919), 30–4. On the Gemeinde's scrupulous avoidance of politics at its meetings even in late Oct., see Protokolle der Plenar-Sitzungen, 20, 24, 27 Oct. 1918, CAHJP, AW, 71/16. Only in early Dec., and then only in protest against nationalist actions, did the Union reappear in the public arena.

[26] Weltsch to Bohemian Zionist District Committee, 10 Oct. 1918, CZA, L6/358. For the Zionist strategy, see Weltsch to ZCO, 2 Oct. 1918; Herrmann to Weltsch, 8 Oct. 1918, both in CZA, Z3/214.

[27] It was used, for example, to stave off threats of refugee expulsion in 1919–20. Already in mid-1917 Leo Herrmann had urged Siegfried Bernfeld to make contact with Lammasch, a move at that time 'prohibited' by Stricker, who apparently remained dubious about its utility. On this meeting and the Zionist tactic of exploiting their international connections, see Weltsch to ZCO, 8 Oct. 1918; Herrmann to Weltsch, 11 Oct. 1918; Weltsch to Herrmann, 28 Oct. 1918, all in CZA, Z3/214; Weltsch, 'Jüdischer Nationalrat für Deutschösterreich', 209; Friedman, 'The Austro-Hungarian Government and Zionism', 244. Meetings were also held with Foreign Ministry officials. See Weltsch to Bohemian Zionist District Committee, 10 Oct. 1918, CZA, L6/358. Isidor Schalit records in his memoirs that the post-war Austrian government approached the Zionists on a number of occasions, hoping to use them as intermediaries to organize loans from foreign Jewish sources to assist the republic's ailing economy. See CZA, A196/62/1; A196/62/4.

basis of nationalist action in the following months. He envisaged a propaganda offensive, massive public demonstrations, an all-empire Zionist conference, and the formation of a Jewish National Council to spearhead the
whole campaign. The moment of truth, he felt, had arrived; the 'possibili-
ties' in Vienna were 'limitless' and it was 'now or never' for the 'Zioniza-
tion' of Austrian Jewry. Weltsch's paramount aim was to ensure official
recognition of Jewish nationality. All else, he felt, would flow from this.[28] In
these initial plans he was optimistic that a connection between Jewish organizations in the successor states could be maintained.[29] While Stricker still
hoped at the end of October for the preservation of such links, to Weltsch it
had already become evident by mid-October that regional Zionists were
intent on pursuing their own course. The Galicians, he wrote to his confidant Leo Herrmann, 'want nothing more to do with us'.[30] In Prague, too,
the Zionists had severed their ties with Vienna, setting up their own
National Council. Stricker's attempts to rescue a centralized Austria, wrote
Max Brod to Herrmann in late October, would be 'catastrophic' for
Bohemian Jewry. Zionist activity in Prague was 'naturally fully independent of Vienna, to whom we merely pass information'.[31] No matter what
relationships emerged between the successor states, it was clear by the end
of October that Viennese Zionism was now primarily a local affair.

Weltsch's ideas met with an overwhelming public response. Mass meetings in the Inner City in mid and late October attracted enormous crowds,
requiring police intervention to maintain order. The Jewish 'masses', trum-
peted the *Jüdische Zeitung*, had 'expressed their will' and 'ushered in a new

[28] Weltsch to ZCO, 2 Oct. 1918; Herrmann to Copenhagen Zionist Office, 17 Oct. 1918;
Weltsch to Herrmann, 28 Oct. 1918, all in CZA, Z3/214; Weltsch to Kaznelson, 28 Sept.; 1 and
6 Oct. 1918, LBIA, RW, AR 7185, box 2, folder 19; Weltsch to Bohemian Zionist District Committee, 10 Oct. 1918, CZA, L6/358. The quotations are from the letters of 2 and 28 Oct.
[29] Herrmann to Weltsch, 8 Oct. 1918, CZA, Z3/850; Herrmann to Weltsch, 8 Oct. 1918;
Weltsch to ZCO, 11 Oct. 1918, both in CZA, Z3/214.
[30] Weltsch to Herrmann, 16 Oct. 1918, CZA, Z3/850. On Stricker's hopes, see Weltsch to
Herrmann, 28 Oct. 1918, CZA, Z3/214.
[31] Brod to Herrmann, 24 Oct. 1918, CZA, L6/366. See also Brod to Herrmann, 23 and 28
Oct. 1918, both in CZA, L6/366; Kieval, *The Making of Czech Jewry*, 188–9. Weltsch had
already complained to Prague about lack of political co-ordination between the two cities
(Weltsch to Bohemian Zionist District Committee, 10 Oct. 1918, CZA, L6/358), although he
encouraged the Czechs to pursue an independent course. See Weltsch to Kaznelson, 28 Sept.
and 18 Oct. 1918, LBIA, RW, AR 7185, box 2, folder 19. Similarly, upon the establishment on
14 Oct. of a Jewish National Council in Bukovina, no mention was made of any continuing link
with Vienna. See *JZ*, 25 Oct. 1918, p. 2; S. A. Soifer, *Das jüdische Wohlfahrtswesen in Czernowitz*
(Czernowitz, 1925), 32–7; Reifer, *Dr. Mayer Ebner*, 74–7.

era for Austrian Jewry'.[32] Central to Weltsch's scheme was the creation of the Jewish National Council, a Jewish version of the National Councils that had sprung up in many parts of the former Habsburg and Russian empires to assume the reins of power. As already noted, the Jewish Councils—nationalist-dominated, although ostensibly pan-Jewish—similarly hoped to usurp the role of the existing Jewish authorities. Sweeping all before them, they rode the post-war nationalist wave to temporary success in Austria, Czechoslovakia, Poland, Ukraine, Lithuania, Hungary, and elsewhere. The Vienna Council announced its existence in late October, arrogating to itself the status of 'sole legitimate representative' of the Jewish 'nation' until a Jewish 'parliament', for which the Council was to prepare the ground, was elected. Encompassing the whole of Jewish society and pursuing 'exclusively Jewish politics', it aspired 'to guide the fate of the Jews'.[33]

Some two weeks elapsed between this announcement and the Council's debut on the public stage in early November, a considerable time in such an eventful period. Yet again, the delay was due in the main to conflicts within the Zionist leadership. Once more, Weltsch and Stricker were at loggerheads, disagreeing sharply about the feasibility and extent of Jewish autonomy in the new situation. Positions were much as they had been during the debates over this issue in the Congress movement. Weltsch, now playing Kaznelson's role, preferred a minimalist approach, advocating limited cultural autonomy—focusing on education and welfare—anchored by constitutional recognition of Jewish nationality. Full national autonomy, cautioned Herrmann, might well be incompatible with the wish of the new nation-states for unlimited sovereignty.[34] 'We can no longer work with the

---

[32] *JZ*, 18 Oct. 1918, p. 1; 25 Oct. 1918, pp. 3–4. Two thousand new recruits, it was claimed, joined the Zionist movement at these meetings. Weltsch commented that the hall was 'almost demolished' by the 'infuriated crowd' left outside at the first meeting. See Weltsch to Herrmann, 16 Oct. 1918, CZA, Z3/850. The first meeting adopted resolutions, formulated by Weltsch in consultation with Herrmann and the Copenhagen Zionist Office, calling for the 'immediate recognition' of Jewish nationality and active involvement of the 'Jewish nation' in the 'reorganization' of Austria. See Weltsch to Herrmann, 2 Oct. 1918, CZA, Z3/214; Herrmann to Weltsch, 8 Oct. 1918, CZA, Z3/850; Herrmann to Weltsch, 8 Oct. 1918, CZA, Z3/214; Weltsch to Kaznelson, 1 Oct. 1918, LBIA, RW, AR 7185, box 2, folder 19. See also the similar resolutions of the Copenhagen Manifesto issued on 25 Oct., in Chasanowitsch and Motzkin, *Die Judenfrage der Gegenwart*, 68–9.
[33] *JZ*, 25 Oct. 1918, pp. 1–2. See also the 27 Dec. 1918 Report of the Jewish National Council in Lemberg, CZA, F3/23.
[34] Herrmann to Weltsch, 8 Oct. 1918, CZA, Z3/214; Herrmann to Weltsch, 8 Oct. 1918, CZA, Z3/850.

slogans "national autonomy" (which is no longer relevant) and "national minority rights"', wrote Weltsch at the end of October. 'It appears that national autonomy has become a territorial matter. . . . How should we fit ourselves into such a scheme? . . . One must realize that we are now dealing only with the German-Austrian administration.' Even cultural autonomy, though, was a risky business in Vienna. Weltsch suspected that the 'anti-semitic Viennese authorities' might well agree to its implementation, but would use it to impose quotas on Jewish enrolments in schools and universities.[35] The collapse of the monarchy, he felt, necessitated a narrowing of horizons and a lowering of expectations with regard to autonomy. Stricker, by contrast, still wished to push for full-blown political autonomy as a national minority, seeing no reason to tamper with the maximalist demands presented to the Austrian government in March 1918.[36]

The delay in publicly launching the Council was a source of chagrin for Weltsch, further diminishing his already jaundiced opinion of his colleagues. 'You know with what kind of material one works here', he wrote to Herrmann. 'It is a pure mad house. . . . all political and organizational work . . . rests exclusively with me.'[37] He complained bitterly of apathy and incompetence, threatening to resign if the locals could not be budged from the habit of running their political affairs from cafés. The reigning system of 'coffee-house prattle' must be overcome, he fumed. 'Everything is inadequate, from the local bureau to the highest leadership.' (Ironically, he respected only Stricker, with whom he was in constant conflict.) It was imperative that the Council declare itself to be the Jewish 'government'.[38] Outlining its demands in early November, the Council carefully avoided any mention of political autonomy, reflecting Weltsch's more modest approach. Naturally, it called for recognition of Jewish nationality and full legal equality; further, it laid claim to 'autonomous administration' of all

[35] Weltsch to Herrmann, 28 Oct. 1918, CZA, Z3/214. Weltsch further pointed out that 'When one expressed these doubts previously, one was accused of anti-national views. As you know, it was over this issue that the Congress collapsed.' Already in early Oct. Weltsch viewed demands for national autonomy as irrelevant. See Weltsch to Kaznelson, 6 Oct. 1918, LBIA, RW, AR 7185, box 2, folder 19.

[36] Weltsch to ZCO, 2 Oct. 1918; Weltsch to Herrmann, 28 Oct. 1918, both in CZA, Z3/214; Herrmann to Weltsch, 1 Nov. 1918, CZA, L6/366; Weltsch, 'Die nationale Revolution im österreichischen Judentum und die jüdischen Nationalräte', 61.

[37] Weltsch to Herrmann, 16 Oct. 1918, CZA, Z3/850.

[38] Weltsch to Herrmann, 28 Oct. 1918, CZA, Z3/214. See also JZ, 1 Nov. 1918, p. 2. On Weltsch's disdain for local activists, see also Weltsch to Kaznelson, 28 Sept.; 1 and 6 Oct. 1918, LBIA, RW, AR 7185, box 2, folder 19.

matters 'exclusively concerning the Jewish people'. But the content of this autonomous administration was described as 'the complete field of Jewish cultural life, above all school and educational affairs' and welfare.[39]

The Council's establishment proved timely. The newly formed Jewish Soldiers' Committee, formed at a mass meeting at the beginning of November, immediately declared its allegiance and put itself at the Council's disposal.[40] Po'alei Zion announced that in such a 'historic hour' it was prepared to collaborate with the 'bourgeois Zionists' in the 'struggle for national rights'. (Vigilance, however, would be necessary in order to guard against the bourgeois tendency to 'flirt' with the Orthodox and engage in *shtadlones*.)[41] Also joining the Council were Viennese representatives of the Galician Jewish Social Democratic Party, along with Hashomer, the Orthodox Zionists of Yishuv Erets Yisrael, and nationalist student and sports organizations.[42] Politicization and nationalism appeared in some rather unlikely places. The administration of a Jewish nursing home, for example, reportedly resigned in the face of an 'assault' by nationally minded young nurses—recently returned from the front—protesting their working conditions.[43] Despite the Council's optimistic assessment that it was 'taking charge of the protection of Jewish interests' and that 'In this decisive moment, the national group within Jewry has assumed leadership', non-nationalist parties (aside from the marginal, Bundist-leaning Galician Jewish Social Democratic Party) were conspicuously absent from its ranks.[44] Weltsch and his allies hoped none the less to generate sufficient momentum

---

[39] *JZ*, 8 Nov. 1918, pp. 1–2. A more detailed version of this manifesto, asking for 'appropriate [Jewish] representation in territorial representative bodies and authorities' and in 'legislative and administrative bodies', was sent to the government on 4 Nov. 1918. See CZA, L6/366. The Council was officially constituted on 4 Nov.

[40] *OW*, 8 Nov. 1918, p. 710; *JZ*, 8 Nov. 1918, p. 4; Bericht über die Tätigkeit des Jüdischen Nationalrates für Deutschösterreich im ersten Monat seines Bestandes, 10 Dec. 1918, CZA, L6/93, claimed that there were 5,000 at the soldiers' meeting.

[41] *YA*, 1 Nov. 1918, p. 1; 8 Nov. 1918, p. 6. Po'alei Zion was represented on the Council presidium by Saul Sokal, a 'rightist' in the party's internal battles. See Singer, *Four Events with a Lesson from the History of the Workers' Movement in Austria*, 24–5. On the Czernowitz-born lawyer Sokal, see Reiss, *The Beginnings of the Jewish Workers' Movement in Galicia*, 200–1.

[42] *JZ*, 8 Nov. 1918, pp. 4–5; 15 Nov. 1918, p. 3; 22 Nov. 1918, p. 5; Leo Herrmann, 'Bericht über meine Reise', Dec. 1918 – Jan. 1919 , CZA, Z3/1696. A meeting organized by Yishuv Erets Yisrael on 5 Nov. attracted an estimated crowd of 1,000. See *JZ*, 15 Nov. 1918, p. 3.

[43] Julius Zappert, 'Kaiserin-Elisabeth-Institut für israelitische Krankenpflegerinnen', in *Festschrift anlässlich des fünfundzwanzigjährigen Bestandes des Israel. Humanitätsvereines 'Eintracht' (Bnai Brith) Wien 1903–1928* (Vienna, 1928), 93–4.

[44] For these claims, see *JZ*, 8 Nov. 1918, pp. 1–2.

and support to persuade the government to give serious consideration to Jewish demands for some form of self-determination.[45]

Initial signs were encouraging. Fortified by the enthusiastic popular response to their initiatives, Council representatives began negotiating with government officials on a range of issues. Talks with Christian Social officials yielded promising signs that Jewish nationality might indeed be recognized. The motivation underlying such a concession, an oft-expressed desire to circumscribe the Jewish presence in public life, was no secret to the Zionists, who were insistent that legal safeguards were necessary to obviate any moves of this kind. High on the Council's agenda were the November pogroms in Galicia. In a vain attempt to persuade the international community to exert pressure on the Polish government to protect Galician Jews, the Council repeatedly intervened with government officials and foreign representatives in Vienna. Further, the Council discussed with the administration the creation of a Jewish defence brigade; the formulation of the new state's citizenship law—protesting against attempts to insert implictly antisemitic clauses; and discrimination against Jewish state functionaries—the refusal, for example, to permit Jewish doctors to swear allegiance to, and thus be employed by, the new state on the grounds that all state employees must be of German-Austrian nationality.[46] By apparently treating the Council as the representative organization of Austrian Jewry in these cases, the government conferred a degree of legitimacy upon the Council's somewhat unwarranted presumption to speak in the name of all Jews.

THE JEWISH MILITIA

Perhaps the most striking example of the revolutionary tenor of Viennese Jewish society in the immediate post-war months was the creation of a Jewish militia in early November 1918. In the last weeks of October the armed forces of the monarchy virtually dissolved, with soldiers deserting from the front to make their way home.[47] Hundreds of thousands of these

[45] Herrmann, 'Bericht über meine Reise'; Situationsbericht des Jüdischen Pressbüros Wien, 10 Dec. 1918, CZA, Z3/1172; Weltsch, 'Österreichische Revolutionschronik', 356–8.

[46] See Bericht über die Tätigkeit des Jüdischen Nationalrates . . . im ersten Monat seines Bestandes, 10 Dec. 1918, CZA, L6/93; Situationsbericht des Jüdischen Pressbüros Wien, 10 Dec. 1918, CZA, Z3/1172. On negotiations with the government, see also *JZ*, 8 Nov. 1918, p. 4; 22 Nov. 1918, p. 6; 6 Dec. 1918, p. 5.

[47] Gunther E. Rothenberg, 'The Habsburg Army in the First World War, 1914–1918', in Béla K. Király and Nándor F. Dreisziger (eds.), *East Central European Society in World War I*, War and Society in East Central Europe, xix (New York, 1985), 296–7; István Deák, 'The Habsburg Army in the First and Last Days of World War I: A Comparative Analysis', ibid. 308–10.

soldiers, often armed and hungry, passed through Vienna, a hub of the rail network. It has been estimated that over 900,000 soldiers arrived in the city during the first three weeks of November, while a further 600,000 war-industry workers in Vienna and the surrounding areas suddenly found themselves unemployed, forming a 'large floating population driven by hunger'. According to B'nai B'rith, some 30,000 Jewish soldiers were in Vienna at this point.[48]

The city's police force was overwhelmed and undermanned, and the Volkswehr, the new state's army, began to form only in the first week of November. Coinciding with this, a powerful tide of revolutionary activism began to challenge Social Democratic control of the Viennese labour move-ment. By early November a communist party, a Red Guards militia, and workers' and soldiers' councils had been established. In the eyes of both Christian Socials and Social Democrats, these constituted a serious threat to public order, liable, as Social Democrat Julius Deutsch (a key figure in the creation of the Volkswehr) feared, 'to unleash civil war'.[49] In an attempt to restore order, the Viennese police formed a paramilitary city guard (the Stadtschutzwache) in the first week of November, quickly recruiting a force of some 2,700 men. Their principal tasks were the 'protection of the securi-ty of persons and property and the maintenance of public order'.[50] The impetus for the formation of the city guard came from the new Christian Social interior secretary, Heinrich Mataja, who had urged his party col-leagues throughout the war to revivify their antisemitism. Mataja con-ceived of the city guard as a counterweight to what he believed would be a socialist-dominated army.[51]

---

[48] See Strong, *Austria (October 1918 – March 1919)*, 144–6. The quotation is on p. 146. On the Jewish soldiers, see *ZBB* 22 (1919), 200.

[49] Julius Deutsch, *Aus Österreichs Revolution* (Vienna, 1921), 35. On the chaotic situation in Vienna in late Oct. and Nov. 1918, see also Plaschka *et al.*, *Innere Front*, ii. 316–28; Rudolf Neck (ed.), *Österreich im Jahre 1918* (Munich, 1968), 88–104, 152–9; Gerhard Botz, *Gewalt in der Poli-tik. Attentate, Zusammenstösse, Putschversuche, Unruhen in Österreich 1918 bis 1938* (Munich, 1983), 26–36. On left-wing activism, see Hans Hautmann, *Geschichte der Rätebewegung in Öster-reich 1918–1924* (Vienna, 1987), 231–61; id., *Die Anfänge der linksradikalen Bewegung und der kommunistischen Partei Deutschösterreichs*, 40–71.

[50] Elisabeth Jelinek, 'Der politische Lebensweg Dr. Heinrich Matajas', Ph.D. diss., Univer-sity of Vienna, 1970, 44. See also *Sechzig Jahre Wiener Sicherheitswache* (Vienna, 1929), 52–3. The Stadtschutzwache was part of the Wiener Sicherheitswache. Evidently, the threat did not come solely from the socialist camp. Paramilitary groups were also formed by German national-ists. See Molisch, *Politische Geschichte der deutschen Hochschulen in Österreich*, 256.

[51] Ludwig Jedlicka, *Ein Heer im Schatten der Parteien* (Graz, 1955), 13; Deutsch, *Aus Öster-reichs Revolution*, 28; Jelinek, 'Der politische Lebensweg Dr. Heinrich Matajas', 43–6. In Sept. 1917 Mataja had called on his party to return to a more pronounced antisemitic line, noting that

Concerned first and foremost about the potential for anti-Jewish violence in such an unstable environment, the Zionists set about organizing a Jewish defence force at the very same time. Herzl's faithful former lieutenant Isidor Schalit, who had remained at the margins of the movement during the war, was now prompted into action in response to a number of serious anti-Jewish outbreaks in the city. Under the aegis of the Jewish National Council, Schalit and Siegfried Bernfeld recruited some 3,000 demobilized Jewish soldiers within the space of a few days.[52] They initially proposed that these soldiers form autonomous Jewish units within the army, an idea rejected by both Julius Deutsch and the German nationalist secretary for the army, Josef Mayer. Following negotiations with Mataja, Mayer, and police chief Johann Schober (with whom Schalit was already acquainted), the Jewish soldiers were incorporated into the city guard as a quasi-independent force, sporting their own nationalist blue-and-white insignia.[53]

The Jewish battalions, as Schalit called them, were immediately posted at strategic points throughout the city. Guarding railway stations and monitoring the bridges leading from the Inner City into the heavily Jewish-populated Leopoldstadt, the battalions marched demonstratively through Leopoldstadt in military formation. Given that the city guard itself had less than 3,000 men at its disposal, the Jewish units provided invaluable reinforcement in keeping the peace in the city at large, concentrating in particular on Leopoldstadt and the adjacent area of Brigittenau. Set up primarily as a Jewish self-defence force, the Jewish soldiers quickly came to bear, by dint of circumstance, considerable responsibility for maintaining law and order in Vienna. From the point of view of the National Council, formal affiliation with the city guard removed the substantial burden of financing and supporting the Jewish troops, since food, accommodation, and remuneration were provided by the government. It was, in addition, important public confirmation of the Council's status and effectiveness; indeed, it

the Christian Socials were 'conceivable only as an antisemitic party'. See *JZ*, 14 Sept. 1917, p. 3; *WH*, 21 Sept. 1917, pp. 4–5. See also Boyer, *Culture and Political Crisis in Vienna*, 432–7; Jelinek, 'Der politische Lebensweg Dr. Heinrich Matajas', 25–6.

[52] Schalit recounts his role in his memoir in CZA, A196/62/1. On recruitment, see *Arbeiter Zeitung*, 5 Nov. 1918, p. 6; *JZ*, 8 Nov. 1918, p. 7. See also the recruiting poster in CZA, Z3/214.

[53] *JZ*, 8 Nov. 1918, p. 2; 15 Nov. 1918, pp. 4–5; Bericht über die Tätigkeit des Jüdischen Nationalrates . . . im ersten Monat seines Bestandes, 10 Dec. 1918, CZA, L6/93; Deutsch, *Aus Österreichs Revolution*, 34; CZA, A196/62/1; Herrmann to Copenhagen Zionist Office, 8 Nov. 1918, CZA, Z3/214. Schober had been police chief in Vienna during the war and twice served as Austrian chancellor, in 1921–2 and again in 1929–30.

was a political triumph.[54] In the very week in which the Council announced its existence, it not only received tacit recognition from the new authorities as a representative Jewish body, but also successfully created something hitherto unknown to Viennese Jewry—a government-sanctioned, armed Jewish militia.

In the ensuing months the new state gradually consolidated its administrative infrastructure and took steps to ease the security situation, regaining control of the streets and returning a semblance of normality to daily life. The anomalous situation in which ethnic militias and paramilitary police patrolled the capital's streets was put to an end when the city guard became one arm of the expanding internal security forces (and, contrary to Mataja's wishes, began to establish closer links with the army). As a consequence, the autonomy of the Jewish units was already curtailed by March 1919. Rather than joining the regular city guard, most Jewish soldiers chose instead to resign, preferring to resume their pre-war, non-military careers. What remained was a much-diminished group of approximately 300, funded by the Gemeinde as well as by nationalist sources, that continued to function as a part-time, semi-autonomous Jewish security force.[55]

The militia marked a radical departure in the history of Viennese Jewry. Bundist and Zionist self-defence had, of course, been a feature of Russian Jewish responses to the wave of violent pogroms of 1903–6.[56] If Austria was not the Pale, Jewish self-defence was nevertheless not unknown in the modern period, even in central Europe. Many of the violent anti-Jewish outbreaks during the 1848 Revolution, for example, were met by armed Jews determined to defend home and hearth. Either in separate units or as part of *ad hoc* citizen militias, Jews fought back in Prague and in other Bohemian, Moravian, and Silesian towns and cities, in Pressburg, and even in

[54] In addition to Schalit's memoir in CZA, A196/62/1, see the accounts by Willy Rosenthal (Uri Nadav), one of the militia's commanders, in YVA, PKA/E-11; *JZ*, 8 Nov. 1918, p. 5; Henisch, *At Home and Abroad*, 167–8; *Arbeiter Zeitung*, 5 Nov. 1918, p. 6; 18 Nov. 1918, p. 3; Paret, Preface to Siegfried Bernfeld, *Sisyphus*, pp. xvi–xvii; Aryeh Sahawi-Goldhammer, *Dr. Leopold Plaschkes. Zwei Generationen des österreichischen Judentums* (Tel Aviv, 1943), 40–1.

[55] On the development of the city guard, see Deutsch, *Aus Österreichs Revolution*, 28; Jelinek, 'Der politische Lebensweg Dr. Heinrich Matajas', 45–6; *Sechzig Jahre Wiener Sicherheitswache*, 53. On the dissolution of the Jewish units, see CZA, A196/62/1; YVA, PKA/E-11. On continued funding for the Jewish group, see Jüdische Zentral-Hilfs-Komitee Bericht, 8 Dec. 1918, CAHJP, AW, 250/5; Protocol of this committee's meeting of 11 Jan. 1919, CAHJP, AW, 586/4; Protokoll der Vertreter-Sitzung, 8 Feb. 1919, CAHJP, AW, 72/17; Protokolle der Plenar-Sitzungen, suppl., 26 May 1919, CAHJP, AW, 71/17.

[56] See Shlomo Lambroza, 'Jewish Self-Defence during the Russian Pogroms of 1903–1906', *Jewish Journal of Sociology*, 23 (1981), 123–34.

Rome and Alsace.[57] These, however, remained isolated instances, dramatic responses to extreme provocation and revolutionary turmoil. In central and western Europe, unlike in the Russian empire, such levels of threat and insecurity were generally considered the exception rather than the rule. Co-ordinated self-defence of this sort was not, in fact, to become necessary again until the similarly fraught post-war months, when a whole slew of Jewish militias was created. It was not just necessity that proved the mother of invention in this case; never before had tens of thousands of war-hardened, recently demobilized Jewish soldiers been on hand. Here was an illustration that the brutality and militarization endemic to the war had seeped into Jewish society. It was evidence, too, of the nationalism and radicalization that had taken hold among central and eastern European Jewry in this period. The Viennese militia, like the National Council that acted as its midwife, was part of a broader movement.

In post-Habsburg Hungary, for example, Jewish soldiers formed a number of Jewish brigades and offered their services to a grateful government. Estimates of the number of troops involved range from 5,000 to a rather extraordinary 11,000 (a figure that may well have included paid non-Jewish recruits). Like their Viennese counterpart, the government-sanctioned Hungarian brigades were a nationalist initiative, popularly known as the Zionist Guards. Commanded by some 200 former army officers and financed by a wide variety of Jewish sources (including some Orthodox organizations), the brigades served in most areas of the country. Far from confining themselves to protecting Jews, in the absence of regular police or army they acted in many places as the pre-eminent enforcers of security and order. As in Vienna, the Jewish brigades were short-lived, voluntarily disbanding at the beginning of March 1919 as the government attempted to regularize its security apparatus. A separate, ethnically or denominationally based mini-army of this sort was no longer acceptable or welcome.[58]

In Galicia violent and deadly pogroms erupted in numerous towns and cities at the end of the war. In Lemberg, where Polish and Ukrainian troops fought bitterly for control of the city, a Jewish militia of some 300 soldiers,

---

[57] Jacob Toury, *Turmoil and Confusion in the Revolution of 1848* (Heb.) (Tel Aviv, 1968), 89–98; Michael Brenner, Stefi Jersch-Wenzel, and Michael A. Meyer, *Emancipation and Acculturation 1780–1871*, vol. ii of Michael A. Meyer (ed.), *German-Jewish History in Modern Times* (New York, 1997), 281–2.

[58] Y. Zvi Zahavi, *A History of Zionism in Hungary* (Heb.) (Jerusalem, 1972), ii. 307–19; Livia Elvira Bitton, 'Zionism in Hungary: The First Twenty-Five Years', *Herzl Year Book*, 7 (1971), 305–9; Löwenheim, 'The Leadership of the Neolog Jewish Congregation of Pest', 105–8.

decked out in Austrian army uniforms with blue-and-white armbands, attempted to protect Jews from the depredations of both sides. As in Hungary, this was a nationalist initiative that received wide support. Recognized by both Ukrainians and Poles, the militia performed sterling service both militarily and in the provision of emergency food and welfare. In Czernowitz, the main city of neighbouring Bukovina, Jewish nationalist soldiers banded together at the end of October 1918 to protect the city's Jews, this time caught between Ukrainian and Romanian forces. Armed with stolen weapons and ammunition, the hundreds of soldiers and officers in this self-defence force formed an important part of a multinational armed force created in Czernowitz in early November. In Pressburg, a force of nearly 200—again, mostly nationalist—Jewish soldiers patrolled the city, focusing particularly on the Jewish quarter. Financed in the main from Jewish sources, not all of whom were sympathetic to Zionism, this Jewish 'Guard' was recognized and approved by the Hungarian authorities. As Czech troops approached Pressburg in December 1918, the Hungarian military requested 100 men to assist in the city's defence. Here too, though, as in Lemberg, the Jews chose to remain scrupulously neutral when faced with a choice between warring national factions. Jewish troops, they argued, ought only to be used for the protection of Jews. Similar units were also formed in Bohemia, Moravia, and Ukraine.[59]

It is clear, then, that the Vienna militia was neither isolated nor unique, but was rather one part of probably the most extensive and impressive network of armed Jewish self-defence in European Jewish history. Jewish military action on this unprecedented scale was first and foremost an improvised response to disaster and semi-anarchy, made necessary and possible only by the dire post-war chaos and the singularly uncommon availability of large reserves of Jewish military manpower. But the nationalist domination of this self-defence effort was not coincidental. Jewish heroism and military prowess were key elements of Zionist ideology and mythology, and the militias formed an integral part of the broader

[59] On Lemberg, see B. Lubotsky (ed.), *The Life of a Fighting Zionist* (Heb.) (Jerusalem, 1947), 33–42; *JZ*, 31 Jan. 1919, pp. 2–3. On Galician pogroms, see Mendelsohn, *Zionism in Poland*, 88–91; *JZ*, 15 Nov. 1918, pp. 1–2; 22 Nov. 1918, pp. 2–4. For Czernowitz, see Schmelzer, 'Die Juden in der Bukowina', 70. (Schmelzer was one of the leaders of the force.) On Pressburg, see S. Komlosi, 'Geschichte der jüdischen Garde anno 1918', in Hugo Gold (ed.), *Die Juden und die Judengemeinde Bratislava in Vergangenheit und Gegenwart* (Brünn, 1932), 151–5. On Ukraine, see Abramson, *A Prayer for the Government*, 82–5. For Bohemia and Moravia, see Lipscher, 'Die Lage der Juden in der Tschechoslowakei nach deren Gründung 1918 bis zu den Parlamentswahlen 1920', 8–9, 29; *JZ*, 15 Nov. 1918, p. 3.

programme of the Jewish National Councils and their strong push for Jewish autonomy in the post-war order.[60]

If under less pressure than its counterparts in Lemberg or Czernowitz, and less imposing in size than the brigades in Hungary, the very existence of the Viennese militia none the less reflected a degree of Jewish defiance and self-assertion inconceivable even a few months previously. Recall, for example, the sum total of the Gemeinde response to the wave of intense antisemitism that reached its height in the summer of 1918: a protest resolution. To be sure, that resolution had hinted at the need for Jewish self-defence. There was, though, a great distance between hints and action, and it was only in the much more threatening and anarchic situation of the post-war months that a far more audacious response became feasible and appropriate. Externally, the new and inexperienced government was casting around for assistance from all available sources; internally, the Gemeinde and its liberal establishment allies were temporarily shell-shocked, lacking a coherent plan. The nationalist militia was a vivid symbol of the changes in Viennese Jewry wrought by the war.

LIBERALISM UNDER SIEGE:
THE BATTLE FOR THE GEMEINDE

For all its success, the National Council did not go unchallenged, and reaction was not long in coming. In contrast to many areas of Poland, and also to Prague, where the National Councils succeeded to a degree in drawing non-nationalists into their orbit, in Vienna neither the liberals nor the Orthodox evinced the slightest inclination to acquiesce in the Council's claims to represent all Viennese Jews.[61] Nationalist support, they repeatedly stressed, was confined to a noisy minority, composed overwhelmingly of east Europeans and youth. 'The outlook of the *Ostjuden*', wrote a Viennese lawyer, 'is inappropriate for Vienna and western Austria. . . . What may be a blessing for them, what they may even see as their salvation [i.e. nationalism], is for western Jews intolerable and downright disastrous.'[62] The east European refugees, echoed a second observer, were only 'guests' in Vienna.[63]

[60] On the importance of heroic models for the nationalists, see Mendelsohn, *On Modern Jewish Politics*, 103–9.

[61] On Poland, see Moshe Landau, *The Jews as a National Minority in Poland 1918–1928* (Heb.) (Jerusalem, 1986), 30–42. On Prague, see Kieval, *The Making of Czech Jewry*, 189–93.

[62] *OW*, 18 Oct. 1918, pp. 659–60.

[63] *OW*, 15 Nov. 1918, p. 722. See also *OW*, 25 Oct. 1918, pp. 674–7; 1 Nov. 1918, p. 689; 22 Nov. 1918, p. 737; 13 Dec. 1918, pp. 785–6; 27 Dec. 1918, pp. 823–4.

The Gemeinde leadership declared in early November that the Council's creation had 'provoked anxiety' among the 'undeniable majority' of Viennese Jews who saw 'social and economic danger in the abandonment of the idea that the Jews are only a religious community'.[64] In early December a group of 'German-Austrian Jews', comprising leading members of the Austrian Israelite Union, B'nai B'rith, and the Gemeinde, issued a statement repudiating the Council 'in the name of the overwhelming majority of our co-religionists' and insisting that 'the bond that unites and maintains Jewry is exclusively confessional. We feel ourselves through *Heimat*, language, and education to be German and to be fully equal citizens of the German-Austrian republic.'[65] At the same time the Union wrote to the government disputing the Council's right to speak on behalf of German-Austrian Jewry and rejecting its call for 'separate or national minority rights'.[66] In late December the Union claimed to have received 'more than ten thousand' letters from 'all strata of Viennese Jewry' in support of its anti-nationalist position.[67]

The Orthodox, too, were aghast at the Council's presumption to speak in their name. The nationalists were 'a small group, pursuing unilateral goals, drawing attention to themselves in all too loud a fashion, trying to seize the reins of leadership, but possessing neither the numbers nor the programme to do so legitimately'.[68] For the Orthodox, though, an equally pressing issue was whether their opposition to the Council should take them further down the path of active political engagement. While it was agreed that in the general political domain a low profile was advisable, the desire to protect Orthodox interests provided the spur—as it had in late 1917—to greater involvement in Jewish politics.[69] In early December Orthodox groups made

[64] *OW*, 8 Nov. 1918, p. 705. Calling the declaration the Gemeinde's 'swansong', the Council responded that anxiety would be engendered only in those who were 'against democracy and for plutocracy'. See *JZ*, 15 Nov. 1918, p. 2.

[65] *OW*, 6 Dec. 1918, pp. 779–80. In response, the Council beat a tactical retreat, protesting that it represented only those Jews who acknowledged the existence of a Jewish nationality. See ibid. 780. Noting that the statement carefully avoided using the term 'nation' in its assertion of German sentiment, the nationalists were particularly galled by the implication that they were not fully loyal to the new state. The protest, they wrote, was 'deceitful and contemptible', an example of 'ghetto psychology', See *JZ*, 6 Dec. 1918, pp. 1–2, 5.

[66] *OW*, 6 Dec. 1918, p. 780. On 9 Dec. a delegation of the Action Committee of German-Austrian Jews reiterated these protests to Karl Seitz, a leading Social Democratic member of the government. See *OW*, 13 Dec. 1918, p. 800. This committee took no further public action.

[67] *OW*, 3 Jan. 1919, pp. 8–10; *JZ*, 10 Jan. 1919, p. 3.

[68] *JK*, 21 Nov. 1918, p. 1. For similar views, see also *JK*, 7 Nov. 1918, pp. 2–3; 5 Dec. 1918, p. 1; *OW*, 20 Dec. 1918, pp. 814–15; *JZ*, 15 Nov. 1918, pp. 3–4.

[69] *JK*, 7 Nov. 1918, pp. 1–3; 14 Nov. 1918, pp. 2–3; 21 Nov. 1918, p. 1.

an abortive attempt to set up an Orthodox counterpart to the Council; its brief was 'to protect Orthodox interests . . . and to act as Orthodoxy's representative'.[70] It was 'imperative', wrote one commentator, 'to politicize Orthodox Jewry', although he added the slightly hesitant rider that this ought to be done only 'to a certain degree'. Only in this way would it be possible to assert Orthodox rights against the 'so-called liberal Jews' controlling the Gemeinde and to battle the 'creeping poison of nationalism' that was making alarming inroads among Orthodox Jewry.[71] Orthodox opinion was at one with the liberals in opposing any form of Jewish autonomy in the new state, asking solely for legal equality and the freedom necessary to pursue a traditional lifestyle.[72]

These disagreements about Jewish status and the Jewish role in the new republic came to a head in a protracted and bitter conflict in the Gemeinde. Following the success of their mass rallies in October the nationalists turned their attention to the Gemeinde, hoping at last to realize their long-standing goal of transforming this symbol of the old order into a democratically elected *Volksgemeinde*.[73] Large and rowdy crowds gathered outside the Gemeinde offices in the Inner City, calling for the resignation of the leadership; armed soldiers threatened to storm the building. The streets, exclaimed one scandalized liberal leader, were 'suddenly full of Jews'.[74] '[T]he democratization of the world', proclaimed the nationalists, 'cannot stop at the doors of Jewish city hall.' The Gemeinde was a 'farce . . . incapable of protecting Jewish interests'.[75] Alarmed at the prospect that the revolutionary tide that had swept away the Habsburgs was also about to wash over the institutions of Jewish society, liberal leaders (including Rudolf Schwarz-Hiller and B'nai B'rith president Salomon Ehrmann, but not, significantly, Alfred Stern) entered into negotiations with the Council in an attempt to avert disaster. In a tacit admission of the weakness of their position, they agreed to replace the Gemeinde's governing board with a Steering Committee made up equally of liberals and nationalists. The Council demanded that democratic elections, open to all Jews resident in

---

[70] *JK*, 5 Dec. 1918, p. 2. Like the liberal Action Committee, this Orthodox initiative was still-born.

[71] *JK*, 19 Dec. 1918, p. 1.   [72] See *JK*, 7 Nov. 1918, pp. 2–3; 5 Dec. 1918, pp. 1–2.

[73] Leo Herrmann, for example, advised Weltsch: 'In my opinion you must now attempt to democratize the Kultusgemeinde by storm and make it the centre of your politics. . . . The Gemeinde must assume a strong national character so that we can carry out our work in it' (Herrmann to Weltsch, 1 Nov. 1918, CZA, L6/366). See also *JZ*, 1 Nov. 1918, p. 3.

[74] *OW*, 8 Nov. 1918, p. 707. See also *JZ*, 24 Jan. 1919, p. 1.   [75] *JZ*, 8 Nov. 1918, p. 1.

Vienna, be held as soon as possible, arguing that since the last elections had been held in 1912, the Gemeinde's board had long since forfeited its mandate to govern. The Steering Committee's primary tasks were to draft new democratic electoral laws and to administer Jewish affairs until new elections were held.[76]

Crucial to the nationalist plan was that Stern, the pre-eminent symbol of the old regime, resign. They threatened, so it was reported to Stern, that 'street battles would result' and 'blood would flow' should he remain at his post. He refused to budge, dismissing the threats of violence: 'One may yield to public violence, but one is not obliged to do so.' To accept the nationalists' demands, he argued, was tantamount to granting legitimacy to the Council, recognizing it not merely as an equal but as a pace-setter, allowing it to dictate its will to Viennese Jewry. He would, he admitted, be prepared to co-opt additional nationalists onto the Gemeinde board and to accept a more democratic electoral system, but not to bow meekly to Council dictates and agree to a compromise that was in reality a capitulation. His colleagues insisted, however, that the threat of bloodshed was indeed real should he persist in his obstruction. For perhaps the first time in his long career Stern bowed to their pressure and submitted his resignation.[77]

In order to avoid a 'catastrophe', as Schwarz-Hiller expressed it, Stern's colleagues had in effect engineered a palace coup and offered the Council an equal role in Gemeinde affairs.[78] In nationalist eyes, this amounted to an admission by the liberals that they no longer enjoyed legitimacy.[79] Overnight the nationalists had made giant strides towards conquering the Gemeinde. Previously holding two of the thirty-six seats on the governing

[76] On the formation of the Steering Committee (Permanenzkommission) and the role of Ehrmann and Schwarz-Hiller, see *JZ*, 8 Nov. 1918, pp. 2, 6; *OW*, 15 Nov. 1918, p. 731; Protokolle der Plenar-Sitzungen, 5 and 13 Nov. 1918, CAHJP, AW, 71/16; Weltsch to Herrmann, 28 Oct. 1918, CZA, Z3/214; Herrmann to Weltsch, 1 Nov. 1918, CZA, L6/366. See also the material in CAHJP, AW, 79. For Schwarz-Hiller's ideas about the Gemeinde, see *OW*, 8 Nov. 1918, pp. 707–8; 29 Nov. 1918, pp. 759–62.

[77] Protokolle der Plenar-Sitzungen, suppl., 5 Nov. 1918, CAHJP, AW, 71/16; *OW*, 8 Nov. 1918, pp. 712–13.

[78] Protokolle der Plenar-Sitzungen, suppl., 5 Nov. 1918, CAHJP, AW, 71/16; IKG Draft Report 1913–1918; *JZ*, 24 Jan. 1919, p. 1; Freidenreich, *Jewish Politics in Vienna*, 38.

[79] The six-member committee (three from each party) included Karl Pollak, former president of the Zionist Central Committee for Western Austria; Leopold Plaschkes, soon to be elected to the Vienna city council on a Jewish nationalist ticket; and liberal anti-nationalist Heinrich Schreiber. Stricker managed to keep out Weltsch's preferred candidate, Adolf Böhm. See Herrmann, 'Bericht über meine Reise'. No agreement could be reached on a successor to Stern. See IKG Draft Report 1913–1918. Schwarz-Hiller reportedly refused an offer to assume the presidency. See *JK*, 14 Nov. 1918, p. 2.

board and none at all in the Vertreter Kollegium, the élite executive commit-tee that was the board's true power centre, they were now equal partners. 'The system of the Kultusgemeinde could not endure,' crowed the *Jüdische Zeitung*, 'because it was built on absolutist bureaucracy and indifference to [the needs of] Gemeinde members. . . . We hope that this day is the begin-ning of a new era for Viennese Jewry. . . . The aged Kultusgemeinde shall make room for a new, youthful, reinvigorated *Volksgemeinde*.'[80]

The removal of Stern, who died only a few weeks later, deprived Jewish lib-eralism in Vienna of its guiding spirit.[81] The liberals' loss of nerve, though, proved only temporary; they soon regrouped and began a spirited rearguard action, led by Heinrich Schreiber, long-time nemesis of the nationalists. The Steering Committee's initial brief was to prepare the ground for elections to be held early in 1919. Upon receipt of the nationalists' draft proposal for new electoral statutes in mid-December, however, Schreiber and his associates requested that discussion be postponed until mid-January, at which time they would present counter-proposals. Their own draft made little effort to bridge the gap between the two sides. While the nationalists suggested democratic elections, open to men and women, with very few franchise restrictions (the right to vote was not to be contingent on payment of communal taxes or long-time residence in Vienna), the liberals wished to exclude non-taxpayers and non-citizens, offered only limited franchise to women and Gemeinde employees, and wanted to retain the two-tier system whereby those paying high taxes were granted a double vote.[82]

To the nationalists, the proposed statutes were scandalous. Lacking the 'slightest concession to the victorious spirit of democracy', they consti-tuted an 'insulting mockery' and 'affront' that would be 'avenged'.[83] Having 'shamelessly broken' the November agreement, the 'Kahalgrossen' were playing for time, regretting their previous weakness now that the 'storms have subsided [and] the commotion has abated'. Parading as liberals and democrats in the general political domain, they erected 'the most reactionary tyranny on the Jewish street'.[84] The liberals' uncompromising stance, how-ever, was not merely a matter of tactics. Rather, it was that their conception of the Gemeinde was diametrically opposed to that of the nationalists.

[80] *JZ*, 8 Nov. 1918, p. 1.
[81] For reactions to Stern's resignation, see *OW*, 15 Nov. 1918, pp. 724–6; *JK*, 14 Nov. 1918, pp. 2–3; *JZ*, 8 Nov. 1918, p. 1.
[82] See *JZ*, 3 Jan. 1919, pp. 1–2; 10 Jan. 1919, p. 1; *OW*, 7 Mar. 1919, pp. 151–4; *JK*, 16 Jan. 1919, p. 1; *WH*, 7 Mar. 1919, pp. 4–6.   [83] *JZ*, 17 Jan. 1919, p. 1.
[84] *JZ*, 24 Jan. 1919, p. 1. For further criticism, see *JZ*, 7 Feb. 1919, pp. 3–4; 14 Feb. 1919, p. 2.

Democracy had no relevance in a voluntary, non-political, religious administrative body such as the Gemeinde. For Schreiber, demands for democracy in such a context were mere 'demagogy'.[85] He declared himself satisfied with the current Gemeinde statutes. In this, he wrote, he was a 'reactionary', although in general he considered himself a staunch 'progressive'.[86]

Further complicating the situation were Orthodox demands, led by the Hungarian-dominated *Schiffschul* and the Association for the Protection of the Interests of Orthodox Jewry, that they too be represented on the Steering Committee. Although expressing their customary ambivalence about involvement in Gemeinde affairs, they were galvanized into action once it became clear that their interests were likely to be directly affected (in much the same way they had responded to the possibility of federal reform of the empire). 'When it is a matter of creating new foundations for the Kultusgemeinde,' wrote one Orthodox commentator, 'the liberals and nationalists have no right to decide unilaterally and arbitrarily; the broad masses of Orthodox Jewry must also have a say.'[87] Maintaining a studied indifference towards the disputing camps, they asked only that their voice, too, be heard in the discussion about reform.[88] Unlike their rivals, though, they possessed neither a sufficiently engaged constituency nor a solid enough institutional base to ensure a hearing for their version of reform—Torah-based and opposed to secular nationalism. Consequently, Orthodox demands were mostly ignored.[89]

Despite an intensification of interest-group politics within the Gemeinde—communal rabbis, non-Orthodox synagogues, and Gemeinde employees all demanded representation and a voice in the reform debates— the main battle was fought out between nationalists and liberals.[90] The

---

[85] *OW*, 8 Nov. 1918, p. 707.

[86] *OW*, 6 Dec. 1918, pp. 77–8. See also *OW*, 7 Mar. 1919, pp. 153–4.

[87] *JK*, 14 Nov. 1918, p. 3. See also *JK*, 5 Dec. 1918, p. 2; 16 Jan. 1919, p. 1; *JZ*, 3 Jan. 1919, p. 6; *OW*, 27 Dec. 1918, p. 824.

[88] *JK*, 20 Mar. 1919, p. 1; 27 Mar. 1919, p. 1; 22 May 1919, p. 2.

[89] See *JK*, 6 June 1919, p. 6; 24 Oct. 1919, p. 1. These moves towards increasing engagement in Gemeinde affairs contributed to the Orthodox decision to run an independent list for the first time in the Gemeinde elections of June 1920. For debate about participation in Gemeinde elections, see *JK*, 25 July 1919, p. 1; 1 Aug. 1919, p. 1; 24 Oct. 1919, pp. 1–2; 14 Nov. 1919, pp. 2–3; 21 Nov. 1919, pp. 1–2; 28 Nov. 1919, pp. 1–2; 18 June 1920, pp. 1–4; 25 June 1920, pp. 1–4; 2 July 1920, pp. 1–2; Freidenreich, *Jewish Politics in Vienna*, 130–1. Galician Orthodoxy (outside the small Mizrahi and other nationalist-leaning circles) remained less organized than the Hungarian Orthodox and did not run an independent list. See Freidenreich, *Jewish Politics in Vienna*, 139–41.

[90] For communal rabbis, see *OW*, 22 Nov. 1918, pp. 738–9. For synagogue associations, see

Steering Committee soon reached a dead end, stalled by the liberals' delaying tactics and the irreducible ideological differences between the two sides. The committee ceded its role as arbiter of Jewish affairs to the Gemeinde's governing board, which now reasserted itself in no uncertain terms.[91] Parity between the parties was thus short-lived, as the nationalists were still only a small minority on the board, notwithstanding the co-option into its ranks of their three Steering Committee members. Months of bitter wrangling about electoral reform ensued, marked by nationalist accusations of treachery and threats of retribution should the 'will of the people' be ignored. Customarily a place of placid administrative business, the Gemeinde chambers were now the scene of political brawling that rivalled the worst days of the Reichsrat. Board meetings on reform, attended by noisy and unruly audiences of Zionist supporters, frequently degenerated into tumult; nationalist walk-outs, shouting, and mutual recriminations were the order of the day.[92]

The result of this conflict was never in doubt. No matter how loudly and vehemently they protested, the nationalists lacked the numbers to carry the day. None the less, their efforts were not entirely wasted. The new electoral laws, in place by May 1919, clearly reflected liberal awareness that the Gemeinde needed to adapt to the democratic post-war order. The two-tier system was discarded; proportional representation introduced; women and Gemeinde employees were given the vote but denied the right to be elected to office; and though the franchise was tied to German-Austrian citizenship (thus excluding many refugees from former Habsburg territories) and to payment of communal taxes, the minimum tax ceiling was lowered.[93] While less than ideal from the nationalists' perspective, the revised statutes

---

OW, 28 Mar. 1919, pp. 198–200. For Gemeinde employees, see *OW*, 9 May 1919, p. 285. See also Palmon, 'The Jewish Community of Vienna between the Two World Wars', 67–9.

[91] To continue the work of drafting new electoral statutes, the board appointed a successor to the defunct Steering Committee, giving the nationalists two of the nine seats on the new body. See *JZ*, 10 Jan. 1919, pp. 1, 3; 17 Jan. 1919, pp. 1, 3; 7 Mar. 1919, p. 2; Protokolle der Plenar-Sitzungen, suppl., 27 Feb. 1919, CAHJP, AW, 71/17; IKG Draft Report 1913–1918.

[92] On these meetings, see *JZ*, 7 Mar. 1919, pp. 1–2; 14 Mar. 1919, pp. 2–3; 21 Mar. 1919, pp. 3–4; *OW*, 7 Mar. 1919, pp. 151–4; 21 Mar. 1919, pp. 184–6; 4 Apr. 1919, pp. 216–18; 11 Apr. 1919, pp. 234–5; 23 May 1919, pp. 316–17; 30 May 1919, pp. 332–3.

[93] Details of the new statutes are in Protokolle der Plenar-Sitzungen, 27 Feb. 1919; 13 Mar. 1919; 26 Mar. 1919, CAHJP, AW, 74/6. See also 'Entwurf einer Wahlordnung . . . vom 27 Feb. 1919', CAHJP, AW, 2924; Palmon, 'The Jewish Community of Vienna between the Two World Wars', 78–9; Freidenreich, *Jewish Politics in Vienna*, 40. Further revisions were undertaken in 1924 and 1932. See Freidenreich, *Jewish Politics in Vienna*, 41, 46, 149–50.

gave them cause to hope for greater success in future elections. The introduction of proportional voting, the *Jüdische Zeitung* noted with exquisite
logic, would 'ensure appropriate minority representation, so that presumably the new governing board will not be exclusively Zionist'.[94] The
Gemeinde was derided in mid-May as 'today more than ever a fiction.
Everything of value and consequence in Jewry takes place outside it. . . .
The Jewish nationalists are now indisputably the representatives of Jewry
in public life. It is an untenable state of affairs that the Gemeinde should be
denied them.'[95] The nationalists' expectation that the Gemeinde, which
remained a central and powerful institution for Viennese Jewry, would simply fall into their hands, a prospect that had appeared imminent in early
November (if only to them), had by this stage well and truly receded. They
did not, in fact, gain control of it until 1932.

Jewish liberalism, though certainly diminished by the buffeting of war
and the collapse of empire, was by no means dead in the water. Quite the
contrary. After a period of initial disarray the liberals proudly reasserted
the vigour and relevance of their integrationist philosophy, modified only
slightly to suit the new circumstances. The core of their *Weltanschauung*—
the dovetailing of a German-Austrian cultural identity with an ethnically
tinged religious Jewish identity—remained intact, although now of course
stripped of its dynastic trappings. Like the nationalists and the Orthodox,
they transferred almost lock, stock, and barrel their pre-war store of ideas
about Jewish society and identity, their solutions to the Jewish Question, to
the post-war period. And in the ethnically homogeneous Austrian republic
Jewish liberalism proved a viable entity until well into the 1930s. The same
cannot be said of Austrian liberalism, which was marginalized by the forces
of socialism and nationalism during the inter-war years.[96]

---

[94] *JZ*, 30 May 1919, p. 3. For the negative Zionist response to the new statutes, see also *JZ*, 13
June 1919, p. 1. There were critical assessments also in *WH*, 4 Apr. 1919, p. 3; 30 May 1919, p. 5;
JK, 6 June 1919, pp. 1–2. Schreiber's more positive response is in *OW*, 6 June 1919, pp. 349–50.

[95] *JZ*, 16 May 1919, p. 5.

[96] See Adam Wandruszka, 'Österreichs politische Struktur', in Heinrich Benedikt (ed.),
Geschichte der Republik Österreich (Vienna, 1954), 291–485.

CONCLUSION

THE end of the Habsburg empire signalled a watershed for its Jews. None had been more devoted to its supranational underpinnings; none grieved more at its passing. Until the last, Jews hoped that the empire would emerge renewed from the war, democratic, tolerant, and pluralistic. Since they had by and large prospered in the old order, and since—unlike almost everyone else—they had no alternative home, Habsburg loyalism died hard among the Jews. At one stroke, they were deprived of a tenaciously held cultural and political identity, and a protective political umbrella—no small matters for a dispersed and dependent minority. For the Jews of Vienna, the loss was doubly traumatic, compounded as it was by the abrupt diminishing of their city. With the notion of Habsburg Austrian Jewry now relegated to the realm of nostalgia, the political culture of Viennese Jewry—like that of Vienna in general—underwent a metamorphosis, its immediate horizons reduced in scope from those of the focal point of an empire to those of a large city in a small nation-state. The collapse of the monarchy brought about a seismic upheaval in Jewish society, an upheaval that can only be understood with reference to the four long years of war and privation that preceded it.

These were years of loss—loss of life above all, but also of established beliefs and certainties about European society and civilization. No less than other Europeans, and perhaps even more (as they so often claimed at the time), Jews were forced to grapple with fundamental questions about society and their place in it. As a minority group, questions of this nature were often formulated as questions of identity, personal and collective. It is a truism that bears repeating that identity is not a fixed category of self-definition, and the case of Austrian Jewry clearly bears this out. One concrete expression of Jewish efforts to come to terms with these large issues was their political culture, which has been a central focus of this book. The Viennese Jewish political landscape, emblematic in this instance of Austrian Jewry as a whole, changed markedly in the course of the war and its aftermath: nationalism and ethnic self-determination grew increasingly powerful, as was true among other minorities in eastern and central Europe. Unlike many regions of eastern Europe, however, where Jewish nationalism continued to hold sway, the reign of the nationalists as the leading force of Viennese Jewry was brief.

Notwithstanding these significant changes, pre-war Jewish ideologies survived almost intact the wholesale transformation of their external environment. Neither the experience of war nor the replacement of the multinational empire by an ethnically homogeneous nation-state led to substantial revision of the underlying ideological premises of Viennese Jewish society and politics; Jewish identities remained firmly grounded in their pre-war assumptions and frameworks, whether nationalist, liberal, or Orthodox. Of course, much did change. The end of empire abruptly put paid to the extra-local agendas that had bulked so large in Viennese Jewish affairs, reflected during the war in the refugee welfare effort and in the Congress and youth movements. Jewish confidence in liberalism as a political home was severely dented. For Jewish liberals, caught for decades between the hammer of anti-semitism and the anvil of Jewish nationalism and Orthodoxy, the war and the monarchy's collapse appeared finally to sweep away the reasonable, rational world they wished for. Yet Jewish liberalism survived and re-emerged in the post-war period with a vigour that Austrian liberals could only envy, remaining an influential movement in Vienna in the 1920s and even into the 1930s. Nationalists lost the multi-ethnic hinterland that played an indispensable role in their political self-conception; at a loss to reformulate their political identity, they anachronistically transferred their pre-war worldview into the utterly different circumstances of the post-war Austrian republic. The Orthodox, like the nationalists, saw their Galician and Bukovinian strongholds disappear. Expecting far less from the non-Jewish world than the liberals and nationalists, though, they needed to make fewer large-scale adjustments. Unlike the nationalists or liberals, the Orthodox sense of self was not inextricably bound up with engagement in the outside society. This afforded the Orthodox a degree of protection from the storms of the day, ensuring a greater degree of stability and continuity. Despite the immense upheavals, the questions that faced the Jewish minority in the new situation remained familiar, or, put another way, the Jewish Question had not disappeared. And as the Jewish Question was the engine of Jewish political culture and its attendant ideologies and identities, these too exhibited resilience and continuity. Austrian Jewish society remained intact to a greater degree than Austrian society at large.

The wartime influx of Galician and Bukovinian refugees accentuated the hybrid east–west nature of Viennese Jewry, intensifying long-standing frictions for Jews and non-Jews alike. This east–west mix was both a direct consequence and an enduring legacy of the city's role as capital of the empire. The perceived threat from the East was a catalyst for the pervasive and threatening antisemitism of the war years, building upon the foundations of decades of Viennese antisemitism and continuing into the post-war period. In turn, the widespread perception of increased vulnerability in the face of this revived antisemitism led to heroic and ultimately futile efforts to unite Viennese and Austrian Jewry, if only on a political level. The failure, or at best the partial success, of these efforts typifies the endemic fragmentation not just of Viennese and Austrian Jewry, but of Jewish society across central and eastern Europe. Despite failure and fragmentation, Jewish parties and ideologies were moderately successful in carving out a niche for themselves in Austrian society and politics in the late nineteenth and early twentieth centuries, an example of what has recently been characterized as a 'broad process of political modernization . . . and a gradual democratization of policymaking and administration' in the empire.[1] Their achievements attest also to the considerable scope for ethnic politics in imperial Austria and, more broadly, for the development and maintenance of ethnic identities. For the Jews, at least, this was no 'prison of nations'.

For Viennese and Austrian Jews, then, the ground beneath their feet certainly shifted, yet did not entirely give way. While the trauma of these years cannot be underestimated, it is also true that 'it was generally assumed by 1921 that for the Jewish people the catastrophe lay behind, not ahead'.[2] This assumption of a restored, if somewhat fragile, stability continued to hold for most of the decade of the 1920s in Vienna for Jews and others. The 1930s, of course, are altogether another story.

---

[1] Gary B. Cohen, 'Neither Absolutism nor Anarchy: New Narratives on Society and Government in Late Imperial Austria', *Austrian History Yearbook*, 29/1 (1998), 55. See also p. 61.

[2] Frankel, 'The Paradoxical Politics of Marginality', 17–18. See also Charles S. Maier, *Recasting Bourgeois Europe: Stabilization in France, Germany, and Italy in the Decade after World War I* (Princeton, 1975), 3: 'If in the turmoil of 1918–1919 a new European world seemed to be in birth by the late 1920's much of the prewar order appeared to have been substantially restored.' Maier stresses, however, that appearances were misleading.

Bibliography

ARCHIVES

Jerusalem
Central Archives for the History of the Jewish People, Archiv Wien (CAHJP, AW)
Central Zionist Archives (CZA)
Yad Vashem Archives (YVA)

New York
Joint Distribution Committee Archives (JDCA)
Leo Baeck Institute Archives, Robert Weltsch Collection (LBIA, RW)

Vienna
Haus-, Hof-, und Staatsarchiv
Österreichisches Staatsarchiv
   Allgemeines Verwaltungsarchiv (AV)
   Archiv der Republik (AR)
Polizeidirektion Wien (PDW)

JOURNALS

Arbeiter Zeitung
Baderekh
Blätter aus der jüdischen Jugendbewegung
Dr. Bloch's Österreichische Wochenschrift
Freie Tribune
Ha'avodah
Hickls Wienerjüdische Volkskalender
Jerubbaal
Der Jude
Jüdische Arbeiter
Jüdische Gemeinschaft
Jüdische Jugendblätter
Jüdische Korrespondenz

Jüdischer Nationalkalender

Jüdische Rundschau

Jüdische Zeitung

Mitteilungsblatt Irgun Olej Merkas Europa

Monatschrift der Österreichisch-Israelitischen Union

Neue Freie Presse

Neue Jüdische Monatshefte

Neue National-Zeitung

Reichspost

Selbstwehr

Volk und Land

Die Wahrheit

Wiener Morgen-Zaytung

Wiener Morgenzeitung

Wiener Zeitung

Yidishe Morgenpost

Yidisher Arbeter

Zweimonats-Bericht für die Mitglieder der österreichisch-israelitischen Humanitätsvereine 'Bnai Brith'

SECONDARY SOURCES

ABELES, OTTO, 'Ein Kongress der Juden Österreichs', *NJM* 2 (1917–18), 287–8.

—— 'Ein Reichsverband der österreichischen Judengemeinden', *NJM* 1 (1916–17), 294–5.

—— *Jüdische Flüchtlinge. Szenen und Gestalten* (Vienna: R. Löwit, 1918).

ABRAMSON, HENRY, *A Prayer for the Government: Ukrainians and Jews in Revolutionary Times 1917–1920* (Cambridge, Mass.: Ukrainian Research Institute and Center for Jewish Studies, Harvard University, 1999).

ALTSHULER, MORDECHAI, 'The Attempt to Organize an All-Jewish Conference in Russia after the Revolution' (Heb.), *He'avar*, 12 (1965), 75–89.

—— 'Russia and her Jews: The Impact of the 1914 War', *Wiener Library Bulletin*, 27 (1973–4), 12–16.

ANDERSON, HARRIET, *Utopian Feminism: Women's Movements in fin-de-siècle Vienna* (New Haven: Yale University Press, 1992).

AN-SKI, S. (Solomon Zainwil Rapaport), *The Destruction of Galicia: The Jewish Catastrophe in Poland, Galicia, and Bukovina*, in An-ski, *Collected Writings* (Yid.), 15 vols., iv–vi (New York, 1921).

ASCHER, ARNOLD, '25 Jahre Eintracht', in *Festschrift anlässlich des fünfundzwanzigjährigen Bestandes des Israel. Humanitätsvereines 'Eintracht' (Bnai Brith) Wien 1903–1928* (Vienna: privately printed, 1928).

ASCHHEIM, STEVEN E., *Brothers and Strangers: The East European Jew in German and German Jewish Consciousness 1800–1923* (Madison: University of Wisconsin Press, 1982).

—— 'Eastern Jews, German Jews and Germany's *Ostpolitik* in the First World War', *LBIYB* 28 (1983), 351–65.

—— 'Nietzsche and the Nietzschean Moment in Jewish Life 1890–1939', *LBIYB* 37 (1992), 189–212.

AVINERI, SHLOMO, *The Making of Modern Zionism: The Intellectual Origins of the Jewish State* (New York: Basic Books, 1981).

BACON, GERSHON C., *The Politics of Tradition: Agudat Yisrael in Poland 1916–1939* (Jerusalem: Magnes, 1996).

BADER-ZAAR, BIRGITTA, 'Women in Austrian Politics 1890–1934: Goals and Visions', in David F. Good, Margarete Grandner, and Mary Jo Maynes (eds.), *Austrian Women in the Nineteenth and Twentieth Centuries: Cross-Disciplinary Perspectives* (Providence, RI: Berghahn, 1996).

BARON, SALO W., 'Aspects of the Jewish Communal Crisis in 1848', *Jewish Social Studies*, 14 (1952), 99–144.

—— *The Russian Jew under Tsars and Soviets*, 2nd edn. (New York: Schocken, 1987).

BARTOV, OMER, *Murder in our Midst: The Holocaust, Industrial Killing, and Representation* (New York: Oxford University Press, 1996).

BATO, LUDWIG, 'Das Kriegsjahr 5678', *JNK* 4 (1918–19), 3–22.

BELLER, STEVEN, 'Patriotism and the National Identity of Habsburg Jewry 1860–1914', *LBIYB* 41 (1996), 215–38.

—— *Vienna and the Jews 1867–1938: A Cultural History* (Cambridge: Cambridge University Press, 1989).

Bericht der Israelitischen Allianz zu Wien (1914–25).

Bericht der Israelitischen Kultusgemeinde Wien über seine Tätigkeit in der Periode 1912–1924 (Vienna: Israelitische Kultusgemeinde Wien, 1924).

Bericht des Vorstandes der Israelitischen Kultusgemeinde in Wien über seine Tätigkeit (1896–1911).

BERNFELD, SIEGFRIED, *Das jüdische Volk und seine Jugend* (Berlin: R. Löwit, 1919).

—— 'Jugendbewegung', *Der Jude*, 5 (1920–1), 351–3.

—— *Kinderheim Baumgarten* (Berlin: Jüdischer Verlag, 1921).

—— 'Die Kriegswaisen', *Der Jude*, 1 (1916–17), 269–71.

—— *Die neue Jugend und die Frauen* (Vienna: Hamönen, 1914).

—— 'Der österreichisch-jüdische Jugendtag in Wien', *Jerubbaal*, 1 (1918–19), 119–20.

BIALE, DAVID, *Gershom Scholem: Kabbalah and Counter-History* (Cambridge, Mass.: Harvard University Press, 1979).

BIHL, WOLFDIETER, 'Die Juden', in Adam Wandruszka and Peter Urbanitsch (eds.), *Die Habsburgermonarchie 1848–1918*, iii: *Die Völker des Reiches*, pt. 2 (Vienna: Österreichische Akademie der Wissenschaften, 1980).

BIRNBAUM, NATHAN, *Den Ostjuden ihr Recht* (Vienna: R. Löwit, 1915).

—— 'Wir und die Flüchtlinge', *JNK* 1 (1915–16), 101–8.

BITTON, LIVIA ELVIRA, 'Zionism in Hungary: The First Twenty-Five Years', *Herzl Year Book*, 7 (1971), 285–320.

BLOCH, JOSEPH SAMUEL, *Erinnerungen aus meinem Leben*, 3 vols. (Vienna: Appel, 1922–33).

—— *Der nationale Zwist und die Juden in Österreich* (Vienna: M. Gottlieb, 1886).

BLUHM, WILLIAM T., *Building an Austrian Nation* (New Haven: Yale University Press, 1973).

BÖHM, ADOLF, *Die zionistische Bewegung*, 2 vols. (Berlin: Welt-Verlag, 1920–1).

BORMAN, YEHOSHUA, 'The "Prague Stream" in the World Zionist Movement 1904–1914' (Heb.), *Gesher*, 15 (1969), 243–50.

BOROCHOV, BER, 'The Vienna Community and Elections to the Executive', in Borochov, *Writings* (Heb.), 3 vols. (Tel Aviv: Hakibuts Hame'uhad, 1955–66).

BOTZ, GERHARD, *Gewalt in der Politik. Attentate, Zusammenstösse, Putschversuche, Unruhen in Österreich 1918 bis 1938* (Munich: Wilhelm Fink, 1983).

BOYER, JOHN W., *Culture and Political Crisis in Vienna: Christian Socialism in Power 1897–1918* (Chicago: Chicago University Press, 1995).

—— *Political Radicalism in Late Imperial Vienna: Origins of the Christian Social Movement 1848–1897* (Chicago: Chicago University Press, 1981).

BRAILSFORD, HENRY NOEL, *Across the Blockade* (New York: Harcourt, Brace & Howe, 1919).

BRAUNTHAL, JULIUS, *In Search of the Millennium* (London: Victor Gollancz, 1945).

BRENNER, MICHAEL, JERSCH-WENZEL, STEFI, and MEYER, MICHAEL A., *Emancipation and Acculturation 1780–1871*, vol. ii of Michael A. Meyer (ed.), *German-Jewish History in Modern Times*, 4 vols. (New York: Columbia University Press, 1996–8).

BREUER, MORDECHAI, *Modernity within Tradition: The Social History of Orthodox Jewry in Imperial Germany*, trans. Elizabeth Petuchowski (New York: Columbia University Press, 1992).

BROUSEK, KARL M., *Wien und seine Tschechen* (Munich: R. Oldenbourg, 1980).

BRUCKMÜLLER, ERNST, 'Die Rolle der Juden in der österreichischen Gesellschaft bis 1918', *Christliche Demokratie*, 7 (1987), 153–7.

BUBER, MARTIN, 'Zion und die Jugend', *Der Jude*, 3 (1918–19), 99–106.

BUDISCHOWSKY, JENS, 'Assimilation, Zionismus und Orthodoxie in Österreich 1918–1938. Jüdisch-politische Organisationen in der Ersten Republik', Ph.D. diss., University of Vienna, 1990.

BUNZL, JOHN, *Klassenkampf in der Diaspora. Zur Geschichte der jüdischen Arbeiterbewegung* (Vienna: Europa, 1975).

BYK, OSWALD, *Dr. Emil Byk. Ein Lebensbild* (Vienna: privately printed, 1907).

CAHNMANN, WERNER J., 'Adolf Fischhof and his Jewish Followers', *LBIYB* 4 (1959), 111–39.

CARSTEN, FRANCIS L., *Fascist Movements in Austria: From Schönerer to Hitler* (London: Sage, 1977).

—— *The First Austrian Republic 1918–1938* (Aldershot: Gower, 1986).

CHASANOWITSCH, LEON, 'Der jüdische Kongress', *Der Jude*, 2 (1917–18), 3–16.

—— and MOTZKIN, LEO (eds.), *Die Judenfrage der Gegenwart* (Stockholm: Bokfoerlaget, 1919).

CHIZIK, MOSHE, *The Unification of Hashomer and Tse'irei Zion* (Heb.) (Haifa: Haifa University, 1984).

COHEN, GARY B., 'Jews in German Liberal Politics: Prague', *Jewish History*, 1 (1986), 55–74.

—— 'Liberal Associations and Central European Urban Society 1840–1890', *Maryland Historian*, 12 (1981), 1–11.

—— 'Neither Absolutism nor Anarchy: New Narratives on Society and Government in Late Imperial Austria', *Austrian History Yearbook*, 29/1 (1998), 37–61.

—— 'Organisational Patterns of the Urban Ethnic Groups', in Max Engman (ed.), *Ethnic Identity in Urban Europe* (New York: New York University Press, 1992).

CONNOR, WALKER, *Ethnonationalism: The Quest for Understanding* (Princeton: Princeton University Press, 1994).

—— 'The Politics of Ethnonationalism', *Journal of International Affairs*, 27 (1973), 1–21.

CORNWALL, MARK, 'News, Rumour and the Control of Information in Austria-Hungary 1914–1918', *History*, 77 (1992), 50–64.

CZEIKE, FELIX (ed.), *Wien in der liberalen Ära* (Vienna: Verein für Geschichte der Stadt Wien, 1978).

DALINGER, BRIGITTE, *'Verloschene Sterne'. Geschichte des jüdischen Theaters in Wien* (Vienna: Picus, 1998).

DANIEK, EDMUND, *Das Judentum im Kriege* (Vienna: Deutsch-nationalen Vereinigung Wien, 1919).

DAVIES, NORMAN, *God's Playground: A History of Poland*, 2 vols. (Oxford: Oxford University Press, 1981).

—— *White Eagle, Red Star: The Polish–Soviet War 1919–1920* (London: Macdonald, 1972).

DEÁK, ISTVÁN, 'The Habsburg Army in the First and Last Days of World War I: A Comparative Analysis', in Béla K. Király and Nándor F. Dreisziger (eds.), *East Central European Society in World War I*, War and Society in East Central Europe, xix (New York: Columbia University Press, 1985).

—— 'The Habsburg Empire', in Karen Barkey and Mark von Hagen (eds.), *After Empire: Multiethnic Societies and Nation-Building. The Soviet Union and the Russian, Ottoman and Habsburg Empires* (Boulder, Colo.: Westview Press, 1997).

—— *Jewish Soldiers in Austro-Hungarian Society*, Leo Baeck Memorial Lecture 34 (New York: Leo Baeck Institute, 1990).

DEUTSCH, JULIUS, *Aus Österreichs Revolution* (Vienna: Wiener Volksbuchhandlung, 1921).

DIAMANT, ALFRED, *Austrian Catholics and the First Republic* (Princeton: Princeton University Press, 1960).

DREISZIGER, NÁNDOR F., 'The Dimensions of Total War in East Central Europe 1914–1918', in Béla K. Király and Nándor F. Dreisziger (eds.), *East Central European Society in World War I*, War and Society in East Central Europe, xix (New York: Columbia University Press, 1985).

Dritter Tätigkeits- und Rechenschafts-bericht der Wohlfahrtsinstitutionen der Frau Anitta Müller für Flüchtlinge aus Galizien und der Bukowina (Vienna: R. Löwit, 1918).

DROR, LEVI, and ROZENZWEIG, YISRAEL (eds.), *The Hashomer Hatsa'ir Book* (Heb.), 2 vols. (Merhavia: Sifriyat Po'alim, 1956).

Dr. Shemariyahu Ellenberg: In Memoriam (Heb.) (Tel Aviv, n.d.).

DUBNOW, SIMON, *Nationalism and History: Essays on Old and New Judaism*, ed. Koppel S. Pinson (Philadelphia: Jewish Publication Society of America, 1958).

DUKER, ABRAHAM G., 'Jews in the World War', *Contemporary Jewish Record*, 2 (Sept.–Oct. 1939), 6–29.

Ein Jahr Flüchtlingsfürsorge der Frau Anitta Müller 1914–1915 (Vienna: R. Löwit, 1916).

EISENMENGER, ANNA, *Blockade: The Diary of an Austrian Middle-Class Woman 1914–1924* (London: Constable, 1932).

ELAZAR, DANIEL J., and COHEN, STUART, *The Jewish Polity: Jewish Political Organisation from Biblical Times to the Present* (Bloomington: Indiana University Press, 1985).

ELEY, GEOFF, 'Remapping the Nation: War, Revolutionary Upheaval and State Formation in Eastern Europe 1914–1923', in Peter J. Potichnyj and Howard Aster (eds.), *Ukrainian–Jewish Relations in Historical Perspective* (Edmonton: Canadian Institute of Ukrainian Studies, 1988).

ENGEL, DAVID JOSHUA, 'Organized Jewish Responses to German Antisemitism during the First World War', Ph.D. diss., University of California, Los Angeles, 1979.

ENGLÄNDER, ARTHUR, 'Die österreichische Wanderbewegung', in Joseph Marcus (ed.), *Tagebuch für jüdische Wanderer 1916–1917* (Vienna: R. Löwit, 1916).

ETTINGER, SHMUEL, 'Jews and Non-Jews in Eastern and Central Europe between the Wars: An Outline', in Bela Vago and George L. Mosse (eds.), *Jews and Non-Jews in Eastern Europe 1918–1945* (Jerusalem: Keter, 1974).

EXNER, FRANZ, *Krieg und Kriminalität in Österreich* (Vienna: Hölder-Pichler-Tempsky, 1927).

FELLNER, FRITZ, 'Die Historiographie zur österreichisch-deutschen Problematik als Spiegel der nationalpolitischen Diskussion', in Heinrich Lutz and Helmut Rumpler (eds.), *Österreich und die deutsche Frage im 19. und 20. Jahrhundert* (Vienna: Geschichte & Politik, 1982).

Festschrift zur Feier des 50-jährigen Bestandes der Union Österreichischer Juden (Vienna: privately printed, 1937).

FISCUS, EMANUEL, 'Aus dem Tagebuch eines Wiener Chaluz', *JJ*, 15 Apr. 1919, pp. 76–8.

FLEISCHMANN, GUSTAV, 'The Religious Congregation 1918–1938', in *The Jews of Czechoslovakia*, 3 vols. (Philadelphia: Jewish Publication Society of America, 1968–84), vol. i.

FRAENKEL, JOSEF (ed.), *The Jews of Austria* (London: Vallentine Mitchell, 1967).

—— *Robert Stricker* (London: Ararat, 1950).

FRANKEL, JONATHAN, 'Crisis as a Factor in Modern Jewish Politics 1840 and 1881–1882', in Jehuda Reinharz (ed.), *Living with Antisemitism* (Hanover, NH: University Press of New England, 1987).

—— 'The Dilemmas of Jewish National Autonomism: The Case of Ukraine 1917–1920', in Peter J. Potichnyj and Howard Aster (eds.), *Ukrainian–Jewish Relations in Historical Perspective* (Edmonton: Canadian Institute of Ukrainian Studies, 1988).

—— 'The Jewish Socialists and the American Jewish Congress Movement', *YIVO Annual*, 16 (1976), 202–341.

—— 'Modern Jewish Politics East and West (1840–1939): Utopia, Myth, Reality', in Zvi Gitelman (ed.), *The Quest for Utopia: Jewish Political Ideas and Institutions throughout the Ages* (Armonk, NY: M. E. Sharpe, 1992).

—— 'The Paradoxical Politics of Marginality: Thoughts on the Jewish Situation during the Years 1914–1921', in Frankel (ed.), *Studies in Contemporary Jewry*, vol. iv.

—— *Prophecy and Politics: Socialism, Nationalism, and the Russian Jews, 1862–1917* (Cambridge: Cambridge University Press, 1981).

—— 'S. M. Dubnov: Historian and Ideologist', in Sophie Dubnov-Ehrlich, *The Life and Work of S. M. Dubnov: Diaspora Nationalism and History*, ed. Jeffrey Shandler (Bloomington: Indiana University Press, 1991).

—— (ed.), *Studies in Contemporary Jewry*, iv: *The Jews and the European Crisis 1914–1921* (New York: Oxford University Press, 1988).

FRANZ, GEORG, *Liberalismus. Die deutschliberale Bewegung in der habsburgerischen Monarchie* (Munich: Georg D. W. Callwey, 1955).

FREI, BRUNO, *Jüdisches Elend in Wien. Bilder und Daten* (Vienna: R. Löwit, 1920).

FREIDENREICH, HARRIET PASS, *Jewish Politics in Vienna 1918–1938* (Bloomington: Indiana University Press, 1991).

—— *The Jews of Yugoslavia: A Quest for Community* (Philadelphia: Jewish Publication Society of America, 1979).

FREUD, A., 'Zum jüdischen Studententag', *JJ*, 15 Mar. 1919, pp. 27–30.

FREUD, ARTHUR, 'Um Gemeinde und Organisation. Zur Haltung der Juden in Österreich', *Bulletin des Leo Baeck Instituts*, 3 (1960), 80–100.

FRIEDMAN, ISAIAH, 'The Austro-Hungarian Government and Zionism 1897–1918', pts. 1 and 2, *Jewish Social Studies*, 27 (1965), 147–67, 236–49.

FRÜHLING, MORITZ (ed.), *Jüdisches Kriegsgedenkblatt* (Vienna: privately printed, 1914–18).

GAISBAUER, ADOLF, *Davidstern und Doppeladler* (Vienna: Böhlau, 1988).

GEISS, IMANUEL, 'The Civilian Dimension of the War', in Hugh Cecil and Peter

H. Liddle (eds.), *Facing Armageddon: The First World War Experience* (London: Leo Cooper, 1996).

GEISS, IMANUEL, 'World War I and East Central Europe: A Historical Assessment', in Béla K. Király and Nándor F. Dreisziger (eds.), *East Central European Society in World War I*, War and Society in East Central Europe, xix (New York: Columbia University Press, 1985).

GELBER, NAHUM MICHAEL, *The History of the Zionist Movement in Galicia 1875–1918* (Heb.), 2 vols. (Jerusalem: Reuven Mass, 1958).

—— 'Die Wiener Israelitische Allianz', *Bulletin des Leo Baeck Instituts*, 3 (1960), 190–203.

Die Gemeinde-Verwaltung der Stadt Wien vom 1 Jänner 1914 bis 30 Juni 1919 (Vienna: Wiener Magistrat, 1923).

GITELMAN, ZVI Y., *Jewish Nationality and Soviet Politics: The Jewish Sections of the CPSU 1917–1930* (Princeton: Princeton University Press, 1972).

GLANZ, RUDOLF, 'Unsere Stellung am Parteitage', *JJ*, 1 May 1919, unpaginated.

GLETTLER, MONIKA, *Die Wiener Tschechen um 1900. Strukturanalyse einer nationalen Minderheit in der Großstadt* (Munich: R. Oldenbourg, 1972).

GOLD, HUGO (ed.), *Zwi Perez Chajes* (Tel Aviv: Olamenu, 1971).

GOLDINGER, WALTER, *Geschichte der Republik Österreich* (Vienna: Geschichte & Politik, 1962).

GRAF, DANIEL W., 'Military Rule behind the Russian Front 1914–1917: The Political Ramifications', *Jahrbücher für Geschichte Osteuropas*, 22 (1974), 390–411.

GRANDNER, MARGARETE, 'Staatsbürger und Ausländer. Zum Umgang Österreichs mit den jüdischen Flüchtlingen nach 1918', in Gernot Heiss and Oliver Rathkolb (eds.), *Asylland wider Willen. Flüchtlinge in Österreich im europäischen Kontext seit 1914* (Vienna: Dachs, 1995).

GRÜN, OSKAR, *Franz Joseph der Erste in seinem Verhältnis zu den Juden* (Zurich: G. V. Ostheim, 1916).

GÜDEMANN, MORITZ, *Nationaljudenthum* (Leipzig: Breitenstein, 1897).

HAAG, JOHN, 'Students at the University of Vienna in the First World War', *Central European History*, 17 (1984), 299–309.

HÄUSLER, WOLFGANG, '"Orthodoxie" und "Reform" im Wiener Judentum in der Epoche des Hochliberalismus', *Studia Judaica Austriaca*, 6 (1978), 29–56.

HAUTMANN, HANS, *Die Anfänge der linksradikalen Bewegung und der kommunistischen Partei Deutschösterreichs 1916–1919* (Vienna: Europa, 1970).

—— *Geschichte der Rätebewegung in Österreich 1918–1924* (Vienna: Europa, 1987).

—— *Die verlorene Räterepublik* (Vienna: Europa, 1971).

HECHT, ALEXANDER, 'Die w. "Eintracht" als Erziehungsstätte', in *Festschrift anlässlich des fünfundzwanzigjährigen Bestandes des Israel. Humanitätsvereines 'Eintracht' (Bnai Brith) Wien 1903–1928* (Vienna: privately printed, 1928).

HEIFETZ, ELIAS, *The Slaughter of the Jews in the Ukraine in 1919* (New York: Thomas Seltzer, 1921).

HELLMANN, ALBRECHT (Siegmund Kaznelson), 'Ein jüdischer Kongress in Österreich', *Der Jude*, 2 (1917–18), 268–74.

—— 'Erinnerungen an gemeinsame Kampfjahre', in Felix Weltsch (ed.), *Dichter, Denker, Helfer. Max Brod zum 50. Geburtstag* (Mährisch-Ostrau: Julius Kittls Nachfolger, 1934).

—— 'Die Geschichte der österreichisch-jüdischen Kongressbewegung', pts. 1–4, *Der Jude*, 5 (1920–1), 204–14, 389–95, 634–45, 685–96.

—— 'National Minderheitsrechte der Juden', *Der Jude*, 4 (1919–20), 481–8.

HENISCH, MEIR, *At Home and Abroad* (Heb.) (Tel Aviv: Ahdut, 1961).

—— 'Galician Jews in Vienna', in Josef Fraenkel (ed.), *The Jews of Austria* (London: Vallentine Mitchell, 1967).

—— 'Galician Jews in Vienna', in Yisrael Cohen and Dov Sadan (eds.), *Aspects of Galicia* (Heb.) (Tel Aviv: Am Oved, 1957).

—— 'Vienna on the Threshold of the Third *Aliyah*', in Yehuda Erez (ed.), *The Third Aliyah Book* (Heb.) (Tel Aviv: Am Oved, 1964).

HERWIG, HOLGER H., *The First World War: Germany and Austria-Hungary 1914–1918* (London: Arnold, 1997).

HESHEL, J., 'The History of Hassidism in Austria', in Josef Fraenkel (ed.), *The Jews of Austria* (London: Vallentine Mitchell, 1967).

HEUBERGER, RACHEL, 'Orthodoxy versus Reform: The Case of Rabbi Nehemiah Anton Nobel of Frankfurt a. Main', *LBIYB* 37 (1992), 45–58.

HILSENRAD, HELEN, *Brown was the Danube* (London: Thomas Yoseloff, 1966).

HÖDL, KLAUS, *Als Bettler in die Leopoldstadt. Galizische Juden auf dem Weg nach Wien* (Vienna: Böhlau, 1994).

HOFFER, WILLI, 'Siegfried Bernfeld and "Jerubbaal": An Episode in the Jewish Youth Movement', *LBIYB* 10 (1965), 150–67.

HOFFMANN-HOLTER, BEATRIX, *'Abreisendmachung'. Jüdische Kriegsflüchtlinge in Wien 1914 bis 1923* (Vienna: Böhlau, 1995).

HÖFLICH, EUGEN, 'Der Volkssozialismus des Hapoel Hazair', *JJ*, 1 Apr. 1919, pp. 45–7.

HOLLEIS, EVA, *Die Sozialpolitische Partei. Sozialliberale Bestrebungen in Wien um 1900* (Munich: R. Oldenbourg, 1978).

HOROWITZ, DAVID, *My Yesterday* (Heb.) (Tel Aviv: Schocken, 1970).

HOROWITZ, S., 'Wie aus zwei Organisationen eine Bewegung ward', *BJJ* (May 1918), 10–13.

JACOBS, JACK, *On Socialists and 'the Jewish Question' after Marx* (New York: New York University Press, 1992).

—— 'Written out of History: Bundists in Vienna and the Varieties of Jewish Experience in the Austrian First Republic', in Michael Brenner and Derek J. Penslar (eds.), *In Search of Jewish Community: Jewish Identities in Germany and Austria 1918–1933* (Bloomington: Indiana University Press, 1998).

JÄGER-SUNSTENAU, HANNS, 'Der Wiener Gemeinderat Rudolf Schwarz-Hiller. Kämpfer für Humanität und Recht', *Zeitschrift für die Geschichte der Juden*, 10 (1973), 9–16.

JANOWSKY, OSCAR, *The Jews and Minority Rights (1898–1919)* (New York: Columbia University Press, 1933).

JÁSZI, OSCAR, *The Dissolution of the Habsburg Monarchy* (Chicago: University of Chicago Press, 1966).

JEDLICKA, LUDWIG, *Ein Heer im Schatten der Parteien* (Graz: Böhlau, 1955).

JELINEK, ELISABETH, 'Der politische Lebensweg Dr. Heinrich Matajas', Ph.D. diss., University of Vienna, 1970.

JENSEN, ANGELIKA, *Sei stark und mutig! Chasak we'emaz! 40 Jahre jüdische Jugend in Österreich am Beispiel der Bewegung 'Haschomer Hazair' 1903 bis 1943* (Vienna: Picus, 1995).

JERUSALEM, WILHELM, *U.O.B.B. Humanitätsverein Wien. Festschrift zur Feier des fünfundzwanzigjährigen Bestandes 1895–1920* (Vienna: B'nai B'rith, 1920).

The Jews in the Eastern War Zone (New York: American Jewish Committee, 1916).

JOCHMANN, WERNER, 'Die Ausbreitung des Antisemitismus', in Werner E. Mosse and Arnold Paucker (eds.), *Deutsches Judentum in Krieg und Revolution 1916–1923* (Tübingen: J. C. B. Mohr, 1971).

JOHN, MICHAEL, and LICHTBLAU, ALBERT (eds.), *Schmelztiegel Wien—Einst und Jetzt. Zur Geschichte und Gegenwart von Zuwanderung und Minderheiten* (Vienna: Böhlau, 1990).

JOSEPH, MAX, 'Jüdische Politik', *Hickls Wienerjüdische Volkskalender*, 17–18 (1918–19), 27–32.

Das jüdische Prag. Eine Sammelschrift (Prague, 1917; repr. Kronberg/Ts.: Jüdischer Verlag, 1978).

Jüdisches Archiv. Mitteilungen des Komitees Jüdisches Kriegsarchiv (Vienna, 1915–17).

JUDSON, PIETER M., *Exclusive Revolutionaries: Liberal Politics, Social Experience, and National Identity in the Austrian Empire 1848–1914* (Ann Arbor: University of Michigan Press, 1996).

KADISCH, HERMANN, 'Das Donaureich und seine Juden', *NJM* 3 (1918–19), 41–3.

—— 'Die Idee des mitteleuropäischen Staatenbundes und das jüdische Volk', *JNK* 1 (1915–16), 94–7.

—— *Die Juden und die österreichische Verfassungsrevision* (Vienna: Moriah, 1918).

—— *Jung-Juden und Jung-Österreich* (Vienna: Adria, 1912).

—— 'Das mitteleuropäische Chaos und die Juden', *Volk und Land*, 1 (12 June 1919), 735–6.

—— 'Die österreichische Nationalitätenfrage und die Juden', *NJM* 1 (1916–17), 300–6.

KALISCH, REUVEN, and STEIN, ARIEH, *Blau–Weiss Austria: The First Zionist Youth Movement in Austria 1911–1914* (Hadera, 1987).

KANN, ROBERT A., *A History of the Habsburg Empire 1526–1918* (Berkeley: University of California Press, 1974).

—— 'German-Speaking Jewry during Austria-Hungary's Constitutional Era (1867–1918)', *Jewish Social Studies*, 10 (1948), 239–56.

—— *The Multinational Empire*, 2 vols. (New York: Columbia University Press, 1950).

KAPLAN, MARION A., *The Making of the Jewish Middle Class: Women, Family, and Identity in Imperial Germany* (New York: Oxford University Press, 1991).

KAPLUN-KOGAN, WLADIMIR W., *Der Krieg. Eine Schicksalsstunde des jüdischen Volkes* (Bonn: A. Marcus & E. Weber, 1915).

KASSNER, SALOMON, *Die Juden in der Bukowina* (Vienna: R. Löwit, 1917).

KASSOW, SAMUEL, 'Jewish Communal Politics in Transition: The Vilna *Kehile* 1919–1920', *YIVO Annual*, 20 (1991), 61–91.

KATZ, JACOB, *A House Divided: Orthodoxy and Schism in Nineteenth-Century Central European Jewry* (Hanover, NH: University of New England Press, 1998).

KATZBURG, NETHANIEL, 'Central European Jewry between East and West', in Yehuda Don and Victor Karady (eds.), *A Social and Economic History of Central European Jewry* (New Brunswick, NJ: Transaction, 1990).

KAZNELSON, SIEGMUND, *The Palestine Problem and its Solution* (Jerusalem: Jewish Publishing House, 1946).

KIEVAL, HILLEL J., *The Making of Czech Jewry: National Conflict and Jewish Society in Bohemia 1870–1918* (New York: Oxford University Press, 1988).

KLEIN, DENNIS B., *Jewish Origins of the Psychoanalytic Movement* (New York: Praeger, 1981).

KLEMPERER, KLEMENS VON, *Ignaz Seipel: Christian Statesman in a Time of Crisis* (Princeton: Princeton University Press, 1972).

—— 'Das nachimperiale Österreich 1918–1938. Politik und Geist', in Heinrich Lutz and Helmut Rumpler (eds.), *Österreich und die deutsche Frage im 19. und 20. Jahrhundert* (Vienna: Geschichte & Politik, 1982).

KOHLBAUER-FRITZ, GABRIELE, 'Jiddische Subkultur in Wien', in Peter Bettelheim and Michael Ley (eds.), *Ist jetzt hier die 'wahre' Heimat? Ostjüdische Einwanderung nach Wien* (Vienna: Picus, 1993).

KOMLOSI, S., 'Geschichte der jüdischen Garde anno 1918', in Hugo Gold (ed.), *Die Juden und die Judengemeinde Bratislava in Vergangenheit und Gegenwart* (Brünn: Jüdischer Buchverlag, 1932).

KRAEMER, MARKUS, 'Am Rande der Geschichte. Aus der Lebens-Chronik von Nathan Eidinger', *Mitteilungsblatt Irgun Olej Merkas Europa*, 17 Oct. 1962, p. 7.

KRAUSS, SAMUEL, *Die Krise der Wiener Judenschaft* (Vienna: Österreichischen Zeitungs- und Druckerei-Aktien-Gesellschaft, 1919).

KREPPEL, JONAS, *Juden und Judentum von Heute* (Vienna: Amalthea, 1925).

—— *Der Weltkrieg und die Judenfrage* (Vienna: Der Tag, 1915).

KUDELA, JIRI, 'Die Emigration galizischer und osteuropäischer Juden nach Böhmen und Prag zwischen 1914–1916/1917', *Studia Rosenthaliana*, suppl., 23 (1989), 119–34.

LACHS, MINNI, *Warum schaust du zurück? Erinnerungen 1907–1941* (Vienna: Europa, 1986).

LAMBERTI, MARJORIE, 'The Attempt to Form a Jewish Bloc: Jewish Notables and Politics in Wilhelmian Germany', *Central European History*, 3 (1970), 73–93.

LAMBROZA, SHLOMO, 'Jewish Self-Defence during the Russian Pogroms of 1903–1906', *Jewish Journal of Sociology*, 23 (1981), 123–34.

LANDAU, MOSHE, *The Jews as a National Minority in Poland 1918–1928* (Heb.) (Jerusalem: Merkaz Shazar, 1986).

LAQUEUR, WALTER Z., *Young Germany: A History of the German Youth Movement* (London: Routledge & Kegan Paul, 1962).

LEDERHENDLER, ELI, *The Road to Modern Jewish Politics: Political Tradition and Political Reconstruction in the Jewish Community of Tsarist Russia* (New York: Oxford University Press, 1989).

LEITER, MOSHE, *Between Hope and Despair* (Heb.) (Vienna: Natan Leiter, 1916).

LEMKE, HEINZ, *Allianz und Rivalität. Die Mittelmächte und Polen im ersten Weltkrieg* (Vienna: Böhlau, 1977).

LEVENE, MARK, *War, Jews, and the New Europe: The Diplomacy of Lucien Wolf 1914–1919* (Oxford: Oxford University Press, 1992).

LEWIN, REINHOLD, 'Der Krieg als jüdisches Erlebnis', *Monatsschrift für Geschichte und Wissenschaft des Judentums*, 63 (1919), 1–14.

LIPSCHER, LADISLAV, 'Die Lage der Juden in der Tschechoslowakei nach deren Gründung 1918 bis zu den Parlamentswahlen 1920', *East Central Europe*, 16 (1989), 1–38.

LIPSKY, LOUIS, *Memoirs in Profile* (Philadelphia: Jewish Publication Society of America, 1975).

LOCKER, BERL, *From Kitov to Jerusalem* (Heb.) (Jerusalem: Hasifriyah Hatsiyonit, 1970).

LOHRMANN, KLAUS, 'Die rechtliche Lage der Juden in Wien zwischen 1848 und 1918', *Austriaca*, 31 (1990), 19–28.

LOW, ALFRED D., *The Anschluss Movement 1918–1919 and the Paris Peace Conference* (Philadelphia: American Philosophical Society, 1974).

LÖWENHEIM, AVIGDOR, 'The Leadership of the Neolog Jewish Congregation of Pest in the Years 1914–1919: Its Status and Activity in the Jewish Community' (Heb.), Ph.D. diss., Hebrew University of Jerusalem, 1991.

LUBOTSKY, B. (ed.), *The Life of a Fighting Zionist* (Heb.) (Jerusalem: Ahiasaf, 1947).

MCCAGG, WILLIAM O. JR., *A History of Habsburg Jews 1670–1918* (Bloomington: Indiana University Press, 1989).

—— 'Jewish Wealth in Vienna 1670–1918', in Michael K. Silber (ed.), *Jews in the Hungarian Economy 1760–1945* (Jerusalem: Magnes, 1992).

MAGOCSI, PAUL ROBERT, *Galicia: A Historical Survey and Bibliographical Guide* (Toronto: University of Toronto Press, 1983).

MAHLER, RAPHAEL, 'The Economic Background of Jewish Emigration from Galicia to the United States', *YIVO Annual*, 7 (1952), 255–67.

MAIER, CHARLES S., *Recasting Bourgeois Europe: Stabilization in France, Germany, and Italy in the Decade after World War I* (Princeton: Princeton University Press, 1975).

MARGALIT, ELKANA, *Hashomer Hatsa'ir: From a Youth Group to Revolutionary Marxism 1913–1936* (Heb.) (Tel Aviv: Tel Aviv University, 1971).

MARGULIES, HEINRICH, 'Bernfeld und Arlosoroff', *JJ*, 20 May 1919, pp. 111–16.

—— 'Jüdische und europäische Politik', *NJM* 3 (1918–19), 496–502.

—— 'Kritik am Deutschtum', *JJ*, 15 Mar. 1919, pp. 23–7.

—— 'Kritik des Zionismus', *NJM* 4 (1919–20), 17–21.

—— 'Politik und Sendung', *JNK* 5 (1919–20), 22–33.

—— 'Wege und Irrwege', *NJM* 2 (1917–18), 271–81.

—— 'Wiener Brief', *Volk und Land*, 1 (28 Aug. 1919), 1098–1102.

—— 'Der zionistische Parteitag', *JJ*, 15 Apr. 1919, pp. 80–2.

MARGULIES-AUERBACH, NANNY, 'Anitta Müller', *NJM* 4 (1919–20), 203–8.

MARRUS, MICHAEL R., *The Unwanted: European Refugees in the Twentieth Century* (New York: Oxford University Press, 1985).

MAURER, TRUDE, *Ostjuden in Deutschland 1918–1933* (Hamburg: Hans Christians Verlag, 1986).

MAY, ARTHUR J., *The Passing of the Hapsburg Monarchy 1914–1918*, 2 vols. (Philadelphia: University of Pennsylvania Press, 1966).

MENDELSOHN, EZRA, 'From Assimilation to Zionism in Lvov: The Case of Alfred Nossig', *Slavonic and East European Review*, 49 (1971), 521–34.

—— 'Jewish Assimilation in Lvov: The Case of Wilhelm Feldman', *Slavic Review*, 28 (1969), 577–90.

—— *Jewish Politics in East Central Europe between the World Wars*, Beiner-Citrin Memorial Lecture (Cambridge, Mass.: Harvard University Library, 1984).

—— *The Jews of East Central Europe between the World Wars* (Bloomington: Indiana University Press, 1983).

—— *On Modern Jewish Politics* (New York: Oxford University Press, 1993).

—— 'Reflections on East European Jewish Politics in the Twentieth Century', *YIVO Annual*, 20 (1991), 23–37.

—— *Zionism in Poland: The Formative Years 1915–1926* (New Haven: Yale University Press, 1981).

—— 'Zionist Success and Zionist Failure: The Case of East Central Europe between the Wars', in Ruth Kozodoy, David Sidorsky, and Kalman Sultanik (eds.), *Vision Confronts Reality: Historical Perspectives on the Contemporary Jewish Agenda* (London: Associated University Presses, 1989).

MENTZEL, WALTER, 'Weltkriegsflüchtlinge in Cisleithanien 1914–1918', in Gernot Heiss and Oliver Rathkolb (eds.), *Asylland wider Willen. Flüchtlinge in Österreich im europäischen Kontext seit 1914* (Vienna: Dachs, 1995).

MINTZ, MATITYAHU, 'Jewish Nationalism in the Context of Multi-National States', in Jehuda Reinharz, Gideon Shimoni, and Yosef Salmon (eds.), *Jewish Nationalism and Politics: New Perspectives* (Heb.) (Jerusalem: Merkaz Shazar, 1996).

—— *Pangs of Youth: Hashomer Hatsa'ir 1911–1921* (Heb.) (Jerusalem: Hasifriyah Hatsiyonit, 1995).

MITTLEMAN, ALAN L., *The Politics of Torah: The Jewish Political Tradition and the Founding of Agudat Israel* (Albany: State University of New York Press, 1996).

MOLISCH, PAUL, *Politische Geschichte der deutschen Hochschulen in Österreich von 1848 bis 1918*, 2nd edn. (Vienna: Wilhelm Braumüller, 1939).

MOMMSEN, HANS, *Die Sozialdemokratie und die Nationalitätenfrage in habsburgischen Vielvölkerstaat* (Vienna: Europa, 1963).

MOSER, JONNY, 'Die Katastrophe der Juden in Österreich 1938–1945. Ihre Voraussetzungen und ihre Überwindung', *Studia Judaica Austriaca*, 5 (1977), 67–133.

MOSSE, GEORGE L., *Germans and Jews* (New York: Howard Fertig, 1970).

—— *German Jews beyond Judaism* (Bloomington: Indiana University Press, 1985).

—— *Toward the Final Solution: A History of European Racism* (New York: Harper, 1978).

MOSSE, WERNER E., and PAUCKER, ARNOLD (eds.), *Deutsches Judentum in Krieg und Revolution 1916–1923* (Tübingen: J. C. B. Mohr, 1971).

MÜLLER, ANITTA, 'Mein Beistand für die Flüchtlinge', *Hickls Wienerjüdische Volkskalender*, 14 (1916–17), 70–5.

NAHIR, EHUD, *The Story of the Viennese Troop* (Heb.) (Givat Havivah: Makhon Zvi Luria, 1984).

NAUTZ, JÜRGEN, and VAHRENKAMP, RICHARD (eds.), *Die Wiener Jahrhundertwende. Einflüsse, Umwelt, Wirkungen* (Vienna: Böhlau, 1993).

NECK, RUDOLF (ed.), *Österreich im Jahre 1918* (Munich: R. Oldenbourg, 1968).

NEUGEBAUER, WOLFGANG, *Bauvolk der kommenden Welt. Geschichte der sozialistischen Jugendbewegung in Österreich* (Vienna: Europa, 1975).

Österreich-Ungarns letzter Krieg, 7 vols. (Vienna: Verlag der militärwissenschaftlichen Mitteilungen, 1930–8).

OSTHEIM-DZEROWYCZ, MARIA, 'Gmünd. Ein Lager ukrainischer Flüchtlinge in Österreich während des Ersten Weltkrieges', in Ilona Slawinski and Joseph P. Strelka (eds.), *Die Bukowina. Vergangenheit und Gegenwart* (Bern: Peter Lang, 1997).

OXAAL, IVAR, POLLAK, MICHAEL, and BOTZ, GERHARD (eds.), *Jews, Antisemitism and Culture in Vienna* (London: Routledge & Kegan Paul, 1987).

—— and WEITZMANN, WALTER R., 'The Jews of Pre-1914 Vienna: An Exploration of Basic Sociological Dimensions', *LBIYB* 30 (1985), 395–432.

PALMON, AVRAHAM, 'The Jewish Community of Vienna between the Two World Wars, 1918–1938' (Heb.), Ph.D. diss., Hebrew University of Jerusalem, 1985.

PARET, PETER, Preface to Siegfried Bernfeld, *Sisyphus; or, The Limits of Education*, trans. Frederic Lilge (Berkeley: University of California Press, 1973).

PAULEY, BRUCE F., *From Prejudice to Persecution: A History of Austrian Anti-Semitism* (Chapel Hill: University of North Carolina Press, 1992).

—— 'The Social and Economic Background of Austria's *Lebensunfähigkeit*', in Anson Rabinbach (ed.), *The Austrian Social Experiment: Social Democracy and Austromarxism 1918–1934* (Boulder, Colo.: Westview Press, 1985).

PAUPIE, KURT, *Handbuch der österreichischen Pressgeschichte 1848–1959*, 2 vols. (Vienna: Wilhelm Braumüller, 1960–6).

PEARSON, RAYMOND, *National Minorities in Eastern Europe 1848–1945* (New York: St Martin's Press, 1983).

PETER, LÁSZLÓ, and PYNSENT, ROBERT B. (eds.), *Intellectuals and the Future in the Habsburg Monarchy 1890–1914* (London: Macmillan, 1988).

PLASCHKA, RICHARD GEORG, HASELSTEINER, HORST, and SUPPAN, ARNOLD, *Innere Front. Militärassistenz, Widerstand und Umsturz in der Donaumonarchie 1918*, 2 vols. (Munich: Geschichte & Politik, 1974).

POPPEL, STEPHEN M., *Zionism in Germany 1897–1933: The Shaping of a Jewish Identity* (Philadelphia: Jewish Publication Society of America, 1977).

PULZER, PETER, 'The Austrian Liberals and the Jewish Question 1867–1914', *Journal of Central European Affairs*, 23 (1963), 131–42.

—— *Jews and the German State* (Oxford: Blackwell, 1992).

—— *The Rise of Political Anti-Semitism in Germany and Austria*, rev. edn. (London: Peter Halban, 1988).

RABINBACH, ANSON, *The Crisis of Austrian Socialism: From Red Vienna to Civil War 1927–1934* (Chicago: University of Chicago Press, 1983).

RABINOWICZ, OSKAR K., 'Czechoslovak Zionism: Analecta to a History', in *The Jews of Czechoslovakia*, 3 vols. (Philadelphia: Jewish Publication Society of America, 1968–84), vol. ii.

RADENSKY, PAUL, 'The Ministry for Jewish Affairs and Jewish Autonomy in Lithuania' (Yid.), *YIVO Bleter*, NS 2 (1994), 127–46.

RAMHARDTER, GÜNTHER, *Geschichtswissenschaft und Patriotismus. Österreichische Historiker im Weltkrieg 1914–1918* (Munich: R. Oldenbourg, 1973).

REDLICH, JOSEPH, *Austrian War Government* (New Haven: Yale University Press, 1929).

REICH, MOSHE, 'The Yishuv Erets Yisrael Association', in Yitzhak Raphael and Shlomo Z. Shragai (eds.), *The Book of Religious Zionism* (Heb.), 2 vols. (Jerusalem: Mosad Harav Kook, 1977), vol. i.

REICHMANN, EVA, 'Der Bewusstseinswandel der deutschen Juden', in Werner E. Mosse and Arnold Paucker (eds.), *Deutsches Judentum in Krieg und Revolution 1916–1923* (Tübingen: J. C. B. Mohr, 1971).

—— 'Wertungen und Umwertungen', in Hans Tramer and Kurt Loewenstein (eds.), *Robert Weltsch zum 70. Geburtstag* (Tel Aviv: Irgun Olej Merkas Europa, 1961).

REIFER, MANFRED, *Dr. Mayer Ebner. Ein jüdisches Leben* (Tel Aviv: Olympia, 1947).

REINHARZ, JEHUDA, *Fatherland or Promised Land: The Dilemma of the German Jew 1893–1914* (Ann Arbor: University of Michigan Press, 1975).

REISS, ANSHEL, *The Beginnings of the Jewish Workers' Movement in Galicia* (Heb.) (Tel Aviv: World Federation of Polish Jews, 1973).

RITTER, HARRY, 'Austro-German Liberalism and the Modern Liberal Tradition', *German Studies Review*, 7 (1984), 227–48.

ROSENBAUM, HEINRICH, 'Die Prager Flüchtlingsfürsorge', in *Das jüdische Prag. Eine Sammelschrift* (Prague, 1917; repr. Kronberg/Ts.: Jüdischer Verlag, 1978).

ROSENFELD, MAX, 'Für eine nationale Autonomie der Juden in Österreich', *Der Jude*, 1 (1916–17), 290–7.

—— 'Die jüdischen Gemeinden in Österreich', *Der Jude*, 2 (1917–18), 152–62.

—— 'Zur Frage der staatlichen Anerkennung der jüdischen Nationalität in Österreich', *NJM* 1 (1916–17), 664–71.

ROSENFELD, MORITZ, *H. P. Chajes' Leben und Werk* (Vienna: privately printed, 1933).

ROSENHEIM, JACOB, *Erinnerungen 1870–1920* (Frankfurt am Main: Waldemar Kramer, 1970).

ROSHWALD, AVIEL, 'Jewish Cultural Identity in Eastern and Central Europe during the Great War', in Aviel Roshwald and Richard Stites (eds.), *European Culture in the Great War: The Arts, Entertainment, and Propaganda, 1914–1918* (Cambridge: Cambridge University Press, 1999).

ROSKIES, DAVID G., *Against the Apocalypse: Responses to Catastrophe in Modern Jewish Culture* (Cambridge, Mass.: Harvard University Press, 1984).

ROTHENBERG, GUNTHER E., 'The Habsburg Army in the First World War, 1914–1918', in Béla K. Király and Nándor F. Dreisziger (eds.), *East Central European Society in World War I*, War and Society in East Central Europe, xix (New York: Columbia University Press, 1985).

ROTHSCHILD, JOSEPH, *Ethnopolitics: A Conceptual Framework* (New York: Columbia University Press, 1981).

—— 'Recent Trends in the Literature on Ethnopolitics', in Ezra Mendelsohn (ed.), *Studies in Contemporary Jewry*, iii: *Jews and Other Ethnic Groups in a Multi-Ethnic World* (New York: Oxford University Press, 1987).

ROZENBLIT, MARSHA L., 'The Assertion of Identity: Jewish Student Nationalism at the University of Vienna before the First World War', *LBIYB* 27 (1982), 171–86.

—— 'The Dilemma of Identity: The Impact of the First World War on Habsburg Jewry', in Ritchie Robertson and Edward Timms (eds.), *The Habsburg Legacy: National Identity in Historical Perspective*, Austrian Studies, v (Edinburgh: Edinburgh University Press, 1994).

—— 'For Fatherland and Jewish People: Jewish Women in Austria during the First World War', in Frans Coetzee and Marilyn Shevin-Coetzee (eds.), *Authority, Identity and the Social History of the Great War* (Providence, RI: Berghahn, 1995).

—— 'Jewish Ethnicity in a New Nation-State: The Crisis of Identity in the Austrian Republic', in Michael Brenner and Derek J. Penslar (eds.), *In Search of Jewish Community: Jewish Identities in Germany and Austria 1918–1933* (Bloomington: Indiana University Press, 1998).

—— 'Jewish Identity and the Modern Rabbi: The Cases of Isak Noa Mannheimer, Adolf Jellinek, and Moritz Güdemann in Nineteenth-Century Vienna', *LBIYB* 35 (1990), 103–31.

—— 'The Jews of the Dual Monarchy', *Austrian History Yearbook*, 23 (1992), 160–80.

—— *The Jews of Vienna 1867–1914: Assimilation and Identity* (Albany: State University of New York Press, 1983).

—— 'The Struggle over Religious Reform in Nineteenth-Century Vienna', *Association for Jewish Studies Review*, 14 (1989), 179–221.

RUDEL, S., 'Poale Zion in Österreich während des Krieges', *Der Jüdische Arbeiter* (Dec. 1927), 30–3.

RUPPIN, ARTHUR, *Soziologie der Juden*, 2 vols. (Berlin: Jüdischer Verlag, 1930–1).

SAHAWI-GOLDHAMMER, ARYEH, *Dr. Leopold Plaschkes. Zwei Generationen des österreichischen Judentums* (Tel Aviv: Irgun Olej Merkas Europa, 1943).

SCHATZKER, CHAIM, 'Martin Buber's Influence on the Jewish Youth Movement in Germany', *LBIYB* 23 (1978), 151–71.

SCHEU, FRIEDRICH, *Ein Band der Freundschaft. Schwarzwald-Kreis und Entstehung der Vereinigung Sozialistischer Mittelschüler* (Vienna: Böhlau, 1985).

SCHMELZER, ARIE LEON, 'Die Juden in der Bukowina 1914–1919', in Hugo Gold (ed.), *Geschichte der Juden in der Bukowina*, 2 vols. (Tel Aviv: Olamenu, 1958–62), vol. i.

SCHMIDL, ERWIN A., *Juden in der k. (u.) k. Armee 1788–1918* (Eisenstadt: Österreichisches Jüdisches Museum, 1989).

SCHNITZLER, ARTHUR, *Tagebuch 1917–1919* (Vienna: Österreichische Akademie der Wissenschaften, 1985).

SCHOEPS, JULIUS H., 'Modern Heirs of the Maccabees: The Beginning of the Vienna Kadimah 1882–1897', *LBIYB* 27 (1982), 155–70.

SCHORSCH, ISMAR, 'Moritz Güdemann: Rabbi, Historian and Apologist', *LBIYB* 11 (1966), 42–66.

SCHORSKE, CARL, *Fin-de-siècle Vienna: Politics and Culture* (New York: Vintage, 1981).

SCHREIBER, HEINRICH, 'Die Wiener Kultusgemeinde und die Fürsorge für die jüdische Flüchtlinge', *Hickls Wienerjüdische Volkskalender*, 14 (1916–17), 66–9.

Sechzig Jahre Wiener Sicherheitswache (Vienna: Bundespolizeidirektion Wien, 1929).

SEEWANN, GERHARD, *Österreichische Jugendbewegung 1900 bis 1938*, 2 vols. (Frankfurt am Main: Dipa-Verlag, 1971).

SEEWANN, HARALD, *Zirkel und Zionsstern. Bilder und Dokumente aus der versunkenen Welt des jüdisch-nationalen Korporationswesens*, 3 vols. (Graz: privately printed, 1990–2).

SELIGER, MAREN, and UCAKAR, KARL, *Wien. Politische Geschichte 1740–1934*, 2 vols. (Vienna: Jugend & Volk, 1985).

SHARFMAN, GLENN RICHARD, 'The Jewish Youth Movement in Germany 1900–1936: A Study in Ideology and Organization', Ph.D. diss., University of North Carolina, Chapel Hill, 1989.

SHEEHAN, JAMES J., *German Liberalism in the Nineteenth Century* (Chicago: University of Chicago Press, 1978; Atlantic Heights, NJ: Humanities Press International, 1995).

SHIMONI, GIDEON, *The Zionist Ideology* (Hanover, NH: University of New England Press, 1995).

SHIMRON, BINYAMIN, *Das Chajesrealgymnasium in Wien 1919–1938* (Tel Aviv, 1989).

SHOSHANI, MOSHE, 'Group 105', in Yehuda Erez (ed.), *The Third Aliyah Book* (Heb.) (Tel Aviv: Am Oved, 1964).

SIEDER, REINHARD J., 'Behind the Lines: Working-Class Family Life in Wartime Vienna', in Richard Wall and Jay Winter (eds.), *The Upheaval of War: Family, Work and Welfare in Europe 1914–1918* (Cambridge: Cambridge University Press, 1988).

SINGER, ISIDOR, *Presse und Judenthum* (Vienna: D. Löwy, 1882).

SINGER, MENDEL, *Four Events with a Lesson from the History of the Workers' Movement in Austria* (Heb.) (Haifa: Mo'etset Po'alei Haifa, 1975).

—— 'The Po'alei Zion Party in Austria in the First World War', in Yisrael Cohen and Dov Sadan (eds.), *Aspects of Galicia* (Heb.) (Tel Aviv: Am Oved, 1957).

SKALNIK, KURT, 'Auf der Suche nach der Identität', in Erika Weinzierl and Kurt Skalnik (eds.), *Österreich 1918–1938*, 2 vols. (Graz: Verlag Styria, 1983), vol. i.

SLUTSKY, YEHUDA, *The Russian Jewish Press in the Nineteenth Century* (Heb.) (Jerusalem: Mosad Bialik, 1970).

SMITH, ANTHONY D., *The Ethnic Revival* (Cambridge: Cambridge University Press, 1981).

SOIFER, S. A., *Das jüdische Wohlfahrtswesen in Czernowitz* (Czernowitz: Krämer, 1925).

SORKIN, DAVID, *The Transformation of German Jewry 1780–1840* (New York: Oxford University Press, 1987).

SPERBER, MANES, *Die Wasserträger Gottes* (Vienna: Europa, 1974).

SPIRA, LEOPOLD, *Feindbild 'Jud'. 100 Jahre politischer Antisemitismus in Österreich* (Vienna: Löcker, 1981).

Staatliche Flüchtlingsfürsorge im Kriege 1914–1915 (Vienna: K. K. Ministerium des Innern, 1915).

STACHURA, PETER D., *The German Youth Movement 1900–1945* (New York: St Martin's Press, 1981).

STADLER, KARL R., *The Birth of the Austrian Republic 1918–1921* (Leiden: A. W. Sijthoff, 1966).

—— 'Die Gründung der Republik', in Erika Weinzierl and Kurt Skalnik (eds.), *Österreich 1918–1938*, 2 vols. (Graz: Verlag Styria, 1983), vol. i.

STAUDINGER, ANTON, 'Christlichsoziale Judenpolitik in der Gründungsphase der österreichischen Republik', in *Jahrbuch für Zeitgeschichte* (Vienna, 1978).

STEIN, EMIL, *Auf dem Wege nach Palästina* (Vienna: Verein Keren Kajemeth Lejisrael, 1919).

STEINBERG, MICHAEL P., 'Jewish Identity and Intellectuality in *fin-de-siècle* Austria: Suggestions for a Historical Discourse', *New German Critique*, 43 (1988), 3–33.

Stenographische Protokolle über die Sitzungen des Hauses der Abgeordneten der öster-reichischen Reichsrates (1917–18).

STILLSCHWEIG, KURT, *Die Juden Osteuropas in den Minderheitenverträgen* (Berlin: Joseph Jastrow, 1936).

—— 'Nationalism and Autonomy among Eastern European Jewry: Origin and His-torical Development up to 1939', *Historia Judaica*, 6 (1944), 27–68.

—— 'Die nationalitätenrechtliche Stellung der Juden im alten Österreich', *Monatsschrift für Geschichte und Wissenschaft des Judentums*, 81 (1937), 321–40.

—— 'Die nationalitätenrechtliche Stellung der Juden in den russischen und öster-reichischen Nachfolgestaaten während der Weltkriegsepoche', *Monatsschrift für Geschichte und Wissenschaft des Judentums*, 82 (1938), 217–48.

STONE, NORMAN, *The Eastern Front 1914–1917* (New York: Charles Scribner's Sons, 1975).

STOURZH, GERALD, 'Galten die Juden als Nationalität Altösterreichs?', *Studia Judaica Austriaca*, 10 (1984), 73–98.

—— *Die Gleichberechtigung der Nationalitäten in der Verfassung und Verwaltung Österreichs 1848–1918* (Vienna: Österreichische Akademie der Wissenschaften, 1985).

STRICKER, ROBERT, *Der jüdische Nationalismus* (Vienna: Wiener Morgenzeitung, n.d.).

—— *Jüdische Politik in Österreich* (Vienna: Wiener Morgenzeitung, 1920).

—— *Wege der jüdischen Politik. Aufsätze und Reden* (Vienna: R. Löwit, 1929).

STRONG, DAVID F., *Austria (October 1918 – March 1919): Transition from Empire to Republic* (New York: Columbia University Press, 1939).

SUBTELNY, OREST, *Ukraine: A History* (Toronto: University of Toronto Press, 1988).

SUVAL, STANLEY, *The Anschluss Question in the Weimar Era: A Study of National-ism in Germany and Austria 1918–1932* (Baltimore: Johns Hopkins University Press, 1974).

SZAJKOWSKI, ZOSA, 'Concord and Discord in American Jewish Overseas Relief 1914–1924', *YIVO Annual*, 14 (1969), 99–158.

—— 'Jewish Relief in Eastern Europe 1914–1917', *LBIYB* 10 (1965), 25–56.

TARTAKOWER, ARIEH, 'Jewish Migratory Movements in Austria in Recent Gener-ations', in Josef Fraenkel (ed.), *The Jews of Austria* (London: Vallentine Mitchell, 1967).

Die Tätigkeit der Wiener Gemeindeverwaltung in der Obmänner-Konferenz während des Weltkrieges (Vienna: Wiener Magistrat, 1917).

THEILHABER, FELIX, *Die Juden im Weltkriege* (Berlin: Weltverlag, 1916).

TIETZE, HANS, *Die Juden Wiens* (Vienna: E. P. Tal, 1933; repr. Vienna: Wiener Journal Zeitschriftenverlag, 1987).

TIMMS, EDWARD, 'Citizenship and "Heimatrecht" after the Treaty of St. Ger-main', in Ritchie Robertson and Edward Timms (eds.), *The Habsburg Legacy: National Identity in Historical Perspective*, Austrian Studies, v (Edinburgh: Edin-burgh University Press, 1994).

TIMMS, EDWARD, *Karl Kraus, Apocalyptic Satirist: Culture and Catastrophe in Habsburg Vienna* (New Haven: Yale University Press, 1986).

TOURY, JACOB, 'Josef Samuel Bloch und die jüdische Identität im österreichischen Kaiserreich', in Walter Grab (ed.), *Jüdische Integration und Identität in Deutschland und Österreich 1848–1918* (Tel Aviv: Tel Aviv University, 1984).

—— *Die jüdische Presse im österreichischen Kaiserreich 1802–1918* (Tübingen: J. C. B. Mohr, 1983).

—— 'Organizational Problems of German Jewry: Steps towards the Establishment of a Central Organization 1893–1920', *LBIYB* 13 (1968), 57–90.

—— 'Troubled Beginnings: The Emergence of the Österreichisch-Israelitische Union', *LBIYB* 30 (1985), 457–75.

—— *Turmoil and Confusion in the Revolution of 1848* (Heb.) (Tel Aviv: Moreshet, 1968).

—— 'Years of Strife: The Contest of the Österreichisch-Israelitische Union for the Leadership of Austrian Jewry', *LBIYB* 33 (1988), 179–99.

TRAU, KUNO, and KREIN, MICHAEL, *A Man in the World: Tsevi Perez Chajes* (Heb.) (Tel Aviv: N. Twersky, 1974).

UNGAR, SHABTAI, 'The Jewish Workers' Movement in Galicia on the Eve of World War One: The Failure to Unify' (Heb.), *Gal-ed*, 10 (1987), 121–46.

—— 'Po'alei Zion in the Austrian Empire 1904–1914' (Heb.), Ph.D. diss., Tel Aviv University, 1985.

Unity in Dispersion: A History of the World Jewish Congress (New York: World Jewish Congress, 1948).

UROFSKY, MELVIN I., *American Zionism from Herzl to the Holocaust* (New York: Doubleday, 1976).

UTLEY, PHILIP L., 'Siegfried Bernfeld's Jewish Order of Youth 1914–1922', *LBIYB* 24 (1979), 349–68.

VIELMETTI, NIKOLAS, 'Liberalismus—Demokratie—jüdische Emanzipation in Österreich', *Christliche Demokratie*, 7 (1987), 166–70.

VITAL, DAVID, 'Diplomacy in the Jewish Interest', in Ada Rapoport-Albert and Steven J. Zipperstein (eds.), *Jewish History: Essays in Honour of Chimen Abramsky* (London: Peter Halban, 1988).

—— *Zionism: The Crucial Phase* (Oxford: Oxford University Press, 1987).

WALLAS, ARMIN A., 'Der Pförtner des Ostens. Eugen Hoeflich—Panasiast und Expressionist', in Mark H. Gelber, Hans Otto Horch, and Sigurd Paul Scheichl (eds.), *Von Franzos zu Canetti. Jüdische Autoren aus Österreich* (Tübingen: Max Niemeyer Verlag, 1996).

WANDRUSZKA, ADAM, 'Österreichs politische Struktur', in Heinrich Benedikt (ed.), *Geschichte der Republik Österreich* (Vienna: R. Oldenbourg, 1954).

WASCHITZ, EPHRAIM, 'Die "Schomrim"', *JNK* 1 (1915–16), 108–11.

WEINBAUM, D., *Nationale-jüdische Zukunftsgedanken* (Zurich: Israelitische Wochenblatt für die Schweiz, 1917).

WEINBERG, DAVID H., *Between Tradition and Modernity: Haim Zhitlowski, Simon*

Dubnow, Ahad Ha-am, and the Shaping of Modern Jewish Identity (New York: Holmes & Meier, 1996).

WEINGARTEN, S. HACOHEN, 'Parallel Organizations to the Mizrahi', in Y. L. Hacohen Fishman (ed.), *The Mizrahi Book* (Heb.) (Jerusalem: Mosad Harav Kook, 1946).

WEISS, ROBERT, 'Jugendbewegung?', *JJ*, 1 Apr. 1919, pp. 41–3.

—— 'Jugendbewegung und Hapoel Hazair', *JJ*, 20 May 1919, pp. 119–25.

WEITZMANN, WALTER R., 'The Politics of the Viennese Jewish Community 1890–1914', in Ivar Oxaal, Michael Pollak, and Gerhard Botz (eds.), *Jews, Antisemitism and Culture in Vienna* (London: Routledge & Kegan Paul, 1987).

WELTSCH, ROBERT, 'Jüdischer Nationalrat für Deutschösterreich 1918', *Michael: On the History of the Jews in the Diaspora*, 2 (1973), 204–15.

—— 'Die nationale Revolution im österreichischen Judentum und die jüdischen Nationalräte', *JNK* 5 (1919–20), 57–68.

—— 'Österreichische Revolutionschronik', *Der Jude*, 3 (1918–19), 350–8.

WHITESIDE, ANDREW G., *The Socialism of Fools: Georg Ritter von Schönerer and Austrian Pan-Germanism* (Berkeley: University of California Press, 1975).

WIERER, RUDOLF, *Der Föderalismus im Donauraum* (Graz: Böhlau, 1960).

WIESENFELD, MOSES, 'Begegnung mit Ostjuden', in Felix Weltsch (ed.), *Dichter, Denker, Helfer. Max Brod zum 50. Geburtstag* (Mährisch-Ostrau: Julius Kittls Nachfolger, 1934).

WILLIAMS, C. E., *The Broken Eagle: The Politics of Austrian Literature from Empire to Anschluss* (London: Paul Elek, 1974).

WININGER, S., *Jüdische National-Biographie*, 7 vols. (Czernowitz: Arta, 1925–36).

WINTER, J. M., 'Catastrophe and Culture: Recent Trends in the Historiography of the First World War', *Journal of Modern History*, 64 (1992), 525–32.

WISER, FRIEDRICH VON, *Staatliche Kulturarbeit für Flüchtlinge* (Vienna: Carl Fromme, 1916).

WISTRICH, ROBERT S., *The Jews of Vienna in the Age of Franz Joseph* (Oxford: Oxford University Press, 1989).

—— *Socialism and the Jews: The Dilemmas of Assimilation in Germany and Austria-Hungary* (London: Associated University Presses, 1982).

WLASCHEK, RUDOLF M., *Juden in Böhmen* (Munich: R. Oldenbourg, 1990).

WOLFSBERG, YESHAYAHU (OSKAR), *Rabbi Dr Nehemiah Tsevi Nobel* (Heb.) (Jerusalem: Hahistadrut Hatsiyonit, 1944).

YERUSHALMI, YOSEF HAYIM, *Freud's Moses: Judaism Terminable and Interminable* (New Haven: Yale University Press, 1991).

ZAAR, BIRGITTA, 'Dem Mann die Politik, der Frau die Familie—die Gegner des politischen Frauenstimmrechts in Österreich 1848–1918', *Österreichische Zeitschrift für Politikwissenschaft*, 16 (1987), 351–62.

ZAHAVI, Y. ZVI, *A History of Zionism in Hungary* (Heb.), 2 vols. (Jerusalem: Hasifriyah Hatsiyonit, 1972).

ZAPPERT, JULIUS, 'Kaiserin-Elisabeth-Institut für israelitische Krankenpflegerinnen', in *Festschrift anlässlich des fünfundzwanzigjährigen Bestandes des Israel. Humanitätsvereines 'Eintracht' (Bnai Brith) Wien 1903–1928* (Vienna: privately printed, 1928).

ZAYIT, DAVID, and SHAMIR, YOSEF (eds.), *Portrait of a Leader as a Young Man: Meir Ya'ari, Chapters from Life 1897–1929* (Givat Havivah: Sifriat Poalim, 1992).

ZECHLIN, EGMONT, *Die deutsche Politik und die Juden im ersten Weltkrieg* (Göttingen: Vandenhoeck & Ruprecht, 1969).

ZEMAN, Z. A. B., *The Break-Up of the Habsburg Empire 1914–1918* (London: Oxford University Press, 1961).

Zentralstelle der Fürsorge für Kriegsflüchtlinge (Vienna, 1917).

ZIPPERSTEIN, STEVEN J., 'The Politics of Relief: The Transformation of Russian Jewish Communal Life during the First World War', in Jonathan Frankel (ed.), *Studies in Contemporary Jewry*, iv: *The Jews and the European Crisis 1914–1921* (New York: Oxford University Press, 1988).

ZWEIG, EGON, 'Von unseren Chaluzim', *JJ*, 1 Apr. 1919, pp. 48–50.

ZWEIG, STEFAN, *The World of Yesterday* (Viking, 1943; repr. Lincoln: University of Nebraska Press, 1964).

Zweiter Tätigkeits- und Rechenschafts-Bericht der Wohlfahrtsinstitutionen der Frau Anitta Müller 1915–1916 (Vienna: R. Löwit, 1917).

Index

A

Adas Jisroel 62
  see also Schiffschul
Agudes Yisroel 20, 61, 63–4, 65, 86, 92
Aliyah Committee 121, 123
Allianz, *see* Israelitische Allianz zu Wien
American Jewish Congress 147
  as model for the Austrian Jewish Congress
    137–40, 153
Anfange, Der 105
Anitta Müller Social Relief Society (Soziale
  Hilfsgemeinschaft Anitta Müller) 88–9
An-ski, S. 69
antisemitism 4–5, 159, 174, 179
  in Austrian youth movements 105–6
  Austrian-Israelite Union and 34
  in German-Austria 173
  Jewish response to 94–7, 99, 134–5
  towards refugees 72, 93–100
Arbeiter Zeitung 5
Arlosoroff, Chaim 121
Association for the Protection of the Interests of
    Orthodox Jewry in Vienna and Lower
    Austria (Verein zur Wahrung der Interessen
    des orthodoxen Judentums in Wien und
    Niederösterreich) 62–6, 184
Austrian Central Committee for the Protection of
    the Civil Rights of the Jewish Population in
    the Northern War Zones (Österreichische
    Zentralkomitee zur Wahrung der
    Staatsbürgerlichen Interessen der jüdischen
    Bevölkerung im nördlichen Kriegsgebiete)
    86
Austrian empire, proposals for reform of 28–32,
    55, 60, 62
Austrian Israelite Union (Österreichisch-
    Israelitische Union) 33–5, 43, 73, 96, 143,
    156, 180
Austrian Jewish Congress 137–59
  Dec. 1916–July 1917 137–42
  Aug. 1917–Jan. 1918 142–50
  Feb.–May 1918 150–60
  Orthodox opposition to 156
  proposed role of women in 148
  Zionist opposition to 138–40
Austrian Jewry, concept of 9–10, 23–4, 26–8
Austrian Social Democratic Party, attitude to
    Jewish refugees 98

B

Balfour Declaration 55
Bar Kochba 115
Bartov, Omer 2
Bauer, Otto 9, 29, 152
Ben-Gavriel, Moshe, *see* Höflich, Eugen
Bernfeld, Siegfried 4, 103, 155 n. 82, 168 n. 27,
    175
  and Jewish youth movements 105–19, 123,
    125–7
Birnbaum, Nathan 28, 51
Blätter aus der jüdischen Jugendbewegung 109, 121
Blau-Weiss 104–5, 107, 127
  contact with Austrian scouting movement 102
Bloch, Joseph Samuel 26, 35, 40, 147
B'nai B'rith 33–4, 72–3, 143, 147, 155–6, 168 n.
    25, 180
  and refugees 83–4, 87
Bohemia, Jewish refugees in 78–9
Böhm, Adolf 54, 108, 120, 155 n. 82, 157, 168,
    183 n. 79
Boyer, John 13
Bratislava, *see* Pressburg
Braunthal, Julius 162
Broch, Hermann 4
Brod, Max 140, 142, 169
Buber, Martin 103, 113–15
  speech at *Jugendtag* 112, 116
Budapest, Jewish refugees in 84
Bukovina:
  Bukovinian Jewish youth groups in Vienna 109
  Jewish politics in during war 52
  Kultusgemeinden in during war 42

C

Central Office for the Welfare of Refugees from
    Galicia and Bukovina (Zentralstelle der
    Fürsorge für die Flüchtlinge aus Galizien
    und der Bukowina) 75–6, 82, 87–8, 123, 127

Chajes, Tsevi Perez 40, 44–5, 56, 167
Christian Social Party 8
    and anti-refugee agitation 95–6, 98
    attitude to Jewish nationality 173
Churchill, Winston 2
Circle of Jerubbaal, see Jerubbaal: Circle of
Committee of Jewish Delegations 10–11
Czernin, Count Ottokar 55, 148, 149 n. 64
Czernowitz, Jewish militia in 178

D
Deák, István 14
Deutsch, Julius 174–5
Deutsche Volkstag 97
Dubnow, Simon 9, 29, 152

E
education, Jewish 107–8, 118–19
    for refugees 105–6
Ehrmann, Salomon 147, 152, 155–6, 181
Eidinger, Nathan 149 n. 64
Executive Committee of United Austrian Zionists
    (Executivkomitee der Vereinigten
    Österreichischen Zionisten) 49–50, 52
Executivkomitee der Vereinigten
    Österreichischen Zionisten, see Executive
    Committee of United Austrian Zionists

F
Federation of Austrian Jewish Youth (Verband
    der jüdischen Jugend Österreichs) 115,
    119–20, 123, 127
Feuchtwang, David 147
Fialla, Hermann 132
First World War:
    consequences for Jews of eastern Europe 1–2
    Jewish historiography on 3
    see also Galicia; refugees, Jewish
Fischhof, Adolf 30
Fleischer, Siegfried 152
Frankel, Jonathan 18
Franz Joseph, Emperor:
    and Jewish refugees in Vienna 71–2
    Jewish veneration of 27
Freie Tribune 60
Freud, Sigmund 3, 4
Friedjung, Heinrich 35

G
Galicia:
    Galician Jews in Vienna 16, 21–3, 71–100

Jewish refugees from 67–83
    Kultusgemeinden in during war 42
Gemeindebund, see General Austrian Israelite
    League
    Galician reluctance to join 131–5
    Orthodox opposition to 130, 132–4
General Austrian Israelite League
    (Gemeindebund) 39, 56, 129–38, 167
Greater Actions Committee (Grosses
    Aktionskomitee) 53
Grosses Aktionskomitee, see Greater Actions
    Committee
Grossman, Meir 54
Grunwald, Max 147, 150–1
Güdemann, Moritz 42–3

H
Habsburg loyalism among Jews 27–8, 187
    see also patriotism, Jewish
Hagibor 118
Hantke, Arthur 51, 55, 138–40, 143–5, 148, 153,
    155
Hapo'el Hatsa'ir 121–3
Hashomer Hatsa'ir 101–2, 104–5, 107, 110,
    112–13, 117, 119, 122–3, 127, 172
hasidim in Vienna 92
Hatchijah 109
Hehaluts, see Pioneer groups
Hellmann, Albrecht, see Kaznelson, Siegmund
Henisch, Meir 50 n. 111, 56 n. 132
Herrmann, Leo 143–4, 149, 155, 166, 168 n. 27,
    169–70, 181 n. 73
Herzl, Theodor 4, 43, 47
Hevesi, Simon 43
Höflich, Eugen (Moshe Ben-Gavriel) 110, 121
Hohenlohe, Prince Konrad von 135
Hungary, Jewish brigades in 177
Hussarek, Max von 135

I
Israelitische Allianz zu Wien 33, 39, 74, 143, 147,
    156
    and welfare of refugees 76–9, 83–4, 87

J
Jabotinsky, Ze'ev 53
Jászi, Oscar 26
Jellinek, Adolf 26, 43
Jerubbaal:
    Circle of 106–7
    Jerubbaal 109–10

Order of 106–7
Jerusalem, Wilhelm 108
Jewish National Association (Jüdische
  Nationalverein) 28 n. 43
Jewish National Council (Jüdischer Nationalrat)
  166–73, 175, 179, 181–2
  liberal opposition to 179–80
  Orthodox opposition to 180–1
Jewish National Councils of 1918–19 11–12
Jewish National Fund, Austrian branch 120
Jewish National Party (Jüdische Nationalpartei)
  28 n. 43
Jewish People's Party (Jüdische Volkspartei)
  28 n. 43
Jewish Soldiers' Committee 172
Jewish State Party 54
Jewish War Archive (Jüdisches Kriegsarchiv) 25
Joint Distribution Committee, relief work in
  Vienna 87–90
Jüdische Korrespondenz 31, 64, 92
Jüdische Nationalpartei, *see* Jewish National Party
Jüdische Nationalverein, *see* Jewish National
  Association
Jüdische Volkspartei, *see* Jewish People's Party
Jüdische Zeitung 28, 53, 56
Jüdischer Nationalrat, *see* Jewish National
  Council
Jüdisches Kriegsarchiv, *see* Jewish War Archive
Jugendtag 105, 109, 111–19

K
Kadimah 46, 50
Kadisch, Hermann 30
Kalischer, Tsevi Hirsch 8–9
Kaminka, Armand 147, 152
Kaplan, Marion 85
Karl I, Emperor 32, 93
Kassner, Salomon 136–7 n. 30
Kaznelson, Siegmund 9
  and the Austrian Jewish Congress 136–59
Kinderheim Baumgarten 126–7
Kohn, Gustav 84
Krauss, Samuel 73, 108
Kreppel, Jonas 64, 91–2, 134
Kulka, Alois 133
Kultusgemeinde 16, 18, 24, 34, 39–41, 43–5, 51,
  53, 61, 167, 176
  challenged by nationalists 36–8
  Orthodox attitude to 61, 184
  post-war challenge to 179–86
  reform in 1919 185–6

response to antisemitism 97, 99
  and welfare of refugees 42, 77, 84, 87–8
Kuranda, Camillo 167

L
Lammasch, Heinrich 168
League of Nations 99
left-wing Jewish movement, absence of in Vienna
  22–3, 57
Leidesdorff, Aron 39
Lemberg, Jewish militia in 177–8
liberalism, Jewish, in Vienna 13, 18–20, 32–46,
  183–4, 186, 188
Lloyd George, David 2
Löwenstein, Nathan von 167
Lueger, Karl 4
Lwów, *see* Lemberg

M
Magnes, Judah 87
Mannheimer, Isak Noa 42–3
Margulies, Heinrich 113, 115–18, 123–7
Marxism 57–8
Mataja, Heinrich 98, 174–5
Mayer, Josef 175
Mendel ben Sabel 39
Mendelsohn, Ezra 19
militia, Jewish 173–9
Minorities Treaties 10–11
Mizrahi 60, 65
Moravia, Jewish refugees in 76–80
Moriah 108–9
Müller, Anitta 85, 89, 108, 155 n. 82

N
nationalism, Jewish 9–12, 19, 46–57, 61–2
  effect of refugees on 92
  Landespolitik 28, 29 n. 45, 47–8, 54, 57
  refugee welfare work and 83–4
  and welfare effort 87–90, 100
  see also Zionism
nationality, Jewish, in Austria 29–30
  and the Austrian Jewish Congress 140, 142,
    145, 150, 153, 155, 157
  Christian Social attitude to 173
  and the collapse of the empire 164
  debate on 168–73
  supported by antisemites 165
Nietzsche, Friedrich, influence on Jewish youth
  movement 126
Nobel, Nehemiah Anton 43, 44

O

Order of Jerubbaal, *see* Jerubbaal: Order of

Order of Youth 106–7

Orthodox Jewry:
  Adas Jisroel 62
  Agudes Yisroel 20, 61, 63–4, 86, 92
  Association for the Protection of the Interests
    of Orthodox Jewry 62–6, 184
  attitude to *Jugendtag* 114–15
  attitude to Kultusgemeinde 61, 184
  hasidim 92
  Mizrahi 60, 65
  opposition to Gemeindebund 130, 132–4
  political attitudes of 20, 60–6
  Verein Jeschurun 114
Österreichische Wochenschrift 24, 26, 35, 95
Österreichische Zentral Komitee zur Wahrung
    der Staatsbürgerlichen Interessen der
    jüdischen Bevölkerung im nördlichen
    Kriegsgebiete, *see* Austrian Central
    Committee for the Protection of the Civil
    Rights of the Jewish Population in the
    Northern War Zones
Österreichisch-Israelitische Union, *see* Austrian
    Israelite Union

P

Palestine, emigration to 103, 112–13, 119–23
Palestine Office in Vienna 120–1, 123
Paris Peace Conference 10–11
patriotism, Jewish 24–5
  see also Habsburg loyalism among Jews
Pioneer groups (Hehaluts) 122–3
Plaschkes, Leopold 182 n. 79
Po'alei Zion 57–60, 92, 104–5, 108, 127, 154, 158,
    172
  and Austrian Jewish Congress 146–7
politics, Jewish 5–9, 13–14, 20
  post-war organizations 10–12
  see also *shtadlones*
Pollak, Karl 50, 182 n. 79
Prague, Jewish refugees in 81–2, 84
Pressburg, Jewish militia in 178

R

Rappaport, Benjamin 40
refugees, Jewish:
  from Austrian army in Galicia 70
  in Budapest 80–1
  camps in Moravia 76–9
  Christian Social agitation against 95–6, 98

and expansion of the Jewish press 91–2
  expulsion from Vienna thwarted 98–100
  Hungarian response to 80–1
  in Moravia and Bohemia 79–80
  in Prague 81–2, 84
  repatriation by Austrian government 74, 79,
    98, 122
  response of Jews to in Budapest and Prague 73
  response of Viennese Jews to 72–3, 83, 90–3
  role of in Jewish youth movement 101–3
  from Russian military rule 67–71
  Social Democratic attitude to 98
  welfare of: government-sponsored 76; as
    instrument of stability of state 75; as a
    political issue 73, 83, 100
  and Yiddish culture in Vienna 91
Reizes, Heinrich 95, 167
Renner, Karl 9, 29, 98, 152
Revisionists 53
Rieger, Eliezer 112–14, 119
Rosenfeld, Max 9, 146, 154
Rothschild, Baron Louis von 41
Russian military rule, expulsions from western
    territories 67–71

S

Salten, Felix 149
Schalit, Isidor 54, 166, 168 n. 27, 175
Schiff, Maximilian Paul 87
Schiffschul 62, 184
  see also Adas Jisroel
Schnitzler, Arthur 3, 4, 164
Schober, Johann 175
Schreiber, Heinrich 27, 84, 133, 163, 166, 182 n.
    79, 183–4
Schwadron, Abraham 71, 122
Schwarz-Hiller, Rudolf 42, 75, 87, 96, 163, 181–2
Seidler, Ernest von 55
Selbstwehr 137
shtadlones 19, 31, 61, 99, 172
Singer, Ludwig 143, 145, 157
Sonne, Abraham 108
Sorkin, David 21
Soziale Hilfsgemeinschaft Anitta Müller, *see*
    Anitta Müller Social Relief Society
Stand, Adolf 45, 52, 55, 139–40, 142
Stein, Emil 120
Steiner, Leopold 78
Stern, Alfred 3, 51, 53, 56, 167
  attitude to youth movements 104
  and Austrian Jewish Congress 146, 150–3, 156

conception of Jewish politics 40–1
and Gemeindebund 130, 132–6
as liberal leader 39–41
and post of Chief Rabbi 44
resignation from Kultusgemeinde leadership
    181–3
Straucher, Benno 55
Stricker, Robert 3, 27, 36, 168–71, 182 n. 79
    attitude to Austria 30, 169
    and Austrian Jewish Congress 138–46, 149,
        151–8
    concept of Jewish autonomy 170–1
    conflict with Robert Weltsch 53–4, 116, 118,
        123–5, 127, 170–1
    and refugee welfare 84
    and youth movements 116, 118, 123–5, 127
    as Zionist leader 52–5
strike of January 1918 58–9
Stürgkh, Karl 78, 136

T

Taglicht, Israel 147
Taussig, Rudolf 50–2, 138, 142–3
Teacher Training Institute 107–8, 118–19
Third Aliyah 120
Tog, Der 91
Toggenburg, Count 55
Torczyner, Harry 108
Tse'irei Zion 101–2
Tur-Sinai, Naphtali Herz, see Torczyner, Harry

U

Union of German Jewish Organizations for the
    Protection of the Rights of the Jews of the
    East (Vereinigung jüdischer Organisationen
    Deutschlands zur Wahrung der Rechte der
    Juden des Ostens) 144
Union of Radical Zionists 53

V

Venetianer, Lajos (Ludwig) 43
Verband der jüdischen Jugend Österreichs, see
    Federation of Austrian Jewish Youth
Verein Jeschurun 114
Verein zur Wahrung der Interessen des
    orthodoxen Judentums in Wien und
    Niederösterreich, see Association for the
    Protection of the Interests of Orthodox
    Jewry in Vienna and Lower Austria
Vereinigung jüdischer Organisationen
    Deutschlands zur Wahrung der Rechte der

Juden des Ostens, see Union of German
    Jewish Organizations for the Protection of
    the Rights of the Jews of the East
Vienna:
    as Austrian Jewish capital 51–2
    Jewish organizations in, see Adas Jisroel;
        Agudes Yisroel; Anitta Müller Social Relief
        Society; Association for the Protection of
        the Interests of Orthodox Jewry in Vienna
        and Lower Austria; Austrian Central
        Committee for the Protection of the Civil
        Rights of the Jewish Population in the
        Northern War Zones; Austrian Israelite
        Union; Blau-Weiss; B'nai B'rith; Executive
        Committee of United Austrian Zionists;
        Federation of Austrian Jewish Youth;
        General Austrian Israelite League; Hapo'el
        Hatsa'ir; Hashomer Hatsa'ir; Israelitische
        Allianz zu Wien; Jerubbaal; Jewish National
        Association; Jewish National Council;
        Jewish National Fund, Austrian Branch;
        Jewish National Party; Jewish People's
        Party; Jewish Soldiers' Committee;
        Kultusgemeinde; Pioneer groups; Po'alei
        Zion; Verein Jeschurun; Yishuv Erets
        Yisrael
    Jewish political movements in 18–66
    Jewish population 16
    Jewish residential areas 17
    refugees in, 1914–20 74–83

W

Wahrheit, Die 30
Wald, Meir, see Ya'ari, Meir
Wandervogel 103
Weiskirchner, Richard 72, 77, 93, 97–8
Weiss, Robert 121, 123–4
Weizmann, Chaim 53
welfare, Jewish, role of women in 85–6
welfare of Jewish refugees in Vienna, see under
    refugees
Weltsch, Robert 155 n. 82, 163, 166
    concept of Jewish autonomy 170–1
    conflict with Robert Stricker 53–4, 116, 118,
        123–5, 127, 170–1
    and Hapo'el Hatsa'ir 122
    and Jewish National Council 168–72
    and youth movements 115–16, 118, 123, 126–7
    as Zionist and political leader 52–4
Wiener Morgen-Zaytung 91–2
Wiener Morgenzeitung 53

women:
    enfranchisement in Kultusgemeinde elections
        183, 185
    exclusion from Jewish leadership 32–3
    proposed role of in Austrian Jewish Congress
        148
    role in Jewish welfare 85–6
World Jewish Congress 159
World Zionist Organization 46, 48, 51, 53, 65,
    121
Wyneken, Gustav 103, 105

Y
Ya'ari, Meir 122–3
Yiddish culture in Vienna 91–2
Yidisher Arbeter 58, 60, 92
Yishuv Erets Yisrael 64–5, 92, 172
youth movements in Vienna, Jewish:
    and education 105–8
    hakhsharah groups 110, 122
    individuals involved in, *see* Bernfeld, Siegfried;
        Margulies, Heinrich; Rieger, Eliezer;
        Stricker, Robert; Torczyner, Harry; Weiss,
        Robert; Weltsch, Robert; Ya'ari, Meir
    journals 109
    Orthodox reaction to 114–15
    see also Blau-Weiss; Federation of Austrian
        Jewish Youth; Hashomer Hatsa'ir;
        Hatchijah; Jerubbaal; Kinderheim
        Baumgarten; Moriah; Pioneer (Hehaluts)
        groups; Teacher Training Institute; Tse'irei

Zion; Verein Jeschurun
Youth Office, Zionist 117–18

Z
Zentralstelle der Fürsorge für die Flüchtlinge aus
    Galizien und der Bukowina, *see* Central
    Office for the Welfare of Refugees from
    Galicia and Bukovina
Zionism:
    Austrian 47–51
    relations between Bukovinian, Galician, and
        Viennese Zionists 52
    'synthetic' 47
    Viennese 48–9, 54
    Zionist youth organizations, *see* Blau-Weiss,
        Hashomer Hatsa'ir; Moriah; Pioneer groups;
        Tse'irei Zion; Youth Office, Zionist
    see also Aliyah Committee; Executive
        Committee of United Austrian Zionists;
        Greater Actions Committee; Jewish
        National Association; Jewish National
        Council; Jewish National Councils of
        1918–19; Jewish National Fund, Austrian
        Branch; Jewish National Party; Jewish
        People's Party; Jewish State Party; Mizrahi;
        nationalism, Jewish; Palestine, emigration
        to; Palestine Office in Vienna; Po'alei Zion;
        Revisionists; Third Aliyah; Union of
        Radical Zionists; Yishuv Erets Yisrael;
        Youth Office, Zionist
Zweig, Egon 120

Printed and bound by CPI Group (UK) Ltd, Croydon, CR0 4YY

13/04/2025

14656581-0006